Environment and Development: Views on Sustainability

Environment and Development: Views on Sustainability

Editors

Dr. Bappa Sarkar
Dr. Kishore Kumar Thapa

ALLIED PUBLISHERS PVT. LTD.

New Delhi • Kolkata • Mumbai • Chennai • Bangalore

ALLIED PUBLISHERS PRIVATE LIMITED

D-5, Sector-2, **Noida**–201 301
Ph. Nos.: 0120-4320295/2542557/4352866 • E-mail: delhi.books@alliedpublishers.com

17 Chittaranjan Avenue, **Kolkata**–700072
Ph.: 033-22129618 • E-mail: cal.books@alliedpublishers.com

15 J.N. Heredia Marg, Ballard Estate, **Mumbai**–400001
Ph.: 022-42126969 • E-mail: mumbai.books@alliedpublishers.com

No. 25/10, Commander-in-Chief Road, Ethiraj Lane (Next to Post Office)
Egmore, **Chennai**–600008
Ph.: 044-28223938 • E-mail: chennai.books@alliedpublishers.com

P.B. No. 9932, No. 15, 3rd Floor (Next to Vijaya Bank), 5th Cross, Gandhinagar,
Karnataka, **Bangalore**–560009, Ph.: 080-41530285 / 22386239
E-mail: bngl.books@alliedpublishers.com

Website: www.alliedpublishers.com

ISBN: 978-93-89934-73-1

Published by Sunil Sachdev and printed by Ravi Sachdev at Allied Publishers Pvt. Ltd.,
D-5, Sector-2, Noida–201 301

DINHATA COLLEGE

Accredited by NAAC (First Cycle) Grade: B+
P.O. DINHATA, DIST. COOCH BEHAR, PIN-736135
Website: www.dinhatacollege.ac.in **Email ID:** principal@dinhatacollege.ac.in **Mob:** 9475104771

Foreword

I am delighted in writing the foreword for the book "Environment and Development: Views on Sustainability," a significant contribution to the discourse on sustainable development. This volume covers discussion on the current crucial environmental and development issues towards sustainability. It reflects our commitment to develop research & knowledge based and its dissemination. The articles in this volume offer valuable insights and practical solutions in areas such as land use, natural resource management, human-nature relationships, tourism, environmental quality, and sustainable management practices. I commend the editors, authors, and contributors for their dedication and hard work. I am confident that this volume will inspire further research and action for a more sustainable future. Dinhata College also acknowledges ICSSR and NABARD for their sponsorship for the National seminar on "Environment and Sustainable Development—A Way of Self Sufficiency" through which this edited volume is generated.

Dr. Abdul Awal
Principal, Dinhata College
West Bengal, India

Preface

The pursuit of sustainable development has never been more crucial, as the challenges we face in balancing economic growth, environmental protection, and social equity become increasingly complex. This edited volume, Environment and Development: Views on Sustainability, comprises a diverse array of research articles offering a comprehensive exploration of various facets of sustainable development, with a particular focus on land use, natural resource management, human-nature relationships, tourism, environmental quality, and sustainable management practices.

In Section A, "Land Use and Sustainable Development," we begin with Dr. Nazrul Islam's insightful analysis, "The Present is the Key to the Past: Unveiling Multiple Geological Events through the Study of Rocks in Western Arunachal Pradesh." This work underscores the significance of geological studies in understanding our planet's history and its implications for future land use. Dr. Debarshi Ghosh and Abdul Momin Hoque delve into "Sustainable Land Use-Cover Dynamics and Livelihood Impacts" through a geospatial analysis of the Kulik River Corridor in Uttar Dinajpur, India. Gopal Das and Dr. Ranjan Sarkar present a "Spatio-temporal Analysis of Land Use and Land Cover in Jalpaiguri District, West Bengal," utilizing remote sensing and GIS approaches. Manash Laha's "Change Detection Analysis Using Landsat Images on Balurghat Municipality, West Bengal, India" completes this section, highlighting the use of satellite imagery in monitoring land use changes.

Section B, "Natural Resources, Practice, and Sustainable Development," features studies that emphasize sustainable agricultural practices. Sanjita Allay explores the potential of "Organic Farming" as a sustainable agricultural opportunity. Sachina Yonzone investigates the "Allelopathic Activity of Medicinal Plants from Darjeeling" in controlling crop weeds, promoting sustainable agricultural production. Sweata Khati examines the "Role of Plant Growth Promoting Fungi in Biocontrol of Plant Diseases and Sustainable Agriculture," while Manjil Gupta's mini-review, "Harnessing Natural Feed Additives to

Mitigate Methane Emissions in Ruminants," addresses the environmental impact of livestock farming.

In Section C, "Human-Nature Relationship," we delve into the intricate interactions between humans and their natural environment. Dr. Mosfudar Rahaman and Mithun Ray provide a case study on "Human-Nature Relationship in Indian Sundarbans," focusing on Chargheri Village, Satjelia Island. Dr. Pinku Das and Dr. Nazrul Islam analyze the "Socio-Economic Status and Sustainable Livelihood Pattern of the Tribal Forest Villagers" in Alipurduar District, West Bengal. Sabita Soren and Dr. Sibabrata study the maternal healthcare services received by tribal mothers in Mayurbhanj District, Odisha, while Bishnu Barman, Sankar Biswas, and Dr. Tamal Basu Roy discuss the challenges and prospects of "Sustainable Tribal Development." Khamnam Michael Meitei and Dr. Biswajit Das provide a district-level analysis of "Literacy Differentials and Educational Development of Manipur."

Section D, "Tourism and Sustainable Development," explores the role of ecotourism in promoting sustainability. Gobinda C. Roy and Anirban Pandey examine "Understanding the Role of Ecotourism and Its Contribution to Sustainable Development," while Sima Biswas discusses "Tourism and Sustainability in Hill Areas of India."

In Section E, "Environmental Quality and Sustainable Development," the focus shifts to the impacts of environmental pollution and management strategies. Mr. Pasang Tshering Dukpa and Miss Neetu Chettri address "Household Air Pollution and Its Impact on Health." Arindam Bhattacharyya investigates the effects of arsenic pollution in South 24 Parganas on human health, while Miss. Jagriti Nandi and Miss. Sova Rani Das emphasize the need to harmonize environmental health with sustainable progress in "The Siliguri Imperative." Keshab Mondal provides a comprehensive review of "Assessing Air Pollution Management in the Context of the UN Sustainable Development Goals," and Dr. Somnath Kundu and Dr. Tapan Sarkar discuss the toxicological impact of cadmium on fish physiology. Mr. Sudarshan Das explores "People's Perception Towards Solid Waste Management and Sustainable Development" in Falakata Municipality, Alipurduar.

Finally, Section F, "Sustainable Management Practice," highlights innovative approaches to sustainable management. Dr. Rumana

Parveen discusses "Designing Sustainable Supramolecular Gels for Self-delivery Application." Partha Das, Roshan Mahato, and Sourav Adhikary provide a critical perspective on the "Heritagization of Cooch Behar Town." Sk Rafikul Alam offers an overview of "Sustainable Resource Management," and Dr. Sapan Tamang engages in an analytical debate on "Political Ideologies and the Issue of Environmentalism."

This collection of scholarly works aims to foster a deeper understanding of sustainable development's multifaceted nature and inspire further research and action towards a more sustainable future. Each contribution offers valuable insights and practical solutions, reflecting the diverse and interdisciplinary approaches required to address the pressing environmental, social, and economic challenges of our time.

We extend our heartfelt gratitude to the authors for their rigorous research and insightful contributions, and to the reviewers for their constructive feedback. We hope this volume serves as valuable resource for researchers, practitioners, policymakers, and students dedicated to the pursuit of sustainable development.

Dinhata
West Bengal, India

Dr. Bappa Sarkar
Dr. Kishore Kumar Thapa

Acknowledgements

The successful completion of this edited volume, "**Environment and Development: Views on Sustainability,**" would not have been possible without the generous support and contributions from various individuals and institutions.

We express our heartfelt gratitude to **Dr. Abdul Awal**, Principal Dinhata College, West Bengal for providing us with his prized foreword for this book. We thank him for his constant support.

First and foremost, we extend our heartfelt gratitude to the Indian Council of Social Science Research (**ICSSR**) and the National Bank for Agriculture and Rural Development (**NABARD**) for their invaluable financial support and encouragement. Their sponsorship has been instrumental in bringing this collection of scholarly works to fruition.

We are deeply thankful to Dinhata College for providing a conducive environment for research and academic discourse. The unwavering support from the College administration, faculty, and staff has been crucial in the successful organization of the seminars and workshops that contributed significantly to this volume.

We express our sincere appreciation to all the contributing authors for their rigorous research and insightful contributions. Their dedication to exploring the multifaceted aspects of sustainable development has enriched this volume and provided a comprehensive understanding of the subject.

Special thanks are due to the editorial team at Allied Publishers, New Delhi, for their diligent efforts in coordinating the various stages of this publication. Their commitment to excellence and attention to detail have been crucial in shaping this volume.

We hope that this volume serves as a valuable resource for researchers, practitioners, policymakers, and students dedicated to the pursuit of sustainable development.

Dr. Bappa Sarkar
Dr. Kishore Kumar Thapa

Our Sponsors

The Indian Council of Social Science Research (ICSSR) holds immense significance in driving research and development within the social sciences domain in India. By providing crucial financial support, including grants, fellowships, and scholarships, ICSSR facilitates the exploration of pertinent societal issues and the formulation of **evidence**-based solutions. Its emphasis on fostering interdisciplinary collaboration encourages researchers to approach complex problems from various angles, leading to comprehensive insights and innovative solutions. Furthermore, ICSSR's focus on marginalized communities ensures that research outcomes are inclusive and address the needs of all sections of society. Through its initiatives, ICSSR not only advances the frontiers of knowledge but also contributes to the socioeconomic development and well-being of the nation as a whole.

NABARD

The National Bank for Agriculture and Rural Development (NABARD) plays a pivotal role in research and development, particularly in the agricultural and rural sectors of India. By providing financial support, grants, and technical assistance, NABARD fosters innovation and sustainable practices that enhance productivity and improve livelihoods. Its initiatives include promoting research on climate-resilient agriculture, water resource management, and rural infrastructure development. NABARD's collaboration with academic institutions, research organizations, and grassroots communities ensures that the research is both relevant and impactful, addressing the real-world challenges faced by farmers and rural entrepreneurs. Through its comprehensive approach, NABARD significantly contributes to the advancement of knowledge and the implementation of effective solutions for sustainable development in rural India.

List of Contributors

1. Mr. Abdul Momin Hoque, Assistant Professor, Department of Geography, Dhupguri Girls' College, West Bengal, India
2. Mr. Anirban Pandey, A.B.N. Seal College, Department of Zoology, Cooch Behar-736101, West Bengal, India
3. Mr. Arindam Bhattacharyya, SACT, Department of Physiology, Sonarpur Mahavidyalaya
4. Mr. Bishnu Barman, SACT, Department of Geography, Dinhata College, Cooch Behar, West Bengal, India.
5. Dr. Biswajit Das, Assistant Professor, Department of Geography, Manipur University
6. Dr. Debarshi Ghosh, Assistant Professor, Department of Geography, Dhupguri Girls' College, West Bengal, India
7. Dr. Gobinda C. Roy, Dinhata College, Department of Zoology, Cooch Behar-736135, West Bengal, India
8. Mr. Gopal Das, Research Scholar, University of North Bengal, Dr. Ranjan Sarkar, Principal , Siliguri College of Commerce, Siliguri, West Bengal
9. Miss Jagriti Nandi, Ph.D Research Scholar, Department of Geography and Applied Geography, University of North Bengal, India.
10. Mr. Keshab Mondal, Assistant Professor, Cooch Behar College, West Bengal
11. Mr. Khamnam Michael Meitei, Research Scholar, Department of Geography, Manipur University
12. Mr. Manash Laha, State Aided College Teacher, Department of Geography, Islampur College, West Bengal, India
13. Mr. Manjil Gupta, Assistant Professor, Department of Zoology, Dinhata College, Dinhata, Cooch Behar-736135
14. Mr. Mithun Ray, Assistant Professor, Department of Geography, Malda College, Malda, West Bengal
15. Dr. Mosfudar Rahaman, Department of Geography, Malda College, Malda, West Bengal

16. Dr. Nazrul Islam, Associate Professor, Department of Geography, Cooch Behar Panchanan Barma University, Dist-Cooch Behar, West Bengal
17. Miss Neetu Chettri, Assistant Professor, Department of Education, Acharya Brojendra Nath Seal College, Cooch Behar-736101
18. Mr. Partha Das, Assistant Professor, Dept. of Geography, Acharya Brojendra Nath Seal College, Cooch Behar
19. Mr. Pasang Tshering Dukpa, Assistant Professor, Department of Physiology, Acharya Brojendra Nath Seal College, Cooch Behar-736101
20. Dr. Pinku Das, Assistant Teacher, Chhatrampur High School, Tufanganj, Cooch Behar
21. Mr. Roshan Mahato (Student) PG Dept. of Geography and Applied Geography, University of North Bengal, Siliguri.
22. Dr. Rumana Parveen, Assistant Professor, Department of Chemistry, Dinhata College, Dinhata-736135. Affiliated to Cooch Behar Panchanan Barma University
23. Dr. Sabita Soren, Ph.D Research Scholar, Dept. of Applied Geography, Ravenshaw University.
24. Dr. Sachina Yonzone, Department of Botany, City College, Raja Rammohan Sarani, Amherst Street, Kolkata, West-Bengal-700009
25. Dr. Sanjita Allay, Department of Botany, Sambhunath College, The University of Burdwan, Birbhum, West Bengal, India,
26. Dr. Sankar Biswas, Research Scholar, Department of Geography and Applied Geography, University of North Bengal, Darjeeling, West Bengal, India
27. Dr. Sapan Tamang, Assistant Professor, Department of Political Science, Dinhata College, Cooch Behar-736135
28. Dr. Sibabrata Das, Professor, Dept. of Applied Geography, Ravenshaw University, Cuttack, Odisha
29. Dr. Sima Biswas, Assistant Professor, Department of Botany, Vidyasagar College for Women, 39 Sankar Ghosh Lane, Kolkata 06, West Bengal, India
30. Sk Rafikul Alam, Assistant Professor, Dinhata College, Dinhata

31. Dr. Somnath Kundu, Assistant Professor, Department of Zoology, Tufanganj Mahavidyalaya
32. Mr. Sourav Adhikary (Student) PG Dept. of Geography, Sikkim University, Gangtok
33. Miss Sova Rani Das, Ph.D Research Scholar, Department of Geography and Applied Geography, University of North Bengal, India.
34. Mr. Sudarshan Das, SACT, Falakata College, West Bengal
35. Dr. Sweata Khati, Department of Botany, Ananda Mohan College, 102/1 Raja Rammohan Sarani, Kolkata-700009, India
36. Dr. Tamal Basu Roy, Assistant Professor, Department of Geography, Raiganj University, Raiganj, West Bengal
37. Dr. Tapan Sarkar, Assistant Professor, Department of Zoology, Raiganj University
38. Dr. Sweata Khati, Department of Botany, Ananda Mohan College, 102/1 Raja Rammohan Sarani, Kolkata-700009

Contents

Foreword .... *v*

Preface .... *vii*

Acknowledgment .... *xi*

Our Sponsors .... *xiii*

List of Contributors .... *xv*

SECTION – A

Land Use and Sustainable Development

1. The Present is the Key to the Past: Unveiling Multiple Geological Events through the Study of Rocks in Western Arunachal Pradesh 3
   Nazrul Islam
2. Sustainable Land Use-Cover Dynamics and Livelihood Impacts: A Geospatial Analysis of the Kulik River Corridor in Uttar Dinajpur, India 17
   Debarshi Ghosh and Abdul Momin Hoque
3. The Spatio-temporal Analysis of Land Use and Land Cover in Jalpaiguri District, West Bengal: A Remote Sensing and GIS Approach 37
   Gopal Das and Ranjan Sarkar
4. Change Detection Analysis Using Landsat Images on Balurghat Municipality, West Bengal, India 54
   Manash Laha

SECTION – B

Natural Resources, Practice and Sustainable

5. Organic Farming for Sustainable Agriculture: Prospects, Practice and Procurement 71
   Sanjita Allay

6. Allelopathic Activity of Medicinal Plants from Darjeeling: *Hydrocotyle nepalensis* Hook.f. and *Rumex nepalensis* Spreng in Controlling Major Crop Weeds for Sustainable Agriculture Production 82
Sachina Yonzone

7. Role of Plant Growth Promoting Fungi in Biocontrol of Plant Diseases and Sustainable Agriculture 90
Sweata Khati

8. Harnessing Natural Feed Additives to Mitigate Methane Emissions in Ruminants: A Mini Review 100
Manjil Gupta

SECTION – C

Human-Nature Relationship

9. Human-Nature Relationship in Indian Sundarbans: A Case Study of Chargheri Village, Satjelia Island 117
Mosfudar Rahaman and Mithun Ray

10. Socio-Economic Status and Sustainable Livelihood Pattern of the Tribal Forest Villagers: A Study of Kalchini and Kumargram C.D. Blocks of Alipurduar District, West Bengal 129
Pinku Das and Nazrul Islam

11. ANC and PNC Services Received by Tribal Mothers from Community Health Workers (CHWs): A Study in Mayurbhanj District, Odisha 145
Sabita Soren and Sibabrata Das

12. Indian Indigenous Tribal Population Sustainable Development and Associated with Their Problems 155
Bishnu Barman, Sankar Biswas and Tamal Basu Roy

13. Literacy Differentials and Educational Development of Manipur: A District Level Analysis 172
Khamnam Michael Meitei and Biswajit Das

SECTION – D
Tourism and Sustainable Development

14. Understanding the Role of Ecotourism and Its Contribution to Sustainable Development 199
Gobinda C. Roy and Anirban Pandey

15. Tourism and Sustainability in Hill Areas of India 205
Sima Biswas

SECTION – E
Environmental Quality and Sustainable Development

16. Household Air Pollution and Its Impact on Health: Problem and Solution 217
Pasang Tshering Dukpa and Neetu Chettri

17. Effect of Arsenic Polluted Environment of South 24 Parganas on the Human Systems of Local Residents 227
Arindam Bhattacharyya

18. Harmonizing Environmental Health Based on Air Pollution with Sustainable Progress: The Siliguri Imperative 240
Jagriti Nandi and Sova Rani Das

19. Assessing Air Pollution Management in the Context of the UN Sustainable Development Goals: A Comprehensive Review 252
Keshab Mondal

20. An Overview of the Toxicological Impact of Cadmium (Cd) on the Physiological Status of Fishes 266
Somnath Kundu and Tapan Sarkar

21. People's Perception Towards Solid Waste Management and Sustainable Development: A Geographical Study of Falakata Municipality, Alipurduar, West Bengal 278
Sudarshan Das

SECTION – F

Sustainable Management Practice

22. Designing Sustainable Supramolecular Gels for Self-delivery Application 293
Rumana Parveen

23. Heritagization of Cooch Behar Town from a Critical Perspective 305
Partha Das, Roshan Mahato and Sourav Adhikary

24. Sustainable Resource Management: An Overview 328
S.K. Rafikul Alam

25. Political Ideologies and the Issue of Environmentalism: An Analytical Debate and Discussion 339
Sapan Tamang

Author Index 349

Section-A

Land Use and Sustainable Development

The Present is the Key to the Past: Unveiling Multiple Geological Events through the Study of Rocks in Western Arunachal Pradesh

Nazrul Islam[1]

ABSTRACT: The principle "Present is the Key to the Past" underscores the significance of present-day geological evidence in unravelling past events. This study examines Gneiss with Ptygmatic Folds, prominent in the North-Eastern Himalayas, particularly around the Nuranang (Jung) Waterfall in Arunachal Pradesh. Through close examination and literature review, the study elucidates the formation processes of Gneiss and ptygmatic folds, considering factors like high pressure, temperature, differential stress, competency variations, and fluid presence. The research reveals insights into the deep burial and tectonic journey of Gneiss during the Himalayan orogeny, shedding light on deformation patterns and regional tectonic stresses. By analyzing present-day geological features, such as ptygmatic folds, researchers gain a deeper understanding of past tectonic events and the geological evolution of the region.

Keywords: *Present is the Key to the Past, Gneiss, Ptygmatic Folds, Himalayas, Tectonic Processes.*

1. Introduction

Present is the Key to the Past, initially proposed by James Hutton (1726–1797) and popularized by Sir Charles Lyell (1797–1875) in his book "Principles of Geology" published in 1830, emphasizes

[1] Associate Professor, Department of Geography, Cooch Behar Panchanan Barma University, Dist-Cooch Behar, West Bengal, India.
E-mail: islamnazrul975@gmail.com

the importance of present-day evidence in understanding past geological events. The evidence of the present led the researcher to explain the multiple events that occurred in the past. Rocks and sediments play a crucial role in deciphering past geological processes and environments (Blatt & Tracy, 1996). Igneous rocks, originating from volcanic activity, serve as indicators of previous tectonic settings and eruption locations—whether at the surface or subsurface—based on their texture and chemistry (Best & Fisher, 2009). Metamorphic rocks, resulting from the transformation of sediments under heat and pressure, offer insights into past mountain-building events and aid in mapping the extent of now-vanished mountain ranges (Vernon, 2004). Sedimentary rocks, on the other hand, provide the most comprehensive record of Earth's history. Factors like sediment size, shape, and the presence of fossils offer valuable clues about the transportation and final depositional environment of sediments (Prothero & Schwab, 2004).

Geological structures like folds, faults, thrusts, joints, and cleavage act as a natural record of a rock's deformational history (Hobbs and Ord, 2011; Fossen, 2016). Folds and thrust faults reveal compressional forces, while faults with displacement indicate past movement and stress direction (Sibson, 2001; Jackson & McKenzie, 1983). Joints and cracks, despite lacking displacement, can still indicate stress fields or weaknesses in the rock (Anderson, 1951; King, 1978). Cleavage in metamorphic rocks indicates directed pressure that realigned mineral grains (Fossen, 2016). By analyzing these features, geologists can reconstruct the sequence of events a rock has endured, providing insights into mountain-building episodes, regional stress patterns, and potential fluid flow paths. Thus, the study of rocks and micro-structures is essential in understanding past geological events.

The formation of the Himalayas dates back to about 48 Ma by the continental collision between the Indian Plate and the Eurasian Plate. The (meta-) sedimentary sequences of Lesser Himalaya deformed multiple times by elastico-frictional (EF) and quasi-plastic (QP)[2]

[2] Collision occurs when two objects interact and apply forces on each other rapidly. There are two main types of collisions: elastic and inelastic/plastic. In elastic collisions, there is no net loss in kinetic energy in the system. Conversely, in inelastic/plastic collisions, kinetic energy is lost, converted into heat energy, and

(Sibson, 1977) processes under different P-T conditions.[3] It depends on the regional strain rate[4] and geothermal gradient[5] (Matin and Majumdar, 2009). From south to north in western Arunachal Pradesh, notable tectonic units include the Himalayan Frontal Thrust (HFT), Bhalukpong Thrust, Lower and Upper Tipi Thrusts, Lower and Upper sections of the Main Boundary Thrust (MBT), Tanga Thrust, Bomdila Thrust, Main Central Thrust (MCT), Sakteng Klippe, Boralum Thrust (BHT), and South Tibetan Detachment (STD). From south to north, the geological formations include alluvium, Kimin-Quaternary Formation, Subansiri + Quaternary Formation, Dafla Formation, Gondwana Formation, Tenga Formation, Dedza Formation, Bomdila Gneiss Formation, Dirang Formation, Sela Group, leucogranite formations, and the Tethys Formation. These formations collectively contribute to the diverse geological makeup of the region. Other features like fold axes (anticlinal and synclinal), lineation, foliation, and bedding offer crucial details about the folding, shearing, and layering of rock strata. Different tectonic and volcanic activities created all the structural components of the eastern Himalayas in the distant past. The rocks are the product of the tectonic events that occurred in the past. Thus, the author tried to explore the tectonic activity, geological history, and processes involved by analyzing rock samples (Ptygmatic fold in Gneiss) abundant in the study area.

---

causes material deformation. At levels above the greenschist transition, where rocks behave almost elastically and cannot absorb significant strains, it's termed as elastico-frictional (EF) collision. Conversely, at lower levels, major rock constituents, like Quartz, can readily deform via crystal plasticity, resulting in quasi-plastic (QP) deformation behavior.

[3] The Pressure-Temperature-Time (P-T-t) path describes the journey of a rock during its metamorphic cycle, from burial and heating to uplift and exhumation. The P-T-t path includes prograde, peak, and retrograde metamorphism, with clockwise and anti-clockwise subtypes.

[4] Strain refers to changes in shape or size due to applied forces, known as deformation. The rate at which this deformation occurs is termed strain rate. Brittle rocks like Quartz or basalt can undergo ductile deformation at the Earth's surface if the strain rate is slow enough.

[5] The geothermal gradient indicates the rate of temperature increase with depth in the Earth's subsurface, typically around 25–30 °C/km (72–87 °F/mi) away from tectonic plate boundaries.

2. Study Area

The study area lies within the easternmost sector of the Himalayan mountain range, extending from 91°30′ E to 96°E longitude and 26°28′ N to 29°30′ N latitude, encompassing the eastern Himalayan syntaxis (Yin *et al.*, 2006; Figure 1). It is confined within the Tawang and West Kameng districts of Arunachal Pradesh (Figure 1). The region is divided into different tectono-morphic zones, including the Shiwalik Himalaya, Lesser Himalaya, Greater Himalaya, and Trans Himalaya. Physiographically, the area is characterized by high altitude, steep slopes, gorges, dissected valleys, and mountain ridges with summits. Annual rainfall ranges from 150 cm to 200 cm, and temperatures vary between 15°C and 30°C. Geographical factors influence the climatic conditions in Arunachal Pradesh, and the region falls within a very high seismic zone (Zone V) due to its geographic location and tectonic activity.

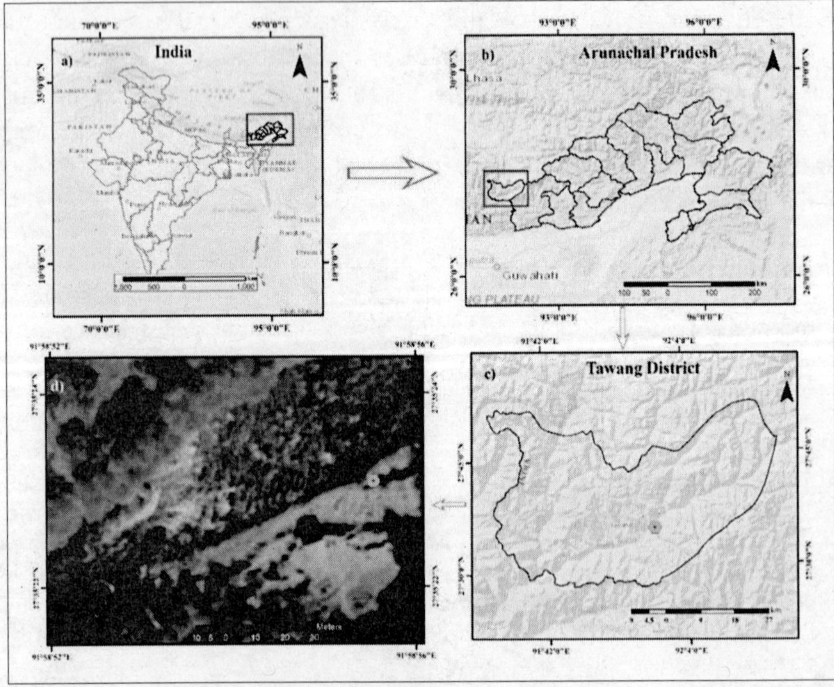

Figure 1: Location of the Study Area from Where Samples have been Collected

During our educational tour of Arunachal Pradesh from November 27th to December 2nd, 2023, we explored Nurananag (Jung) Waterfall in the foothills of the North-Eastern Himalayas, situated at 27°35′23″ N latitude and 91°58′56″ E longitude. Among the geological features observed, Gneiss with Ptygmatic Folds stood out prominently.

3. Geology of the Study Area

Western Arunachal Pradesh, which is separated by the Assam Plain and encompasses the West Kameng and Tawang districts, is characterized by high complexity, featuring three distinct mountain systems: the Himalayan range, the Naga-Patkai-Arakan range, and the Mishmi hills. Previous geological studies primarily relied on field surveys, lacking comprehensive structural and geochronological analyses (Yin, 2006). Drained by the Subansiri River, Kameng River, Dirang River, and their tributaries, the region provides a comprehensive depiction of its intricate geological composition.

The region predominantly consists of sedimentary rocks from the Siwalik group, with the Main Boundary Thrust (MBT) serving as a demarcation line separating this region from the Lesser Himalayas (Figure 2). The Lesser Himalayan range exhibits a diverse array of rocks spanning different geological ages, delineated by thrust faults (Singh *et al.*, 2014). Thus, the region is characterized by the crystalline formations of the Se La group, comprising Kyanite-sillimanite bearing garnet-biotite schist, Psammatic Gneiss, streaky Gneiss, tourmaline-bearing leucogranite, and amphibolites, dating back to the Archaean and Palaeozoic eras (Mishra, 2007; Sharma *et al.*, 2022; Figure 2). Another significant rock system is the Bomdila group, featuring argillaceous, arenaceous, metamorphic, and penecontemporaneous basic volcanic rocks, categorized into the Dedza and Dirang formations (Bhushan *et al.*, 1991; Srivastava *et al.*, 2011). The gneissic and schist formations exhibit various folds, symmetric and asymmetric structures, fault scars, shear plains, and linear and non-linear structures. Meso-scopic shear zones have been identified over schists and migmatitic gneisses (Srivastava *et al.*, 2011).

On the other hand, the Gondwana supergroup overlays the quartzite-carbonate-phyllite sequence (Singh *et al.*, 2014). A noticeable shift in geomorphic features occurs along local and regional discontinuities. The Tawang section's topography is characterized by steep slopes with glacial geomorphic features attributed to faults and thrusts (Srivastava *et al.*, 2011). The Tawang Thrust, roughly parallel to the Main Central Thrust (MCT), marks a significant discontinuity between the Se La and Tawang sectors. Satellite observations have identified another significant thrust south of the Se La pass, separating the Se La sector from the Senge sector. The Se La thrust is discernible through the presence of Knick points and abrupt changes in the drainage system originating from high-altitude regions (Kumar, 1997). Further, the region is characterized by diverse fold axes (anticlinal and synclinal), lineation, foliation, and bedding, which offer crucial details about the folding, shearing, and layering of rock strata (Figure 2).

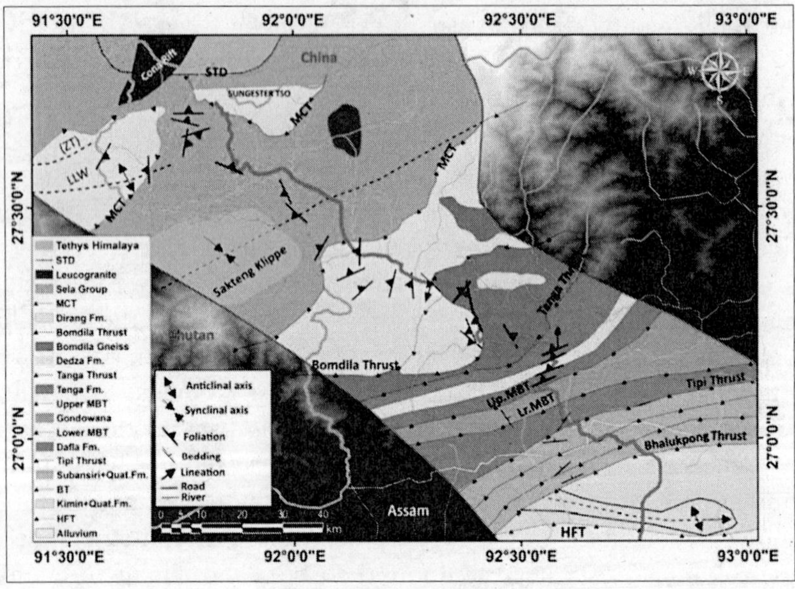

Figure 2: Geology of Western Arunachal Pradesh.
Adapted from Saha *et al.* (2023), p. 100158

4. Methodology

This paper presents the results of close examinations and evaluations of the relationships between Gneiss with Ptygmatic folds within contact zones surrounding the Nuranang (Jung) Waterfall along the

Nuranang River in the Himalayan region of Arunachal Pradesh. The study primarily focuses on ptygmatic features associated with Gneiss rock. The methodology involves identifying the rock as Gneiss with Ptygmatic Folds and conducting a literature review to comprehend the formation processes involved. Based on this research, assumptions are made about the geological conditions and processes contributing to the formation of Gneiss with Ptygmatic Folds. These assumptions are then analyzed and interpreted to develop a coherent understanding of the rock's origin, evolution, and regional geology.

5. Result and Discussion

5.1 *Gneiss as a Metamorphic Rock*

Metamorphic rocks undergo a process known as metamorphism, derived from the Greek words "meta", meaning "change", and "morphé" meaning "form." This transformation involves the solid-state recrystallization of existing igneous, sedimentary, and metamorphic rocks due to changes in physical and chemical conditions, notably heat, pressure, and the introduction of chemically active fluids and gases (Haldar & Tišljar, 2014). (Figure 1). These alterations can result in changes to the mineral composition, texture, and overall appearance of the rock, including the formation of new minerals such as garnet, kyanite, and chlorite. The original rocks affected by metamorphic changes are referred to as protoliths[6].

Gneiss (as an example in this case) is a coarse-grained metamorphic rock characterized by its alternate dark and light-coloured banded appearance, formed through high-grade regional and plutonic metamorphism from various igneous and sedimentary precursors such as granite, shale, or schist (Best, 2003). These layers often vary in composition, reflecting the mineralogy of the original rock and the metamorphic processes involved (Yardley, 2021).

The terms "orthogneiss" and "paragneiss" denote gneisses originating from igneous and sedimentary rocks, respectively. Orthogneissic rocks display medium to coarse foliation and significant recrystallization, similar to granite mineral composition. Paragneiss

[6] A protolith is the original, unmetamorphosed rock from which a given metamorphic rock is formed, e.g. shale or mudstone is the protolith in slate.

contains quartz, feldspar, and other minerals like sillimanite, kyanite, cordierite, andalusite, and staurolite, which are typical clay-rich sediments. Various gneiss varieties exist based on mineral composition, including quartz-feldspar, muscovite, biotite, sillimanite, and cordierite gneiss, characterized by "eye" or porphyroblastic texture, often with granoblastic or granolépidoblastic texture and gneissic structure development.

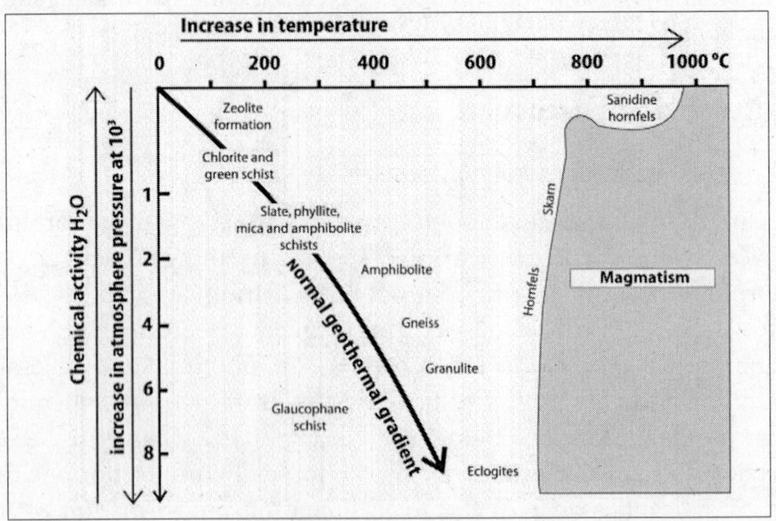

Figure 3: Major Mineral Communities (metamorphic facies) with Increasing Pressure, Temperature, Depth, and Magma Heating (After Haldar & Tišljar, 2014)

5.2 *Ptygmatic Fold*

The small crumpling of Gneissic or migmatitic rocks, termed "ptygmatic" by Sederholm (1907, 1926), was initially described by Milch (1900), who stated that 'Ptygmas' have the general appearance of highly disharmonic, extremely tortuous folds. The ptygmatic fold is a distinctive fold characterized by high amplitude-to-wavelength ratios. It often takes on highly irregular and complex shapes that resemble intestines (Ghosh, 2000). It forms within Gneiss due to ductile deformation[7] under high pressure and temperature conditions

[7] *Ductile deformation* refers to the tendency of rock to deform to large strains without macroscopic fracturing. Such behaviour occurs at greater depths in all rock types,

(Ramsay & Lisle, 2000). During this process, the rock exhibits plastic behaviour, allowing the less competent layers (e.g., mica-rich) to flow and fold around the more competent layers (e.g., feldspar-rich) under the influence of shearing forces (Ghosh, 2000). Thus, a Ptygmatic fold involves several processes, including injection along meandering cracks (Read, 1931), viscous flow (Sederholm, 1926), injection into an incompetent host and crumpling where the ribbon of magma meets resistance (Wilson, 1952), and anatectic growth in a passive host (Dietrich, 1959).

5.2.1 *Characteristics of Ptygmatic Fold*

The ptygmatic folds discussed in the paper exhibit distinct characteristics. It is mainly composed of quartz along with potassium and/or plagioclase feldspar, and these folds are commonly found within biotite-rich gneisses of injection zones, xenoliths[8], or roof pendants associated spatially with quartz-bearing phanerites. The host gneisses are primarily composed of biotite, quartz, albite, oligoclase, and/or potassium feldspar, with or without gross compositional banding. Ptygmatic folds can trend parallel or at any angle to the host rock's foliation, with high concentrations of biotite observed adjacent to some folds. These folds present highly disharmonic and extremely tortuous folds, with sporadic, nearly straight segments, contrasting with the host rock's predominantly quartz and feldspar composition. These characteristics offer valuable insights into the mineralogy, occurrence, orientation, and appearance of ptygmatic fold within gneissic rocks, contributing to a comprehensive understanding of their geological significance and formation processes. Various hypotheses have been proposed to explain the formation of ptygmatic features, including spreading and/or laminar flow, replacement-expansion flowage, metasomatism, filling of tortuous fissures, aberrant injection, tectonic deformation, syntectonic injection, volume reduction of the host rock by squeezing, plastic deformation, and magmatic flowage

---

where higher temperatures promote crystal plasticity and higher confining pressures (Fossen, 2010).

[8] Xenoliths are rock fragments enveloped within larger rocks during solidification, commonly found in igneous rocks during magma ascent and eruption. They typically comprise mineral assemblages such as clinopyroxene, phlogopite, and K-richterite.

(Dietrich, 1959). While some ptygmatic folds may have originated from processes like syntectonic magmatic flowage, each hypothesis encounters challenges when applied to most ptygmatic features.

5.2.2 *The Formation of Ptygmatic Fold in Gneiss*

The formation of the Ptygmatic fold in Gneiss involves several geological processes. Initially, the protolith, or the original rock from which the Gneiss formed, undergoes metamorphism due to tectonic forces, such as mountain-building processes or the collision of tectonic plates. This metamorphism causes the minerals within the protolith to recrystallize and reorganize, leading to the development of the characteristic banding observed in Gneiss.

On the other hand, Ptygmatic folds formed under different specific conditions:

1. ***High Pressure and Temperature:*** These folds result from ductile deformation under high temperatures (typically above 300°C) and pressures (several kilobars). At these conditions, rocks become more pliable and can deform plastically, forming complex folds.
2. ***Differential Stress:*** Unequal stress, commonly found in convergent plate boundaries or shear zones within the Himalayas (Kumar, 1997), leads to differential movement of rock layers, resulting in varying degrees of deformation and the formation of folds (Ramsay & Lisle, 2000).
3. ***Competency Variations:*** The presence of layers with contrasting competencies within the rock is essential. As mentioned earlier, Gneiss often exhibits this characteristic, with feldspar-rich layers being more competent and mica-rich layers less competent. This difference in competency allows the less competent layers to flow and fold around the more resistant layers, creating intricate ptygmatic structures.
4. ***Presence of Fluids:*** Fluids like water can act as lubricants and further facilitate the flow of less competent layers during deformation, promoting ptygmatic fold development.
5. ***Deformation Rate:*** The deformation rate can also influence the formation of ptygmatic folds. Slower deformation rates may allow for more pronounced fold development than rapid deformation events.

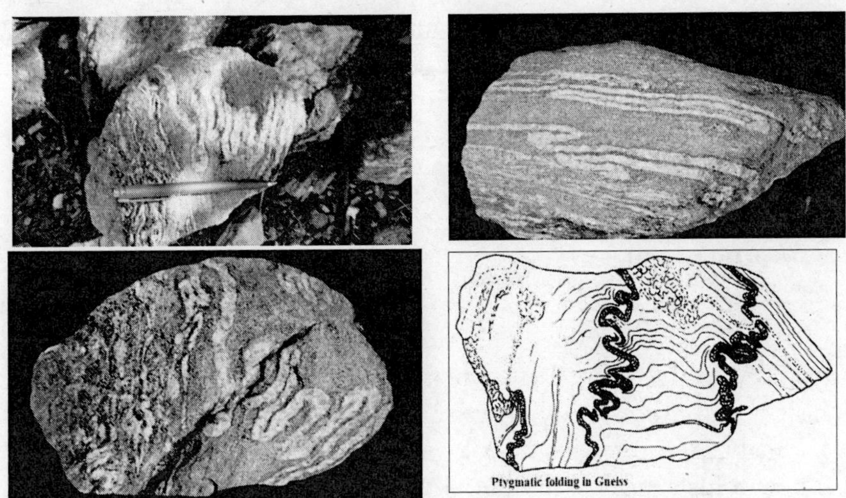

Photo 1: Gneiss with Ptygmatic Fold (Field Photo & Sketch)

5.3 *Provenance of Gneiss with Ptygmatic Fold*

The provenance of the protolith (Country or original rock), whether sedimentary, igneous, or metamorphic, hinted at the geological context in which it originated, offering clues to the ancient environments and processes at play. The provenance of the protolith of Gneiss can vary, depending on the region's geological history. It could originate from sedimentary rocks like shale or sandstone, igneous rocks like granite, or even pre-existing metamorphic rocks like schist. The specific composition and mineralogy of the protolith influence the characteristics of the resulting Gneiss, including its banding and foliation.

6. Significance of the Study

The presence of ptygmatic folds on Gneiss in the high-altitude setting of Arunachal Pradesh carries significant geological implications. Firstly, their formation suggests deep burial of the Gneiss, indicating that these rocks once resided at considerable depths within the Earth's crust, likely during the Himalayan orogeny (Kumar, 1997). Secondly, Ptygmatic folds provide evidence of the intense shearing forces the Gneiss endured during its tectonic journey within the Himalayas and offer valuable insights into deformation patterns and prevalent tectonic stresses in the region (Ghosh, 2000). By examining these geological features, researchers can glean a deeper understanding of the tectonic processes shaping the high-altitude terrain of Arunachal Pradesh, particularly in the context of the broader regional geology of the Tethyan Himalayas.

7. Conclusion

The study of Gneiss with Ptygmatic folds in the high-altitude setting of Arunachal Pradesh underscores the principle that "the Present is the Key to the Past." Researchers can unravel the complex geological history and processes that have shaped the region over millions of years by analyzing present-day geological features such as ptygmatic folds. These folds suggest deep burial of the Gneiss during the Himalayan orogeny, providing insights into past tectonic events. Additionally, the formation of ptygmatic folds highlights the intense shearing forces and tectonic stresses experienced by the Gneiss, shedding light on deformation patterns within the Himalayas. Through this study, we gain a deeper understanding of the region's geological evolution and its significance in the broader context of the Tethyan Himalayas. As we continue to explore and analyze present-day geological features, we enhance our understanding of past events, demonstrating the timeless relevance of the principle "the Present is the Key to the Past" in geological research. In conclusion, the rock, along with the multiple events we encountered during our tour, serves as a tangible reminder of the ever-changing nature of our planet and the profound geological forces that have shaped its landscapes over millennia.

References

[1] Anderson, E.M. (1951). The dynamics of faulting, New York; Hafner, reprinted, 1972.

[2] Best, M.G. (2013). *Igneous and metamorphic petrology*. John Wiley & Sons.

[3] Best, M.G. and Fisher, R.V. (2009). Igneous and metamorphic petrology (2nd ed.). Blackwell Publishing.

[4] Bhushan, S.K., Bindal, C.M. and Aggrawal, R.K. (1991). Geology of Bomdila Group in Arunachal Pradesh. *Himalayan Geology*, 2(2), 207–214.

[5] Blatt, H. and Tracy, R.J. (1996). Petrology: igneous, sedimentary, and metamorphic rocks (2nd ed.). Freeman, W.H. & Company.

[6] Dietrich, R.V. (1959). Development of ptygmatic features within a passive host during partial anatexis. Beiträge zur Mineralogie und Petrographie, 6(6), 357–365. http://dx.doi.org/10.1007/bf01206337

[7] Fossen, H. (2010). *Structural geology.* Cambridge (UK): Cambridge University Press. https://doi.org/10.1017/CBO9780511777806

[8] Ghosh, S.K. (1993). Structural Geology: Fundamentals and Modern Developments, Pergamon Press. Oxford, UK.

[9] Haldar, S.K. and Tišljar, J. (2014). Metamorphic Rocks. In Introduction to Mineralogy and Petrology (pp. 213–232). http://dx.doi.org/10.1016/b978-0-12-408133-8.00006-7

[10] Hobbs, B.E. and Ord, A. (2011). Microstructures in deforming–reactive systems. Geological Society, London, Special Publications, 360(1), 273–299. https://doi.org/10.1144/SP360.16

[11] Jackson, J. and McKenzie, D. (1983). The geometrical evolution of normal fault systems. Journal of Structural Geology, 5(5), 471–482. https://doi.org/10.1016/0191-8141(83)90053-6

[12] King, G.C.P. (1978). Geological Faults: Fracture, Creep and Strain. Philosophical Transactions of the Royal Society A: Mathematical, *Physical and Engineering Sciences,* 288(1350), 197–212. https://doi.org/10.1098/rsta.1978.0013

[13] Kumar, G. (Ed.). (1997). Geology of Arunachal Pradesh. Geological Society of India. Reprinted in 2013.

[14] Matin, A. and Mazumdar, S. (2009). Deformation mechanisms in the frontal Lesser Himalayan Duplex in Sikkim Himalaya, India. *Journal of Earth System Science, 118*(4), 379–390. http://dx.doi.org/10.1007/s12040-009-0033-6

[15] Milch, L. (1900). On dynamometamorphic phenomena on a Nordic granite gneiss. New Yearbook for Mineralogy, 2, 29–51.

[16] Mishra, D.K. (2007). Evidence of Neotectonic activity along active faults in Arunachal Himalaya, NE India. Himalayan Geol, 28(2), 75–78.

[17] Ramsay, J.G. and Lisle, R.J. (2000). The techniques of modern structural geology, volume 3: Applications of continuum mechanics in structural geology [Softback]. Academic Press. London.

[18] Read, H.H. (1928). A note on "ptygmatic folding" in the Sutherland granite complex. Memoirs of the Geological Survey of Scotland. Summary of Progress for 1927, 2, 72–77.

[19] Saha, S., Bera, B., Shit, P. K., Sengupta, D., Bhattacharjee, S., Sengupta, N., ... and Adhikary, P. P. (2023). Modelling and predicting

of landslide in Western Arunachal Himalaya, India. Geosystems and Geoenvironment, 2(2), 100158. https://doi.org/10.1016/j.geogeo.2022.100158

[20] Schwab, F. and Prothero, D. (2014). Sedimentary Geology (3rd ed.). New York, NY: W. H. Freeman and Company.

[21] Sederholm, J.J. (1907). On granites and gneisses. Bulletin of the Geological Commission of Finland, 23, 1–110.

[22] Sederholm, J.J. (1926). On migmatites and associated Precambrian rocks of southwestern Finland, 2. Bulletin of the Geological Commission of Finland, 77, 69–81.

[23] Sharma, S., Baruah, S. and Sarma, J.N. (2022). Neotectonic evidence of some major rivers of North East India. Current Science, 122(8), 918–933.

[24] Sibson, R.H. (2009). Rupturing in overpressured crust during compressional inversion—the case from NE Honshu, Japan. Tectonophysics, 473(3–4), 404–416.

[25] Sibson, R.H. (1977). Fault rocks and fault mechanisms, Journal of the Geological Society, v. 133; p. 191–213, http://dx.doi.org/10.1144/gsjgs.133.3.0191

[26] Singh, C.D., Kohli, A. and Kumar, P. (2014). Comparison of results of BIS and GSI guidelines on macrolevel landslide hazard zonation—A case study along the highway from Bhalukpong to Bomdila, West Kameng district, Arunachal Pradesh. Journal of the Geological Society of India, 83, 688–696. https://doi.org/10.1007/s12594-014-0101-7

[27] Srivastava, H.B., Srivastava, V., Srivastava, R.K., *et al.* (2011). Structural analyses of the crystalline rocks between Dirang and Tawang, West Kameng district, Arunachal Himalaya. *Journal of the Geological Society of India*, 78, 45. https://doi.org/10.1007/s12594-011-0066-8

[28] Vernon, R.H. (2004) A Practical Guide to Rock Microstructure. Cambridge University Press, Cambridge. http://dx.doi.org/10.1017/CBO9780511807206

[29] Wilson, G. (1952). Ptygmatic structures and their formation. *Geological Magazine,* 89(1), 1–21.

[30] Yardley, B. (2021). An Introduction to Metamorphic Petrology (2nd edition) [Hardcover]. Cambridge University Press, India.

[31] Yin, A., Dubey, C.S., Kelty, T.K., Gehrels, G.E., Chou, C.Y., Grove, M. and Lovera, O. (2006). Structural evolution of the Arunachal Himalaya and implications for asymmetric development of the Himalayan orogen. *Current Science,* 195–206. https://www.jstor.org/stable/24088981

Sustainable Land Use-Cover Dynamics and Livelihood Impacts: A Geospatial Analysis of the Kulik River Corridor in Uttar Dinajpur, India

Debarshi Ghosh[1] **and Abdul Momin Hoque**[1]

ABSTRACT: Human activities profoundly influence river characteristics over spatial and temporal scales. The primary flow of the river, alongside its associated wetlands or oxbow lakes, plays a vital role in the livelihoods of the local populations. Within the Kulik river corridor, changes in land use and cover have significantly altered the ecological balance and human reliance on the river. From 1990 to 2021, there was a notable increase in settlements within the corridor from 2% to 8.61%. Similarly, agricultural land expanded by 1.38% from 2001 to 2021. This expansion in agriculture, particularly with the introduction of boro paddy and maize in the post-monsoon season, has increased water demand. This study examines how the changing landscape influences local residents' dependence and strategies for adapting to their evolving environment. A model for detecting and simulating changes in land use and cover was developed to understand both current and future dynamics. Factor analysis was conducted to evaluate the shifting dependencies of the local population. The first factor score, representing direct dependency, accounts for 81.1% of the variance in water scarcity. Typically observed beyond urban centers, direct dependency on the river has decreased markedly among urban populations. This reduction in dependency has led to less use of oxbow lakes and abandoned channels for fish breeding. Domestic reliance on the river has also significantly decreased, from 0.8% to 0.62%. A non-parametric test clearly demonstrates the decline in river dependency among the current generation.

[1] Assistant Professor, Department of Geography, Dhupguri Girls' College, West Bengal, India.

Keywords: *River Corridor; Rural Livelihood; Anthropogenic Impact; Non-parametric Test, Factor Analysis.*

1. Introduction

Rivers play a crucial role in human civilization, offering multiple utilities such as water sources, transportation routes, geographical boundaries, pollution absorbers, and shaping local environments (Mouton *et al.*, 2011). As pivotal ecological assets, they endure significant stress due to their vital contributions (Beißler and Hack, 2019). Increasing anthropogenic pressures are transforming river systems, forcing them to adapt to new equilibrium conditions and behavioral shifts (Hajek & Wolinsky, 2012; Han *et al.*, 2020). Many rivers, especially in temperate regions, have lost their pristine states due to prolonged human impacts, making them among the most endangered ecosystems globally (Bowen & Waltermire, 2002; Rogers *et al.*, 2021). Assessing and managing the ecological health of rivers, as emphasized by the European Water Framework Directive 2000/ 60/EC (Loos, 2012), is therefore critical. River corridors, particularly vulnerable to both direct and indirect human influences, traverse densely populated megacities and urban areas (Golfieri *et al.*, 2018). These corridors require specific land allocations to support the river's natural stability and dynamic equilibrium (Kearsley *et al.*, 2005; Tranmer *et al.*, 2020), offering essential ecosystem services to a large human demographic (Mazzorana *et al.*, 2018). The tropical river corridors, with their rich biodiversity, play a significant role in maintaining high habitat quality (Magdaleno & Fernández-Yuste, 2011).

Population growth and urbanization along riverbanks intensify stress on river ecosystems, leading to severe water crises, exacerbated by unsustainable irrigation, industrialization, and inadequate water management (Ahmad *et al.*, 2018). The construction of dams, riverbank concretization, and other modifications contribute to channel instability and alter hydraulic geometries, resulting in long-term ecological damage (Mahadevan *et al.*, 2020; Deng *et al.*, 2015; Hajek and Wolinsky, 2012; Subramani *et al.*, 2013; Wei, Taubenböck, and Blaschke, 2017; Rodriguesda *et al.*, 2020; Rukhsana *et al.*, 2021). The pressure on river systems has also led to a shift in rural livelihoods, which increasingly rely on the ecological richness of rivers (Talukdar *et al.*, 2020; Yao *et al.*, 2021). Changes in land use affect hydrological processes, altering evapotranspiration rates, soil water retention, and runoff patterns, which, in turn, influence river flows (Mandal *et al.*, 2021).

The Kulik River, essential to the livelihoods in Uttar Dinajpur District, faces degradation due to dense settlement along its banks post the India-Pakistan partition and the 1971 Bangladesh liberation movement, which brought a surge of refugees (District Human Development Report, 2010; Sarkar and Pal, 2018; Sarkar and Mondal, 2020). This study aims to analyze the impact of human activities on this river's ecosystem by examining the effects of land-use changes along its corridor. It will also explore how these changes influence rural livelihood adaptations based on local perceptions of the evolving river-based economy. If not addressed with appropriate management and conservation strategies, the region could face significant water shortages and increased flood risks.

2. Study Area

The Kulik River, a transboundary waterway between Bangladesh and India, is the focus of this study, which spans from Panduabeel to the confluence with the Nagar River, all within Indian territory (Figure 1). This segment stretches geographically from 25°33′27″N to 25°44′27″N and from 88°13′57″E to 88°02′41″E. The river traverses a broad, flat alluvial plain with a modest elevation change of 20–25 meters from the source to the mouth. The river's path is notably winding in this region, characterized by various geomorphological features such as offshoots, paleo-channels, chute and neck cut-offs, point bars, and a convex-concave bank slope, along with a typical pool-riffle sequence. The climate here is sub-humid monsoon with annual rainfall ranging from 1550 to 2280 mm. The basin predominantly consists of sandy to sandy-loam soil textures, often inundated, leading to deposits locally known as 'Khaddar' (Chen *et al.*, 2019; Gao *et al.*, 2020; Siddiqui *et al.*, 2018), which are conducive to cultivating crops like paddy, jute, maize, sugarcane, and potatoes. Along its banks lies the Raiganj Wildlife Sanctuary, one of Asia's prominent bird sanctuaries, hosting about 164 species and attracting 70,000 to 80,000 migratory birds annually (Pramanik *et al.*, 2010). For this study, a buffer zone extending 1500 meters along both sides of the bank was delineated, within which intensive and direct utilization of river water for agriculture and other domestic purposes was observed during field investigations.

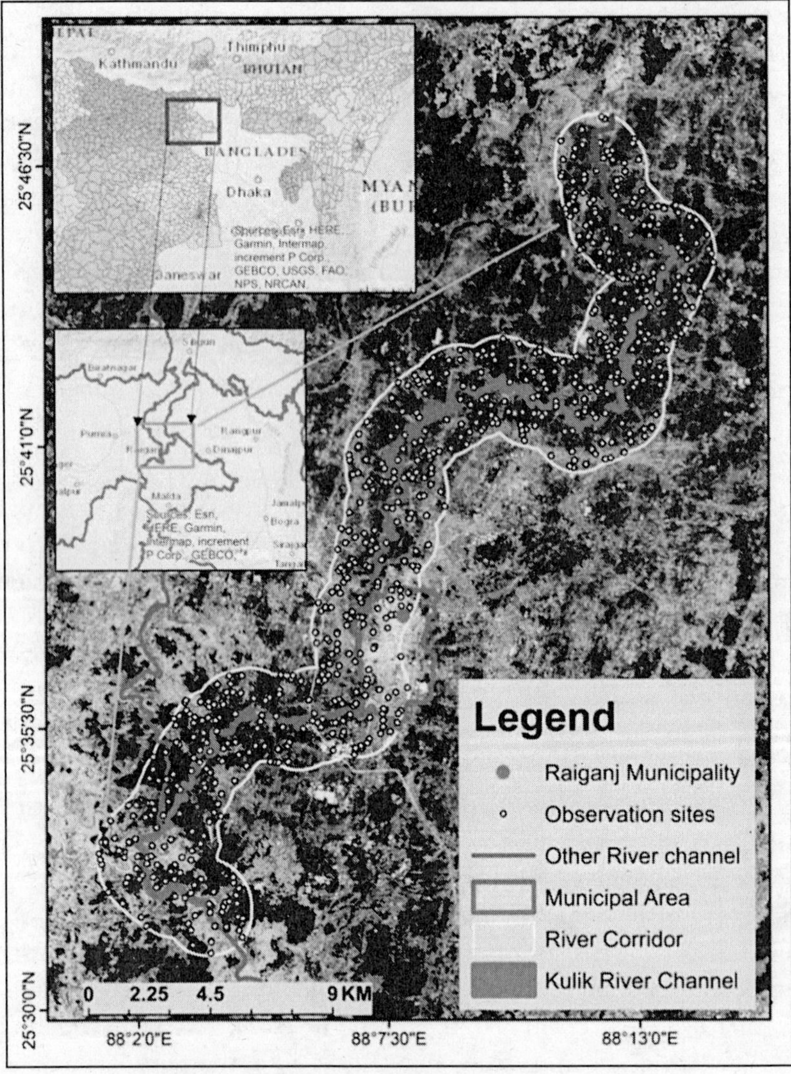

Figure 1: Location of the Study Area Emphasizing Lateral Buffer Belt and Channel form of River Kulik

3. Methodology

3.1 *Change Detection Analysis*

The livelihood patterns within a region can vary significantly with changes in landscape characteristics. Remote sensing and Geographic Information Systems (GIS) serve as essential tools for effectively monitoring and managing land-use changes, which are critical in areas experiencing increasing anthropogenic pressure (Ewane and Lee, 2020; Saddique, Mahmood, and Bernhofer, 2020). Image classification and change detection techniques play pivotal roles in observing the dynamics of land use, particularly within riparian zones (Figure 2). For this analysis, non-thermal bands were utilized to create False Color Composite (FCC) images, which help in distinguishing different land use categories by their unique color signatures. These images were classified to generate land use maps for the years 2001, 2010 and 2020 (Figure 3a, b, and 4a). The Maximum Likelihood Classification

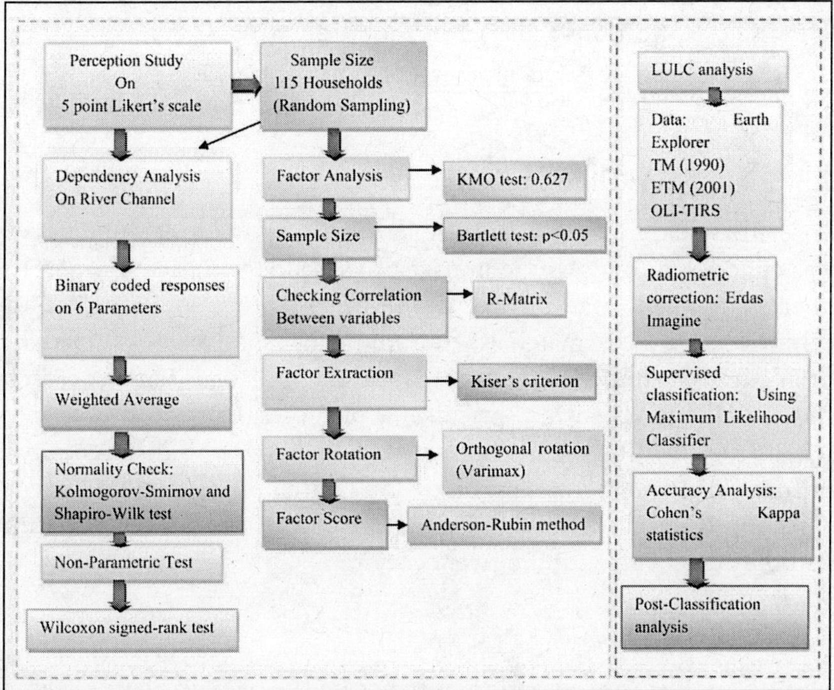

Figure 2: Flow-Chart on Methodological Course of Action for the Study

(MLC) algorithm, a widely recognized method for its probabilistic approach to pixel classification, was employed to ensure each pixel was accurately categorized into its respective land-use class (A. Sarkar & Chouhan, 2020).

3.2 Accuracy Assessment

To validate the accuracy (Figure 2) of each land use map, reference data were compiled using stratified random sample points from Google Earth for the years 2001 and 2010, supplemented by topographical maps (Survey of India, No. 78C/3). The accuracy assessment process involved examining 40 pixels per category through ground-truthing to ensure reliability. The results were cross-tabulated against the ground truth data, with outcomes presented in an error matrix format. To further quantify the classification accuracy and address both diagonal and off-diagonal elements of the confusion matrix, a non-parametric Kappa test was performed. This statistical method is crucial for assessing the consistency and precision of the land use classifications achieved in the study.

$$\text{Cohen's Kappa} = \frac{\text{Overall accuracy} - \text{Expected Accuracy}}{1 - \text{Expected accuracy}} \quad \ldots (1)$$

3.3 *Field-based Data Collection*

A detailed field investigation complemented by a photographic survey was conducted to assess the impact of anthropogenic activities on the river. The focus was on key environmental stressors such as the extraction of bed materials, dumping of solid waste, riverbank protection efforts, construction of bridges and roads, and encroachment of the riverbed for agricultural purposes. Historical data were reconstructed using a comparative analysis between old series Survey of India (SOI) topographical maps and contemporary satellite images. This approach allows for a detailed evaluation of changes over time and the current state of the river ecosystem.

3.4 *Perception Study*

During the field investigation, a structured survey was conducted to explore local perceptions regarding livelihood dependencies and the intergenerational shifts in reliance on the Kulik River. The survey included 115 households, strategically selected and geographically represented in Figure 1. A dependency ratio was established based on several critical parameters: Drinking Water, Domestic Use, Irrigation, Fishing, Transport, and Jute Retting. This ratio was designed to quantitatively assess the extent and nature of the community's reliance on the river for these essential aspects of their daily lives and economic activities.

3.5 *Intergenerational Dependency Analysis*

The study examines intergenerational dependencies on the river channel, focusing on evolving livelihood patterns. A perception survey categorized respondents into older and younger generations, with binary-coded responses collected on key aspects of dependency. Dependency ratios were calculated based on six aspects, and statistical tests revealed significant deviations from normality. A non-parametric Wilcoxon signed-rank test was used to identify differences in dependency ratios between generational groups, indicating a departure from the null hypothesis of zero median differences.

3.6 *Factor Analysis Approach*

Factor analysis (Figure 2) was conducted to investigate seven key variables influencing river dependency: (a) River water pollution (F1), (b) River water scarcity (F2), (c) Reduction in fish supply in the river (F3), (d) Issues with irrigation facilities (F4), (e) Land loss (F5), (f) Changing attitudes of people (F6) and (g) Availability of water from alternative sources (F7). This analysis aimed to accomplish three objectives: understanding the structure of the variable set, designing a questionnaire to gauge an underlying variable, and reducing the dataset to a more manageable size while preserving essential information (A. Sarkar & Chouhan, 2021).

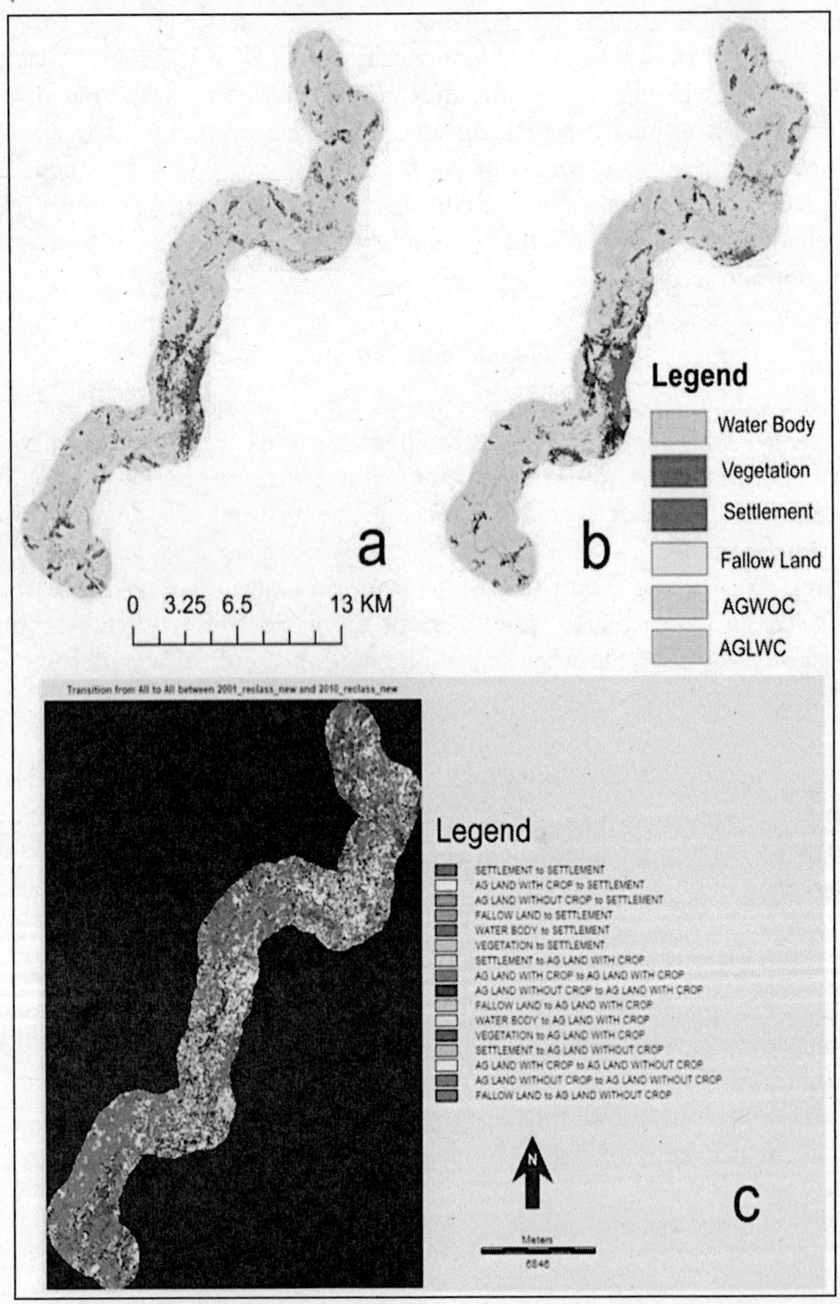

Figure 3: LULC and Transition Layers: a. LULC Map of 2001, b. LULC Map of 2010, c. Transition Map from All Classes to Settlement

4. Results

4.1 *Land Use Simulations for Kulik Corridor*

The Kulik, a trans-boundary river between Bangladesh and India, has experienced significant urban expansion over the last two decades due to rapid economic development. This trend, coupled with population increases, is projected to continue, reshaping the urban landscape significantly in the coming years. The Land Use and Land Cover (LULC) maps from 2001 (Figure 3a), 2010 (Figure 3b) and 2020 (Figure 4a) illustrate these changes, showing a pronounced expansion of urban areas. The accuracy of these maps for the years 2001, 2010 and 2020 are 79.57%, 88.29%, and 89.13% respectively, with the overall kappa statistic values for land use at 0.793 in 1990, 0.823 in 2001 and 0.876 in 2020. As the landscape evolves, so does the livelihood pattern of those residing in the floodplains, necessitating that decision-makers adapt and plan for future scenarios. To assist in predicting and managing these changes, a land-use land cover simulation model using a multilayer Perceptron neural network algorithm has been implemented. This model aims to provide insights into future land-use shifts under various basin management and planning scenarios, evaluating the impact of increased settlement patches within the river corridor on the dynamics of land use and cover change (LUCC).

4.2 *Land-Use Change Simulation for Raiganj Township Expansion*

In response to Raiganj township's expansion, a specialized sub-model was developed to analyze transitions from various land use and land cover (LULC) categories to settlement areas. This sub-model relied on proximity rasters—such as distance to roads, railways, rivers, and urban amenities—as key variables. The evidence likelihood method assessed transformation likelihood, with Cramer's V statistics indicating a strong correlation (>0.5) between these variables and urban land shifts, confirmed as statistically significant (p-value = 0). The model, considering each driver variable static, used a multilayer perceptron (MLP) neural network to simulate 2020 LULC changes, achieving Root Mean Square (RMS) accuracy rates of 44.57% in training and 45.25% in testing, with an overall accuracy of 68.34%. The transition potential map showed a 9.95% chance of land shifting from agricultural use to settlements between 2000 and 2010, underscoring the dynamic changes linked to urban expansion.

4.3 *Transition Modeling Using MLP-ANN Algorithm*

The transition sub-model, utilizing MLP-ANN, generates a Transition Potential Map (TPM) assessing land use conversions, particularly focusing on shifts to settlements from 2001 to 2010. Spatial trends in land use and land cover changes are analyzed. Simulating land use for 2020 validates settlement expansion in the river corridor using class-to-class transition matrices. Cross-validation with classified maps enhances reliability. The model highlights human encroachment in floodplains, aiding understanding of river channel degradation. Results show significant transformations, notably from agricultural land to settlements (9.95%) and a shift in agricultural land use to fallow (34.55%).

4.4 *Land Use Changes and Impacts on the Kulik River Corridor*

The river corridor, intersecting with urban areas, faces environmental pressures from development, leading to significant land-use changes. From 2001 to 2020, agricultural and forested lands were largely converted to settlements, with agricultural areas shrinking and built-up areas expanding. The study highlights the decline in water bodies and vegetation, with a projection of continued urban sprawl and habitat fragmentation (Figure 5 a, b, c & d). The expansion of settlements is expected to impact the river corridor's ecology adversely, affecting the local community's reliance on the river for essential resources.

4.5 *Generational Changes in Dependency on the Kulik River*

The dependency on the Kulik River among the current generation has significantly decreased, with the dependency ratio dropping from 0.66 to 0.44. The use of river water for drinking has declined due to better access to alternative sources and pollution concerns, decreasing from a ratio of 0.8 to 0.62. Similarly, fishing dependency has reduced from 0.87 to 0.80 due to overfishing and diminished fish stocks. In contrast, irrigation dependency slightly increased from 0.58 to 0.62, thanks to improved irrigation technology and practices. Statistical analysis confirms a significant shift in river dependency between generations, marked by. a p-value of 0.00 and a notable z-score of 7.969.

Table 1: Amount of Change in Different Land Use-Cover Categories in the Kulik River Corridor (2001–2040)

Land Use-Cover (LULC) Categories	*Change 2001–2020*		*Change 2020–2040*	
	Sq. km	*%*	*Sq. km*	*%*
Settlement	9.94	6.40	7.50	4.91
Agriculture land With Corp	–1.14	–0.81	–5.60	–3.38
Agriculture land without crop	3.09	1.97	–2.76	–1.70
Fellow land	–0.43	–0.28	0.00	0.00
Water Body	–6.95	–4.49	–0.30	–0.17
Vegetation	–3.65	–2.36	–0.53	–0.33
Total	0.00	0.00	0.00	0.00

Source: Computed by the authors.

Table 2: Land Use-cover Change Based on Simulation Model

Land Use-cover (LULC) Categories	*2020*		*2030*		*2040*	
	Sq. km	*%*	*Sq. km*	*%*	*Sq. km*	*%*
Settlement	20.19	12.98	25.99	16.82	26.99	17.47
Agriculture land with Corp	84.15	54.12	80.45	52.06	79.55	51.48
Agriculture land without crop	31.20	20.06	29.8	19.29	29.44	19.05
Fellow land	0.89	0.57	0.09	0.06	0.09	0.06
Water Body	8.06	5.18	7.84	5.07	7.76	5.02
Vegetation	11.01	7.08	9.34	6.025806	9.68	6.24
Total	155	100	155	100	155	100

Source: Computed by the authors.

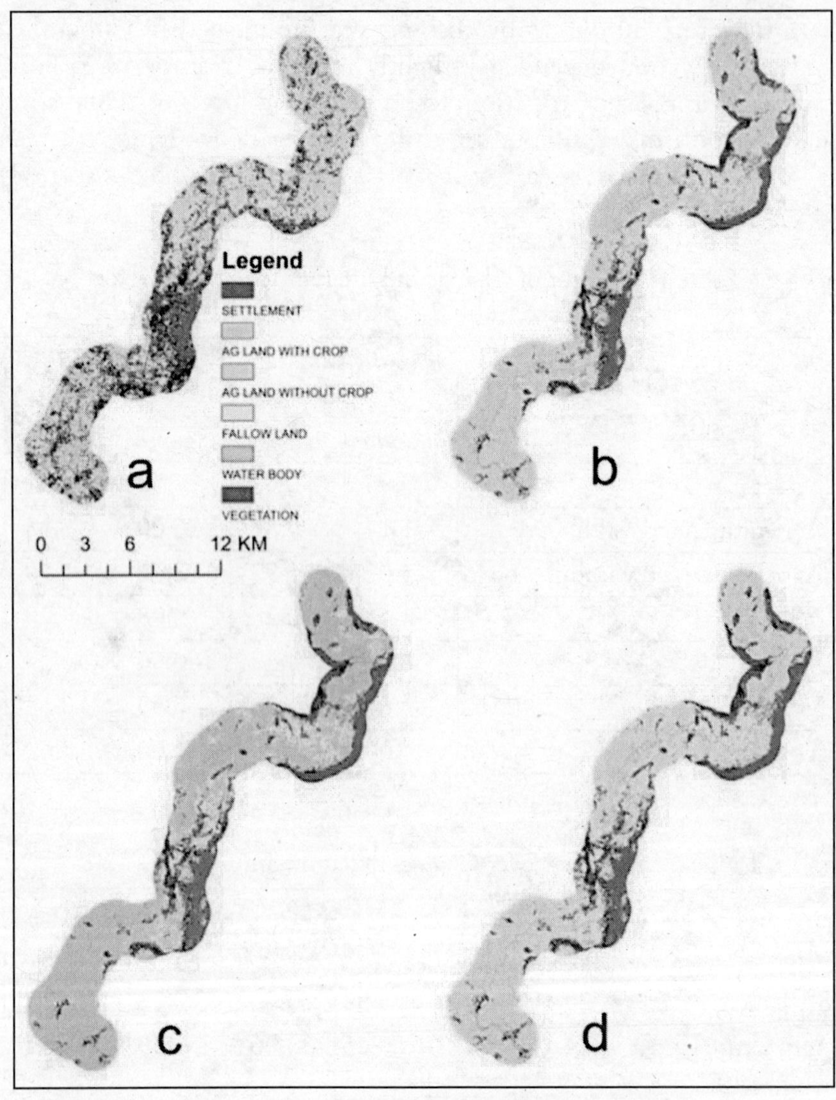

Figure 4: Changes in Class Category: a. Land Use Classified Land Use 2020, b. Simulated Land Use 2020, c. Simulated Land Use 2030, d. Simulated Land Use 2030 Based on Sub-model

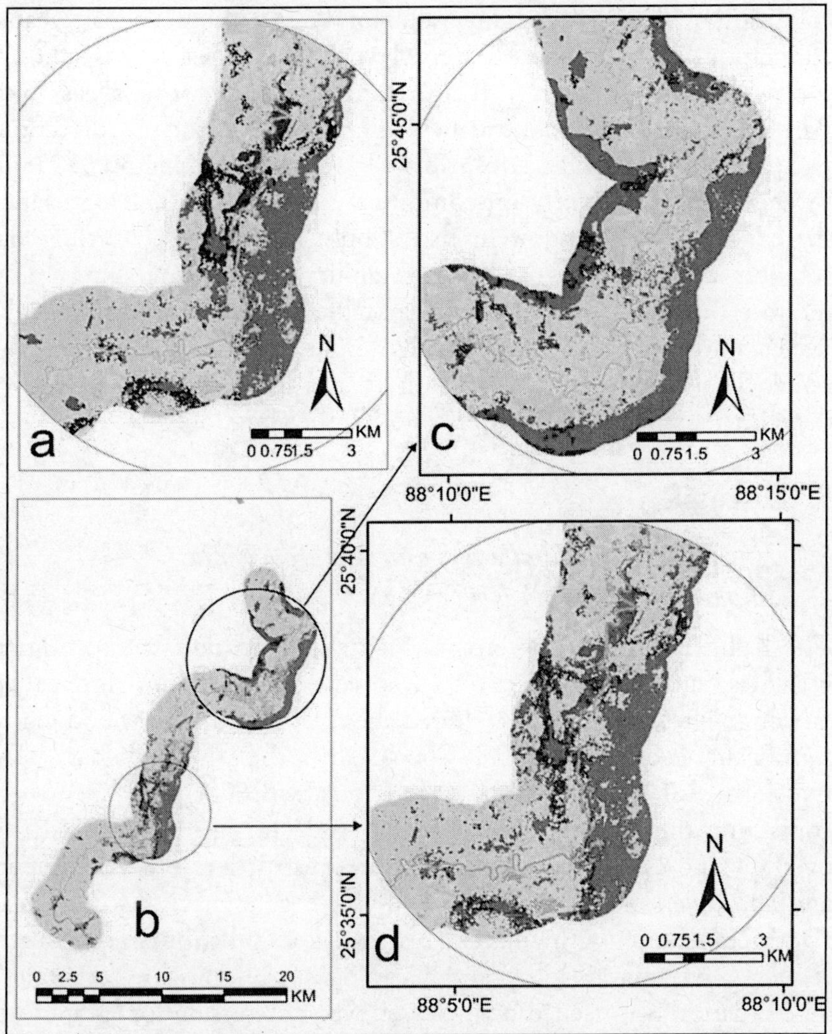

Figure 5: Trend of settlement expansion in Kulik corridor: a. settlement expansion in and around Raiganj municipality from 2020 simulated map, b. projected LULC of 2040, c. edge expansion of settlement in the upper part of corridor, d. settlement expansion in and around Raiganj municipality in 2040.

4.6 *Factor Analysis Results and Interpretations*

The study presents a correlation matrix with coefficients ranging from 0.3 to 0.9, suggesting moderate correlations and minimal multicollinearity. The determinant value of 0.292 indicates manageable correlation levels. The Kaiser-Meyer-Olkin measure is 0.627, supporting the adequacy of the sample for factor analysis, and Bartlett's test confirms the data's suitability for structure detection. Factor analysis extracted two principal factors explaining 39.329% of the variance, with significant communalities such as a 63.0% variance shared by the 'Reduction in fish supply in the river.' Orthogonal rotation improved factor interpretability, identifying direct and indirect dependency factors, with notable loadings on variables like 'River water scarcity' and 'Problem in irrigation facility from the river'. The analysis reveals both direct and indirect impacts on river dependency, supported by robust statistical validation.

5. Discussion

5.1 *Environmental Challenges and Anthropogenic Impacts on the Kulik River*

The Kulik River is facing environmental degradation due to human activities, such as construction, riverbed cultivation, and intensified farming. These actions have altered the river's natural flow and led to significant ecological shifts. Specifically, the riverbed has been transformed for boro-paddy cultivation, with 73 plots identified, converting the riverbed into elevated land and heightening risks of overflow and erosion. Furthermore, the construction of embankments and the diversion of water through sluice gates have disrupted the river's connection with adjacent oxbow lakes and tributaries, severely reducing water availability and harming surrounding water bodies. The situation is worsened by increased water extraction for agriculture, driven by decreased flood frequency and the shift towards high-water-demand crops like boro paddy and maize, replacing traditional crops such as pulses, potatoes, and vegetables.

5.2 *Socio-Economic Shifts and Livelihood Adjustments*

Local communities have adapted to these environmental changes by altering their livelihood strategies. Many fishermen have abandoned their traditional occupations due to reduced fish stocks, compounded by river pollution and narrowing river widths, particularly under bridges where debris and pollutants accumulate. As a result, direct dependency on the river for traditional livelihoods like fishing and jute retting has decreased, while indirect dependencies, such as using the river for irrigation during the dry season, have increased.

5.3 *Factor Analysis of Dependency on the River*

The factor analysis to understand local dependencies on the Kulik River revealed two main factors accounting for 55.23% of the variance in river interaction. The first factor (F1), contributing 28.98% of the variance, is driven by 'river water scarcity,' indicating a high direct dependency on the river for water resources. This dependency is particularly strong from Ratanpur to Gayas, where inhabitants rely heavily on the river for irrigation. On the other hand, in areas like Raiganj Municipality and Dakshin Kasba, cultural shifts have led to reduced direct dependencies on the river, as reflected in the second factor, which focuses on indirect dependencies such as irrigation and water extraction. The expansion of settlements, especially near Raiganj Municipality, continues to threaten the river's ecological health, with land use and land cover (LULC) models projecting increased urbanization and further reduction in natural habitats and water bodies along the river corridor by 2040.

6. Conclusion

The Kulik River corridor is experiencing significant environmental degradation due to human activities such as land-use changes, development of transportation networks, and construction projects. These activities have led to pollution, reduced water levels, and a decrease in fish populations, impacting the livelihoods of local communities that depend on the river. Urban residents near Raiganj municipality are moving away from traditional river-dependent occupations due to the deteriorating river conditions. Additionally, agricultural practices are adapting to water scarcity, with an increased reliance on groundwater irrigation. Analysis indicates that while natural dependency on the river remains higher in rural areas, it is diminishing across generations, with the current generation showing a significant reduction in river reliance compared to their predecessors. This shift underscores the urgent need for collaborative efforts to restore the river's health and protect the rural livelihoods it supports. Local communities, government entities, and NGOs must work together to implement sustainable practices that mitigate environmental degradation. To ensure the river's sustainability and the well-being of its dependent communities, it is crucial to promote community-based management, enhance education and awareness programs, enforce environmental regulations strictly, and adopt advanced wastewater treatment technologies. These measures will help preserve the river's ecological health, cultural heritage, and the livelihoods that have developed around it, maintaining a balance between growth and environmental sustainability.

References

[1] Aarthi, A.D. and Gnanappazham, L. (2018). Urban growth prediction using neural network coupled agents-based Cellular Automata model for Sriperumbudur Taluk, Tamil Nadu, India. *Egyptian Journal of Remote Sensing and Space Science*, *21*(3), 353–362. https://doi.org/10.1016/j.ejrs.2017.12.004

[2] Ahmad, I., Zhang, F., Tayyab, M., Anjum, M.N., Zaman, M., Liu, J., Farid, H.U. and Saddique, Q. (2018). Spatiotemporal analysis of precipitation variability in annual, seasonal and extreme values over upper Indus River basin. *Atmospheric Research*, *213*, 346–360. https://doi.org/10.1016/j.atmosres.2018.06.019

[3] Amoako Johnson, F., Hutton, C. and William Hutton, C. (2010). Hazard, vulnerability and risk on the Brahmaputra Basin: a case study of river bank erosion Dependence on agriculture and ecosystem services for livelihood in Northeast India and Bhutan: vulnerability to climate change in the Tropical River Basins of the Upper Brahmaputra. *Springer*, *127*(1), 107–121. https://doi.org/10.1007/s10584-012-0573-7

[4] Beißler, M.R. and Hack, J. (2019). A Combined Field and Remote-Sensing Based Methodology to Assess the Ecosystem Service Potential of Urban Rivers in Developing Countries.

[5] Bowen, Z.H. and Waltermire, R.G. (2002). Evaluation of light detection and ranging (LIDAR) for measuring river corridor topography. *Journal of the American Water Resources Association*, *38*(1), 33–41. https://doi.org/10.1111/j.1752-1688.2002.tb01532.x

[6] Chen, Y., Li, X., Liu, X., Huang, H. and Ma, S. (2019). Simulating urban growth boundaries using a patch-based cellular automaton with

economic and ecological constraints. *International Journal of Geographical Information Science, 33*(1), 55–80. https://doi.org/10.1080/13658816.2018.1514119

[7] Deng, X., Xu, Y., Han, L., Yu, Z., Yang, M. and Pan, G. (2015). Assessment of river health based on an improved entropy-based fuzzy matter-element model in the Taihu Plain, China. *Ecological Indicators, 57*, 85–95. https://doi.org/10.1016/j.ecolind.2015.04.020

[8] Ewane, B.E. and Lee, H.H. (2020). Assessing land use/land cover change impacts on the hydrology of Nyong River Basin, Cameroon. *Journal of Mountain Science, 17*(1), 50–67. https://doi.org/10.1007/s11629-019-5611-8.

[9] Gao, C., Feng, Y., Tong, X., Lei, Z., Chen, S. and Zhai, S. (2020). Modeling urban growth using spatially heterogeneous cellular automata models: Comparison of spatial lag, spatial error and GWR. *Computers, Environment and Urban Systems, 81*(July 2019), 101459. https://doi.org/10.1016/j.compenvurbsys.2020.101459

[10] Golfieri, B., Surian, N. and Hardersen, S. (2018). Towards a more comprehensive assessment of river corridor conditions: A comparison between the Morphological Quality Index and three biotic indices. *Ecological Indicators, 84* (September 2017), 525–534. https://doi.org/10.1016/j.ecolind.2017.09.011

[11] Hajek, E.A. and Wolinsky, M.A. (2012). Simplified process modeling of river avulsion and alluvial architecture: Connecting models and field data. *Sedimentary Geology, 257–260*, 1–30. https://doi.org/10.1016/j.sedgeo.2011.09.005

[12] Han, H., Zhang, K. and Jinglai Zhang (2020). Evaluating the health of an urban river combining DPSIR framework and an improved fuzzy matter-element extension model: A case study from the jinshui river. *Polish Journal of Environmental Studies, 29*(3), 2211–2223. https://doi.org/10.15244/pjoes/111239

[13] Huang, X. and Xu, G. (2021). *Optimization of a Novel Urban Growth Simulation Model Integrating an Artificial Fish Swarm Algorithm and Cellular Automata for a Smart City.*

[14] Islam, A., Talukdar, S., Mahato, S., … S. K.-G. 2021, undefined. (n.d.). Flood susceptibility modelling using advanced ensemble machine learning models. *Elsevier*. Retrieved March 24, 2021, from https://www.sciencedirect.com/science/article/pii/S1674987120302073

[15] Itzkin, A., Scholes, M.C., Kumar Clifford-Holmes, J., Rowntree, K., van der Waal, B. and Coetzer, K. (2021). A Social-Ecological Systems Understanding of Drivers of Degradation in the Tsitsa River

Catchment to Inform Sustainable Land Management. *Mdpi.Com.* https://doi.org/10.3390/su13020516

[16] Kearsley, M.J.C., Cobb, N.S., Yard, H.K., Lightfoot, D.C., Brantley, S.L., Carpenter, G.C. and Frey, J.K. (2005). Inventory and Monitoring of Terrestrial Riparian Resources in the Colorado River Corridor of Grand Canyon: An Integrative Approach. *Unpublished Report, April 2014.*

[17] Lin, L., Wang, F., Chen, H., Fang, H., Zhang, T., Indicators, W.C.-E. and 2021, undefined. (n.d.). Ecological health assessments of rivers with multiple dams based on the biological integrity of phytoplankton: A case study of North Creek of Jiulong River. *Elsevier*. Retrieved March 24, 2021, from https://www.sciencedirect.com/science/article/pii/S1470160X20309377

[18] Loos, R. (2012). Analytical Methods for the new proposed Priority Substances of the European Water Framework Directive (WFD). *JRC Technical Report*, 71.

[19] Magdaleno, F. and Fernández-Yuste, J.A. (2011). Meander dynamics in a changing river corridor. *Geomorphology*, *130*(3–4), 197–207. https://doi.org/10.1016/j.geomorph.2011.03.016

[20] Mahadevan, H., Krishnan, K.A., Pillai, R.R. and Sudhakaran, S. (2020). Assessment of urban river water quality and developing strategies for phosphate removal from water and wastewaters: Integrated monitoring and mitigation studies. *SN Applied Sciences*, *2*(4), 1–14. https://doi.org/10.1007/s42452-020-2571-0

[21] Mandal, T., Saha, S., Das, J. and Sarkar, A. (2021). Groundwater depletion susceptibility zonation using TOPSIS model in Bhagirathi river basin, India. *Modeling Earth Systems and Environment*, 1–21. https://doi.org/10.1007/s40808-021-01176-7

[22] Mazzorana, B., Nardini, A., Comiti, F., Vignoli, G., Cook, E., Ulloa, H. and Iroumé, A. (2018). Toward participatory decision-making in river corridor management: two case studies from the European Alps. *Journal of Environmental Planning and Management*, *61*(7), 1250–1270. https://doi.org/10.1080/09640568.2017.1339593

[23] Megahed, Y., Cabral, P., Silva, J. and Caetano, M. (2015). Land cover mapping analysis and urban growth modelling using remote sensing techniques in greater Cairo region-Egypt. *ISPRS International Journal of Geo-Information*, *4*(3), 1750–1769. https://doi.org/10.3390/ijgi4031750

[24] Mouton, A.M., Alcaraz-Hernández, J.D., de Baets, B., Goethals, P.L.M. and Martínez-Capel, F. (2011). Data-driven fuzzy habitat

suitability models for brown trout in Spanish Mediterranean rivers. *Environmental Modelling and Software*, *26*(5), 615–622. https://doi.org/10.1016/j.envsoft.2010.12.001

[25] Munoth, P. and Goyal, R. (2020). Impacts of land use land cover change on runoff and sediment yield of Upper Tapi River Sub-Basin, India. *International Journal of River Basin Management*, *18*(2), 177–189. https://doi.org/10.1080/15715124.2019.1613413

[26] Pramanik, A.K., Santra, K.B. and Kumar Manna, C. (2010). Abundance and Diversity of Plants and Animals in the Abundance and Diversity of Plants and Animals in the Kulik Bird Sanctuary, Raiganj, West Bengal, India. *Article in Journal of Biodiversity*, *1*(1), 13–17. https://doi.org/10.1080/09766901.2010.11884714

[27] Rodriguesda, C., Doria, C., Dutka-Gianelli, J., Brasil De Sousa, S.T., Chu, J. and Garlock, T.M. (2020). Understanding impacts of dams on the small-scale fisheries of the Madeira River through the lens of the Fisheries Performance Indicators. *Elsevier*. https://doi.org/10.1016/j.marpol.2020.104261

[28] Rogers, D.B., Newcomer, M.E., Raberg, J.H., Dwivedi, D., Steefel, C., Bouskill, N., Nico, P., Faybishenko, B., Fox, P., Conrad, M., Bill, M., Brodie, E., Arora, B., Dafflon, B., Williams, K.H. and Hubbard, S.S. (2021). Modeling the Impact of Riparian Hollows on River Corridor Nitrogen Exports. *Frontiers in Water*, *3*(February). https://doi.org/10.3389/frwa.2021.590314

[29] Rukhsana, Haldar, A., Alam, A. and Satpati, L. (2021). Habitat, Ecology and Ekistics: An Overview. In *Advances in Asian Human-Environmental Research*. https://doi.org/10.1007/978-3-030-49115-4_1

[30] Saddique, N., Mahmood, T. and Bernhofer, C. (2020). Quantifying the impacts of land use/land cover change on the water balance in the afforested River Basin, Pakistan. *Environmental Earth Sciences*, *79*(19). https://doi.org/10.1007/s12665-020-09206-w

[31] Sarkar, A. and Chouhan, P. (2019). Dynamic simulation of urban expansion based on Cellular Automata and Markov Chain Model: a case study in Siliguri Metropolitan Area, West Bengal. *Modeling Earth Systems and Environment*, *5*(4), 1723–1732. https://doi.org/10.1007/s40808-019-00626-7

[32] Sarkar, A. and Chouhan, P. (2020). Modeling spatial determinants of urban expansion of Siliguri a metropolitan city of India using logistic regression. *Modeling Earth Systems and Environment*, *6*(4), 2317–2331. https://doi.org/10.1007/s40808-020-00815-9

[33] Sarkar, A. and Chouhan, P. (2021). COVID-19: District level vulnerability assessment in India. *Clinical Epidemiology and Global Health*, *9*(August 2020), 204–215. https://doi.org/10.1016/j.cegh.2020.08.017

[34] Sarkar, D. and Mondal, P. (2020). Flood vulnerability mapping using frequency ratio (FR) model: a case study on Kulik river basin, Indo-Bangladesh Barind region. *Applied Water Science*, *10*(1). https://doi.org/10.1007/s13201-019-1102-x

The Spatio-temporal Analysis of Land Use and Land Cover in Jalpaiguri District, West Bengal: A Remote Sensing and GIS Approach

Gopal Das[1] and Ranjan Sarkar[2]

ABSTRACT: The Spatio-temporal analysis of land use and land cover and its future prediction have become significant concerns for researchers, planners and academicians due to their multidimensional impact on the environment and sustainability. The rapid population growth and urbanisation are changing the landscape pattern, eventually degrading the ecosystem. This study aims to analyse the spatial pattern of land use and land cover and their temporal changes in the Jalpaiguri district of West Bengal. The study area is located in the Piedmont zone of the northeastern sub-Himalayan region. Jalpaiguri district is one of the essential parts of the Bengal-doors region. The study is based on satellite imageries of Landsat-TM and Landsat-OLI/TIRS to obtain the historical dynamics of LULC. Primary and secondary data were collected from different sources, such as maps, journals, articles, books, etc. Supervised image classification with maximum likelihood classifier was applied to produce LULC maps for 1990, 2000, 2010 and 2020. The accuracy level of classified maps was assessed by kappa accuracy assessment, which many researchers admit in their study. The result of the study revealed that the land use and land cover pattern of Jalpaiguri district has been changed from earlier to the present, mainly due to anthropogenic factors. Population growth and urban expansion are marked as the main driving factors for land use and land cover changes. The result also demonstrated a continuous development of

---

[1] Research Scholar, University of North Bengal, India.
E-mail: dasgopalgeo@gmail.com

[2] Principal, Siliguri College of Commerce, Siliguri, West Bengal, India.
E-mail: ranjangeo@gmail.com

the built-up areas from 1990 to 2020, which is expected to increase further. The vegetation cover has been reduced considerably. The result also showed a decreasing trend in cropland from 1990 to 2020. However, the present work indicates a probability of future land use and land cover changes that may result from human activity.

Keywords: Lulc, Urbanization, Supervised Image Classification, Transition Probability, Built-up Area.

1. Introduction

Land use and land cover change in a region are important indicators of human interference in the natural environment (Biswas *et al.*, 2019). Many researchers have contributed their perspectives in this field by using GIS remote sensing and satellite data, which is regarded as a crucial and pertinent source of information for predicting and forecasting land use dynamics of any part of the world (Mazhar, 2019). Land use and cover are closely linked (Das & Sarkar, 2019). Land cover is related to the bio-physical features, and land use exhibits the anthropogenic uses of those features, primarily accompanied by the transformation of green space into domicile or built-up space (Naikoo *et al.*, 2020). Change refers to either modification within one type of land cover or converting one category to another. Many natural and socio-economic factors are responsible for land use and cover changes. Unprecedented population growth, over-exploitation of natural resources, and unplanned urbanization are drivers of the change in land use and cover (Adingo *et al.*, 2020). The rapid growth of urban population and urban growth has persuaded an unpropitious modification in the landscape. Many studies have argued that the change in land use and land cover, particularly the conversion of vegetation into built-up areas, has escalated the earth's surface temperature, finally affecting the world's climate (Nayak, 2019). The land surface temperature is negatively correlated with the vegetation cover whereas the growth of built-up areas positively impacts LST (Dhar *et al.*, 2019).The study of the spatial pattern of lulc and its temporal changes may be considered to develop suitable land management strategies and policies (Mazhar, 2019). Landscape dynamics also influence the hydrological cycle of the earth's terrestrial surface as the surface runoff and groundwater discharge are appreciably determined by the level of land cover alteration (He *et al.*, 2013; Nagarajan & Poongothai, 2011). The spatiotemporal variation of land use and land cover with changing probabilities are considered the prerequisite for regional development in developing and developed countries (Palaniyandi & Nagarathinam, 1997). The approach for the classification of land has been improved from the past to the present time, and present day approaches are more inclined towards the application of RS and GIS techniques, which is more reliable and time-saving as well as cost effective (Chen *et al.*, 2003; Dhinwa *et al.*, 1992; Rawat & Kumar, 2015). The change in land use pattern is a multidimensional facet of man-environment interaction. Many researchers have reported that the encroachment of built-up areas into the marginal land at the expanse of vegetation or green spaces is a major cause of lulc alteration and threats to sustainable land utilization (Abebe *et al.*, 2021). Much research has been done in different parts of India, showing a drastic transformation of vegetation cover into built-up areas, accelerating biodiversity loss (Moulds *et al.*, 2018). In India, most parts have seen a significant change in land use, essentially triggered by changes in socio-economic conditions and urbanization (Prasad & Ramesh, 2019). The rate of urbanization is higher in South Asian countries, in which India is not exceptional, and many researchers in this country have asserted the consequences of the urbanization process on land use and land cover change (Bera & Chatterjee, 2019; Mandal *et al.*, 2021). The country's tourism sector also contributed to a substantial change; in fact, the depletion of natural resources and degradation of land ultimately lead to land use and land cover modification through the enrichment of impervious surfaces (Saha & Paul, 2020). Many studies on land use and land cover have also been done from the West Bengal perspective. Chamling and Bera have shown the pattern of land use and land cover and how it has been changed due to anthropogenic factors during the last few decades in the Bhutan—Bengal foothill region. The present study attempts to analyze the temporal patterns of land use and land cover in Jalpaiguri District, which is also recognized as one of the dooars regions of West Bengal. This region significantly witnessed a negative relation between the Spatiotemporal distributions of green space and those of built-up areas (Hoque & Lepcha, 2019).

The Spatio-temporal distribution of land use and land cover in the study area, based on the years 1990, 2000, 2010 and 2020, was examined using high-resolution satellite imagery obtained from the USGS Earth Explorer portal free of cost. Image classification accuracy is normally affected by the temporal aspect of data acquisition (Islam *et al.*, 2023). Most of the images for this study were acquired during the dry season to minimize the effect of clouds on classified maps. Accuracy assessment or validation is a significant step in retrieving the geospatial data. It establishes the validity and reliability of classified data by comparing the classified pixels corresponding to the ground truth data. For the present study, supervised image classification, which is considered one of the most frequently used processes for analyzing and quantifying satellite images (Rwanga & Ndambuki, 2017), has been applied.

2. Study Area

The present study has been conducted in Jalpaiguri District (divided), which is located within the geographical extension of 26°15′47″N to 26°59′34″ N Latitude and 88°23′2″E to 89°7′30″ E Longitude. The

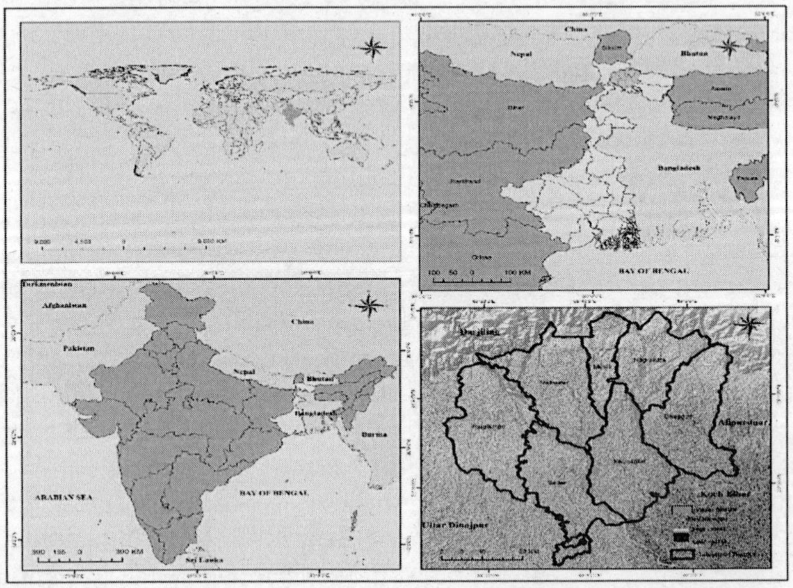

Figure 1: Location Map of Study Area

District covers an area of approximately 3386.18 sq. km. Jalpaiguri District was established on 1st January 1869, and it is the HQ of the entire North Bengal. The district is drained by several perennial and non-perennial rivers that originate in the outer range of the Himalayas. The area is significantly characterized by its diversity and richness concerning luxuriant vegetation cover, flora, fauna and cultural heritage. The area has been divided into seven community development blocks, among which the Rajganj block is the largest, covering 616 sq. km area, and Meteli is the smallest block, covering 200 sq. km. area. Other blocks are Jalpaiguri Sadar, Maynaguri, Malbazar, Dhupguri and Nagrakata.

3. Materials and Methods

To attain the study's objectives, four different years with equal time intervals have been considered to evaluate the temporal pattern of land use and land cover and its changing trends. Landsat images for 1990, 2000, 2010 and 2020 were derived from the access USGS Earth Explorer portal (https://earthexplorer.usgs.gov). For 1990, 2000 and 2010, the Landsat 5 (TM) data, while for 2020, Landsat 8 (OLI/TIRS) data have been downloaded. The path and row are 138, 139, 41 and 42, respectively. Images were collected from October to December of the respective year to minimize cloud effects. All images were processed by using the ArcGIS 10.3.1 version. Image layers were composited with an image analysis tool and then converted into FCC colour bands. These images were geo-referenced to the World Geodetic System (WGS84) and projected to UTM zone 45. A shape file of Jalpaiguri District has been prepared and digitized using the existing map to restrict the study area. After that, the study area was extracted from all satellite images using the extract-by-mask tool.

Table 1: Data Properties of Satellite Images

Period	*Month*	*Satellite*	*Sensor*	*Path*	*Row*	*Spatial Resolution*	*Datum*	*Projection*	*Zone*
1990	December	Landsat 5	TM	138,139	41,42	30 m	WGS84	UTM	45
2000	December	Landsat 5	TM	138,139	41,42	30 m	WGS84	UTM	45
2010	December	Landsat 5	TM	138,139	41,42	30 m	WGS84	UTM	45
2020	November	Landsat 8	OLI/TIRS	138,139	42	30 m	WGS84	UTM	45

3.1 *Image Classification*

Supervised image classification with maximum likelihood classifier technique was applied to produce the final land use and land cover map of Jalpaiguri District. The entire district has been categorised into seven classes: vegetation, crop land, built-up area, water bodies, plantation, grassland, and sand fill. Training samples with random selection were developed to generate the signature file, which was used to run the classification process.

3.2 *Accuracy Assessment*

The accuracy assessment is another essential part of land use and land cover classification. This compares the classified information with real data or, in other words, accuracy assessment verifies the pixels of the categorised images to that of features on the earth's surface (Jin *et al.*, 2015). The kappa accuracy method is the most useful measure to evaluate the accuracy of land use and land cover maps, and many researchers have applied this technique to assess the accuracy of classified maps (Chuang *et al.*, 2011; Hua, 2017; Verma *et al.*, 2020). In the present study, the kappa accuracy technique has been used to assess accuracy for all land use and land cover maps using some randomly selected points, which were adopted in such a way that should cover almost every lulc class with equal proportion. The ground truth data were collected from Google Earth Pro. Field verification was also done for 2020, excluding the areas with either no access or difficulty access. Kappa accuracy, user's accuracy (UA), producer's accuracy (PA) and overall accuracy (OA) were calculated based on an error matrix using the following equation (Acharya *et al.*, 2016; Bera & Chatterjee, 2019).

4. Results and Discussion

4.1 *Accuracy Assessment of Classified Images*

The accuracy assessment was effectuated for LULC maps by generating confusion or error matrix in each land use and land cover class of 1990, 2000, 2010, and 2020. The overall accuracy has been estimated as 90.48%, 89.00%, 92.86% and 82.00% for the years 1990, 2000, 2010 and 2020, respectively. The results signify the acceptability and suitability of classified image for reliable and rational change analysis and model building for future prediction. The kappa coefficient also shows reliable values, which have been calculated as 0.89, 0.87, 0.92 and 0.79 for the years of 1990, 2000, 2010 and 2020, respectively. The user's and producer's accuracy indicates that the vegetation and cropland categories are associated with high user accuracy, whereas cropland, built-up, plantation and grassland were marked as high producer accuracy for all temporal periods. The lowest user's accuracy was found for the class of sand fill (1990), water bodies (2000) and built-up area (2010 and 2020). Water bodies (1990, 2000, 2020) and vegetation (2010) procured the lowest producer's accuracy.

4.2 *Spatio-temporal Analysis of Land Use and Land Cover Status*

The historical status of Jalpaiguri district land use and land cover has been analysed based on LULC classified maps prepared by supervised image classification technique with maximum likelihood classification through ArcGIS 10.3.1. The land use and land cover changes have been estimated by using a land change modeller embedded in TerrSet Geospatial Monitoring and Modelling System software. The LULC dynamics for each period were appraised using quantitative measures in sq. km. and area in percentage.

Table 3a: Land Use and Land Cover Area in sq.km and in %

Land Use Class	*Area in Sq. Km.*				*Area in Percentage*			
	1990	*2000*	*2010*	*2020*	*1990*	*2000*	*2010*	*2020*
Vegetation	356.24	294.28	303.92	350.63	10.64	8.79	9.08	10.47
Crop land	1672.21	1265.82	1066.98	1035.22	49.95	37.81	31.87	30.92
Built up area	199.48	297.47	369.22	463.29	5.96	8.89	11.03	13.84
water bodies	148.57	251.71	157.65	146.65	4.44	7.52	4.71	4.38
Plantation	332.67	388.83	322.35	378.08	9.94	11.61	9.63	11.29
Grassland	559.99	757.8	1046.42	909.38	16.73	22.64	31.26	27.16
Sand fill	78.58	91.84	81.21	64.5	2.35	2.74	2.43	1.93

In 1990, 1672.21 sq. km area was covered by cropland, which was 49.95% of the total area, followed by grassland (559.99 sq. km.), which was 16.73% of the total area. The total area built up increased continuously from 1990 to 2020. The built-up area accounted for

5.96% in 1990, which has increased by 13.84% in 2020. Vegetation cover decreased from 356.24 sq. km. to 294.28 sq. km from 1990 to 2000. Afforestation contributed to an increase of 9.64 sq. km. forest cover from 2000 to 2010, and interestingly, the forest cover increased by 46.71 sq. km. from 2010 to 2020. The area covered by grassland has also increased from 559.99 sq. km. in 1990 to 909.38 sq. km. in 2020. The lowest percentage of share was associated with the sand fill class, which was marked as 2.35% in 1990 and 1.93% in 2020. The change percentage and rate of change was also calculated for the analysis. The present study has shown a significant change in various land use and land cover in Jalpaiguri district. The area has been dominated by two major land use and land cover groups as more than 50% area has been covered by crop land and grassland from 1990 to 2020. Among all classes only built up area shows an increasing trend from 1990 to 2020 which indicates the fact that the urbanization and urban expansion was continuously occurred whereas the crop land indicates a decreasing trend during the same period. The vegetation cover decreased by 0.17% from 1990–2020. The plantation area has increased by 1.35% from 1990 to 2020. The area covered by sand fill has decreased by 0.42% from 1990 to 2020. A significant changes were seen in crop land, built up area, plantation and grassland.

Figure 3 shows the spatial pattern of land use and land cover in the study area. The built-up area has grown tremendously from 1990 to 2020 in every block of Jalpaiguri district. The highest growth of the built-up area was observed in the Dhupguri block, followed by the Rajganj and Maynaguri blocks. The growth of the built-up area was lower in Nagrakata and Meteli block, which is characterised by mountainous and undulating topography, and this may be the driving factor for less growth in this class. The vegetation cover has been reduced in Dhupguri, Malbazar and Sadar block. 18.6 sq. km. area under vegetation has diminished in the Dhupguri block from 1990 to 2020. The growth of the built-up area significantly impacts vegetation in the Dupguri, Malbazar, and Sadar blocks. The vegetation density has increased in Rajganj block, followed by Maynaguri, Mateli, and Nagrakata. Many water bodies have been depleted in the Sadar block from 1990 to 2020. The Highest grassland expansion was encountered in Rajganj block, whereas Meteli block marked the lowest grassland growth from 1990–2020.

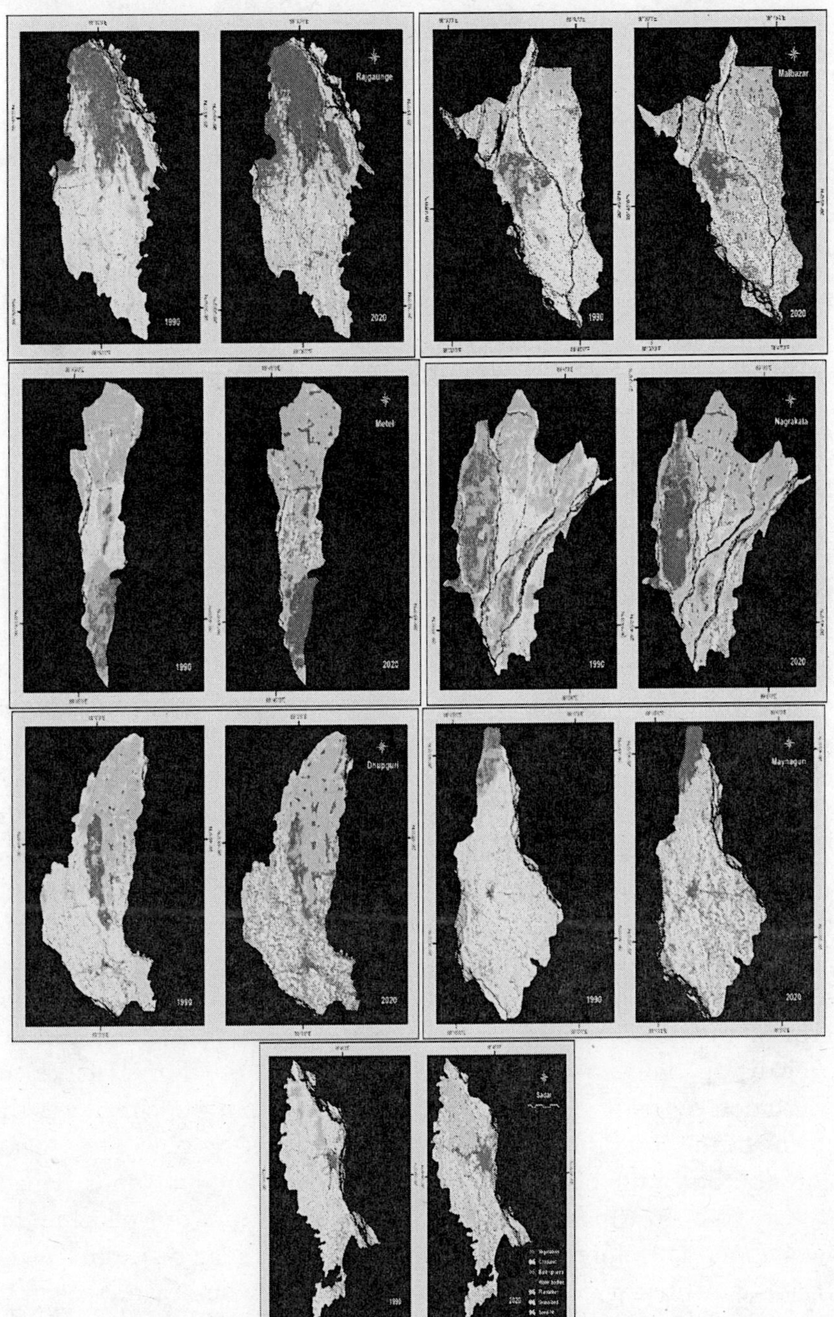

Figure 3: Spatial Analysis of Lulc in Jalpaiguri District from 1990 to 2020

4.3 *The Spatiotemporal Analysis of Gain and Loss of Land Use and Land Cover Classes*

The gain and losses of land use and land cover from 1990 to 2020 were acquired from the LCM change modeller, which is associated with TerrSet Geospatial Monitoring and Modelling System software. Overall gain and loss for different periods have been presented in Figure 4a. The grassland category observed the largest gain, followed by the built-up area. Grassland and built-up areas gained by 19.43% and 11.46%, respectively, from 1990 to 2020. The smallest gain occurred in sand fill (1.47%), vegetation (2.55%) and water bodies (2.81%). The area covered by cropland has gained by 5.35%, whereas plantation gained by 6.94% from 1990 to 2020. In the case of loss of land use and land cover area, the cropland diminished (24.36%) significantly. The vegetation cover lost its area extension by 2.71% from 1990 to 2020, but the grassland reduced by 9.00% during the same study periods. Among all categories of land use and land cover, the sand fill marked the lowest reduction, i.e. 1.89%. The aerial coverage of the plantation has decreased by 5.58%. The positive change occurred in built-up areas, plantations and grassland, among which the grassland coverage has gained the most. The net negative change took place in the case of vegetation, cropland, water bodies, and sandfill. Cropland was the main contributor to grassland. About 56.46% of cropland has been transformed into grassland, which also marked a decrease in agricultural land. The industrial development in this district during the last few years demotivated people to engage in agricultural activity the unprofitable price of agricultural products brought about a change in economic activities in this area. The rapid growth of urban population and urban expansion impacts the net growth of built-up coverage. Deforestation, or the clearance of vegetation cover for making plantations and/or built-up areas, was the main factor for the depletion of vegetation cover. The major contributors to the built-up area were grassland and croplands. This is due to the growing rate of population size and the demand for habitation. Therefore, the anthropogenic factors may be treated as the major contributor to the change of land use and land cover in Jalpaiguri district from 1990 to 2020. The aerial coverage of the plantation has grown up in the northern part of the district, which

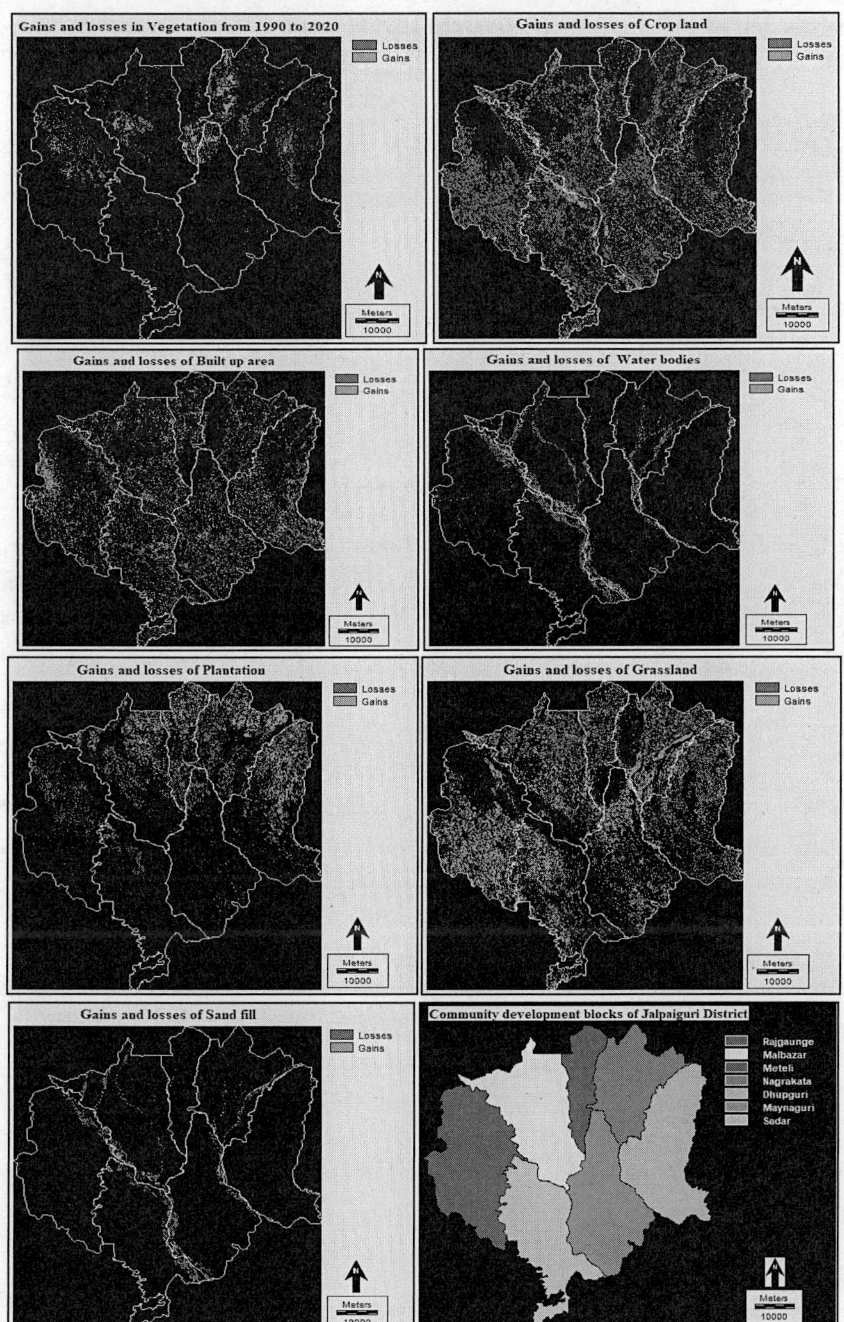

Figure 4a: Spatial Status of Gain and Loss in LULC from 1990–2020

Table 4: Gain and Loss in LULC from 1990 to 2020

LULC Classes	*Gain and loss in LULC from 1990–2020*			
	Gain in sq. km.	*Gain in %*	*Loss in Sq. Km.*	*Loss in %*
Vegetation	85.33	2.55	90.95	2.71
cropland	179.27	5.35	816.27	24.36
Built up area	384.01	11.46	120.19	3.59
Water bodies	94.14	2.81	96.06	2.87
Plantation	232.47	6.94	187.07	5.58
Grassland	651.09	19.43	301.71	9.00
Sand fill	49.35	1.47	63.43	1.89

includes the Malbazar, Meteli, Nagrakata and Dhupguri blocks. The loss of water bodies was marked in the Malbazar and Sadar blocks, but the gain in this category occurred in the Maynaguri block. The grassland gained a lot in Rajganj block, followed by Sadar, Maynaguri, and Nagrakata. Dhupguri block has the lowest gain in grassland, which is often converted into tea plantations.

The transition probability matrix has been calculated between 1990–2000 and 2000–2010 for understanding the trend. The transition probability matrix is a cross tabulation of two consecutive images. In transition probability matrix, the diagonal value indicates the probability of land use and land cover category will remain unchanged from 1990 to 2020 and off diagonal value shows the probability of a given land use and land cover will undergo a change from one category to another. The row value represents the previous LULC category and the column value represents the later LULC class. The transition area matrix records the pixel value that area expected to transform from one category of land use to other category over the specific interval of time.

5. Conclusion

The present study analyses the spatial pattern of land use and land cover and its temporal changes in Jalpaiguri district using different dependent and independent variables and geospatial techniques from

1990 to 2020. Seven land use and land cover categories were identified using supervised classification, which is considered a robust technique for land use and land cover analysis. Landsat images from 1990, 2000, 2010, and 2020 were used to extract the land use and land cover maps. LCM is also applied to estimate the gain and loss of each category and the spatial trend of land use and land cover dynamics. The result of the study confirms the change in land use and land cover during the last few decades. Several factors like elevation, slope, proximity to major roads, distance from rivers and distance from urban centres significantly influenced the spatial pattern of land use and land cover. The high positive correlation between temporal periods and built-up areas implies a rapid growth of urban areas from 1990 to 2020. The population growth and urban area expansion in this district significantly enhanced the rate of urbanization. The new formation of the Maynaguri municipality also endorsed the opinion of expeditious urbanization, which was perhaps driven in an unplanned way. The growth of built-up areas is negatively correlated with cropland. Therefore, it can be said that most of the cropland is converted into built-up land. The changes in land use and land cover are ascribed to transformation, intense socio-economic development and continuous sprawling of urban areas, which ultimately threaten the loss of natural resources and biodiversity of this region. Rapid landscape changes are extremely detrimental to environmental sustainability, which needs to be conserved using adequate measures. The grassland increased from 16.73% in 1990 to 27.16% in 2020, which implies a positive sign in order to increase the percentage of cropland as the grassland may be converted into cultivable land by taking suitable and sustainable measures through a planned way. However, the vegetation class after 2010 was more or less stable, which indicates the fact of growing awareness towards green cover. The water area is expected to decrease in future. Human interventions like the construction of embankments, bridges, revetment, channel diversion, soil erosion and deposition have brought substantial changes in the normal flow of rivers in this district. Plantation farming decreased in 2010, but after that, it has further increased and is expected to increase in the future. The spatial pattern of land use and land cover transformation showed a general degree of change, which may have the probability of amplification in coming decades. The concentration of spatial trend for vegetation, cropland and built-up area was very high in the middle part of the district during 1990–2020, whereas it is predicted to be shifted in the north, south-east and north-west, respectively, in the coming decades. The shifting trend was also observed in Plantation, which has begun to translocate from the north-east towards the middle part of the district. Other classes, such as grassland, water bodies, and sandfill, did not show a substantial change in the concentration of spatial trends. So it may be conceded that the land use and land cover dynamics in Jalpaiguri district were not and will not be modified temporarily, but the modification will appear spatially. Anthropogenic factors mostly constrained Jalpaiguri district's land use and land cover dynamics. They may be apprised distinctly by applying remote sensing and GIS techniques using satellite images. The present work will provide policymakers and planners with a perception of the present scenario of land use and land cover status and its future prediction to formulate a comprehensive framework with sustainable policy for future development without hampering this region's environmental and natural conditions. The study will also facilitate scholars and researchers to investigate further in this direction. However, the government and administrators may apprised that they should have some sustainable measures and strategies for the overall development of this area, which is significantly renowned for its beauty and diversity.

References

[1] Abebe, G., Getachew, D. and Ewunetu, A. (2021). Analysing land use/land cover changes and its dynamics using remote sensing and GIS in Gubalafito district, Northeastern Ethiopia. *SN Applied Sciences, December*. https://doi.org/10.1007/s42452-021-04915-8

[2] Acharya, T.D., Lee, D.H., Yang, I.T. and Lee, J.K. (2016). *Identification of Water Bodies in a Landsat 8 OLI Image Using a J48 Decision Tree*. 1–16. https://doi.org/10.3390/s16071075

[3] Adingo, S., Li, X. and Yu, X.L.J. (2020). *Analysis of Land-Use and Land-Cover Changes in YongDeng County Using Remote Sensing and GIS. 10*(6), 175–186. https://doi.org/10.7176/JEES/10-6-15

[4] Bera, S. and Chatterjee, N. Das. (2019). Mapping and monitoring of land use dynamics with their change hotspot in North 24 - Parganas district, India: a geospatial—and statistical—based approach. *Modeling Earth Systems and Environment, September*. https://doi.org/10.1007/s40808-019-00601-2

[5] Biswas, M., Banerji, S. and Mitra, D. (2019). of Markov model: A case study of Eastern part of Kolkata. *Environment, Development and Sustainability, 0123456789.* https://doi.org/10.1007/s10668-019-00387-4

[6] Chen, J., Gong, P., He, C., Pu, R. and Shi, P. (2003). *Land-Use/Land-Cover Change Detection Using Improved Change-Vector Analysis. 69*(4), 369–379.

[7] Chuang, C., Lin, C., Chien, C. and Chou, W. (2011). Application of Markov-chain model for vegetation restoration assessment at landslide areas caused by a catastrophic earthquake in Central Taiwan. *Ecological Modelling, 222*(3), 835–845. https://doi.org/10.1016/j.ecolmodel.2010.11.007

[8] Das, S. and Sarkar, R. (2019). Predicting the land use and land cover change using Markov model: A catchment level analysis of the Bhagirathi-Hugli River Predicting the land use and land cover change using Markov model: A catchment level analysis of the Bhagirathi-Hugli River. *Spatial Information Research, January 2020.* https://doi.org/10.1007/s41324-019-00251-7

[9] Dhar, R.B., Chakraborty, S., Chattopadhyay, R. and Sikdar, P.K. (2019). Impact of Land-Use/Land-Cover Change on Land Surface Temperature Using Satellite Data: A Case Study of Rajarhat Block, North 24-Parganas District, West Bengal. *Journal of the Indian Society of Remote Sensing, 1.* https://doi.org/10.1007/s12524-019-00939-1

[10] Dhinwa, P., Patiian, S.K, Sasiry, S.V.C., Rao, M., Majumder, K.L., Chotani, M.L., Singh, J.P. and Sinha, R.L.P. (1992). Land Use Change Analysis of Bharatpur District Using GIS. *Journal of the Indian Society OfRemote Sensing, 20*(4), 237–250.

[11] He, Y., Lin, K. and Chen, X. (2013). *Effect of Land Use and Climate Change on Runoff in the Dongjiang Basin of Effect of Land Use and Climate Change on Runoff in the Dongjiang Basin of South China. February 2016.* https://doi.org/10.1155/2013/471429

[12] Hoque, I. and Lepcha, S.K. (2019). *A geospatial analysis of land use dynamics and its impact on land surface temperature in Siliguri Jalpaiguri development region, West Bengal.*

[13] Hua, A.K. (2017). *Application of CA-Markov Model and Land Use/Land Cover Changes in Malacca River Watershed. 15*(4), 605–622.

[14] Islam, M.R., Miah, M.G. and Inoue, Y. (2023). *Analysis of Land Use and Land Cover Changes in the Coastal Area of Bangladesh Using Landsat Imagery. March.* https://doi.org/10.1002/ldr.2339

[15] Jin, G., Li, Z., Lin, Q., Shi, C., Liu, B. and Yao, L. (2015). *Land Use Suitability Assessment in Low-Slope Hilly Regions under the Impact of Urbanization in Yunnan, China. 2015.*

[16] Mandal, J., Ghosh, N. and Mukhopadhyay, A. (2021). Urban Growth Dynamics and Changing Land-Use Land-Cover of Megacity Kolkata and Its Environs Urban Growth Dynamics and Changing Land-Use Land-Cover of Megacity Kolkata and Its Environs. *Journal of the Indian Society of Remote Sensing, July 2019.* https://doi.org/10.1007/s12524-019-01020-7

[17] Mazhar, F. (2019). *A Time Series Analysis of Satellite Imageries for Land Use & Land Cover (LULC) Change Detection of Gujranwala City, Pakistan from 1999–2019. December.* https://doi.org/10.17485/ijst/2019/v12i46/148606

[18] Moulds, S., Buytaert, W. and Mijic, A. (2018). *Data Descriptor: A spatio-temporal land use and land cover reconstruction for India from.* 1–11.

[19] Nagarajan, N. and Poongothai, S. (2011). *Identification of Land use and Land cover Changes using Remote Sensing and GIS. 3*(5), 570–576.

[20] Naikoo, M.W., Rihan, M. and Ishtiaque, M. (2020). Analyses of land use land cover (LULC) change and built-up expansion in the suburb of a metropolitan city: Spatio-temporal analysis of Delhi NCR using landsat datasets. *Journal of Urban Management, 9*(3), 347–359. https://doi.org/10.1016/j.jum.2020.05.004

[21] Nayak, S. (2019). Examining the impact of regional land use and land cover changes on temperature•: the case of Eastern India. *Spatial Information Research.* https://doi.org/10.1007/s41324-019-00263-3

[22] Palaniyandi, M. and Nagarathinam, V. (1997). Land Use/Land Cover Mapping and Change Detection Using Space Borne Data. *Journal of the Society of Remote Sensing, 25*(I), 27–33.

[23] Prasad, G. and Ramesh, M.V. (2019). Spatio-Temporal Analysis of Land Use/Land Cover Changes in an Ecologically Spatio-Temporal Analysis of Land Use/Land Cover Changes in an Ecologically Fragile Area—Alappuzha District, . *Natural Resources Research, October 2018.* https://doi.org/10.1007/s11053-018-9419-y

[24] Rawat, J.S. and Kumar, M. (2015). Monitoring land use/cover change using remote sensing and GIS techniques: A case study of Hawalbagh block, district Almora, Uttarakhand, India. *Egyptian Journal of Remote Sensing and Space Science, 18*(1), 77–84. https://doi.org/10.1016/j.ejrs.2015.02.002

[25] Rwanga, S.S. and Ndambuki, J.M. (2017). *Accuracy Assessment of Land Use/Land Cover Classification Using Remote Sensing and GIS. 2017*, 611–622. https://doi.org/10.4236/ijg.2017.84033

[26] Saha, J. and Paul, S. (2020). An insight on land use and land cover change due to tourism growth in coastal area and its environmental consequences from West Bengal, India. *Spatial Information Research*. https://doi.org/10.1007/s41324-020-00368-0

[27] Srivastava, P.K., Han, D., Rico-ramirez, M.A. and Bray, M. (2012). *Selection of classification techniques for land use/land cover change investigation. 50*, 1250–1265.

[28] Verma, P., Raghubanshi, A. and Srivastava, P.K. (2020). Appraisal of kappa—based metrics and disagreement indices of accuracy assessment for parametric and nonparametric techniques used in LULC classification and change detection. *Modeling Earth Systems and Environment, 0123456789*. https://doi.org/10.1007/s40808-020-00740-x

Change Detection Analysis Using Landsat Images on Balurghat Municipality, West Bengal, India

Manash Laha[1]

ABSTRACT: The major focus of the current study is a spatio-temporal analysis of land-use and land-cover changes in Balurghat Municipality, West Bengal, using remote sensing and geographic information systems (G.I.S.) from 1990 to 2020. The primary goals are to identify changes in land-use and land-cover and to look at the key influences and how they affect the dynamics of the landscape. The Landsat images of the study area are classified into five categories with the help of GIS software and Google verified and validated by the process of accuracy assessment. An image has been classified digitally with the help of the Supervised Image Classification method under Maximum Likelihood Classification techniques which also helps to identify the transformation of land from vegetation cover to built-up area. The paper assesses the spatial growth of the urban region from 1990 to 2020, as well as changes in land-use and land-cover (LULC). The LULC Change demonstrated that the unsustainable built-up growth trend remained in this region. A substantial loss of vegetative cover of about 19.74 percent was caused by the 15.83 percent increase in the built-up area. According to the study, it is helpful to determine current and projected urban growth and development so that local planning authorities may control growth and development in accordance with the region's ecological or environmental carrying capacity.

Keywords: Accuracy Assessment, Change Detection, Land-use and Land-cover Change, Major Problem, Population Growth, Probable Solution.

1. Introduction

The land is a product of nature and it is an example of three-dimensional dynamic complex bodies. A part of land developed

---

[1] State Aided College Teacher, Department of Geography, Islampur College, West Bengal, India. E-mail: manashlaha05@gmail.com

through the interaction of lithology, structure, drainage, climate, vegetation, and the geomorphological processes operating through time. As a result, different types of landforms have evolved in different parts of the earth (Roy & Shaikh, 2021). Land-cover refers to the physical coverage of land. It describe how the land is covered, e.g., natural vegetation, water. Land-Use refers to the use or management of land by humans. It describes how the land is being used, e.g., residential, commercial. Changes in Land-Use and Land-Cover have significant impacts on local physical environmental conditions and economic and social welfare. A landscape is a natural arrangement on interrelated tracts of land which is very complicated in nature, the study of landscape dynamics it is very much relevant for land-use land-cover planning management (De & Jana, 1997). Recent research on land-use and land-cover change detection has drawn attention of many researchers (Liang *et al.,* 2002; Ayele *et al.,* 2016).Change detection has a significant process for managing and monitoring natural resources and urban development mainly due to the provision of quantitative analysis of the spatial distribution based on a temporal scale. There are a lot of available techniques that serve the purpose of detecting and recording differences and might also be attributable to change (Singh, 1989). Remote Sensing (RS) and Geographic Information System (GIS) are now providing new tools for advanced ecosystem management. Balurghat is the head quarter of the Dakshin Dinajpur District but in 60 years ago it had been a mere village, in the historical context of the partition of India and East Pakistan(1971), overnight made its appearance as a town and today it has been turned into a Class-I urban centre of district. Due rapid urbanization, still different problems such as population growth, dramatically changed land-cover and land-use pattern, urban environmental degradation and gaps are related to the development, don't use any kind statistical based and satellite image based study on urban growth and landscape dynamics of this town area (Kundu, 2018).

2. Objectives

The present study focused on the following major objectives:

(a) To examine the pattern of population growth.

(b) To identify the land use and land cover change detection.

(c) To identify major land use and land cover problems and provide some probable solutions.

3. Study Area

The name of the town Balurghat has been probably derived from 'BALUKAKIRNAGHAT' meaning a *'ghatfull of sand'* (Roy, 2000). The study area is Balurghat Municipality under Balurghat community development block of South Dinajpur district. Khadimpur, Chakbhabani, Sanket, saheb kachari, Biwas para, Rathtala, Power house more, Mangalpur Bongi, Narayanpur, Raghunathpur, part of Hosseinpur, and Dakra are all included in the Balurghat Municipality area. It is lies between 25°12′29"N to 25°16′17"N and 88°44′48"E to 88°47′27"E. (Figure 1). The study area had 153279 people living

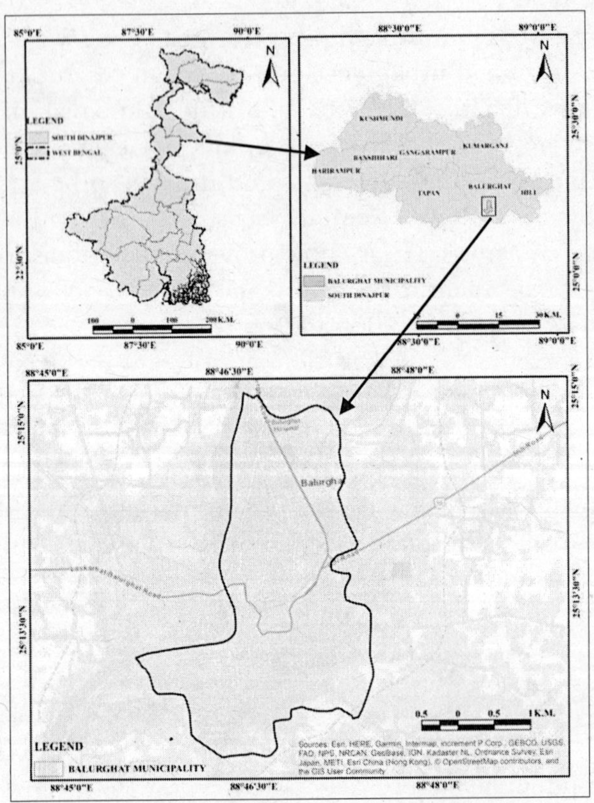

Figure 1: Location Map of the Study Area

there as of the 2011 Census, covering an area of just under 10.74 sq. km. 23 wards are available in this Municipality and river Atreyee runs across the city, dividing it into disproportionate halves. On the eastern bank of the river is where the city's vital administrative, cultural, and entertainment units are located. The border between India and Bangladesh is 3 km away from the township (Kundu, 2018).

4. Database & Methodology

This research is based on cloud free, error free satellite images from USGS data archive on various dates (Table 1). For the improving the image accuracy, satellite images should be preprocessed before using. GIS mapping techniques, cartographic techniques and various statistical analyses have been done to fulfill our research objectives. Arc GIS 10.2 and QGIS 2.18 have been used for location map, supervised image classification with maximum likelihood algorithm and transformation of land characteristics. MS-Excel (07) and Power Bi software have been used for statistical calculation and cartographic techniques. Figure 2's flow chart of methodology illustrates the approach used in the current study.

Table 1: Secondary Data Source of this Research

Spatial Data	*Data*	*Data Source*	*Date of Acquisition*
Satellite Image	Landsat 5 TM	USGS Earth Explorer	30.01.1990
	Landsat 8 OLI/ TIRS	PATH : 138/ ROW:48	20.02.2020
Administrative Area	Village Shape file	https://sedac.ciesin.columbia.edu	01.07.2022
Non Spatial Data	South Dinajpur District Census Hand Book, 2001 & 2011		
	District Statistical Hand Book South Dinajpur 2014		

Source: Prepared by author, 2022.

4.1 *Supervised Image Classification*

The goal of image classification is to classify all of the pixels in digital image into various land-use and land-cover classes. There are two forms of classification, depending on how the computer and interpreter interact during the process. When an image analysis has extensive expertise of the field, supervised classification one of the two main approaches of picture classification is typically selected. The analyst performs these classifications using a three-stage method that includes training input, classification, and output. In this research supervised image classification method has been adopted to demonstrate the change detection over a 30-year period. In this classification five different land-use and land-cover features have been identify to validate our research goal. Each and every image is independently classified in a supervised classification method with the help of a maximum likelihood algorithm using Arc GIS (10.2) software.

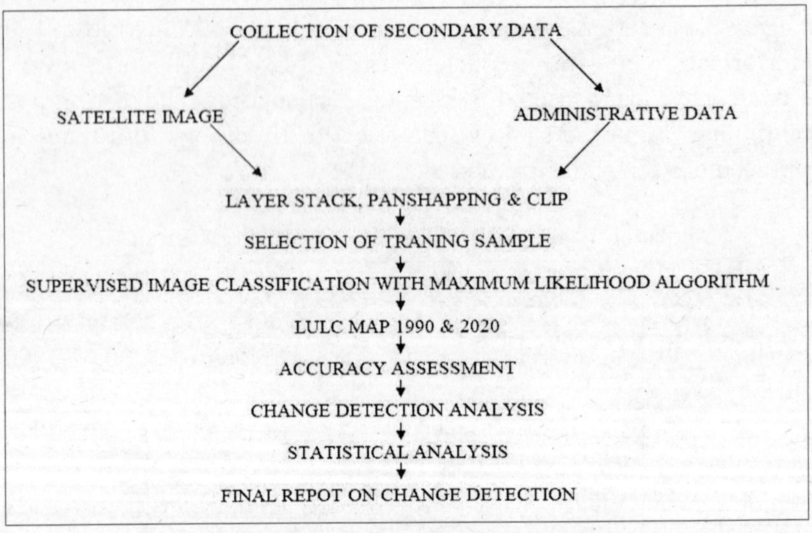

Figure 2: Flowchart of Methodology

4.2 *Accuracy Assessment*

The most popular method for determining accuracy is error matrix analysis (Khorram *et al.,* 2013). The change detection process relies heavily on individual classifications. As a result, a through examination of accuracy must include a report on overall accuracy, user accuracy, and producer accuracy, all of which were examined using the Kappa coefficient (Table 3).

Table 2: Status of Kappa (Rwanga, 2017)

Value of Kappa	*Status of Kappa*
< 0	Poor
0–0.2	Slight
0.21–0.4	Fair
0.41–0.6	Moderate
0.61–0.8	Good
> 0.81	Very good

Source: Prepared by author, 2022 & Das & Sahu, 2020.

4.3 *Statistical Calculation*

Correlation analysis is a statistical analysis which allows researchers to explore the degree of association within independent and dependent variables (Schober & Schwarte, 2018; Senthilnathan, 2019).

$$r = \frac{\Sigma(X_i - \bar{x})(Y_i - \bar{y})}{\sqrt{(X_i - \bar{x})^2 \Sigma(Y_i - \bar{y})^2}}$$

Where, 'r' is the Pearson's product moment correlation coefficient, 'x_i' is values of x variable in a sample, '$\bar{x}_i$' is mean values of x variable, y_i is the value of y variable in a sample and '$\bar{y}_i$' is mean values of y variable.

5. Result and Discussion

5.1 *Population Growth*

The political reasons for the country's split in 1947 and in 1971 as a result of the Bangladesh war are the key factors that led to the formation of Balurghat Town. This area was first incorporated in East Pakistan by British attorney Sir Radcliff. Later, Radcliff was forced to reverse his choice as a result of the persistent efforts of Mr. Satindranath Basu and Dr. Sushil Ranjan Chatterjee. So, three days later, on August 18, 1947, Balurghat experienced the taste of independence and it was designated as the administrative centre of the West Dinajpur District. Previously a little settlement patches were converted into Balurghat Municipality status in 1951 at a small room of the "1928 Club" by Notification No. M1M-40/50 (1) dt. 24th May, 1951 with a population of 18121 and an area of 6.37 sq. km. The Municipality began operations formally on June 18, 1951, with five wards operating under a nominated authority (Kundu, 2018). The population data are collected from census handbook of South Dinajpur District showing the continuous population growth in Balurghat Municipality from 1951 to 2011 and r^2 value (0.9679) showing the population growth over time. According to Census (2011), present Municipality has 23 wards with 10.74 sq.km total area and total population is 153279. The town is primarily an administrative town having overall population density 6213 persons per sq km. According to census highest decadal growth rate had been recorded in the year 1971, which was 148.48% due to independence war of Bangladesh. Figure 3 line graph illustrates the continuous flow of population growth.

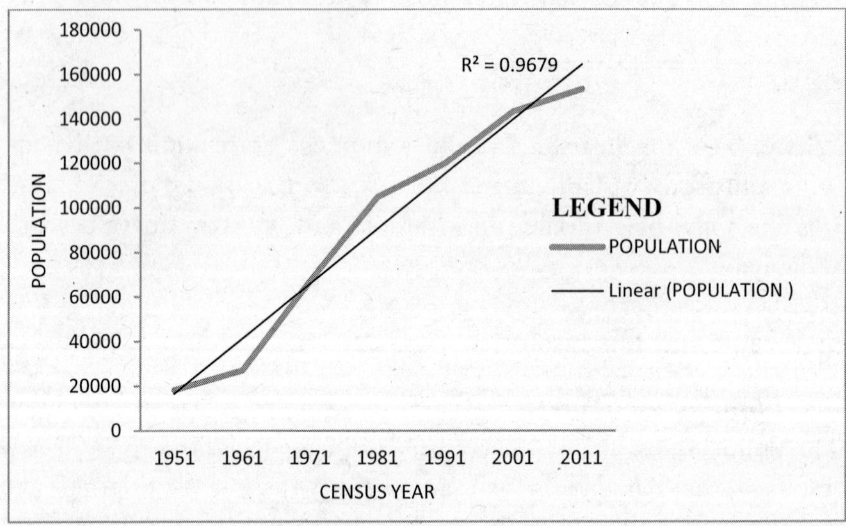

Figure 3: Population Growth of Study Area from 1951 to 2011

Infrastructural development is the major threshold area on which developments depends upon in an area (Arif, 2018). It is one of the most significant pull factor for the migrate people. The phenomenon of urbanization therefore occurs on an area and involves links and nodes to create a total system (Sharma, 2012).

$$\text{Degree of urbanization} = \frac{\text{Urban Population}}{\text{Total Population}} \times 100$$
$$= (153279/248907) \times 100$$
$$= 61.58\%$$

5.2 *Land-Use and Land-Cover Change*

Detection of changes in the land-use/land-cover involves use of at least two period data sets (Jenson, 1996). Therefore, spatial changes including surface organization of the land-use and land-cover and their inter-relationship with a focus on direction and spread are well explained (Patra and Gavsker, 2021). A substantial portion of the research region is revealed to be urban in nature, with little in the way of greenery or open space (Figure 4).

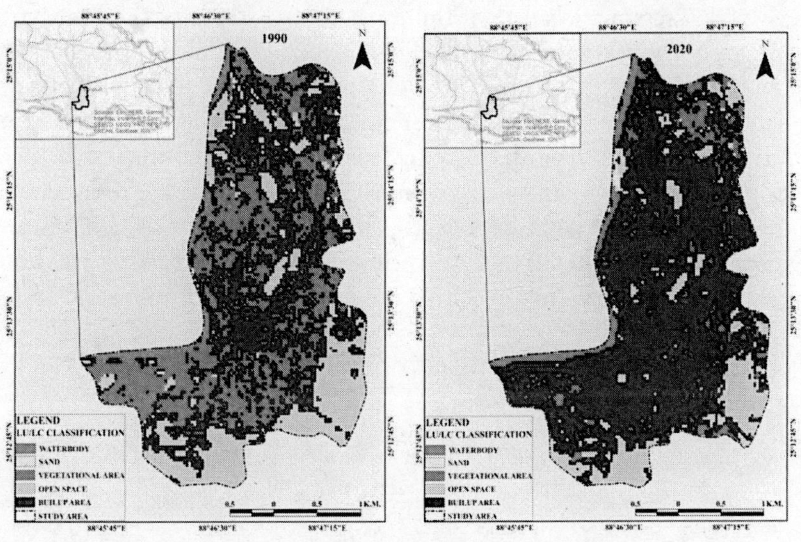

Figure 4: Land Use and Land Cover Map of the Study Area from 1990 to 2020

5.2.1 *Land-use and Land-Cover Classification 1990*

Based on the land-use land-cover map of 1990 the area and percentage of areas as classified are water bodies 2.88% (0.31 Sq.Km.), sand 0.93% (0.1 Sq.Km.), vegetation area 33.79% (3.63 Sq.Km.), open space 16.79% (1.8 Sq.km.) and built-up area 45.62% (4.9 Sq.Km.).

The dominated land-use class was built-up area and main land-cover type was vegetation cover. (Table 4)

5.2.2 *Land-use and Land-Cover Classification 2020*

In other hand based on the land-use land-cover map of 2020 the area and percentage of areas as classified are water bodies 4.18% (0.45 Sq.Km.), sand 1.86% (0.2 Sq.Km.), vegetation area 14.05% (1.51 Sq.Km.), open space 18.43% (1.98 Sq.Km.), and built-up area 61.45% (6.6 Sq.Km.). The dominated land use class was built up area and main land cover type was vegetation cover. In case of spatio temporal change it is very indicated that most part of the vegetation cover and open space are transform into or built up area. (Table 4)

5.3 *Accuracy Assessment*

Accuracy assessment is one of the most crucial stages of the research to confirm our work with genuine earth. Kappa coefficient analysis is one of the most helpful approaches to determine the accuracy evaluation of a study. For the accuracy assessment random sampling method has been used over 100 samples, collected samples are compared between Google Earth image and Landsat images and Table 2 are represent the kappa value which was express the level of accuracy of our research (Kaimais & Patidar, 2016). According to Rwanga's (2017) classification (Table 2) the values of kappa are under good to very good scale.

Table 3: Summary of Accuracy Assessment from 1990 to 2020

LU/LC Classification Type	*1990*		*2020*	
	User's Accuracy	*Producer's Accuracy*	*User's Accuracy*	*Producer's Accuracy*
Waterbody	0.78	0.88	0.8	0.94
Sand	0.8	0.75	0.82	0.87
Vegetation	0.76	0.76	0.8	0.92
Open	0.8	0.85	0.85	0.85
Buil-Up Area	0.92	0.81	0.92	0.81
Overall Accuracy	0.815		0.881	
Kappa	0.769		0.834	

Source: Prepared by author, 2022.

5.4 Change Detection

Boriah *et al.,* (2008) have performed a new change detection technique for the land-use land-cover change detection, especially for remote sensing data. An important aspect of change detection is to determine, which is actually changing to what extent, in other words to check, which land-use class is changing. The outcome results will reveal both the desirable and undesirable changes along with relatively stable categories overtime. This information works as a vital tool in management decisions (Opeyemi, 2006). In this section the attempt is made to check the trend, rate and magnitude of changes in land-use/land-cover of study area. Table 4 and Figure 4 are representing the spatial change over study area.

Table 4: Summary of Accuracy Assessment from 1990 to 2020

LU/LC Categories	*1990*		*2020*		*Area Change*		*Value of R Square*
	Area	*%*	*Area*	*%*	*Area*	*%*	
Waterbody	0.31	2.88	0.45	4.18	0.14	1.3	0.826
Sand	0.1	0.93	0.2	1.86	0.1	0.93	0.89
Vegetation Cover	3.63	33.79	1.51	14.05	–2.12	–19.74	0.858
Open Space	1.8	16.79	1.98	18.43	0.18	1.64	0.79
Built-Up Area	4.9	45.62	6.6	61.45	1.7	15.83	0.811

Source: Prepared by author, 2022.

Waterbody

A river called River Atreyee flows from north to south direction in this region. In 1990 the water bodies hold 0.31 sq.km areas which were almost 2.88% of the total area. But in 2020 the water bodies hold 0.45 sq.km areas which were almost 4.18% of the total area. So it's clear that from 1990 to 2020 total areas of water bodies continuously increasing nearly 1.3% and the r^2 value of water body is 0.826 which indicates the rate growth of water body within this time (Table 4 and Figure 5).

Sand area mainly found in the river floodplain. Sand covered 0.1 sq. km in 1990, or roughly 0.93% of the total area but in the 2020 sand holds 0.2 sq.km areas which were almost 1.86% of the total area. Therefore, it is evident that total sand areas was increased by roughly 0.93% between 1990 and 2020, and the r^2 value 0.89, so it is shows the pace at which sand will expand during this period (Table 4 and Figure 5).

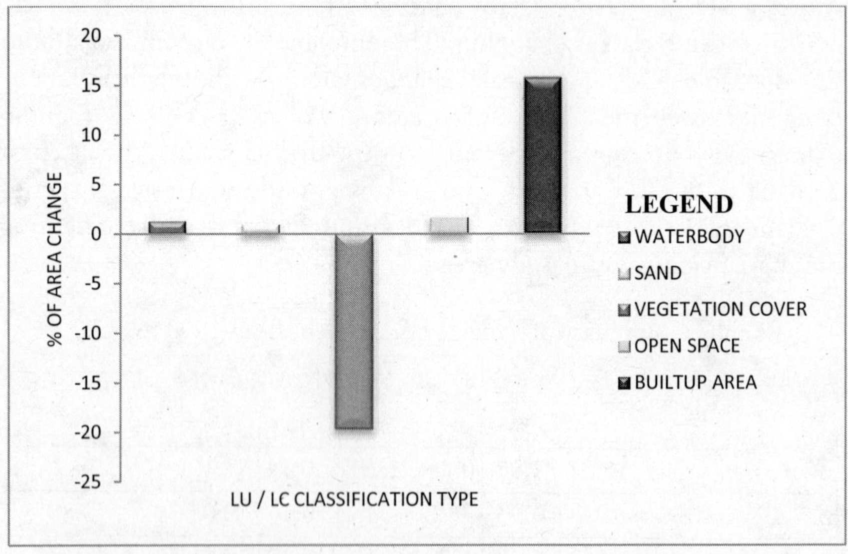

Figure 5: Change Detection of the Study Area from 1990 to 2020

- Sand
- Vegetation Cover

North Eastern, South and South Western parts of the region are covered by dense forest (Figure 4). In 1990 the vegetation cover was 3.63 km^2 areas, about 33.79% of the total area. But the area decreased to 1.51 km^2 (14.05%) in 2020. Hence it's clearly analyzed that from 1990 to 2020 the amount of vegetation cover continuously decreased nearly -19.74% of area. Also the r^2 value of vegetation cover is 0.858 which indicates the rate of extensive declining of vegetation cover within this time (Table 4 and Figure 5).

Open Space

Stadium, Play Ground, Park, Recreational spot, Project area and under construction area etc are categorized as open area in LULC map. Generally this natural open area has been converted into urban sector and few of them remain static. This area experience a little change with an aerial extent of 1.8 km^2 in 1990 which was 16.79% of the total area and 1.98 km^2 (18.43%) in 2020. Value of r^2 open area is 0.79 indicating the low positive value and showing its significant level of complexness according to time (Table 4 and Figure 5).

Built-up Area

An urban sector's area are includes residential, commercial, and other administrative buildings. Accordingly the area included under built-up area was 4.9 km^2 in 1990 which was 45.62% of the total area and in the year 2020 the area is 6.6 km^2 (61.45%) of the total area respectively. The transformation and growth of built-up areas mainly from eastern to south eastern part of the Municipality area (Figure 4). Value of r^2 Built-up area is 0.811 is the indication of highly positive development of built-up area within time and roughly 15.83 percentage area had been take a positive change (Table 4 and Figure 5).

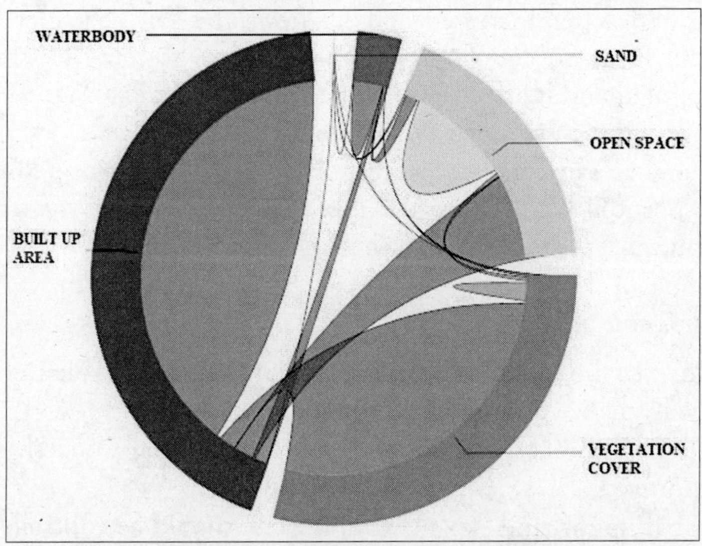

Figure 6: Transformation of Land Characteristics of The Study area from 1990 to 2020

Figure 6 is useful for determining the rate of change, whereas Table 4 and Figure 5 primarily aid in identifying the region of change during the course of the research. The primary land characteristics have shifted from vegetation cover (2.44%) and open space (0.63%) to built-up area.

5.5 *Major Problem Associated with Land Use and Land Cover Changes*

- Clearing of forest areas in some parts of Balurghat city as a result increased the level of carbon-di-oxide. It causes a general *rise in temperature.* It is also observed that due to concretization of the open land the area is now becoming heat islands.
- *Water logging* in the rainy season is one of the most important problems in the town as a result of unplanned rapid urbanization.
- Construct residential apartment is major crime to *encroaching of water bodies* in my study area.
- Land is one of the most precious natural resources on the planet. Due to the sprawling and unplanned growth the fetching of ground water increased and it affects the soil character of the land. Due to the improper management system the soil gets polluted and it affects the soil health and microbial statues of the soil, and the *quality of soil is degraded* over time.
- Many areas of the study area have *traffic congestion,* particularly in portions where there are encroachments. Most of the traffic in Balurghat is made up with slow moving vehicles.

5.6 *Probable Solution*

- The *new underground drainage* system should be made to control the hygienic condition of the environment.
- The system of *collection and management of solid wastes* should be improved.
- Urban sprawl and expansion of the city should be controlled.
- Large scale afforestation programmes should be undertaken by the Balurghat municipality.
- *One way transportation system* should be made to control the overcrowding.

6. Conclusion

This study pinpoints the fundamental issue and suggests some potential solutions. It mostly focuses on change detection from 1990 to 2020. According to the research, Balurghat Municipality policy makers should be concerned about future urban growth and create a detailed strategy for environmentally friendly construction. According to the study, it is helpful to local planning authorities may control growth and development in accordance with the region's ecological or environmental carrying capacity.

References

[1] Arif, M. and Gupta, K. (2018). Mapping peri-urbanization in a non-primate city: A case study of Burdwan, India. *European Academic Research, V* (11), 6065–6081.

[2] Ayele, G.T., Demessie, S.S., Mengistu, K.T., Tilahun, S.A. and Melesse, A.M. (2016): Multitemporal Land Use/Land Cover Change Detection for the Batena Watershed, Rift Valley Lakes Basin, Ethiopia. In: Melesse, A.,Abtew, W. (eds.) Landscape Dynamics, Soils and Hydrological Processes in Varied Climates. *Springer Geography.* Springer, https://doi.org/10.1007 /978-3-319-18787-7_4

[3] Boriah, Shyam, Kumar, Vipin, Steinbach, Michael., Potter, Christopher.s and Klooster Steven (2008): Land Cover Change Detectin: A Case Study. http://cucis.ece.northwestern.edu/projects/DMS/publications/BoriahBKSPK2008.pdf

[4] Briassoulis, H. (2000). Analysis of Land Use Change: Theoretical and Modeling Approaches. *The Web Book of Regional Science, West Virginia University.* http://www.rri.wvu.edu/WebBook/Briassoulis/contents.html

[5] Census of India, 1990 & 2011: District Census Handbook, Dakshin Dinajpur District.

[6] District Statistical Hand Book South Dinajpur 2014.

[7] De, N.K. and Jana, N.C. (1997). *The Land Multifaced Appraisal and Management.* Calcutta: Sribhumi Publication Company.

[8] Jensen, J.R. (1996). *Introductory digital image processing: A remote sensing perspective.* Prentice-Hall Inc.

[9] Kaimaris, D. and Patias, P. (2016). Identification and Area Measurement of the Built-up Area with the Built-up Index. *International Journal of Advanced Remote Sensing and GIS, 5* (6), 1844–1858

[10] Khorram, S., Nelson, S., Cakir, H. and Wiele, C.V. (2013). Digital Image Processing: Post-processing and Data Integration. (J. N. Pelton, S. Madry and S. C. Lara, Eds.) *Handbook of Satellite Applications, Springer*, 839–862. DOI 10.1007/ 978-1-4419-7671-0.

[11] Kundu, T. (2013). Urbanization in the South-East Resource Region of India—A Case Study of Jharkhand, Orissa and Chattisgarh : 1901–2001. (N.C. Jana and L. Sivaramakrishnan, Eds.) *Reources and Development Issues and Concerns*, 280–298

[12] Kundu, P.K. (2018). Emergence of Balurghat as a Class-i City: Demographic Impact of Partition and Bangladesh Liberation War. *International Journal of Research and Analytical Reviews*, *5* (3), 955Z–964Z.

[13] Patra, S. and Gavsker, K.K. (2021). Land use and land cover change-induced landscape dynamics: a geospatial study of Durgapur Sub-Division, West Bengal (India). AUC Geographica 56(1), 79–94 https://doi.org/10.14712/23361980.2021.3

[14] Roy, D. (2000). *River is the another name of Creation: The Atreyee River* (in Bengali) in *Dadhichi Uttaradhikar Balurghat,* eds. by M. Chakraborty, Banerjee Press, Balurghat, pp. 4–17.

[15] Roy, S.K. and Shaikh, A.S. (Dec. 2021). Spatio – temporal change—An analytical Geospatial study using satellite data—Farakka block,Murshidabad district,West Bengal(India). *Territorio Della Ricercasu Insediamenti e Ambiente International Journal of Urban Planning*. 27 (2/2021) 111–126.

[16] Rwanga, S.S. and Ndambuki, J.M. (2017). Assessment of Land Use/Land Cover Classification Using Remote Sensing and GIS. *International Journal of Geosciences. Accuracy*. (8): 611–622. https://doi.org/10.4236/ijg.2017.84033

SECTION-B

Natural Resources, Practice and Sustainable Development

Organic Farming for Sustainable Agriculture: Prospects, Practice and Procurement

Sanjita Allay[1]

ABSTRACT: Demand for agricultural product is increasing at an alarming rate as the world's population is also growing. Agricultural operations if managed sustainably can improve soil health and environment. But unsustainable practices are proving to have a dangerous impact on people and the environment. An adaptable agriculture system is required which can boost up the crop yield without harming the environment. The focal point of this paper includes the benefits and constraints of organic farming which mainly includes maintaining the natural balance of the environment, improving soil health, cutting out on expensive fertilizers and chemicals, good return on investments developing rural economy, nutritious food and the ability to compete with conventional farming. More research has to be implemented to understand the ecological process for creating a safe and pleasant environment for sustainable agricultural development.

Keywords: *Organic Farming, Sustainable, Environment.*

1. Introduction

The world population is quickly escalating and in 2023 it reached 8.01 billion with India having the l largest population count of 1.43 billion (PRB). Meeting the future demand for food has become a global challenge (Borlaug, 2002). In order to complement the food supply, the green revolution in farming was introduced. The use of chemicals increased for growing crops and as a result

[1] Assistant Professor, Department of Botany, Sambhunath College, The University of Burdwan, Birbhum, West Bengal, India. E-mail: sanjiava@gmail.com

conventional farming became popular. This method uses less land with more yield and profit. Mechanization like tractors, harvesters, etc. are used increasing productivity but decreasing labour (Conventional farming, 2023). But this growth did not seem to be sustainable. Brundtland Report (1987) introduced the concept of sustainable development and has guided the principles for sustainable development as it is understood today. Farmers are slowly shifting towards sustainable farming methods after noticing gradual decrease in the soil nutrient and food quality. There has been a threefold increase in land under organic cultivation from 5,28,171 ha in 2007 to 1.2 million ha in 2014 (www.idronline.org/article). Madhya Pradesh started the first organic crop production in India. Mango, banana, pineapple, papaya organic fruits are grown in Maharashtra and Madhya Pradesh (Kulhade *et al.*, 2016).

2. Government Schemes for Organic Farming in India

The Government of India is providing several schemes to promote organic and natural farming. 1. Paramparagat Krishi Vikas Yojana (PKVY). Rashtriya Krishi Vikas Yojana (RKVY), Mission Organic MOVCDNER) Scheme for Organic Farming Value Chain Development for North Eastern Region (, National Programme for Organic Production (NPOP), National Project on Organic Farming (NPOF), Capital Investment Subsidy Scheme under SHM (Soil Health Management Scheme), National Mission on Oilseeds and Oil Palm (NMOOP) Scheme for Organic Farming and National Horticulture Mission (NHM) (www.agrifarming.in/government-schemes-for-organic-farming-in-india)

Indian government has also initiated a scheme named Pradhan Mantri Fasal Bima Yojana (PMFBY), since January 2016, aiming towards sustainable agriculture and protection of farmers (pmfby.gov.in).

3. Organic Farming in West Bengal

People are becoming more health conscious nowadays and hence are aware of the negative impacts of hybrid farming affecting the food we consume. Organic farming is steadily growing in India. Bengal is getting more involved in this new-age natural agriculture and has shown a considerable growth in organic food business becoming the second largest market after north India. Organic farming is usually supported by local bodies so they mostly operate on a smaller scale. Supporting these local farmers helps to keep up the economy preserve rural communities. Sufal Bangla Programme and Susthai Krishi Programme are such programme which is helping to spread and promote sustainable agriculture. Lalmati, Murshidabad, Malda, Dinajpur and Jangal Mahal are a few places where organic farming is already initiated. But due to the lower yield of organic farming, many farmers are reluctant to make a changeover as yet. Paddy is the principle crop of West Bengal so many movements are taking place to promote the usage of natural seeds to hybrid ones (www.getbengal.com).

4. Concept and Component of Organic Farming

Concept: Organic farming uses natural techniques and practices instead of synthetic pesticides and fertilizers for agricultural production. Organic farming aims at preserving and enhancing soil quality by using techniques such as crop rotation, composting and natural pest control. These practices also promote biodiversity and reduce the use of non-renewable resources such as fossil fuels. As Food and Agriculture organization (FAO) (1999) says, "Organic agriculture is a holistic production management system which promotes and enhances agro-ecosystem health, including biodiversity, biological cycles and soil biological activity. It emphasises the use of management practices in preference to the use of off-farm inputs, taking into account that regional conditions require locally adapted systems".

Component: Organic farming mainly includes the following components which are discussed briefly.

1. **Crop residue**: Crop residue are the residues which are left in the field after the main crop is harvested. It is considered to be an effective anti erosion measure. It improves soil aeration by promoting free exchange of gases between the soil and the atmosphere. It can also be used in biofuel production (Science Direct). Crop residues improves water conservation and storage, nutrient availability and crop yields (Bharti, 2021).
2. **Crop rotation**: Different plants have different nutritive needs. Rotation of nutritive demanding crops must be followed by

leguminous crops which help to replenish the soil with nitrogen content. Crop rotation is the practice of growing different crops in regular succession in the same field. It improves the physical and chemical properties of soil maintaining soil quality and ability to break the disease cycle. It also helps fight against erosion (Shah *et al.*, 2021).

3. **Organic manure**: Organic manure is mainly plant and animal waste which is used as a source of plant nutrients.it improves the physical properties of soil as compared to chemical fertilizers. Organic manures aids in the direct growth of crop and assimilation of humic substances promoting soil productivity through the activity of soil microorganisms.
4. **Integrated pest management**: Healthy plants are likely to be more resistant to pest and diseases so it is important to maintain conditions to keep the plant healthy (Yadav *et al.*, 2020). Non chemical biological pest management can be implemented which does not have any harmful effect to the environment and plant. Application of oil cakes which have insecticidal properties, use of green leaf manures such as Calotropis are some of the measures used in organic farming to reduced the incidence of pests and diseases (Ravisankar *et al.*, 2021).
5. **Non-chemical weed control measures**: Weed control is a huge challenge in farming. Mechanical weed control is the best method to control weed growth especially in row crops. Cultural biological and physical methods should be resorted to herbicides (ecourse online.iasri.res.in)
6. **Biofertilizer:** Biofertilizers have a substantial capacity for nitrogen fixation, solubilizing phosphates and promoting soil microbial activity. Biofertilizers are now being extensively used in organic farming as it is proving to be an effective way to increase crop yield and soil health (Mehata, *et al.*, 2023). Bioinoculants such as arbuscular mycorrhizal fungi has been found to augment the population of favourable microbial interaction and providing resistance to unfavourable biotic and abiotic stress (Allay, *et al.*, 2021). Soil and water contamination is primarily caused by the extensive application of chemical fertilizers. It is also responsible for the rise in pest and disease incidence and degradation of soil

fertility (Mishra *et al.*, 2013). Biofertilizers are cost effective and easily available so the farmers can afford biofertilizer over chemical fertilizer (Kumar and Kumar, 2019).

7. **Vermicompost**: Vermicomposting is a natural method for producing compost by using earthworms. It is an eco-friendly process as organic wastes are converted to compost. Soil that is treated with vermicompost has greater water retention, aeration, better electrical conductivity and organic matter improving crop yield (Lim *et al.*, 2015). Bhat *et al.* (2018) has discussed how the strong metabolic system of the microbes and chloragocyte cells in earthworms have the ability to detoxify heavy metals in industrial wastes and thereby help in plant growth and development. Vermicompost amended soil has a greater pH as compared to farmyard manure or mineral fertilizers (Drinkwater *et al.*, 1995; Gopinath *et al.*, 2008).
8. **Limiting nutrient losses**: Care should be taken in organic farming so that nutrient in the soil is maintained. Better recycling and handling of organic wastes should be rendered. Organic matter should be applied at the right time in the appropriate manner and quantity. Organic matter can also be conserved by decreasing burning of crop residues. (ecourse online.iasri.res.in). Cropping pattern should also be taken care of by growing mixed crops and practicing soil management by manuring after harvesting crops as the soil is prone to lose most of its nutrients after growing one crop. Proper fertility can be managed by balancing the macro and micro nutrients in the soil.
9. **Livestock production**: Farm animals which include domestic or domesticated animals helps in maintaining the sustainability of farms. Livestock not only provide food, helps in non-mechanized ploughing and income generation but also provide dung which is used as organic matter as they are rich in nutrients and urine which is a good source of nitrogen (Kumar, 2021; Nandhini and Suganthi, 2018).

5. Challenges and limitations in Organic Farming

People are slowly shifting towards organic products as a result organic farming is gaining popularity. But despite its advantage over conventional farming, India is facing a big challenge in shifting towards organic farming (Soni *et al.,* 2022). One of the reasons being pests. Plants are easily attacked by pests and diseases where pesticides are not used. Organic pesticides are more expensive than chemical pesticides. Therefore the high cost is proving to be a major disadvantage in organic farming (Muscanescu, 2013).

The cost of organic resources like neem cakes, groundnut cakes, cowdung, earthworms are highly priced. That is why farmers are choosing chemical fertilizers over organic fertilizers (Wani *et al.*, 2017). It is therefore obvious that organic products are much pricey and not everyone is willing to pay the price for it. (http://www.akmindia.in/organic-farming-pros-cons).

Yadav (2010), has stated that the use of organic manures in organic farming is high so it may have a high risk of contamination. But, Gopalakrishnan (2019) stated that organic foods have more healful nutrients similar to antioxidants and also people who was allergic to food with chemicals and preservatives found their symptoms lessen or disappeared after consuming organically grown food. Moreover, research has shown that it is safe to consume organically produced foods (Yadav *et al.,* 2020).

Proper education, awareness, skills and knowledge of proper farming methods is lacking among the farmers (Mukherjee *et al.*, 2022). Eventually, the dquantity of organic products is less and not sufficient enough to meet the demands of the people. Lack of supply is also one of the most disadvantages of organic farming in India (Wani *et al.*, 2017).

Organic farming is more labour intensive as farmers have to keep a close watch in the aeration, drainage, fertility, watering and weeding. Certain practices must be met to retain the organic label otherwise the farm will lose their organic certification (Meena *et al.*, 2013).

6. Principles of Organic Farming

There are four main Principles of organic agriculture which form the growth and development of organic farming. They are inter-connected and lends to the contribution and vision in improving agriculture (www.ifoam.bio/why-organic/shaping-agriculture/four-principles-organic; www.agritech.tnau.ac.in).

1. ***Principle of health:*** The health of the ecosystem and individuals should be sustained as well as producing high quality nutritious food to maintain the health and well-being of all.
2. ***Principle of Ecology:*** Correct ecological balance should be maintained between the environment and ecosystem by reducing inputs, reusing and recycling materials and energy to maintain environmental quality and conserve resources.
3. ***Principle of Fairness:*** Everyone should be provided with a good quality of life in accordance with their physiology, natural behaviour and well-being be it human beings or animals. There should be fairness in production, distribution and trade.
4. ***Principle of Care:*** Precautionary and responsible management practices has to be managed to protect the health and well-being of the current and future generations and the environment.

7. Organic Farming *vs.* Conventional Farming

There are two common methods of farming i.e. organic farming and conventional farming. They both aim to produce food but differ greatly in their approaches, methods and outcomes which has been highlighted in Table 1.

Table 1: Comparative Analysis of Organic Farming and Conventional Farming

Sl. No.	*Organic Farming*	*Conventional Farming*
1.	Based on ecological framework	Based on chemical framework
2.	Improves soil fertility	Deteriorate soil fertility
3.	Uses biofertilizers	Uses chemical fertilizers
4.	Causes no pollution	Causes air, water and soil pollution
5.	Irrigation requirements reduced	Intensive irrigation needed
6.	Products are chemical free	Chemical residues present in products
7.	Harmony with nature	Domination of nature
8.	Restraint nature	Exploitation of nature

Sl. No.	*Organic Farming*	*Conventional Farming*
9.	Improve the ecosystem	Impact on ecosystem
10.	Uses organic inputs to increase production	Uses synthetic inputs to increase production
11.	Focus on sustainability	Focus only on yield and not on sustainability
12.	No health risks due to absence of harmful chemicals	Extensive health risks due to heavy use of fertilizers
13.	Weed control by mechanical, crop rotation and cultural practices	Weed control by herbicides
14.	Promotes biodiversity	Does not promote biodiversity
15.	Creates healthier soils	Depletes soil of nutrition
16.	Combats soil erosion as organic farms have thicker topsoil	Soil erosion more likely to happen
17.	Significantly reduces greenhouse gases	Greenhouse gases more likely to increase

Source courtesy: www.slideshare.net

8. Procurement of Certification

Without the proper certification organic products cannot be sold at a proper rate and it needs to attain certain standards prescribed by Certifying Agencies. One has to take several precautions to obtain such standard organic products such as soil, weed, water, pest & disease management etc. Maintaining of biodiversity is also an important component. Fulfilling all such components one can apply for certification of organic farming. In India, it is handled by the National Programme for Organic Production (NPOP) which is overseen by Agricultural and Processed Food Products Export Development Authority (APEDA). The certifying agencies of organic farming are INDOCERT, ECOCERT India, and SGS India etc. It needs various steps to get the certification. After procurement of certificate one has easy market access, premium pricing, trust of the buyer and contribution to environment. The organic farming is preferred subject to population growth.

9. Conclusion

Organic farming uses techniques to achieve good quality crop with maximum yield keeping in mind the safety and health of the people as well as conserving nature and the environment. Organic farming is focused more in providing nutritious, healthy and tasty food. But there is an imperative need to understand soil science and ecology in order to lock the fertility and health of the soil. More research has to be implemented in order to identify the thrust area in increasing the yield using safe biological methods so that not only the consumers but also the producers may get maximum benefit. Organic farming should not only benefit the environment but also human health.

References

[1] Allay, S., Thapa, K. and Chakraborty, B.N. (2021). Mycorrhizal association and root colonization of *Citrus reticulata, Citrus medica* and *Citrus limonia* grown in Darjeeling hills and foot hills Journal of Mycopathological Research, 59(4), 375–384

[2] Bharti, K. (2021). Crop residues and their impact on crop production: a review. *Journal of Emerging Technologies and Innovative Research.* 8(5) 613–618

[3] Bhat, S.A., Singh, S., Singh, J., Kumar, S., Bhawana and Vig, A.P. (2018). Bioremediation and detoxification of industrial wastes by earthworms: Vermicompost as powerful crop nutrient in sustainable agriculture. Bioresource technology, 252, 172–179. https://doi.org/10.1016/j.biortech.2018.01.003

[4] Borlaug, N.E. (2002). Feeding a world of 10 billion people: The miracle ahead. *In Vitro Cellular and Developmental Biology—Plant* 38(2), 221–228. https://doi.org/10.1079/IVP2001279

[5] Drinkwater, L.E., Letourneau, D.K., Workneh, F., Van Bruggen, H.C. and Shennana, C. (1995). Fundamental differences between conventional and organic tomato agroecosystems in California. *Ecological Applications*, 5, 1098–1112.

[6] FAO/WHO Codex Alimentarius Commission, 1999

[7] Gopalakrishnan, R. (2019). Advantages and Nutritional Value of Organic Food on Human Health. *International Journal of Trend in Scientific Research and Development*, 3(4), 242–245. 10.31142/ijtsrd 23661.

[8] Gopinath, K.A., Saha, S., Mina, B.L., Kundu, S., Pande, H., Gupta, H.S. (2008). Influence of organic amendments on growth, yield and

quality of wheat and soil properties during transition to organic production. *Nutrient Cycling in Agroecosystems*, 82, 51–60.

[9] http://www.akmindia.in/organic-farming-pros-cons/

[10] https://www.agrifarming.in/government-schemes-for-organic-farming-in-india

[11] https://www.agrifarming.in/government-schemes-for-organic-farming-in-india

[12] https://www.agritech.tnau.ac.in

[13] https://www.ecourseonline.iasri.res.in

[14] https://www.fao.org/organicag

[15] https://www.getbengal.com

[16] https://www.ifoam.bio/why-organic/shaping-agriculture/four-principles-organic

[17] https://www.pmfby.gov.in

[18] https://www.sciencedirect.com

[19] https://www.slideshare.net

[20] Khushdil, B. (2021). Crop residues and their impact on crop production: a review. *JETIR*, 8(5), 613–618

[21] Kulhade, A., Gupta, A.D., Mishra, A. and Singh, S.R.K. (2016). Role of organic farming in indian agriculture. *Flora and Fauna*. 22(1), 41–48

[22] Kumar, M. and Kumar, K. (2019). Role of Bio-fertilizers in Vegetable Production: A review. *Journal of Pharmacognosy and Phytochemistry*. 8(1), 328–334

[23] Kumar, V. 2021. Organic Farming: Goals, Principles and Components. Just Agriculture multidisciplinary e-newsletter. 1(10) Article ID: 53, 1–5

[24] Lim, S.L., Wu, T.Y., Lim, P.N. and Shak, K.P.Y. (2015). The use of vermicompost in organic farming: Overview, effects on soil and economics. Journal of the Science of Food and Agriculture, (6), 1143–1156. https://doi.org/10.1002/jsfa.6849

[25] Meena, R.P., Meenal, H.P. and Meena, R.S. (2013). Organic Farming: Concept and Components. Popular Kheti, 1(4), 5–14

[26] Mehata, D.K., Kattel, I., Sapkota, P., Ghimire, N.P. and Mehta, R.K. (2023) Biofertilizers: A sustainable strategy for organic farming that would increase crop production and soil health. Plant Physiology and Soil Chemistry, 3(2), 35–39

[27] Mishra, D.J, Rajvir, S., Mishra, U.K. and Kumar, S.S. (2013). Role of Bio-Fertilizer in Organic Agriculture: A Review. *Research Journal of Recent Sciences,* 2, 39–41. http://isca.in/rjrs/archive/special_issue2012/8.ISCA-ISC2012-1AFS-32.pdf

[28] Mukherjee, K., Konar, A. and Ghosh, P. (2022). Organic farming in India: A brief review. *International Journal of Research in Agronomy*, 5(2), 113–118

[29] Muscanescu, A. (2013). Organic Versus Conventional: Advantages and Disadvantages of Organic Farming. *Economic Engineering in Agriculture and Rural Development*, 13(1), 253–256.

[30] Nandhini, D.U. and Suganthi S. (2018). Livestock Importance in Organic Farming. Approaches in Poultry, Dairy & Veterinary Sciences. *Approaches in Poultry, Dairy & Veterinary Sciences*, 5(1). 394–396 10.31031/apdv.2018.05.000602.

[31] Ravisankar, N., Ansari, M.A., Panwar, A.S., Aulakh, C.S., Sharma, S.K., Suganthy, M., Suja, G. and Jaganathan, D. (2021). Organic farming research in India: Potential technologies and way forward. *Indian Journal of Agronomy* 66, 142–162.

[32] Santhoshkumar, M., Reddy, G.C. and Sangwan, P. (2017). A Review on Organic Farming-Sustainable Agriculture Development. *International Journal of Pure and Applied Bioscience* 5(4), 1277–1282.

[33] Shah, K.K., Modi, B., Pandey, H.P, Subedi, A., Aryal, G., Pandey, M. and Shrestha, J. (2021). Diversified Crop Rotation: An Approach for Sustainable Agriculture Production. *Advances in Agriculture* 2021, 1–9 https://doi.org/10.1155/2021/8924087.

[34] Soni, R., Gupta, R., Agarwal, P. and Mishra, R. (2022). Organic Farming: A Sustainable Agricultural Practice. *Vantage: Journal of Thematic Analysis*, 3(1), 21–44.

[35] Wani, S.A., Wani, M.A., Mehraj, S., Padder, B.A. and Chand, S. (2017). Organic farming: Present status, scope and prospects in northern India. *Journal of Applied and Natural Science*, *9*(4), 2272–2279. https://doi.org/10.31018/jans.v9i4.1523.

[36] World Commission on Environment and Development. (1987). Report of the World Commission on Environment and Development: Our Common Future (The Brundtland Report). Osl

[37] Yadav, A.K. (2010). Organic Agriculture (Concept, Scenario, Principals and Practices), National Project on Organic farming Department of Agriculture and Cooperation, Govt. of India. 1–60. http://ncof.dacnet.nic.in

[38] Yadav, P., Pandiaraj, T., Kumar, V., Yadav, V. and Singh, P. (2020). Concepts, Present Status, Prospective and Myth and Reality of Organic Farming with Special Reference to Indian Context. *International Journal of Current Microbiology and Applied Sciences*, 9(08), 3742–3748. https://doi.org/10.20546/ijcmas.2020.908.432

Allelopathic Activity of Medicinal Plants from Darjeeling: *Hydrocotyle nepalensis* Hook.f. and *Rumex nepalensis* Spreng in Controlling Major Crop Weeds for Sustainable Agriculture Production

Sachina Yonzone[1]

ABSTRACT: The present study was aimed to determine and elucidate about the allelopathic potentiality of two medicinal plants; *Hydrocotyle nepalensis* Hook.f. and *Rumex nepalensis* Spreng on *Oryza sativa* L. seed germination percentage and seedling growth (length of radicle verses length of plumule). Different concentrations of aqueous extract of leaves of two selected medicinal plants were prepared and examined and was noted to have a considerable inhibitory effects on target plant germination. The effect at 15%, 20% and 25% was found to be significantly higher than that at the lower concentration (5%, 10%) and control. Plumule and radicle growth of the selected crop was also reduced significantly over control. Aqueous extract of leaf of *Hydrocotyle nepalensis* showed more inhibitory effect on seed germination percentage of targeted crop as compared to aqueous leaf extract of *Rumex nepalensis.* Besides its physiological attributes, some biochemical test was also taken into account to corroborate the allelopathic stress posed by the plant. Therefore tests for proline, peroxidase, protein contents and α-amylase of the target plant (*Oryza sativa* L.) was also found out under laboratory condition, which showed higher proline yield and peroxidase activity under stress and lower enzymatic activity of α-amylase in the seed treated with higher concentrations of leaf extract.

---

[1] Assistant Professor, Department of Botany, City College, Raja Rammohan Sarani, Amherst Street, Kolkata, West-Bengal-700009, India.
E-mail yonzonesachina@gmail.com

Keywords: *Allelopathy, Hydrocotyle Nepalensis, Rumex Nepalensis, Oryza Sativa, Inhibitory, Stress, α-amylase.*

1. Introduction

Allelopathy is the biological phenomenon by which one plant interferes upon neighbouring plants or their associated micro-flora and/or macro-flora by the release of bioactive chemicals (8). These bioactive chemicals are known as allelochemicals which may have both beneficial (positive allelopathy-antimicrobial effects (6) or detrimental (negative allelopathy) effects on the target organisms (both crop and weed species). These allelochemicals are classified as secondary plant metabolites (such as alkaloids, isoprenoids, phenolics, flavonoids, terpenoids and glucosinolates etc.)(13). These chemicals may be present in all parts of a plant like leaves, flowers, fruits, stems, roots, rhizomes, seeds and pollens etc (4, 9, 13, 15,). So when released into the surrounding environment (atmosphere or rhizosphere) through a number of ways by leaching, politization, root exudation and residue decomposition of certain plants on germination and seedling growth of the associated plants may suppress the germination, growth, yield and establishment of neighbouring plants, even the donor species itself directly by affecting their physiological properties (18, 20) or indirectly by modifying the rhizosphere soil properties through influencing the microbial biomass carbon and microbial community (10, 19, 21).

Allelochemicals of different plants species have also been reported to affect enzymes responsible for plant hormone synthesis in addition to inhibition of nutrient and ion absorption by affecting plasma membrane permeability (24), inhibition of biological nitrogen fixation. Thus allelopathic substances play a vital role in regulating the structure of plant communities (16) and thus could be used to lead for bio-degradable herbicide production (5, 17).

Medicinal plants are considered as an important source of secondary metabolites having strong allelopathic activity i.e. herbicidal potential (9). Keeping in view, two medicinal plants *Hydrocotyle nepalensis* Hook.f. and *Rumex nepalensis* Spreng have been selected to examine their biological and allelopathic activity in controlling major crop weeds for sustainable agricultural production.

2. Materials and Methods

Plant Collection and Identification: The arial plant parts of *Hydrocotyle nepalensis* Hook.f. and *Rumex nepalensis* Spreng. were collected from Darjeeling hill areas of West Bengal, when only the vegetative parts of the plants were available. The plants were identified by Lloyd Botanical Garden, Darjeeling.

Preparation and extraction of plant material: The fresh leaves of the above two plants were collected, cleaned, cut into small pieces and allowed to air dry. The dry leaves were crushed into fine powder using mortar and pestle and was sieved which were then stored in air tight glass bottles. 10gm of powder drug of both *Hydrocotyle nepalensis* Hook.f. and *Rumex nepalensis* Spreng was soaked in 100 ml of distilled water and kept for 24 hrs at room temperature. Then the extracts were filtered using Whatmans no 1 filter paper and the volume of the filtrate was made 100 ml (Dhawan and Narwal, 1994). From stock solutions different dilutions of the extract was prepared (5%, 10%, 15%, 20%, 25%). These different dilutions and distilled water as a control was used to study the allelopathic effect on the germination, seedling growth in the form of plumule length and radicle length dry weight of crop.

Healthy seeds of *Oryza sativa* L. were selected, washed thoroughly with distilled water and kept overnight. On the second day, washed and dry seeds were surface sterilized with 0.1% mercuric chloride solution for 2 minutes and washed twice with dist. water and kept for germination. Fifty sterilized seeds were taken in each case and were placed equispaced in sterilized Petri dish with filter paper. Each fifty sterilized seeds was moistened uniformly with respective concentrations of leaf extract of *Hydrocotyle nepalensis* and *Rumex nepalensis* and distilled water and all the petri-dish were kept under diffused sunlight at room temperature. The number of seeds germinated in each treatment was counted and calculated from subsequent days till the achievement of 50% germination percentage. After the seeds achieved 50% germination, biochemical tests related to physiological stress were also carried out such as proline, protein, peroxidise and α-amylase content of the target plant.

3. Results and Discussion

Allelochemicals were universally present in plants and its functions are to defence against its enemies. Although toxic metabolites are distributed throughout the plant (15), but the leaves and bark are their most potential source (1, 2). In nature water is the solvent extraction medium (7), that is why aqueous extracts are used in the present experiment. As these chemicals are bio-degradable in short time, their persistence in plants or soil system will not cause problems like pesticides.

Effect of aqueous extract on seed germination: Aqueous leaf extracts of both *Hydrocotyle nepalensis* and *Rumex nepalensis* inhibited seed germination of the test crop (Table 1&2). The germination percentage was decreased with the increased concentrations (20% &25%) i.e. the germination is not considerably inhibited in the mild concentrations of the leaf extracts as seen in the case of 5%, 10%, 15% viz not much difference lies between control and the other three. When the effects of the two medicinal plants are considered, then negative allelopathy is observed to the maximum degree in case of leaf extracts taken from *Hydrocotyle nepalensis. Rumex nepalensis* leaf extract is somewhat not too much inhibitory (Table 1, 2).

Table 1: Effects of Various Concentrations of Aqueous Extracts of *Hydrocotyle nepalensis* Hook.f. on Germination Percentage

Con of Leaf Extracts	*Days*											
	4 Days		*6 Days*		*8 Days*		*10 Days*		*12 Days*		*14 Days*	
	No. of Seeds Germinated	*Germination %*	*No. of Seeds Germinated*	*Germination %*	*No. of Seeds Germinated*	*Germination %*	*No. of Seeds Germinated*	*Germination %*	*No. of Seeds Germinated*	*Germination %*	*No. of Seeds Germinated*	*Germination %*
0%	15	30%	21	42%	23	46%	24	48%	27	54%	29	58%
5%	6	12%	14	28%	20	40%	15	30%	17	34%	17	34%
10%	4	8%	10	20%	15	30%	14	28%	16	32%	21	42%
15%	1	2%	2	4%	5	10%	6	12%	11	22%	9	18%
20%	0	0%	1	2%	2	4%	4	8%	5	10%	8	16%
25%	0	0%	0	0%	1	2%	2	4%	3	6%	6	12%

Table 2: Effects of Various Concentrations of Aqueous Extracts of *Rumex nepalensis* Spreng. on Germination Percentage

Con of Leaf Extracts	*Days*											
	4 Days		*6 Days*		*8 Days*		*10 Days*		*12 Days*		*14 Days*	
	No of seeds germinated	*Germination %*	*No of seeds germinated*	*Germination %*	*No of seeds germinated*	*Germination %*	*No of seeds germinated*	*Germination %*	*No of seeds germinated*	*Germination %*	*No of seeds germinated*	*Germination %*
0%	8	16%	18	36%	22	44%	24	48%	22	44%	25	50%
5%	7	14%	15	30%	22	44%	23	46%	22	44%	24	48%
10%	6	12%	15	30%	19	38%	23	46%	21	42%	22	44%
15%	2	4%	12	24%	18	36%	21	42%	20	40%	21	42%
20%	4	8%	11	22%	19	38%	16	32%	17	34%	18	36%
25%	1	2%	8	16%	13	26%	17	34%	15	30%	14	28%

Effect on length of plumule and radical: Effect of various aqueous concentrations of leaf extracts of *H. nepalensis* and *R. Nepalensis* on the length of plumule and radicle showed drastic effects. There is gradual decrease in length of both plumule and radicle as the concentrations of the extracts increased over the succeeding days (Table 3). From this table, it is clearly corroborates the fact that leaf extracts of *H. nepalensis* leads to decreased in growth of plumule and radicle but not as found in case of *R. Nepalensis.* But as the concentrations of leaf extracts increases, the length of plumule and radicle decreases which means that the leaf leachate obviously suppresses the natural physiological growth and development of the seedlings.

Estimation of proline, peroxidase, α-amylase and protein: There was a relative increase in the yield of proline (Mg/ml) with increase in leaf extracts of two studied medicinal plants. Such biochemical findings support the negative allelopathic effects of these plants towards the target plants. Similarly there is increase in peroxidase activity, also with the increase in the leaf extracts concentrations and yield being highest in case of *H. Nepalensis* leaf leachate treated plants and lowest in R. *Nepalensis.*

Table 3: Effects of Various Concentrations of Aqueous Extracts of *Hydrocotyle nepalensis* Hook.f. *and Rumex nepalensis* Spreng on Plumule and Radicle Length (mm) after Different Days of Intervals

Con of Leaf Extracts	*Hydrocotyle Nepalensis Hook.F.*						*Rumex Nepalensis Spreng*					
	10 Days		*12 Days*		*14 Days*		*10 Days*		*12 Days*		*14 Days*	
	Length of radicle	*Length of plumule*	*Length of radicle*	*Length of plumule*	*Length of radicle*	*Length of plumule*	*Length of radicle*	*Length of plumule*	*Length of radicle*	*Length of plumule*	*Length of radicle*	*Length of plumule*
0%	14.8	16.0	20.5	25.4	22.2	27.8	6.1	10.1	12.6	13.2	14.2	16.4
5%	14.2	12.6	13.8	17.3	15.4	17.8	5.4	8.6	7.6	8.2	12.5	14.0
10%	11.4	9.6	12.4	16.5	14.1	17.5	5.0	8.0	10.2	11.0	11.4	11.9
15%	10.4	9	10.3	14.2	11.6	15.0	4.6	7.6	8.7	9.3	9.0	10.6
20%	5.2	4.3	2.5	3.7	3.0	6.2	4.4	7.2	6.42	6.5	8.2	9.2
25%	2	1.5	3	3.2	3.2	6.3	3.8	5.0	4.8	5.5	6.0	8.1

Activity of α-amylase in the target plants was lowest in the *H. Nepalensis* leaf extract treatment. In case of *R. Nepalensis* treated seedlings, same type of results was found. Total protein content of the target plant under stress was increased with relative increment of leaf extract treatment. Studies conducted so far indicate that stressful conditions adversely affect the metabolism in plants and in all different types of environmental stresses, new stress specific proteins are synthesized. Therefore more protein production may be attributed to higher production of stress proteins.

4. Conclusion

The present study reports to have negative allelopathic effect of two medicinal plants *Hydrocotyle nepalensis* and *Rumex nepalensis* on the target plant *Oryza sativa* L although other medicinal studied showed a wide range of activities from complete inhibition to stimulation (Qasem 11, 12). There were significance differences between the test treatments and control. Out of two medicinal plants, *Hydrocotyle nepalensis* has more negative effects on the germination rate, seedling length than *Rumex nepalensis* leaf extracts studied. Therefore it is clear that there is immense prospect of allelopathic medicinal plants for the isolation and identification of allelochemicals and applies them as a tool for new bio-herbicide development. In future too, more and more emphasis should be given by the researchers to examine their bioactivity under laboratory and field conditions. If satisfy both then recommend them to use as a tool for new natural herbicides development for the evergreen world.

Acknowledgement

We are indebted to PG Department of Botany, Darjeeling Government College for allowing laboratory facilities in carrying out these experiments.

References

[1] Bhatt, B.P. and Chauhan, D.S., "Allelopathic effects of Quercus spp. on crops of Garhwal Himalaya" *Journal of Allelopathy,* 2000, pp. 265–272

[2] Bhatt, B.P., Kaletha M.S. and Todaria, N.P., "Allelopathic exclusion of understory by some agro forestry tree crops of Garhwal Himalaya" *Journal of Allelopathy,* 1997, pp. 321–328.

[3] Duke, S.O. and Lydon, J., "Herbicides from natural compounds" *Weed Technology,* 1987, pp.122–128.

[4] Duke, S.O., Baerson, S.R., Rimando, A.M., Pan, Z., Dayan, F.E. and Belz, R.G., "Biocontrol of weeds with allelopathy: Conventional and transgenic approaches. In: Novel Biotechnologies for Biocontrol Agent Enhancement and Management" (Eds., M. Vurro and J. Gressel). Springer, Dordrecht, The Netherlands, 2007, pp. 75–85.

[5] Duke, S.O., Dayan, F.E., Romagni, J.G. and Rimando, A.M., "Natural Products as Sources of Herbicides: Current Status and Future Trends" *Weed Research,* 2000, pp. 99–111.

[6] Erez, M.E., Battal, P., "Determination of Allelopathic and antimicrobial effects of four different plants species" International Journal of Nature and Life Science, 2022, pp. 79–89.

[7] Hill, E.C., Ngauajio, M. and Nair, M.G., "Differential response of weeds and vegetable crops to aqueous extracts of hairy wetch and cowpea" *Horticultural Science,* 2006, pp. 695–700.

[8] IAS International Allelopathy Society (2018). http://allelopathy-society.osupytheas.fr/about/

[9] Islam, A.K.M.M., Yeasmin, S., Qasem, J.R.S., Juraimi, A.S., Anwar, M.P., "Allelopathy of Medicinal Plants: Current Status and Future Prospects in Weed Management" *Agricultural Sciences,* 2018, pp. 1569–1588.

[10] Meier C.L. and Bowman, W.D., "Phenolic-Rich Leaf Carbon Fractions Differentially Influence Microbial Respiration and Plant Growth" *Oecologia*, 2008, pp. 95–107.

[11] Qasem, J.R., "A Survey on the Phytotoxicity of Common Weeds, Wild Grown Species and Medicinal Plants on Wheat" *Allelopathy Journal,* 2017, pp.179–194.

[12] Qasem, J.R., "Allelopathic Effects of Selected Medicinal Plants on *Ama retroflexus* and *Chenopodium murale*" *Allelopathy Journal,* 2002, pp. 105–122.

[13] Rawat, L.S., Maikhuri, R.K., Negi, V.S., Bahuguna, Y.M., Pharswan, D.S., Maletha, A., "Allelopathic Performance of Medicinal Plants on Traditional Oilseed and Pulse Crop of Central Himalaya, India" *Natural Academy of Science Lett,* 2016, pp. 141–144.

[14] Rice, E.L., "Allelopathy an-update". *The Botanical Review,* 1979, pp. 15–109.

[15] Rice, E.L., "Allelopathy" 2nd edition. Academic Press. New York, 1984.

[16] Smith, A.E., and Martin, L.D., "Allelopathic Characteristics of Three Cool-Season Grass Species in the Forage Ecosystem" *Agronomy Journal,* 1994, pp. 243–246.

[17] Vyvyan, J.R., "Allelochemicals as Leads for New Herbicides and Agrochemicals" *Tetrahedron,* 2002, pp. 1631–1646.

[18] Weir, T.L., Park, S.W., and Vivanco, J.M., "Biochemical and Physiological Mechanisms Mediated by Allelochemicals" *Current Opinion in Plant Biology*, 2004, pp. 472–479.

[19] Xingjun Y.U., Yu, D., Zhijun, L.U. and Keping, M.A., "A New Mechanism of Invader Success: Exotic Plant Inhibits Natural Vegetation Restoration by Changing Soil Microbe Community" *Chinese Science Bulletin,* 2005, pp. 1105–1112.

[20] Yu, J.Q., Ye, S.F., Zhang, M.F. and Hu, W.H., "Effects of Root Exudates and Aqueous Root Extracts of Cucumber (*Cucumis sativus*) and Allelochemicals, on Photosynthesis and Antioxidant Enzymes in Cucumber" *Biochemical Systematics and Ecology*, 2003, pp. 129–139.

[21] Zhou, B., Kong, C.H., Li, Y.H., Wang, P. and Xu, X.H., "Crabgrass (*Digitaria sanguinalis*) Allelochemicals That Interfere with Crop Growth and the Soil Micro-bial Community" *Journal Agriculture Food Chemistry,* 2013, pp. 5310–5317.

Role of Plant Growth Promoting Fungi in Biocontrol of Plant Diseases and Sustainable Agriculture

Sweata Khati[1]

ABSTRACT: Plant production in agriculture has traditionally been associated with the use of inorganic fertilizers and synthetic pesticides for rapid growth in crop productivity. However, in the long term, such practices may negatively affect the quality of the soil and also favour pollution. Plant-growth-promoting fungi (PGPF) resident microorganisms residing in the rhizosphere soil of various crop plants are one of the effective and ecologically friendly derivatives to inhibit or eradicate plant diseases. They are known for improving the defence mechanisms and growth in plants. Numerous direct and indirect mechanisms, including solubilization of minerals, synthesis of phytohormones, production of volatile organic compounds, exploitation of microbial enzymes, increases in nutrient uptake, amelioration of abiotic stresses and suppression of deleterious phytopathogens are involved. These wide ranges of interconnected mechanisms help PGPF to maintain rhizosphere competence and stability in host performance. The application of PGPF not only suppresses the use of agrochemicals but also prevents it from a variety of biotic and abiotic stresses without environmental contamination. The biotechnological technique is sustainable and effective in stimulating the interaction between PGPF and plant root exudates, which is required to improve the abundant production of crops and promote soil health. Therefore, the need for superior PGPF to supplement inorganic chemical fertilizers is one of the crucial steps in moving toward organic farming practices.

Keywords: *Plant Growth Promoting Fungi (PGPF), Abiotic Factors, Biotic Factors, Plant Growth, Sustainable Agriculture.*

---

[1] Assistant Professor, Department of Botany, Ananda Mohan College, 102/1 Raja Rammohan Sarani, Kolkata-700009, India. E-mail: sweatak@yahoo.com

1. Introduction

Agriculture provides a significant proportion of the household economy worldwide. People rely on agriculture to feed their families, earn a living, and start a business, no matter how small (Dorosh and Thurlow, 2016; Abhilash *et al.*, 2021). This industry has been a source of income for many individuals in developing and developed countries, with construction programs, drainage systems, suppliers, and more (Bennett *et al.*, 2013). Agriculture has brought a plethora of benefits, and its significance should not be overlooked. It has basic, economical, and developmental benefits. It enriches every country in the world in some form while playing a critical role in both developed and developing countries when it comes to the way of life (Christiaensen *et al.*, 2011; Dubey *et al.*, 2022). The rapid increase in the requirement for food couldn't be achieved by using traditional methods, and people have invented more ways to use natural processes. But now, it has exceeded the natural boundaries of the environment and caused so many adverse effects due to not following sustainable ways. The cost of environmental quality cannot be sustainable in the future because of the adverse changes being caused to the environment and ecosystem. The necessity of having an alternative agriculture method that can function in a friendly ecosystem while sustaining and increasing productivity is the demand of this day. Fortunately, plant roots harbour an abundant association of beneficial micro-organisms. The uniqueness of microorganisms and the dynamic part they play in sustaining agricultural ecosystems have made them likely candidates for playing a central role in organic-based modern agriculture. Root exudates are the largest source of carbon that attracts microbial populations and allows them to forge an intimate association with host plants (Vacheron *et al.*, 2013). In response, the rhizosphere microbial populations play versatile roles in transforming, mobilizing and solubilizing soil nutrients, which are crucial for plant growth and development. Among the diverse rhizosphere microbial population, fungi known as plant growth-promoting fungi (PGPF) have received growing attention in recent days.

2. Plant Growth Promoting Fungi (PGPF)

PGPF are soil-dwelling, non-pathogenic saprophytes and are reportedly beneficial to many crop plants, not only by promoting plant growth but also by serving in disease protection (Begum *et al.*, 2019; Liu & Zhang, 2015). Moreover, PGPF encompasses a diverse taxonomic group compared to mycorrhiza. They are often involved in a range of complex interactions with plants and develop distinct strategies to mediate improvements in seed germination, seedling vigor, plant growth, flowering and productivity of host plants. PGPF is not only associated with the root mediating positive effects on plant growth and development but also has beneficial effects on suppressing phytopathogenic microorganisms (Hossain *et al.*, 2007). Not every organism identified as PGPF will improve plant growth under all conditions or in association with all plant hosts (Hyakumachi & Kubota, 2004). Some PGPF biocontrol inoculants usually contain necrotrophic mycoparasites such as Trichoderma spp. (Kaewchai *et al.*, 2009), while a limited number, such as Sphaerodes mycoparasitica is biotrophic mycoparasitic agents (Vujanovic and Goh, 2012). Therefore, PGPF is considered one of the potential active ingredients in both biofertilizer and mycofungicide formulation.

3. Impact of PGPF in Plant Disease Management

Plant-growth-promoting fungi (PGPF) resident microorganisms residing in the rhizosphere soil of various crop plants, in which tomato plants are not left out, are one of the effective and ecologically friendly derivatives scientists investigated to inhibit or eradicate plant diseases. They were known for improving the defence mechanisms and growth in plants (Zhou *et al.*, 2014). PGPF applications suppress the usage of agrochemicals and likewise prevent plants from biotic and abiotic stresses (Yadav *et al.*, 2011). Various studies reported the following PGPF genera (Gliocladium *et al.*) to improve tomato (Zhou *et al.*, 2014), orange (Hyakumachi & Kubota, 2004), apple (Islam *et al.*, 2014), pear (Khan *et al.*, 2011), cucumber (You *et al.*, 2015), carrot (Salas *et al.*, 2011), and other plants' growth and further promote the plants' innate immunity and the production of various necessary secondary metabolites by the plants. PGPF perform the following functions in plants: antagonistic or biocontrol potential by competing for space and nutrients (Hyakumachi & Kubota, 2004), growth hormone production (Waqas *et al.*, 2015), mineral solubilization, mycoparasitic and saprophytic resistance, root colonization, induced systemic resistance (ISR) in plants (Ignatova *et al.*, 2015) and also SAR ISR is mediated through the activation of the jasmonate pathway (Cong & Lingyun, 2019). SAR (Systemic *et al.*) is regulated by the salicylic acid-dependent signalling pathway, and its activation involves local and systemic increases in endogenously synthesized salicylic acid (SA), leading to the promotion of the pathogenesis-related (PR) proteins (Backer *et al.*, 2019).

4. Effect of AMF in the Rhizosphere of Crop Plants

Arbuscular mycorrhizas are mutualistic associations which are formed between the roots of 80 per cent of terrestrial plant species and fungi belonging to the small phylum Glomeromycota (Schubler *et al.*, 2001). The ancient mutualist and biotroph of plants, Arbuscular mycorrhizal fungi (AMF), has been found to improve the supply of water and nutrients, such as phosphate and nitrogen, to its host plant. In its exchange, it takes a part of photosynthate sugar to complete its life cycle. Although it has its own immune system, the plant, upon pathogen attack, gets weakened and needs reinforcement to fight back and become stabilized in the battleground. AMF fulfils the needs of the host plants and provides support in many ways by inducing attenuated defence signalling to fight against phytopathogens. This increase not only makes the plants more tolerant towards the attack of phytopathogens but also enhances the genetic, biochemical, and signalling factors responsible for their defence purposes. According to (Mahadevan *et al.*, 1982) AMF forms symbiotic association with the roots of most terrestrial plants, including many agricultural crops. VAM fungi are known to improve the nutrient status of plants, increase growth and development, protect plants against pathogens and fight drought and salinity. AMF dwelled in the host plants without effecting danger and were known to elicit the toleration of various stresses. AMF have also displayed their adaptation in plants when exposed to various conditions of habitats, especially those affected by abiotic stresses, such as drought, chilling, salinity, high temperature, heavy metals, and flooding (Igiehon & Babalola, 2017). Furthermore, AMF has been reported to contribute to the improvement of salt tolerance, employing various methods which constitute regulating the rate of K+/Na+ in plant cells, the production of growth hormones, the development of the rhizosphere and other soil conditions, the transfer of ion salts to the vacuoles, and, likewise, the promotion of photosynthetic water use effectiveness (Sofy *et al.*, 2021).

5. PGPF Formulation

Trichoderma spp., a well-known PGPF, have many success stories as a plant growth-promoting agent and appears to have much potential as a commercial formulation. As reported by (Abdel-Fattah *et al.*, 2007), direct foliar application of T. harzianum was also foundto reduce the disease severity and appreciably improve grain yield, total grain carbohydrate and protein, in addition to a significant improvement in the total photosynthetic pigments in rice leaves. The application of the formulation of seed saw a significant increase in growth promotion in chickpeas (Singh & Nautiyal, 2012). The use of Trichoderma spp., a well-known mycoparasite, can help by improving nutrient uptake and mobilization, enhancing nitrogen use efficiency, promoting root growth and plant biomass, and improving tolerance to various physiological stresses, including soil salinity and drought through the reduction of oxidative damage that stresses cause according to (Harman, 2011; Shoresh *et al.*, 2010). A talc-based formulation was developed for T. harzianum to supply concentrated conidial biomass of the fungus with high colony-forming units (CFU) and long shelf life ((Singh & Nautiyal, 2012)). A composted cattle manure-based Trichoderma biofertilizer was developed and tested in the field. Plots fertilized with biofertilizer had the greatest aboveground biomass of any treatment and were significantly more productive than non-amended plots and plots fertilized with any rate of organic fertilizer (Zhang *et al.*, 2018). Effective formulation of P. indica was prepared in talcum powder or vermiculite with 20% moisture. The talcum-based formulations performed significantly better as bioinoculant over vermiculite-based formulations in glass-house experiments (Sarma *et al.*, 2011).

6. Applicability for Sustainable Agriculture

Microbial communities coexist in inter-relationships with the roots of crop plants. Plant-growth-promoting microorganisms (PGPMs) have been employed in the stimulation of resistance in plants against pathogen invasion aside from promoting the development of crop plants (Adedayo *et al.*, 2022). The introduction of these microbes is one of the ecologically friendly management methods of disease that is durable as a result of the stimulation of innate immunity in plants. The multi-inoculations regime in the field trials is highly needed. These inocula integration of different species possessing variable benefits to the crop plants may be of greatest value. These treatments may reduce the chemical application of pesticides to crop plants. Multifunctional biofertilizers is another strategy to reduce chemical fertilizers, diseases and to increase soil fertility in tea (Nepolean *et al.*, 2012). Various forms of fungal inoculum can be used for inoculating tree seedlings, but the most recommended form is vegetative mycelium (Tikhonovich & Provorov 2011). Gliocladium species are soil dwellers saprobes and some species have been described to be parasites of several plant pathogens (Mendes *et al.*, 2013). The effectiveness of Coniothyrium minitans can be enhanced by combinations with Trichoderma spp. (Park *et al.*, 2017). The non-pathogenic species of Fusarium are known to have effective biocontrol activity (Kottb *et al.*, 2015).

7. Conclusion

Because of current concerns over the adverse effects of agrochemicals, there is a growing interest in improving our understanding of the role and application of beneficial microbes in agriculture. At present, effective microorganisms are increasingly used as inoculants for biocontrol and biofertilization because the reduction of fungicides and fertilizers used in the agricultural field is in topmost demand to improve sustainable agriculture and to maintain the ecosystem. The use of Plant Growth Promoting Fungi formulations has helped reduce the problems encountered in the production of crops and the endeavour of pest-free crops with no or minimal applications of chemical fertilizers and pesticides. This review portrays how Plant Growth Promoting Fungi can improve not only the sustainability of agricultural products but also the fertility of the soil. If we are able to search deeply into the complex rhizosphere environment, the mechanisms of action of PGPF and the practical aspects of its mass production, inoculant formulation and delivery increase, more PGPF products will become available in the coming future.

References

[1] Abdel-Fataah, G.M., Shabana, Y.M., Ismail, A.E. and Rashad, Y.M. *Trichoderma harzianum*: a biocontrol agent against *Bipolaris oryzae. Mycopathol*, 164: 81–99, 2007.

[2] Abhilash, P., Bastianoni, S., Chen, W., DeFries, R., Fraceto, L., Fuckar, N., Hashimoto, S., Hunter, D., Keesstra, S., Merah, O., O'Farrell, P., Singh, S., Smith, P., Stringer, L. and Turner, II B. Introducing 'Anthropocene Science': A New International Journal for Addressing Human Impact on the Resilience of Planet Earth. *Editorial, Anthropocene.* 2021.

[3] Adedayo, A., Fadiji, A. and Babalola, O. The Effects of Plant Health Status on the Community Structure and Metabolic Pathways of Rhizosphere Microbial Communities Associated with Solanum lycopersicum. *Horticulturae*, 8: 404, 2022.

[4] Backer, R., Naidoo, S. and den Berg, N. The Non Expressor of Pathogenesis-Related Genes 1) NPR1(and Related Family: Mechanistic Insights in Plant Disease Resistance. *Frontiers in Plant Science.* 10: 102, 2019.

[5] Begum, N., Qin C., Ahanger, M.A. and Raza, S., Role of Arbuscular Mycorrhizal Fungi in Plant Growth Regulation: Implications in Abiotic Stress Tolerance. *Frontiers in Plant Science.*10: 1068, 2019.

[6] Bennett, A. Chi-ham, C., Barrows, G. and Sexton, S., Agricultural Biotechnology: Economics, Environment, Ethics, and the Future, 249–281, 2013.

[7] Christiaensen, L., Demery, L. and Kuhl, J., The (evolving) role of agriculture in poverty reduction-An empirical perspective. *J. Dev. Econ.* 96: 239–254, 2011.

[8] Cong, Z. and Lingyun, Z., An account of in silico identification tools of secreted effector proteins in bacteria and future challenges. *Briefings in Bioinformatics.* 20: 110–129, 2019.

[9] Dubey, P., Singh, A., Merah, O. and Abhilash, P. Managing agro-ecosystems for food and nutrition security. Editorial. *Curr. Res. Environ. Sustain.* 4: 100127, 2022.

[10] Dorosh, P. and Thurlow, J. Beyond agriculture versus non-agriculture: Decomposing sectoral growth–poverty linkages in five African countries. 2016.

[11] Harman, G.E., Trichoderma—not just for biocontrol anymore. *Phytoparasi.* 39(2):103–108, 2011.

[12] Hossain, M., Sultana, F., Kubota, M., Koyama, H. and Hyakumachi, M., The plant growth-promoting fungus Penicillium simplicissimum

GP17–2 induces resistance in Arabidopsis thaliana by activation of multiple defense signals. *Plant & Cell Physiology.* 48:1724–1736, 2007.

[13] Hyakumachi, M. and Kubota, M., Fungi as plant growth promoter and disease suppressor. *Fungal Biotechnology in Agricultural, Food, and Environmental Applications.* 21: 101–110, 2004.

[14] Igiehon, O. and Babalola, O., Biofertilizers and sustainable agriculture: Exploring arbuscular mycorrhizal fungi. *Appl. Microbiol. Biotechnol.* 101: 4871–4881, 2017.

[15] Ignatova, V., Brazhnikova, V., Berzhanova, Z. and Mukasheva, D., Plant growth-promoting and antifungal activity of yeasts from dark chestnut soil. *Microbiological Research.* 175:78–83, 2015.

[16] Islam, S., Akanda, M., Sultana, F. and Hossain, M., Chilli rhizosphere fungus Aspergillus spp. PPA1 promotes vegetative growth of cucumber (Cucumis sativus) plants upon root colonisation. *Archives of Phytopathology and Plant Protection.* 47:1231–1238, 2014.

[17] Kaewchai, S., Soytong, K. and Hyde, D., Mycofungicides and fungal biofertilizers. *Fungal Diversity.* 38:25–50, 2009.

[18] Khan, L., Hamayun, M., Kim, H., Kang, M., Lee, H. and Lee, J., Gibberellins producing endophytic Aspergillus fumigatus sp. LH02 influenced endogenous phytohormonal levels, plant growth and isoflavone biosynthesis in soybean under salt stress. *Process Biochemistry, 46:*440–447, 2011.

[19] Kottb, M., Gigolashvili, T., Großkinsky, D.K. and Piechulla, B., Trichoderma volatiles effecting Arabidopsis: from inhibition to protection against phytopathogenic fungi. *Frontiers in Microbiology*, 6: 995, 2015.

[20] Liu, X.-M. and Zhang, H., The effects of bacterial volatile emissions on plant abiotic stress tolerance. *Frontiers in Plant Science*, 6: 774, 2015.

[21] Mahadevan, N. and Shridhar, R.. Methods in physiological plant pathology. *2nd Ed. SivakaniPubl., India,* 242, 1982.

[22] Mendes, R., Garbeva, P. and Raaijmakers, J.M., The rhizosphere microbiome: significance of plant beneficial, plant pathogenic, and human pathogenic microorganisms. *FEMS Microbiology Reviews.* 37: 634–663, 2013.

[23] Nepolean, P., Jayanthi, R., Pallavi Vidhya, R. and Balamurugan, A., Role of biofertilizers in increasing tea productivity. *Asian Pac J. Trop Biomed*, S1443–S1445, 2012.

[24] Park, S., Leonid, T., Seung, Y.L .and Chang, G.B., Mycobiology New Recorded Species in Three Genera of the Sordariomycetes in Korea. *Mycobiology.* 45: 64–72, 2017.

[25] Salas-Marina, A., Silva-Flores, A., Cervantes-Badillo, G., Rosales-Saavedra, T., Islas-Osuna, A. and Casas-Flores, S., The plant growth-promoting fungus Aspergillus ustus promotes growth and induces resistance against different lifestyle pathogens in Arabidopsis thaliana. *Journal of Microbiology and Biotechnology*. 21: 686–696, 2011.

[26] Sarma, M., Kumar, V., Saharan, K., Srivastava, R., Sharma, A. and Prakash, A., Application of inorganic carrier-based formulations of fluorescent pseudomonads and Piriformospora indica on tomato plants and evaluation of their efficacy. *Journal of Applied Microbiology*, 111: 456–466, 2011.

[27] Schubler, A., Schwarzott, D. and Walker, C., A new fungal phylum, the Glomeromycota: phylogeny and evolution. *Mycol. Res.*. 105: 1413–1421, 2001.

[28] Shoresh, M., Harman, G.E. and Mastouri, F., Induced systemic resistance and plant responses to fungal biocontrol agents. *Ann. Rev. of Phytopathol.* 48: 21–43, 2010.

[29] Singh, P. and Nautiyal, C., A novel method to prepare concentrated conidial biomass formulation of Trichoderma harzianum for seed application. *Journal of Applied Microbiology*. 113:1142–1450, 2012.

[30] Sofy, R., Aboseidah, A., Heneidak, A. and Ahmed, R., ACC deaminase containing endophytic bacteria ameliorate salt stressin Pisum sativum through reduced oxidative damage and induction of antioxidative defense systems. *Environ. Sci. Pollut.* Res. 28: 40971–40991, 2021.

[31] Tikhonovich, I.A. and Provorov, N.A., Microbiology is the basis of sustainable agriculture: an opinion. *Annals of Applied Biology*, 159: 155–168, 2011.

[32] Vacheron, J., Desbrosses, G., Bouffaud, L., Touraine, B., Moënne-Loccoz, Y. and Muller, D., Plant growth-promoting rhizobacteria and root system functioning. *Frontiers in Plant Science*, 4:356, 2013.

[33] Vujanovic, V. and Goh, K., qPCR quantification of Sphaerodes mycoparasitica biotrophic mycoparasite interaction with Fusarium graminearum: in vitro and in planta assays. *Archives of Microbiology*, 194:707–717, 2012.

[34] Waqas, M., Khan, L., Hamayun, M., Shahzad, R., Kim, H. and Choi, S., Endophytic infection alleviates biotic stress in sunflower through regulation of defence hormones, antioxidants and functional amino acids. *European Journal of Plant Pathology*, 141:803–824, 2015.

[36] Yadav, J., Verma, P. and Tiwari, K., Plant growth promoting activities of fungi and their effect on chickpea plant growth. *Asian Journal of Biological Sciences*, 4:291–299, 2011.

[37] You, H., Kwak, W., Kang, M., Lee, C. and Kim, G., Aspergillus clavatus Y2H0002 as a new endophytic fungal strain producing gibberellins isolated from Nymphoides peltata in fresh water. *Mycobiology,* 43:87–91, 2015;

[38] Zhang, F., Huo, Y., Cobb, A., Luo, G., Zhou, J. and Yang, G., Trichoderma biofertilizer links to altered soil chemistry, altered microbial communities, and improved grassland biomass. *Frontiers in Microbiology,* 9: 848, 2018.

[39] Zhou, Z., Zhang, C., Zhou, W., Li, W., Chu, L. and Yan, J., Diversity and plant growth-promoting ability of endophytic fungi from the five flower plant species collected from Yunnan, Southwest China. *Journal of Plant Interactions*, 9:585–591, 2014.

Harnessing Natural Feed Additives to Mitigate Methane Emissions in Ruminants: A Mini Review

Manjil Gupta[1]

ABSTRACT: Climate change poses a critical threat to global ecosystems, driven in part by methane emissions from the livestock sector. Enteric fermentation in ruminants accounts for a substantial portion of these emissions, necessitating effective mitigation strategies. Feed additives have emerged as a promising approach to reducing methane production in the rumen. This mini review examines the use of natural feed additives in lowering methane emissions, focusing on herbal extracts, propolis, yeast, algae, enzymes and organic acids. Natural feed additives modulate rumen fermentation, microbial populations, and methane production pathways by enhancing propionate production, inhibiting hydrogen-producing bacteria, disrupting methanogenic archaea and protozoa populations, and indirectly regulating methane production via hydrogen utilization. Despite their potential, challenges remain in identifying specific bioactive compounds, improving palatability, and ensuring economic viability. Standardized measures and in vivo trials are necessary to validate the efficacy and safety of natural feed additives for practical use.

Keywords: Ruminants, Methane, Methanogens, Feed Additives, Global Warming.

1. Introduction

Climate change poses a significant threat to our planet due to a growing population and increasing economic demands. The International Panel of Climate Change (IPCC) warns that the current

---

[1] Assistant Professor, Department of Zoology, Dinhata College, Dinhata, Cooch Behar, West Bengal-736135, India. E-mail: manjilslg@gmail.com

rate of climate change surpasses anything seen in the last millennium, with projected global temperature increases of 1.8 to 4.0°C within the next 90 years (Yatoo *et al.,* 2012). This rapid change threatens the well-being of both present and future generations. One major contributor to greenhouse gas emissions, particularly carbon dioxide (CO_2) and methane (CH_4), is the livestock sector (Gerber *et al.,* 2014; Ghanbari Maman *et al.,* 2022). Livestock emit CH_4 primarily through enteric fermentation and nitrous oxide (N_2O) from manure management. Methane, produced in the rumen by methanogenic archaea during feed fermentation, accounts for a significant portion of global emissions, with 95 million tons emitted annually by domestic animals (Knapp *et al.,* 2014). These emissions, predominantly from ruminant livestock, contribute to 17% of global CH_4 and 3.3% of greenhouse gas emissions (Patra *et al.,* 2014). Feed additives are incorporated into animal diets to enhance feed quality, promote growth, address nutrient deficiencies, neutralize toxins, mitigate the effects of anti-nutritional factors, and decrease methane production in the rumen. Over the past decade, extensive research has focused on finding effective ways to reduce enteric methane (CH_4) emissions from livestock, particularly through dietary adjustments, rumen manipulation, and chemical inhibitors (Beauchemin *et al.,* 2022). However, the results of these mitigation strategies have been inconsistent, and some chemical additives may have negative impacts on animals or offer only short-lived efficacy (Kumar *et al.,* 2014). To promote ethical, sustainable, and environmentally friendly livestock production, there is growing interest in utilizing feed-additive technology that harnesses bioactive substances with antimethanogenic properties (Wang *et al.*, 2019). Natural resources such as essential oils, marine algae, and plant extracts have shown promise as additives in ruminant diets, offering benefits without disrupting rumen fermentation or endangering animal health (Kim *et al.,* 2013; Patra and Yu, 2012). These natural feed additives must meet criteria such as safety for both livestock and consumers, sustained efficacy across various feed types, affordability, and enhancement of overall livestock productivity. This mini review examines the use of natural feed additives in lowering methane emissions, focusing on herbal extracts, propolis, yeast, algae, enzymes and organic acids.

2. Methane Production in the Rumen

The ruminant stomach comprises the rumen, reticulum, omasum, and abomasum, with the rumen being the largest chamber. It acts as a fermentation chamber where microbial flora break down fibrous feed, enabling ruminants to derive nutrients from otherwise indigestible plant material. Rumen microorganisms, including bacteria, protozoa, fungi, and methanogenic archaea, thrive in symbiotic anaerobic conditions (Qi *et al.,* 2010). This microbial population, ranging from bacteria to viruses, plays a crucial role in degrading diverse substrates, producing short-chain fatty acids (SCFA), methane (CH_4), carbon dioxide (CO_2), ammonia, lactic acid, microbial protein, and vitamins. Methane is generated by methanogenic bacteria through the reduction of CO_2 with hydrogen as an energy source for their growth (Patra, 2012). The composition and function of rumen micro-organisms are influenced by factors such as host species, diet, management practices, and geographical location. SCFA and ammonia produced through microbial fermentation are absorbed through the rumen epithelium, eructated as gases, or exit to the small intestine for further absorption (McCann *et al.,* 2014). Acetate, propionate, and butyrate are the primary SCFA used as energy sources, with acetate being the most abundant. Propionate is converted to glucose, while butyrate is metabolized into ketone bodies. Ammonia is metabolized to urea in the liver or recycled through saliva, and microbial protein is digested and absorbed in the small intestine. Methane production by methanogenic bacteria represents an energy loss for ruminants, ranging from 2 to 12% of energy intake, but it is essential for maintaining optimal rumen fermentation conditions (Morgavi *et al.,* 2010).

3. Feed Additives in Reducing Methane Emissions

3.1 *Herbal Extracts*

In recent years, plant and herbal extracts have emerged as successful alternatives to antibiotics and feed additives in the livestock industry. Essential oils, saponins, tannins, and organosulfides have demonstrated promising results in improving rumen microbial populations, nitrogen metabolism, and overall animal health (Patra *et al.,* 2019; Adegbeye *et al.*, 2019; Zhou *et al.*, 2020). For instance, studies have shown that certain plant extracts, like those from heather and European blueberry, can reduce methane emissions in red deer and sheep (Pérez-Barbería *et al.*, 2020). Essential oils from anise and capsicum have been found to modify rumen fermentation patterns and increase dry matter intake (Fandino *et al.*, 2020). Additionally, thyme, mint, and orange oils have been shown to decrease methane and CO_2 production in the rumen (Canbolat *et al.*, 2011; Jahani *et al.*, 2019; Pedraza-Hernandez *et al.*, 2019). Similarly, extracts from moringa and brewer's yeast, as well as combinations of plant extracts like acacia, grape seed, and green tea extracts, have demonstrated methane reduction effects. Bamboo grass pellets and eucalyptus oil have also been linked to decreased methane production (Sinz *et al.*, 2019, Wann *et al.*, 2019; Abdelrahaman *et al.*, 2019). However, it's important to note that while some extracts may inhibit methane production, excessive use could potentially harm rumen microorganisms and reduce overall fermentation and methanogenesis.

3.2 *Propolis*

Propolis, a bee-collected plant product, has gained attention as a dietary additive in animal nutrition. It promotes rumen microorganism activity, leading to increased consumption of hydrogen and alterations in total volatile fatty acids (VFAs). There is growing interest in studying the potential of propolis to mitigate methane emissions, considering factors such as phytogeography, botanical origin, climate, and collection methods. Phenolic compounds in propolis have been shown to enhance rumen fermentation, reduce ammonia levels, and decrease methane emissions (Santos *et al.*, 2016). Studies by Morsy *et al.*, 2021 and Kara *et al.*, 2014 have demonstrated the anti-methanogenic effects of propolis extract, indicating its potential to reduce methane production in the rumen.

3.3 *Yeast*

Yeast supplementation has become popular in ruminant diets due to its numerous benefits for health, performance, and ruminal fermentation. A meta-analysis of 110 studies revealed that *Saccharomyces cerevisiae* supplementation increased dry matter intake, milk yield, rumen pH, and volatile fatty acid concentrations while reducing lactic acid levels (Desnoyers *et al.,* 2009). While in vivo experiments on yeast's impact on methane (CH_4) production in ruminants are limited, in vitro studies have shown promising results. Yeast culture enhances acetate production by acetogenic bacteria in the rumen, leading to reduced CH_4 emissions (O'brien *et al.,* 2014). However, the effectiveness of yeast in reducing CH_4 output can vary depending on factors like substrate type, yeast dosage, and experimental conditions.

Studies on dairy and beef cattle have yielded mixed results regarding yeast's effect on CH_4 production, with some showing no significant impact (Munoz *et al.,* 2017; Oh *et al.,* 2019). In contrast, experiments with sheep and goats have demonstrated positive effects, with yeast culture reducing CH_4 emissions by up to 10.19% and CH_4 per dry matter intake by 6.85% (Mwenya *et al.,* 2004, Lu *et al.,* 2016). The potency of yeast culture appears to be dose-dependent, with higher doses leading to greater reductions in CH_4 emissions. While the exact mechanism of yeast's CH_4 mitigation remains unclear, it is believed to involve increased propionate production, thereby reducing methanogenesis (Mutsvangwa *et al.,* 1992; Dai *et al.,* 2022). Further research is necessary to fully understand the effects of yeast on CH_4 production in ruminants, considering variables like yeast dosage, basal diets, and forage/concentrate ratios.

3.4 *Algae*

Micro- and macroalgae have shown promising potential as feed additives, as highlighted in studies by Anele *et al.,* 2016 and Brooke *et al.,* 2020. Initial research by Machado *et al.,* 2014, identified red algae as effective in reducing methanogenesis, with bromoform ($CHBr_3$) identified as the most potent compound for methane inhibition. However, further investigation is needed to understand the effects of bromoform on animal health and atmospheric chemistry. Concerns have also been raised regarding the sustainable production of seaweeds and their potential negative impacts on rumen digestibility and health (Min *et al.,* 2021).

3.5 *Enzymes*

Enzymes with fibrolytic or proteolytic activities are commonly added to ruminant diets to improve plant cell wall digestibility and production performance. However, their impact on methane (CH_4) production varies. In vitro studies show conflicting results: cellulase reduces CH_4 production per unit of degraded dry matter (Tang *et al.*, 2013), while xylanase increases CH_4 in some substrates (He *et al.*, 2015). In vivo studies have also yielded mixed findings. Proteolytic enzyme supplementation in beef cattle diets doesn't significantly affect CH_4 production, but improves dry matter digestibility (Mc Ginn *et al.*, 2004). Conversely, dairy cattle given higher doses of fibrolytic enzyme exhibit increased CH_4 production, suggesting greater energy loss during fermentation (Chung *et al.*, 2012). Some studies find no effect of cellulase and xylanase on CH_4 in growing goats or exogenous enzymes in dairy cattle (Lu *et al.*, 2016). However, fibrolytic enzymes may reduce CH_4 production and the acetate/propionate ratio in dairy cattle (Arriola, 2011). Further research is needed to understand these varying responses, considering enzyme activity, dosage, diet, and substrate.

3.6 *Organic Acids*

Organic acids, such as formic and fumaric acid, are utilized in animal diets to enhance acidity, preserving feed quality like silage, and promoting nutrient absorption by regulating microbial balance in the digestive system. Formic acid, when used in low doses, reduces total gas production, but higher doses may have the opposite effect. Additionally, formic acid exhibits a significant inhibitory effect on gas production (Kara *et al.*, 2015). Fumaric acid shows promise in reducing methane emissions from ruminants and improving environmental conditions when used sustainably (Palangi *et al.*, 2021).

4. Mechanisms of Lowering Methane Production

The regulatory mechanisms of natural feed additives in lowering methane production in the rumen involves several key aspects:

4.1 *Regulation of Rumen Fermentation*

Many compounds in natural feed additives modify rumen fermentation characteristics, improving dry and organic matter degradation, fiber digestibility, and gas production (Hamid *et al.*, 2020; Kim *et al.*, 2014). They alter the volatile fatty acid (VFA) profile by increasing propionate production and reducing acetate, consequently lowering the acetate-to-propionate ratio and methane production.

4.2 *Regulation of Rumen Bacteria Ecosystem and Propionate Pathway*

Some feed additives influence the composition and abundance of bacteria in the rumen, promoting propionate-producing bacteria while inhibiting hydrogen-producing bacteria. This shift towards propionate synthesis competes with methanogenesis for available hydrogen, reducing methane production (Salami *et al.*, 2018). Additionally, many compounds may inhibit specific bacteria, such as *Ruminococcus albus*, known for hydrogen production, further decreasing methane formation (Kim *et al.*, 2015).

4.3 *Regulation of Rumen Methanogenic Archaea and Protozoa Population*

Bioactive compounds can inhibit the growth and activity of methanogenic archaea and protozoa in the rumen. They disrupt protozoa cell membranes, reducing protozoal-associated methanogens and hindering hydrogen transfer. By targeting these methane-producing microorganisms, they indirectly lower methane emissions (Hassan *et al.*, 2020; Reddy *et al.*, 2020).

4.4 *Regulation of the Hydrogenotrophic Pathway*

Some compounds indirectly regulate methane production by manipulating rumen fermentation and the availability of hydrogen. They promote propionate formation as an alternative sink for hydrogen, diverting it away from methanogenesis. This shift in hydrogen utilization reduces methane production without directly diminishing rumen methanogens (Newbold and Rode, 2006).

5. Problems and Prospects

Biological formulations and extracts contain diverse and complex compounds, making it challenging to identify specific compounds responsible for methane mitigation (Adeleye *et al.,* 2021). Blends of multiple plant varieties or extracts often show positive effects, complicating the attribution of anti-methanogenic properties to individual compounds. Utilizing omics technologies can help elucidate the interactions between bioactive compounds and rumen micro-organisms, guiding targeted extraction and processing of active ingredients for industrial-scale purposes. Some phytochemicals in medicinal plants have bitter or unpleasant tastes, which may reduce feed intake and negatively impact animal performance (Ban *et aL.,* 2022). Improving palatability through methods such as crushing into fine powder, encapsulation, or fermentation with probiotics can enhance acceptance by livestock. Coating technology and microbial fermentation may also help mask undesirable flavors while enhancing antimethanogenic activity (Aderojo *et al.,* 2019). Extracting bioactive ingredients from medicinal plants can be complex and costly, potentially limiting their widespread adoption. Further, utilizing natural feed additives and exploring cost-effective extraction processes are essential to ensure economic viability (Pai *et al.,* 2022). Additionally, standardized measures are needed to guarantee the quality and safety of feed additives for practical use on a large scale. Lastly, many studies for methane mitigation rely on in vitro trials, which may not fully capture the complexity of the rumen ecosystem or predict long-term effects accurately. In vivo trials are necessary to validate in vitro findings and assess the sustained effectiveness of medicinal plants in reducing methane emissions in ruminants over time (Malik *et al.,* 2017).

6. Conclusion

Addressing methane emissions from ruminant livestock is crucial for mitigating the impact of agriculture on climate change. Livestock, particularly ruminants, contribute significantly to methane production through enteric fermentation, posing environmental challenges. The utilization of feed additives offers a promising approach to reducing methane emissions while improving animal health and performance. The development and application of feed additives offer promising opportunities to mitigate methane emissions from ruminant livestock, contributing to sustainable and environmentally responsible agricultural practices. Continued research and innovation in this field are essential for developing effective strategies to address methane emissions while supporting animal welfare and productivity.

References

[1] Abdelrahman, S.M., Li, R.H., Elnahr, M., Farouk, M.H. and Lou, Y. (2019). Effects of different levels of eucalyptus oil on methane production under in vitro conditions. *Polish Journal of Environmental Studies,* 28, 1031–1042.

[2] Adegbeye, M.J., Elghandour, M.M., Monroy, J.C., Abegunde, T.O., Salem, A.Z., Barbabosa-Pliego, A. and Faniyi, T.O. (2019). Potential influence of Yucca extract as feed additive on greenhouse gases emission for a cleaner livestock and aquaculture farming—A review. *Journal of Cleaner Production*, 239, 118074.

[3] Adejoro, F.A., Hassen, A. and Akanmu, A.M. (2019). Effect of lipid-encapsulated acacia tannin extract on feed intake, nutrient digestibility and methane emission in sheep. *Animals*, 9, 863. https://doi.org/10.3390/ani9110863

[4] Adeleye, O.A., Bamiro, O.A., Bakre, L.G., Odeleye, F.O., Adebowale, M.N., Okunye, O.L. and Menaa, F. (2021). Medicinal plants with potential inhibitory bioactive compounds against coronaviruses. *Advanced Pharmaceutical Bulletin*, 12, 7–16. https://doi.org/10.34172/apb.2022.003

[5] Anele, U.Y., Yang, W.Z., McGinn, P.J., Tibbetts, S.M. and McAllister, T.A. (2016). Ruminal in vitro gas production, dry matter digestibility, methane abatement potential, and fatty acid biohydrogenation of six species of microalgae. *Canadian Journal of Animal Science,* 96, 354–363. https://doi.org/10.1139/cjas-2015-0132

[6] Arriola, K.G., Kim, S.C., Staples, C.R. and Adesogan, A.T. (2011). Effect of fibrolytic enzyme application to low-and high-concentrate diets on the performance of lactating dairy cattle. *Journal of Dairy Science,* 94, 832–841.

[7] Ban, C., Paengkoum, S., Yang, S., Tian, X., Thongpea, S. and Purba, R.A.P. (2022). Feeding meat goats mangosteen (Garcinia mangostana L.) peel rich in condensed tannins, flavonoids, and cinnamic acid

improves growth performance and plasma antioxidant activity under tropical conditions. *Journal of Applied Animal Research*, 50, 307–315. https://doi.org/10.1080/09712119.2022.2068557

[8] Beauchemin, K.A., Ungerfeld, E.M., Abdalla, A.L., Alvarez, C., Arndt, C., Becquet, P. and Kebreab, E. (2022). Invited review: Current enteric methane mitigation options. *Journal of Dairy Science*, 105, 9297–9326. https://doi.org/10.3168/jds.2022-22091.

[9] Brooke Charles, G., Roque Breanna, M., Shaw, C., Najafi, N., Gonzalez, M., Pfefferlen, A., De Anda, V., Ginsburg David, W., Harden Maddelyn, C., Nuzhdin Sergey, V., *et al.* (2020). Methane reduction potential of two pacific coast macroalgae during in vitro ruminant fermentation. *Frontiers in Marine Science*, 7, 561. https://doi.org/10.3389/fmars.2020.00561

[10] Canbolat, Ö., Kalkan, H., Karaman, S. and Filya, I. (2011). The effect of essential oils on the digestibility, rumen fermentation and microbial protein production. *Kafkas Üniversitesi Veteriner Fakültesi Dergisi*, 17, 557–565.

[11] Chung, Y.H., Zhou, M., Holtshausen, L., Alexander, T.W., McAllister, T.A., Guan, L.L. and Beauchemin, K.A. (2012). A fibrolytic enzyme additive for lactating Holstein cow diets: Ruminal fermentation, rumen microbial populations, and enteric methane emissions. *Journal of Dairy Science,* 95, 1419–1427. https://doi.org/10.3168/jds.2011-4905

[12] Dai, X., Kalscheur, K.F., Huhtanen, P. and Faciola, A.P. (2022). Effects of ruminal protozoa on methane emissions in ruminants—A meta-analysis. *Journal of Dairy Science*, 105, 7482–7491. https://doi.org/10.3168/jds.2021-21095

[13] Desnoyers, M., Giger-Reverdin, S., Bertin, G., Duvaux-Ponter, C. and Sauvant, D. (2009). Meta-analysis of the influence of Saccharomyces cerevisiae supplementation on ruminal parameters and milk production of ruminants. *Journal of Dairy Science*, 92, 1620–1632. https://doi.org/10.3168/jds.2008-1663

[14] Fandiño, I., Ferret, A. and Calsamiglia, S. (2020). Dose and combinations of anise oil and capsicum oleoresin as rumen fermentation modifiers in vitro and in vivo with high concentrate diets fed to Holstein beef heifers. *Animal Feed Science and Technology*, 260, 114363.

[15] Gerber, P., Vellinga, T., Opio, C. and Steinfeld, H. (2011). Productivity gains and greenhouse gas emissions intensity in dairy systems. *Livestock Science*, 139, 100–108.

[16] Ghanbari Maman, L., Palizban, F., Fallah Atanaki, F., Elmi Ghiasi, N., Ariaeenejad, S., Ghaffari, M.R. and Kavousi, K. (2020). Co-abundance analysis reveals hidden players associated with high methane yield phenotype in sheep rumen microbiome. *Scientific Reports,* 10, 4995. https://doi.org/10.1038/s41598-020-61942-y.

[17] Hamid, M.M.A., Moon, J., Yoo, D., Kim, H., Lee, Y.K., Song, J. and Seo, J. (2020). Rumen fermentation, methane production, and microbial composition following in vitro evaluation of red ginseng byproduct as a protein source. *Journal of Animal Science and Technology*, 62, 801–811. https://doi.org/10.5187/jast.2020.62.6.801

[18] Hassan, F., Arshad, M.A., Ebeid, H.M., Rehman, M.S., Khan, M.S., Shahid, S. and Yang, C. (2020). Phytogenic additives can modulate rumen microbiome to mediate fermentation kinetics and methanogenesis through exploiting diet–microbe interaction. *Frontiers in Veterinary Science*, 7. https://doi.org/10.3389/fvets.2020.575801

[19] He, Z.X., Yang, L.Y., Yang, W.Z., Beauchemin, K.A., Tang, S.X., Huang, J.Y. and Tan, Z.L. (2015). Efficacy of exogenous xylanases for improving in vitro fermentation of forages. *Journal of Agricultural Science,* 153, 538–553.

[20] Jahani-Azizabadi, H., Durmic, Z., Vadhanabhuti, J. and Vercoe, P.E. (2019). Effect of some Australian native shrubs essential oils on in vitro rumen microbial fermentation of a high-concentrate diet. *Journal of Animal and Plant Sciences*, 29, 8–15.

[21] Kara, K., Aktuğ, E., Çağrı, A., Güçlü, B.K. and Baytok, E. (2015). Effect of formic acid on in vitro ruminal fermentation and methane emission. *Turkish Journal of Agriculture—Food Science and Technology,* 3, 856–860. https://doi.org/10.24925/turjaf.v3i10.856-860.304

[22] Kara, K., Güçlü, B.K. and Oğuz, F.K. (2014). Use of propolis and phenolic acids in ruminant nutrition. *Erciyes University Faculty of Veterinary Medicine Journal,* 11, 43–53.

[23] Kim, E.T., Guan, L.L., Lee, S.J., Lee, S.M., Lee, S.S., Lee, I.D., Lee, S.K. and Lee, S.S. (2015). Effects of flavonoid-rich plant extracts on in vitro ruminal methanogenesis, microbial populations and fermentation characteristics. *Asian-Australasian Journal of Animal Sciences*, 28, 530–537. https://doi.org/10.5713/ajas.14.0692

[24] Kim, E.T., Min, K.-S., Kim, C.-H., Moon, Y.H., Kim, S.C. and Lee, S.S. (2013). The effect of plant extracts on in-vitro ruminal fermentation, methanogenesis and methane related microbes in the rumen. *Asian-Australasian Journal of Animal Sciences,* 26, 517–522. https://doi.org/10.5713/ajas.2012.12480.

[25] Knapp, J.R., Laur, G.L., Vadas, P.A., Weiss, W.P. and Tricarico, J.M. (2014). Enteric methane in dairy cattle production: Quantifying the opportunities and impact of reducing emissions. *Journal of Dairy Science,* 97, 3231–3261.

[26] Kumar, S., Choudhury, P.K., Carro, M.D., Griffith, G.W., Dagar, S.S., Puniya, M., ... Puniya, A.K. (2014). New aspects and strategies for methane mitigation from ruminants. *Applied Microbiology and Biotechnology,* 98, 31–44. https://doi.org/10.1007/s00253-013-5365-0.

[27] Lu, Q., Wu, J., Wang, M., Zhou, C., Han, X., Odongo, E.N. and Tang, S. (2016). Effects of dietary addition of cellulase and a Saccharomyces cerevisiae fermentation product on nutrient digestibility, rumen fermentation and enteric methane emissions in growing goats. *Archives of Animal Nutrition*, 70, 224–238. https://doi.org/10.1080/1745039X.2016.1173322

[28] Machado, L., Magnusson, M., Paul, N.A., de Nys, R. and Tomkins, N. (2014). Effects of marine and freshwater macroalgae on in vitro total gas and methane production. PLoS ONE, 9, e85289. https://doi.org/10.1371/journal.pone.0085289

[29] Malik, P.K., Kolte, A.P., Bakshi, B., Baruah, L., Dhali, A. and Bhatta, R. (2017). Effect of tamarind seed husk supplementation on ruminal methanogenesis, methanogen diversity and fermentation characteristics. *Carbon Management,* 8, 319–329. https://doi.org/10.1080/17583004.2017.1357403

[30] McCann, J.C., Wickersham, T.A. and Loor, J.J. (2014). High-throughput methods redefine the rumen microbiome and its relationship with nutrition and metabolism. Bioinformatics and Biology Insights, 8, 109–125.

[31] McGinn, S.M., Beauchemin, K.A., Coates, T. and Colombatto, D. (2004). Methane emissions from beef cattle: Effects of monensin, sunflower oil, enzymes, yeast, and fumaric acid. *Journal of Animal Science,* 82, 3346–3356.

[32] Min, B.R., Parker, D., Brauer, D., Waldrip, H., Lockard, C., Hales, K. and Augyte, S. (2021). The role of seaweed as a potential dietary supplementation for enteric methane mitigation in ruminants: Challenges and opportunities. *Animal Nutrition*, 7, 1371–1387. https://doi.org/10.1016/j.aninu.2021.07.010

[33] Morgavi, D.P., Forano, E., Martin, C., Newbold, C.J., Anderson, R.C., Rasmussen, M.A. and Morrison, M. (2010). Microbial ecosystem and methanogenesis in ruminants. Animal, 4, 1024–1036.

[34] Morsy, A.S., Soltan, Y.A., El-Zaiat, H.M., Alencar, S.M. and Abdalla, A.L. (2021). Bee propolis extract as a phytogenic feed additive to enhance diet digestibility, rumen microbial biosynthesis, mitigating methane formation and health status of late pregnant ewes. *Animal Feed Science and Technology*, 273, 114834. https://doi.org/10.1016/j.anifeedsci.2021.114834

[35] Muñoz, C., Wills, D.A. and Yan, T. (2017). Effects of dietary active dried yeast (Saccharomyces cerevisiae) supply at two levels of concentrate on energy and nitrogen utilisation and methane emissions of lactating dairy cows. Animal Production Science, 57, 656–664. https://doi.org/10.1071/AN16522

[36] Mutsvangwa, T., Edwards, I.E., Topps, J.H. and Paterson, G.F.M. (1992). The effect of dietary inclusion of yeast culture (Yea-Sacc) on patterns of rumen fermentation, food intake and growth of intensively fed bulls. *Animal Science*, 55, 35–40.

[37] Mwenya, B., Santoso, B., Sar, C., Gamo, Y., Kobayashi, T., Arai, I. and Takahashi, J. (2004). Effects of including 1–4 galacto-oligosaccharides, lactic acid bacteria or yeast culture on methanogenesis as well as energy and nitrogen metabolism in sheep. *Animal Feed Science and Technology*, 115, 313–326. https://doi.org/10.1016/j.anifeedsci.2004.01.017

[38] Newbold, C.J. and Rode, L.M. (2006). Dietary additives to control methanogenesis in the rumen. *International Congress Series*, 1293, 138–147. https://doi.org/10.1016/j.ics.2006.03.047

[39] O'Brien, M., Navarro-Villa, A., Purcell, P.J., Boland, T.M. and O'Kiely, P. (2014). Reducing in vitro rumen methanogenesis for two contrasting diets using a series of inclusion rates of different additives. *Animal Production Science*, 54, 141–157. https://doi.org/10.1071/AN13242

[40] Oh, J., Harper, M., Melgar, A., Compart, D.P. and Hristov, A.N. (2019). Effects of Saccharomyces cerevisiae-based direct-fed microbial and exogenous enzyme products on enteric methane emission and productivity in lactating dairy cows. *Journal of Dairy Science*, 102, 6065–6075. https://doi.org/10.3168/jds.2018-15636

[41] Pai, S., Hebbar, A. and Selvaraj, S. (2022). A critical look at challenges and future scopes of bioactive compounds and their incorporations in the food, energy, and pharmaceutical sector. *Environmental Science and Pollution Research*, 29, 35518–35541. https://doi.org/10.1007/s11356-022-19423-4

[42] Palangi, V. and Macit, M. (2021). Indictable mitigation of methane emission using some organic acids as additives towards a cleaner

ecosystem. *Waste and Biomass Valorization*, 12, 4825–4834. https://doi.org/10.1007/s12649-020-01158-w

[43] Patra, A.K. (2012). Enteric methane mitigation technologies for ruminant livestock: A synthesis of current research and future directions. *Environmental Monitoring and Assessment*, 184, 1929–1952.

[44] Patra, A. K. (2014). Trends and projected estimates of GHG emissions from Indian livestock in comparisons with GHG emissions from world and developing countries. *Asian-Australasian Journal of Animal Sciences*, 27, 592–599.

[45] Patra, A.K. and Yu, Z. (2012). Effects of essential oils on methane production and fermentation by, and abundance and diversity of, rumen microbial populations. *Applied and Environmental Microbiology*, 78, 4271–4280. https://doi.org/10.1128/AEM.00309-12

[46] Patra, A.K., Min, B.R. and Saxena, J. (2012). Dietary tannins on microbial ecology of the gastrointestinal tract in ruminants. In Dietary Phytochemicals and Microbes (pp. 237–262). Springer.

[47] Pedraza-Hernandez, J., Elghandour, M.M.M.Y., Khusro, A., Camacho-Diaz, L.M., Vallejo, L.H., Barbabosa-Pliego, A. and Salem, A.Z.M. (2019). Mitigation of ruminal gases production from goats using Moringa oleifera extract and live yeast culture for a cleaner agriculture environment. *Journal of Cleaner Production*, 234, 779–786.

[48] Pérez-Barbería, F.J., Mayes, R.W., Giráldez, J. and Sánchez-Pérez, D. (2020). Ericaceous species reduce methane emissions in sheep and red deer: Respiration chamber measurements and predictions at the scale of European heathlands. Science of The Total Environment, 714, 136738.

[49] Qi, M., Jakober, K.D. and McAllister, T.A. (2010). Rumen microbiology. In R. J. Hudson (Ed.), Animal and plant productivity. Encyclopedia of Life Support Systems (EOLSS), Oxford, p. 462.

[50] Reddy, P.R.K., Elghandour, M.M.M.Y., Salem, A.Z.M., Yasaswini, D., Reddy, P.P.R., Reddy, A.N. and Hyder, I. (2020). Plant secondary metabolites as feed additives in calves for antimicrobial stewardship. *Animal Feed Science and Technology*, 264. https://doi.org/10.1016/j.anifeedsci.2020.114469

[51] Salami, S.A., Valenti, B., Bella, M., O'Grady, M.N., Luciano, G., Kerry, J.P., Jones, E., Priolo, A. and Newbold, C.J. (2018). Characterization of the ruminal fermentation and microbiome in lambs supplemented with hydrolysable and condensed tannins. *FEMS Microbiology Ecology*, 94. https://doi.org/10.1093/femsec/fiy061

[52] Santos, N.W., Zeoula, L.M., Yoshimura, E.H., Machado, E., Macheboeuf, D. and Cornu, A. (2016). Brazilian propolis extract used

as an additive to decrease methane emissions from the rumen microbial population in vitro. *Tropical Animal Health and Production,* 48, 1051–1056. https://doi.org/10.1007/s11250-016-1076-2

[53] Sinz, S., Marquardt, S., Soliva, C.R., Braun, U., Liesegang, A. and Kreuzer, M. (2019). Phenolic plant extracts are additive in their effects against in vitro ruminal methane and ammonia formation. *Asian-Australasian Journal of Animal Sciences*, 32, 966. https://doi.org/10.5713/ajas.18.0772

[54] Tang, S.X., Zou, Y., Wang, M., Salem, A.Z.M., Odongo, N.E., Zhou, C.S. and Kang, J.H. (2013). Effects of Exogenous Cellulase Source on In Vitro Fermentation Characteristics and Methane Production of Crop Straws and Grasses. *Animal Nutrition and Feed Technology*, 13, 489–505.

[55] Wang, W.J., Wang, S.P., Luo, D.M., Zhao, X.L., Yin, M.J., Zhou, C.F. and Liu, G.W. (2019). Effect of Chinese herbal medicines on rumen fermentation, methanogenesis and microbial flora in vitro. *South African Journal of Animal Science,* 49, 63. https://doi.org/10.4314/sajas.v49i1.8

[56] Wann, C., Wanapat, M., Mapato, C., Ampapon, T. and Huang, B. (2019). Effect of bamboo grass (Tiliacora triandra, Diels) pellet supplementation on rumen fermentation characteristics and methane production in Thai native beef cattle. *Asian-Australasian Journal of Animal Sciences*, 32, 1153–1160. https://doi.org/10.5713/ajas.18.0506

[57] Yatoo, M.I., Kumar, P., Dimri, U. and Sharma, M.C. (2012). Effects of climate change on animal health and diseases. *International Journal of Livestock Research*, 2, 15–24.

[58] Zhou, R., Wu, J., Lang, X., Liu, L., Casper, D.P., Wang, C., Zhang, L. and Wei, S. (2020). Effects of oregano essential oil on in vitro ruminal fermentation, methane production, and ruminal microbial community. *Journal of Dairy Science,* 103, 2303–2314.

SECTION-C

Human-Nature Relationship

Human-Nature Relationship in Indian Sundarbans: A Case Study of Chargheri Village, Satjelia Island

Mosfudar Rahaman[1] **and Mithun Ray**[1]

1. Introduction

The Sundarbans is the world's largest mangrove forest, spanning the borders of Bangladesh and India. It is also a UNESCO World Heritage site recognized for its ecological uniqueness and importance to all humanity. The Sundarbans are home to diverse species and some of the poorest twelve million people in the world. Entire communities in the Sundarbans depend directly and indirectly on the forest and its waterways for their livelihood, from fisheries to honey production. Almost 85 percent of the people living in Sundarban depend on agriculture (Roy and Alam, 2015). The possession of the land heavily determines socioeconomic status. There is also a socioeconomic divide in the fisherman community because only some fishermen own boats and can obtain official fishing licences (Islam, 2010). The lives of Sundarban residents are frequently affected by human-animal conflicts; a few tiger and crocodile attacks every year are common. Because of issues such as deaths and injuries due to human-animal conflict, overfishing, and deforestation, the state imposed several restrictions on livelihood strategies (Das and Bandopadhyay, 2012). The state forest department has tried to reduce the local people's dependency on the forest for their livelihood by taking on infrastructure development projects such as building roads and jetties, excavating irrigation channels and ponds, providing solar lamps and establishing a few

[1] Assistant Professor, Department of Geography, Malda College, Malda, West Bengal, India.

medical facilities. The Sundarbans are very vulnerable to various anthropogenic activities (Ghosh, 2015). In this situation, understanding the human-nature relationship is very important in the conservation of Sundarbans and policy making. Nature can be seen as beautiful and harmonious, but it also inspires fear in man who has had to fight it to survive. Now, nature is threatened by man, who has become detached from it (Schultz, 2002). Technology has endowed humans with the power of a major geological agency, which may act on a continental or even planetary scale (e.g. acid rain, photochemical smog, radioactive contamination, stratospheric ozone depletion, climate change). These man-made environmental problems cannot all be solved by technology alone. Changes in human behaviour are necessary; hence, there is a need for codes of conduct based on the ethics of the environment. The relationship between man and nature must be reconsidered (Bourdeau, 2004). It is well documented that biodiversity resources have been declining at an alarming rate across different regions of the world, posing a threat to the future of humanity and other species (Higgins *et al.*, 2013). Means and measures drawn from different schools of thought have yet to find solutions for sustainable natural resource management that would lead to a sustainable conservation process, secured livelihood options for the stakeholders, and a balanced ecosystem. Selfish resource exploitation threatens societies and livelihoods, contributing to a serious imbalance in the ecosystem (Battersby 2017). The situation is even worse in developing countries where the continuous pressures have already caused the extinction of numerous biodiversity resources. Sundarbans is no exception in this case (Titumir *et al.*, 2020). The Sundarbans is a unique ecosystem that provides humanity with a range of services, including food, water, and protection from natural disasters (Nishat, 2021). The Sundarbans is an area of global ecological significance. However, it is also one of the most vulnerable regions impacted by climate change (Vyas, 2015; Rahaman, 2017). The health of Sundarban is critical for the survival of many species of plants and animals, including the Royal Bengal Tiger. Raha (2016) predicts an enhanced human-wildlife/tiger-human conflict threatening the long-term conservation of the highly endangered Bengal tiger population in the world's largest delta. Human–tiger conflict (HTC) is a serious public health issue in Sundarban Reserve Forest, India (Chowdhury, 2008).

2. Database and Methodology

2.1 *Questionnaire Design*

A questionnaire survey is the main instrument used for collecting the required household data for the study. The questionnaire was divided into four sections. The first section was for household identity, and the second included questions about basic socio-demographic characteristics. The third section was for information regarding the households' economic status and forest dependency. The fourth section assessed the human-nature attachment and consisted of eighteen items with a five-point Likert scale: five for strongly agree, four for agree, three for neither agree nor disagree, two for disagree and one for strongly disagree for favourable items and vice versa for non-favourable items.

2.2 *Survey Design and Sampling*

For the convenience of the study door, a door survey has been conducted in the study area. Systematic random sampling was applied to select ideal representatives to produce reliable results.

2.3 *Data Structure*

The present study is based on both primary and secondary data. Primary data has been collected through questionnaire surveys, and secondary data has been collected mainly from the District Census Handbook of South 24 Parganas.

2.4 *Statistical Techniques and Data Representation*

The collected data has been classified and tabulated with the help of a master table. Cross-tabulation was made according to the requirement. Descriptive statistics such as mean, median, and percentage were applied. Vertical and horizontal bar graphs and pie diagrams were used in the present study for the graphical presentation of data.

2.5 *Study Area*

The Sundarbans is the world's largest mangrove forest, spanning the borders of Bangladesh and India. It is also a UNESCO World Heritage site recognized for its ecological uniqueness and importance to all humanity. It symbolises majestic beauty and tranquillity, a wilderness of nature and a biodiversity hotspot. It is located at the great delta of the Ganges, Brahmaputra and Meghna (GBM) rivers at the edge of

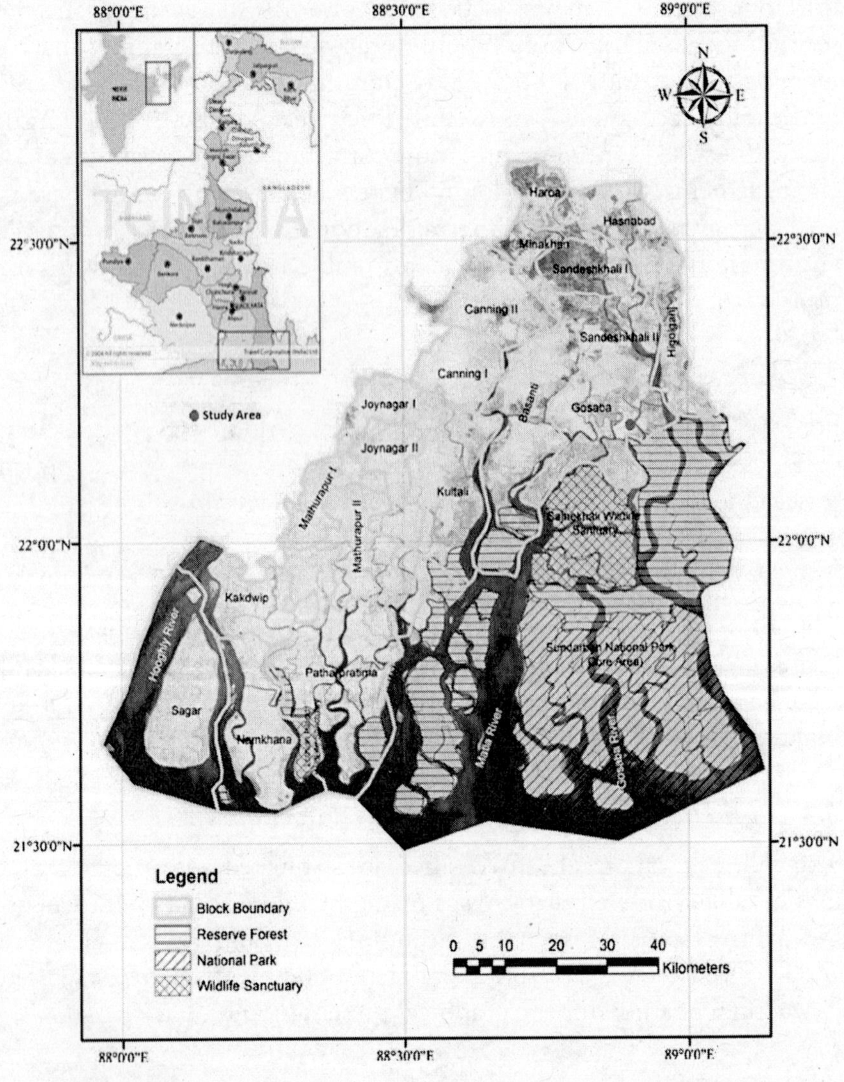

the Bay of Bengal and is the largest contiguous single-tract mangrove ecosystem in the world. It is located in the southwest corner of Bangladesh. A significant part of the total area of this mangrove swamp lies within India (West Bengal State). The Bangladesh portion is more important than India's, with an area of 6, 071 km2 (62% of the total area).

3. Result and Discussion

3.1 *Socio-Economic Profile of Chargheri Village*

Approximately 4.5 million people live in the Sundarbans of West Bengal, and another 7.5 million in Bangladesh. They rely on fishing, wood, honey, wax collection, prawn seed collection, and shrimp farming for income. However, these activities could be more sustainable. Despite their profitability, prawn seed numbers are decreasing, and shrimp farming is damaging natural barriers. A micro-level study in Chargheri village, Satjelia Island, South 24 Parganas, India, severely affected by cyclone Aila, highlights these challenges.

Demographic data offers valuable insights into communities' present status, history, and future prospects. In Chargheri village, males make up 54.95% of the population, mirroring national and state trends. The age structure skews towards adults aged 19–50. At the same time, a significant population (23.08%) over 51 years old suggests a low birth and death rate, typical of the fourth stage of demographic transition theory. Literacy is crucial for economic development. However, 45.05% of the village needs formal education, while only 45% have studied up to the secondary level, with few pursuing higher education. This underscores the importance of addressing educational disparities for societal advancement.

Social structural characteristics provide insights into how individuals are situated within society and how societal structures influence their behaviour, experiences, and attitudes. They also help understand social change and its impact on the labor market, health, environment, and politics. Furthermore, they aid in studying behavioural and attitudinal differences among different social groups. In Chargheri village, the majority (76.74%) belong to the SC community, with all surveyed individuals adhering to Hinduism, though a small Muslim population is reported. Marriage status shows 55.49% married, 25.82% unmarried, and 24.73% widowed or divorced. Joint families (69.53%) are prevalent, fostering strong bonds and equal sharing of prosperity and adversity, contrasting with nuclear families (30.47%). Migration history is significant, with 79.07% of current residents born in the area. In comparison, 20.93% are refugees from Bangladesh, especially after the Marichjhapi incident in 1979, spurred by the West Bengal government's efforts to rehabilitate Bengali-speaking refugees. Understanding the economic background of respondents is vital in social science studies, aiding in gauging economic conditions and individual personality patterns. Chargheri village's economic profile reveals a reliance on primary activities, with over 60% engaged in agriculture and 7.14% in fishing. Most farmers are marginal or tiny landholders, cultivating paddy with chemical inputs. Domestic animal husbandry is prevalent, including high-demand turkey breeds. Housing primarily comprises semi-pucca structures (42%) and kutcha houses (28%). Nearly all households have electricity (98%), and a majority have toilet facilities (84%). Dependency on the mangrove forest is high, with varied resource collection activities. Human-tiger conflict affects 14% of households due to forest resource collection, highlighting the need for conservation strategies.

3.2 *Assessment of Ecological Awareness and Effectiveness*

3.2.1 *Ecological and Environmental Awareness*

Ecological and Environmental Awareness (henceforth, EAW) is a key element in assessing the state of the HN relationship. EAW then refers to individuals' social consciousness in relation to the sphere of the natural environment as perceived by humans. High levels of EAW have been observed to be strongly related to a number of psychographic and sociodemographic factors, such as nature engagement during childhood and adulthood, involvement in growing food, and outdoor experiences.

3.2.2 *Understanding Nature*

Understanding nature is an essential aspect of the cognitive dimension of the HN relationship, and the topic has been discussed from a wide variety of perspectives. On the one hand, humans have often viewed nature as a provider of resources, rationalizing nature as a good that can be managed and utilised for human profit. This way of conceiving nature constitutes one of the basic principles of the currently dominating capitalist-based neoliberal society; other perspectives of individuals' understanding of nature may come from an understanding based on spiritual beliefs.

Table 1: Participants' Understanding of Nature

Item	*Mean*	*SD*	*Min*	*Max*
I don't like natural environments because I I find them dangerous.	2.25	1.40	1	5
The establishment of a natural biosphere reserve near my house prevents my personal development	3.20	1.22	1	5
I don't like natural/protected areas because they have many restrictions.	2.75	1.25	1	5
Human beings have the right to use natural resources in the way we want.	2.86	1.39	1	5
Nothing I do will improve problems in other places on the planet.	2.41	1.18	1	5
Animals and plants have fewer rights than humans.	2.82	1.61	1	5

Source: Field Survey, 2023.

Adverse conditions in the Sundarbans are indeed a cause for fear. Most people think the establishment of a natural biosphere reserve near my house prevents my personal development. Most of the people of the Sundarbans do not like all the protections currently being provided to protect the Sundarbans. It could hurt their livelihood. Just as some people think of using the natural resources here as they wish, some think it is not right to use the natural resources as they wish. Most people do not want their actions to cause any harm to the other world.

3.2.3 *Nature Appreciation*

Nature appreciation has shaped the HN relationship since the beginning of humankind. Since prehistoric times, nature appreciation has played an essential role in shaping the interaction between humans and their environment. The items of the scale included in this sub-dimension reflect ways of valuing and appreciating nature from a utilitarian point of view, as we believe this is still the dominant perspective in today's society. About 67.44% strongly agreed regarding respect to nature, while 27.91% agreed, 2.33% either agreed or disagreed, and 2.33% fully disagreed with this statement. From here, their nature is proved to be love. Because they respect this nature enough no matter how many problems there are.

Table 2: Participants' Appreciation of Nature

Item	*Mean*	*SD*	*Min*	*Max*
I observe/respect nature wherever I am	4.30	1.07	1	5
I watch wildlife wherever I am	4.25	1.15	1	5

Source: Field Survey, 2023.

3.2.4 *Perception of Nature*

Individuals' perception of nature can be considered a highly complex phenomenon influenced by sensorial (e.g., sight and smell) and non-sensorial components, such as cultural beliefs of nature, personal experiences related to nature, and moral and ethical principles guiding their perceptions. Very importantly, people's perception of nature has also been related to the development of cognitive functions such as learning and memory because it triggers the development of solid observational skills. The respondents of the study area feel that their activities really harm the environment, but they have to do something to survive. Apart from respecting nature, most of them also appreciate the intelligence of every living organism.

Table 3: Participants' Perception of Nature

Item	*Mean*	*SD*	*Min*	*Max*
I always think about how my Actions affect the environment	3.68	1.14	1	5
I recognize and appreciate the intelligence of other living organism	3.98	0.95	1	5

Source: Field Survey, 2023.

3.3 *Ecological and Environmental Affectiveness*

Ecological (and Environmental) Affectiveness (henceforth EAF) is here understood as the development of an array of emotions and feelings (i.e. affective factors) toward nature, including our love of nature, emotional reactions to environmental changes, the feelings Stemming from a sense of being part of nature, the sense of "socio-territorial belonging", and other kinds of cosmovisions relating to nature. These feelings may contribute to the development of positive attitudes and the emergence of positive emotional reactions toward the independent requirements of living organisms and attributes of nonliving elements of the natural world. In this light and for this study, three sub-dimensions have been considered—empathy, enjoyment, and connectedness—as expressions of effectiveness.

3.4 *Empathy for Nature*

Not surprisingly, a number of studies have shown that by helping to develop empathy for nature, people report higher levels of engagement with environmental problems and positive attitudes toward nature, which is why including empathy as one way in which we measure effectiveness is very valuable. In this study, we depict empathy for nature as a unifying construct involving both emotional and cognitive processes that trigger different feelings of caring about nature's well-being or destruction.

Table 4: Participants' Empathy for Nature

Item	*Mean*	*SD*	*Min*	*Max*
People who pollute nature make me angry	4.11	1.22	1	5
I feel sad when animals are hurt and plants are harmed	4.18	0.75	2	5
Taking care of plants and animals is important to me	4.45	0.91	1	5
I like to see wild animals living in their natural environment	4.43	0.94	1	5

Source: Field Survey, 2023.

3.5 *Enjoyment of Nature*

As an expression of affectiveness, enjoyment of nature is here viewed as the values and feelings that emerge from one's contact with nature. Thus, these values and feelings may be connected to the enjoyment of, for example, doing outdoor activities and adventure sports, for which nature becomes a source of, for instance, positive emotions, and inspiration in arts. In this context, we view enjoyment of nature as a pivotal aspect of the HN relationship that can boost intervention efforts of conservation of natural areas and threatened species.

Table 5: Participants' Enjoyment of Nature

Item	*Mean*	*SD*	*Min*	*Max*
I like to be outdoors, even in Bad Weather	3.41	1.37	1	5
When I feel sad, I like to go out and enjoy nature	3.95	1.30	1	5

Source: Field Survey, 2023.

3.6 *Connectedness to Nature*

The concept of connectedness refers to the idea of having a bond or being in touch with something and has been examined in different ways in the fields of geography and environmental studies, among others. Moreover, a number of studies have shown that connectedness plays an essential role in the HN relationship. A strong relationship between connectedness, mindfulness, and pro-environmental behaveours has been established, demonstrating that connectedness to nature plays a major role in the HN relationship and, therefore, is a valuable dimension to incorporate into any scale that examines this relationship.

Table 6: Participants' Connectedness to Nature

Item	*Mean*	*SD*	*Min*	*Max*
I feel that all the inhabitants of the Earth, human and nonhuman, share a common place	4.18	0.81	2	5
I feel part of the nature surrounds me	4.41	0.83	1	5

Source: Field Survey, 2023.

In spite of various unfavorable conditions, most of the villagers love the Sundarbans enough. It is as if they have considered this adversity as a part of daily life. It is as if they don't see this breath of nature as a form of nature and think it is a gift of nature. So they are living here in spite of all these happenings. It was also learned from them whether they would go if they were ever given an opportunity to move to another place. Most of them answered 'No'. Some of them want to stay there because of the place of birth, some because of their relatives, memories of dead husbands, and some because of the nature, the environment, and the animals. Love for nature can be observed in every aspect of their life. To protect nature, villagers have planted mangrove trees there. The people of Sundarbans have repeatedly proved their love for nature and their ability to fight and survive against adversity.

4. Conclusion

Humans need to interact with the environment to obtain our food, water, fuel, medicines, building materials and many other things. Advances in science and technology have helped us to exploit the environment for our benefit, but we have also introduced pollution and caused environmental damage. In the present study, Chargheri village of Gosaba Island of Indian Sundarbans has been surveyed, which is situated close to the forest area and is almost entirely dependent on forest produce. The uniqueness of Sundarban is not only over exploitation of natural resources but it is also a fact that people lose their lives in great numbers by transgressing the habitat of Royal Bengal Tiger. The risks associated with activities like honey collection, crab hunting and fishing are well known to the local communities. In response, the communities have adapted with their traditions and rituals which are backed by a strong socio-religious belief system. This gives them the psychological strength to go inside the forest. Although it has been widely established that forest conservation adversely impacts local livelihoods and results in dispossession from subsistence resources, it is indeed imperative to understand that in legitimizing forested landscapes as 'protected' and inviolate, survival of different communities is also at stake.

References

[1] Battersby, S. (2017). Can humankind escape the tragedy of the commons? Proceedings of the National Academy of Sciences, 114(1), 7–10.

[2] Bourdeau, P. (2004). The man-nature relationship and environmental ethics. Journal of environmental radioactivity, 72(1–2), 9–15.

[3] Das, Chandan Surabhi and Sunando Bandyopadhyay (2012). Sharing Space: Human-Animal Conflicts in the Indian Sundarban. Progressive Publishers.

[4] Ghosh, Priyanka (2015). Conservation and conflicts in the Sundarban biosphere reserve, India. *Geographical Review*. 105 (4): 429–440.

[5] Hasenkamp, M.L. and Sun, Z. (2022). Rethinking human–nature relationships: Daoism's contribution to transcultural sociotechnical imaginaries. *The Professional Geographer*, 75(2), 269–277.

[6] Higgins, P., Short, D. and South, N. (2013). Protecting the planet: a proposal for a law of ecocide. Crime, Law and Social Change, 59, 251–266.

[7] Islam, S.N. (2010). Threatened wetlands and ecologically sensitive ecosystems management in Bangladesh. *Front. Earth Sci.*, 4 (4), 438–448.

[8] Roy, A.K.D. and Alam, K. (2012). Participatory Forest Management for the Sustainable Management of the Sundarbans Mangrove Forest. *American Journal of Environmental Science*, vol. 8(5), 549–555.

[9] Schultz, P.W. (2002). Inclusion with nature: The psychology of human-nature relations. *Psychology of sustainable development*, 61–78.

[10] Schultz, P.W. (2002). Inclusion with nature: The psychology of human-nature relations. Psychology of sustainable development, 61–78.

[11] Seymour V. (2016). The Human– Nature Relationship and Its Impact on Health: A Critical Review. *Front. Public Health* 4, 1–12.

[12] Soga Masashi and Gaston Kevin J. (2020). The ecology of human–nature interactions. *Proc. R. Soc. B.*, 1–10.

Socio-Economic Status and Sustainable Livelihood Pattern of the Tribal Forest Villagers: A Study of Kalchini and Kumargram C.D. Blocks of Alipurduar District, West Bengal

Pinku Das[1] **and Nazrul Islam**[2]

ABSTRACT: The livelihood of individuals and groups is a product of the natural, social, and economic environment. A sustainable livelihood is resilient enough to withstand and recover from various stresses and shocks. Livelihoods of forest villagers are particularly vulnerable to shocks and stresses due to their dependence on natural resources. Sustainable livelihoods in these communities require a balance between using natural resources for economic gain and conserving these resources for future generations. This can be achieved by adopting sustainable forest management practices, community-based resource management and developing alternative livelihood options. This study explores socio-economic status and sustainable livelihood pattern of the tribal forest villagers of Kalchini and Kumargram C.D. Block of Alipurduar district. Kalchini and Kumargram blocks are located in the north-eastern part of Alipurduar district. The geographical area of the Kalchini and Kumargram blocks are 1229.29 sq. km. The present study concerns the 11 selected forest villages (6 villages from Kalchini and 5 villages from Kumargram Block). Sample villages are selected on the basis of percentage of schedule tribe household, population density and area of the villages. A simple random sampling technique is used to select sample household for the field survey and the sample size is

---

[1] Assistant Teacher, Chhatrampur High School, Tufanganj, Cooch Behar, India. E-mail: geopinku100@gmail.com

[2] Associate Professor, Department of Geography, Cooch Behar Panchanan Barma University, Cooch Behar, West Bengal, India. E-mail: islamnazrul975@gmail.com

394. Primary as well as secondary data were used for this present study. Descriptive statistics like frequency, percentage are used to analyze collected data.

Keywords: *Socio-economic Status, Sustainable Livelihood Pattern, Tribal Forest Villagers, Kalchini and Kumargram Block.*

1. Introduction

Tribal people of West Bengal are facing a large scale economic and livelihood insecurity due to the lack of employment opportunities in villages. There are numerous issues of sustainable livelihood among the scheduled tribe population in this region. On-going pressure on forest resources is leading to a decline in their traditional occupation. Government control and the exchange of forest land are weakening valuable tribal land (Sonar, 2023). Less number of the institutional opportunities was given by the government to upgrade income opportunities of the tribals. Forest degradation, institutional disappointments, absent of government strategies, poor communication, absence of social services like health care, education, employment etc. have cut down the livelihood options and quickly expanding poverty (Mallik, 2013).

Socio-economic conditions are often broadly discussed as satisfying needs, well-being, good or bad working conditions and other indicators (Pal *et al.*, 2015). The socio-economic conditions and sustainable livelihood pattern of the tribal forest villagers of Kalchini and Kumargram C.D. Blocks of Alipurduar district, West Bengal, are the focus of this article. The surveyed households comprise various tribes residing in forest villages, including Santal, Oraon, Munda, Asur, Rabha, Tamang, Mal Paharia, and Mech. By exploring their living conditions, income levels, and overall well-being, this research highlights these communities' challenges and opportunities, contributing valuable insights to support their sustainable livelihoods.

2. Location of the Study Area

Kalchini and Kumargram blocks are located in the north-eastern part of the Alipurduar district and lie between 26°43'7•N to 26°86'N latitude and 89°20'E to 89°80'E longitude. The western part of the study area is bounded by Madarihat-Birpara and Falakata blocks, and the southern part is by the Alipurduar-I and II block and Koch Bihar district. The eastern part shares its boundary with the state of Assam, and the northern part has an international border with Bhutan. The geographical area of the Kalchini and Kumargram block is 1229.29 sq. km, and the total population is 4, 98, 067, of which 2, 57, 421 are male and 2, 40, 646 are female (2011 Census).

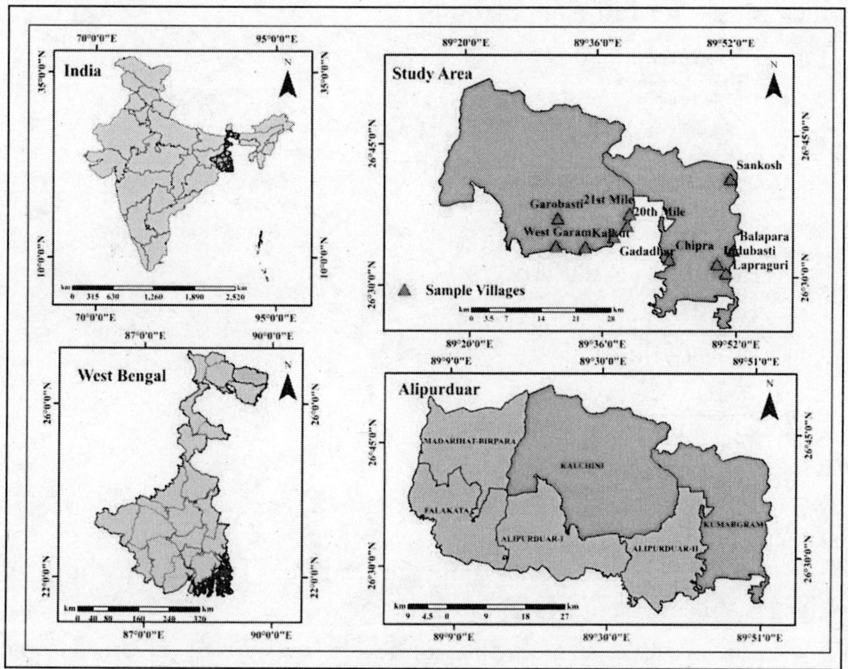

Map 1: Location Map of the Study Area

3. Methodology

3.1 *Selection of Sample Village*

The researchers conducted the study in the tribal concentrated forest villages of Kalchini and Kumargram C.D. block of Alipurduar District. Sample villages are selected based on the percentage of Scheduled Tribe (ST) households, area of the village, and population density. From Kalchini block, 6 villages were chosen (West Garam, Kalkut, Garobasti, Gadadhar, 20th Mile and 21st Mile) and from Kumargram block, 5 villages were selected (Chipra, Sankosh, Lapraguri, Indubasti and Balapara) using these criteria.

3.2 *Determination of Sample Size and Selection of Sampling Technique*

As the researchers knows the sample villages' total household and population, the sample size is determined using Slovin's formula, which is used for finite populations.

$$n = \frac{N}{1 + N(e)^2}$$

$$n = \frac{1064}{1 + 1064(0.04)^2}$$

$$n = \frac{1064}{1 + 1064 \times 0.0016}$$

$$n = \frac{1064}{1 + 1.70240}$$

$$n = \frac{1064}{2.70240}$$

$$n = 393.72410$$

$$n = 394$$

n = Sample Size, N = Population Size (Total Household of Selected Villages), e = Margin of Error.

So the sample size is 394 at a 4% margin of error. Sample households were selected from the sample villages by using simple random sampling. Finally, data were collected from the sample households through a pre-tested interview schedule.

3.3 *Selection of the Number of Sample Households from Selected Villages*

The total household of the sample villages is 1064, out of which 793 are from Kalchini and 271 from Kumargram block. The sample size is 394, i.e., 37% of the total households of sample villages. The number of sample households from each sample village of both blocks is calculated and presented in Table 1. The table showed that 294 sample households were selected from the Kalchini block, comprising 12 from West Garam, 52 from Kalkut, 80 from Garobasti, 109 from Gadadhar, 31 from 20th Mile, and 10 from 21st Mile. Apart from that, 100 sample households were selected from the Kumargram block, of which 16 were from Chipra, 36 were from Sankosh, 19 were from Lapraguri, 14 were from Indubasti, and 15 were from Balapara.

Table 1: Village-wise Sample Household

Kalchini C.D. Block						
Sl. No.	*Division*	*Range*	*Beat*	*Name of the Forest Village*	*Total Household*	*Sample Household*
1.	BTR (West)	WDPO	West Garam	West Garam	33	12
2.		EDPO	Checko	Kalkut	141	52
3.		WRVK	WRVK	Garobasti	216	80
4.		ERVK	Gadadhar	Gadadhar	293	109
5.			Panbari (S)	20th Mile	83	31
6.			Panbari (N)	21st Mile	27	10
Total					**793**	**294**
Kumargram C.D. Block						
Sl. No.	*Division*	*Range*	*Beat*	*Name of the Forest Village*	*Total Household*	*Sample Household*
1.	BTR (East)	South Rydak	Chipra	Chipra	44	16
2.		Kumargram	Sankosh	Sankosh	98	36
3.		Bholka	Barobisha	Lapraguri	52	19
4.			Ghoramara	Indubasti	37	14
5.			Balapara	Balapara	40	15
Total					**271**	**100**
Grand Total					**1064**	**394**

Source: Computed by the Researchers.

3.4 *Data Sources*

Both primary and secondary data were used in this study. Primary data were collected from tribal forest dwellers of the selected forest villages of the study area through a well-structured interview schedule specially prepared for the study. The schedule was pre-tested during the preparatory survey for further improvement. Mainly quantitative methods were used for the collection of primary data and information. These include household surveys through pre-tested interview schedules and personal interviews. All the surveys and interviews were arranged with tribal forest dwellers of the selected forest villages of the study area and with various forest officials of Buxa Tiger Reserve (BTR). Secondary data were collected from a wide variety of sources like Office of the Deputy Field Director Buxa Tiger Reserve (East and West Division), Annual Administrative Report of BTR, Management-Cum-Working Plan of BTR (2000–01 to 2009–10), District Statistical Hand Book, Primary Census Abstract, topic related various books and journals.

3.5 *Data Analysis and Representation*

Finally, all collected data from both sources have been classified and tabulated systematically. Then these tabulated data were analyzed and interpreted with descriptive statistics like frequency and percentage. Maps were prepared based on collected data with the help of Arc GIS.

4. Result and Discussion

4.1 *Social Status of the Tribal Forest Villagers*

4.1.1 *Age Structure*

Table 2 shows the age distribution of the surveyed respondents. The researcher divided the population into four age groups: 0 to 14, 15 to 34, 35 to 59 and above 59. The working-age population is 15–59. Overall, 69.37% of the total respondents belong to the working age group (15–59), and 30.63% are dependent population. In Kalchini block, the maximum population belongs to the age group of 15–34 (40.20%), followed by the 35–59 age group (27.93%), 0–14 age group (24.77%) and minimum in the age group of above 59 (7.10%). Similarly, in Kumargram block highest percentage of people belong to the age group of 15–34 (40.14%), followed by the 35–59 age group (32.95%), 0–14 age group (17.86%) and the lowest in the above 59 age group (9.05%).

4.1.2 *Marital Status*

Generally, marital status is divided into four classes- married, unmarried, divorcee and widow. In the study area, 55.70% of people are married, 40.59% are unmarried, and only 2.78% are widows. The event of divorce is very uncommon among surveyed tribals. Only 0.93% of people have mutual separation established by society because legal divorce is still not popular among tribes of the study area. Married and unmarried people are more or less the same in Kalchini and Kumargram blocks, but the widow percentage is slightly higher in Kumargram (3.71%) than in Kalchini (2.47%). The rate of divorce is very low in both block, but Kalchini (1.16%) hold the edge over Kumargram (0.23%) block (Table 2).

4.1.3 *Literacy Rate*

Education is one of the most important indirect variables affecting socio-economic behaviour and a population's labour force participation (Gogoi, 2016).

Literacy is defined differently from country to country. UNESCO characterizes literacy as utilizing printed and written materials to identify, understand, interpret, create, communicate, and compute within various contexts. It encompasses a range of learning experiences that empower individuals to attain their objectives, enhance their knowledge and abilities, and engage actively in their communities and society. The definition of literacy and its assessment method may vary from source to source in India, like the Census of India, the National Literacy Mission (NLM), the National Sample Survey Organization (NSSO), and the National Family Health Survey (NFHS). Still, the definition given by the Census of India is extensively accepted. Census of India (2011) defined literacy as *"a literate person is defined as an individual aged seven years and above who can read and write with comprehension in any language."* It has also been mentioned that literacy can be attained through the adult education system or any non-formal educational system. Blind people who can read in braille can also be treated as literate. The overall development of any village depends on the literacy rate of the dwellers (Mandal & Sengupta, 2016).

Lack of infrastructure, work participation at an early age, poverty and lack of supportive education culture at home are the main causes behind the low literacy rate and high early dropout rate among the tribal people in the study area (Roy, 2008).

Table 2 shows the percentage of tribal literacy rate in the study area. The overall literacy rate is 66.67%, and in Kalchini, 65.06%, whereas it is 71.39% in the case of Kumargram block. So Kumargram block is more developed than Kalchini in terms of literacy rate.

4.1.4 *Level of Education*

Table 2 shows most of the literate tribal people left their studies after completing upper primary (41.21%), primary (25.80%) and secondary level (21.64%). Very few people completed their higher education, like higher secondary (7.94%), under graduation (3.13%), and post-graduation (0.28%). The percentage of literate tribal people who completed their primary and upper primary education is higher in Kalchini, 27.63% and 42.54%, than in Kumargram block 20.91% and 37.63%. In the case of secondary, higher secondary and under graduation, Kumargram block recorded higher percentages 22.65%, 12.20%, and 5.56% than Kalchini block, 21.27%, 6.36%, and 2.20%. Post-graduate tribal people are only in the Kumargram block (1.05%).

Most of the forest villages of Kalchini block are located in the core area of BTR. Road connectivity of those villages is very poor, and educational infrastructure is not up to the mark in all the villages, whereas most of the forest villages of Kumargram block are located in the buffer zone of BTR. Those villages are well connected by road, and educational infrastructure is comparatively more developed. Because of that percentage of people who completed higher education is more in Kumargram than in Kalchini block.

4.1.5 *Mother Tongue*

According to Table 2, most surveyed tribal people speak the Rabha language. Overall, the mother tongue of 44.92% of families is Rabha. Kurukh is the second most common language in the study area. As a whole, the mother tongue of about 25.13% of the families is Kurukh, followed by Santali (11.93%), Boro (7.36%), Mundari (4.06%), Tamang (3.30%), Asuri (2.54%) and Mal Paharia only 0.76%.

48.30% of surveyed families in the Kalchini block speak the Rabha language as their mother tongue. The second most common language spoken in the Kalchini block is Kurukh (21.43%), followed by Santali (15.99%), Mundari (5.44%), Tamang (4.42%), Asuri (3.40%) and Mal Paharia (1.02%). In Kumargram block, 36% of surveyed families speak the Kurukh language, followed by Rabha (35%) and Boro (29%).

4.1.6 *Religion*

The study area's religious affiliation is displayed in Table 2. Hindu, Christian and Buddhist are the three main religious groups in the study region. As a whole, Hinduism makes up 50.76%, followed by Christianity at 47.72% and Buddhism at only 1.52%. Hinduism is the most prevalent religion in the Kalchini block (55.10%), Christianity is the second most important religion in the Kalchini block (42.86%), and only 2.04% of families practice Buddhism. In the Kumargram block, Christianity is the predominant religion (62.00%), and the remaining 38% are Hindu.

4.1.7 *Housing Pattern*

Within the total number of households studied, kutcha house covers 54.06%, pucca 10.41%, semi-pucca 24.37%, and wooden 11.16%. For the Kutcha house, the Kalchini block (55.44%) has a little greater percentage than the Kumargram block (50.00%). The Kumargram block is slightly higher than the Kalchini block for pucca, semi-pucca, and wooden houses. In both blocks, the number of kutcha houses is greater because of their poor economic Condition.

4.1.8 *Household Asset*

Table 2 shows the wealth status of the surveyed household. In Kalchini block, 53.06% of households have T.V., 36.39% fan, 72.79% bi-cycle, 9.52% bike and 87.07% have mobile phones. On the other hand in Kumargram block, 46% of households have a T.V., 35% have a fan, 56% bi-cycle, 19% bike and 89% have a mobile phone.

4.1.9 *Family Type*

Table 2 shows that about 53.81% of the surveyed households are joint, and the rest of 46.19% belong to the nuclear family. The percentage of joint families is higher in the Kumargram block (61%) than in the Kalchini block (51.36%). In the case of the nuclear family, the percentage is higher in Kalchini (48.64%) than in Kumargram block (39%).

4.1.10 *Family Size*

According to Table 2, 4–6 family members are in around 72.08% of the surveyed homes. The fundamental reason for big family sizes is an agriculture-based economy. About 22.08% of households have 3 or fewer members in the family. There are more than 6 family members in only 5.84% of households. More than 70% of surveyed households have 4–6 family members in both blocks. The percentage of households having more than 6 family members is higher in Kalchini (6.46%) than in Kumargram block (4%). In the case of 3 or fewer members in the family, Kumargram block (26%) holds the edge over Kalchini (20.75%).

4.1.11 *Sanitation*

Access to a sanitary facility is available to every family in the study area and is presented in Table 2. Overall, kutcha sanitary accounts for 42.89% of the total households examined, followed by semi-pucca (35.29%), pucca (17.51%) and wooden (4.31%). In Kalchini block, the proportion of kutcha sanitation is highest (47.28%), followed by semi-pucca (33.33%), pucca (17.35%) and wooden (2.04%). On the other hand, in Kumargram block, the proportion of semi-pucca sanitation was highest (41%), followed by kutcha (30.00%), pucca (18.00%) and wooden (11.00%).

4.1.12 *Drinking Water*

The tube well serves as the primary drinking water source for most people in the study area. Overall, 85.03% of the surveyed families depend on tube wells for their drinking water supply, while 11.67% also rely on wells, and 3.30% get their water from tap. Table 2 shows that in Kalchini block, 98.98% of all surveyed families depend on tube well for drinking water, whereas just 0.68% depend on well and 0.34% on tap. About 44.00% of the families in the Kumargram block depend on tube well and well, respectively, while the remaining 12.00% are on tap.

4.1.13 *Electricity*

Table 2 shows the presence of electricity in surveyed households in the study area. Overall, 92.39% of all surveyed households have access to electricity, whereas 7.61% household have no access to electricity. About 91.50% of the surveyed households in the Kalchini block and 95.00% of the surveyed households in the Kumargram block have access to electricity. On the other hand, 8.50% of the surveyed families in Kalchini do not have electricity, compared to 5.00% in the Kumargram block.

4.1.14 *Food Habit*

Food habits describe how various people choose, prepare, serve, and consume food that is accessible to them. An individual is affected by other people's or groups' behaviours, responses and thoughts. Personal preferences and societal, cultural, and economic factors collectively shape our dietary choices. Peer pressure, persuasion, marketing, sales and conformity are examples of social influence (Paroi *et al.*, 2020).

The main food of the tribal people in the study area is rice, various wild edible vegetables, fish, meat, noodles, pickle and chutney. Their food preparation process was different from that of non-tribal people.

Table 2 shows that out of the entire households surveyed, 46.19% include wine in their meals, whereas 53.81% do not. These communities consume their homemade wine. In Kalchini block, 50.68% of households drink wine as a tradition, whereas 49.32% don't consume it regularly as a part of food. The situation of wine consumption in Kumargram block is just somewhat favourable. Only 33.00% of households consume wine as a part of food, and the remaining 67.00% are not consuming wine as a part of food.

4.1.15 *Source of Medical Treatment*

As seen in Table 2, traditional healers provided medical care to around 12.93% of all surveyed households in Kalchini and 20.00% in Kumargram block. Regarding the percentage of residents obtaining medical care from dispensaries, Kumargram block (39.00%) outpaces Kalchini block (14.63%). Among the 294 families in the Kalchini block, 69.39% obtained medical care at the health centre; in the case of Kumargram, it was 68.00%. The percentage of households that received medical treatment from Government hospitals was much higher in Kalchini block (90.48%) than in Kumargram block (77.00%). A significant percentage of households also received medical care from private doctors, 23.47% in Kalchini and 28.00% in Kumargram block. Only 9.00% household of Kumargram block can receive medical care from nursing homes.

4.2 *Economic Status of the Tribal Forest Villagers*

4.2.1 *Income and Expenditure*

Income, typically in monetary terms, is the spending and saving opportunity acquired by an entity within a given duration (Barr, 2012). Conceptually, income is hard to define, and different fields may have distinct definitions. For instance, a person's income may differ from their income as defined by law and in an economic sense (McCaffery, 2012). Costs associated with resources or goods depleted or consumed daily are known as expenditures. Because we consume food, housing, clothing, energy, and other resources daily, expenses recur, which means they happen repeatedly. A budget deficit occurs when revenue is insufficient to cover expenses, leaving you with insufficient funds to meet your requirements or wants. A budget deficit is not fiscally viable and cannot be sustained. The only options are to increase income, cut expenses, or borrow to make up the difference to reduce the deficit. Although borrowing might appear like the simplest and fastest answer, it raises costs since it adds a new expense: interest. Borrowing to close a deficit will only make it bigger unless revenue can also be increased.

Monthly Household Income

The monthly income status of the surveyed families is displayed in Table 2. The researchers divide respondents into five income groups. The highest percentage of people in the surveyed households are in the Rs. 5001–10000 income group (58.63%), followed by up to Rs.

5000 income group (21.32%), Rs. 10001–15000 (11.68%), Rs. 15001–20000 income group (4.82%) and above Rs. 20000 income group (3.55%). In both Kalchini and Kumargram blocks, the highest income group for the surveyed families is Rs. 5001–10000, while the second highest range is up to Rs. 5000. Few percentage of working people have monthly income of above Rs. 20000 in both blocks.

Monthly Household Expenditure

The researchers divided monthly expenses into five groups: Rs. 3000, Rs. 3001–5000, Rs. 5001–7000, Rs. 7001–9000 and Rs. Above 9000. About 31.22% of households spend Rs. 5001–7000 per month, 28.17% spend Rs. 3001–5000 and 15.74% spend less than Rs. 3000 monthly. Only 24.87% of families spend Rs. 7001 or more every month. Families with Rs. 7001–9000 and above expenditures were 27.21% in the Kalchini block and 18.00% in the Kumargram block. About 72.79% of families in Kalchini block have monthly expenses under Rs. 7000, compared to 82% in Kumargram block.

4.3 *Occupational Structure*

The proportion of a country's workforce involved in various economic activities is called its occupational structure. The occupational structure of a country can be analyzed to ascertain the proportion of the working population involved in various sectors. This includes determining the percentage of individuals engaged in agriculture and related activities and the percentage working in manufacturing and service industries. Such an examination provides valuable insights into the nation's economic composition and workforce distribution. In India, the manufacturing and service sectors are believed to employ only 10 and 15–20% of the country's workers, respectively, while the agriculture sector has the greatest workforce participation rate. This rate typically reached 70–75%. The study of occupational structure is crucial because it offers fundamental knowledge about the organization of the local economy. Knowing the many jobs, such as farming, fishing, manufacturing etc., is easier by understanding occupational structure. The occupational structure also reveals the labour available in that area. It helps to show people's financial situations, what kinds of activities are engaged in making money, or how a region makes money.

4.3.1 *Workers and Non-Workers*

Only 55.47% of the respondents are workers, and 44.53% are dependents. Both blocks contain a significant dependent population. The proportion of workers is slightly greater in the Kalchini block (57.10%) than in the Kumargram block (50.58%). About 42.90% of respondents in Kalchini block and 49.42% in Kumargram block are non-workers.

4.3.2 *Primary Sources of Livelihood*

The researchers categorize the professions into the following groups: agriculture, daily wage earner, NTFPs collection, business, service, cattle rearing and traditional healer. Agriculture (32.25%) is the highest-ranking out of all occupations, followed by NTFPs collection (22.13%), daily wage earner (18.48%), cattle rearing (14.51%), business (6.16%), service (4.38%) and traditional healer (2.09%).

In Kalchini block, the highest percentage of workers are engaged in agriculture (30.14%), followed by NTFPs collection (24.32%), daily wage earner (16.89%), cattle rearing (15.54%), business (6.89%), service (4.19%) and traditional healer (2.03%). On the other hand, in Kumargram block, the maximum working people are engaged in agriculture (39.45%), followed by daily wage earner (23.85%), NTFPs collection (14.68%), cattle rearing (11.01%), service (5.05%), business (3.67%) and traditional healer (2.29%).

4.3.3 *Subsidiary Sources of Livelihood*

Half of the working population (50.25%) uses NTFPs collection as a subsidiary occupation. Cattle rearing (22.08%), daily wage earner (13.45%), agriculture (7.87%) and business (6.35%) are the next four most common subsidiary occupations.

In Kalchini block, 45.97% of workers engaged in NTFPs collection as a subsidiary occupation, followed by cattle rearing (24.50%), daily wage earner (15.44%), agriculture (7.55%) and business (6.54%). Whereas, in Kumargram block, 63.54% of workers engaged in NTFPs collection as a subsidiary occupation, followed by cattle rearing (14.58%), agriculture (8.85%), daily wage earner (7.29%) and business (5.74%).

4.3.4 *Job from Forest Department*

Only 32.99% of the total surveyed household had employment with the forest department. The forest department does not employ a total of 67.01% of households. Only 35.03% of households in Kalchini block were employed by the forest department, and the remaining 64.97% were not. In Kumargram block, only 27% of the surveyed households were employed by the forest department, and the remaining 73.00% received no employment from the forest department.

5. Conclusion

In this article, an attempt has been made to discuss the socio-economic status and sustainable livelihood pattern of tribal forest villagers of Kalchini and Kumargram block of Alipurduar district. Demographic characteristics like marital status and age structure are discussed along with literacy rate, education level. Religion and the mother tongue of the tribals are also discussed. Household characteristics are analyzed, including family type and size and household assets. Living conditions, house and sanitation types and sources of drinking water are also explained. Sources of Livelihood, including primary and subsidiary sources, monthly household income and expenditure also presented in a subsequent section. Food habits and multiple aspects of health conditions are also presented.

The socio-economic Condition of any society reflects economic development. It is one of the important characteristics of the social well-being of any tribal community. The collection of non-timber forest products (NTFPs) is the primary source of subsidiary occupation for many communities. Human being experimented through the ages by using natural forest products. They earn money through NTFPs sale for the betterment of their livelihood. On the other hand, it deals with the dependency on forest products for their basic needs and fulfills economic growth demands. The income from the forest products lies behind the livelihood pattern of the tribal forest villagers of the Kalchini and Kumargram C.D. blocks.

References

[1] Barr, N. (2012). *Economics of the Welfare State*. Oxford University Press.

[2] Census of India. (2011). Office of the Registrar General and Census Commissioner, India. Retrieved from http://censusindia.gov.in

[3] Gogoi, M.C.P. (2016). A Socio-Economic study of the slum dwellers of Assam.

[4] Mallik, R.M. (2013). *Tribal Livelihood, Food Security and Poverty in India*. SSDN Publishers & Distributors.

[5] Mandal, J. and Sengupta, P. (2016). Socio-Economic status of tribe: A case study of Porobasti, Alipurduar, West Bengal. *Imperial Journal of Interdisciplinary Research*, 2(5), 536–541.

[6] McCaffery, E. J. (2012). *The Oxford Introductions to U.S. Law: Income Tax Law*. Oxford University Press.

[7] Pal, B., Goswami, A. and Biswas, S. (2015). Socio-economic status of some selected tribes in West Bengal, India. *International Journal of Current Research*, 7(4), 14292–14295.

[8] Paroi, S., Islam, A.A., Hasanat, M.A. and Zohora, F.T. (2020). Food habits of the adolescents in relation with socio-demographic variables in a selected high school in Khulna City. *Mediscope*, 7(1), 38–43. https://doi.org/10.3329/mediscope.v7i1.47138

[9] Roy, S.K. (2008). *Work participation of Tribal women and marginalization: The case of Tribes in North Bengal.* Levant Books, Kolkata, p. 8.

[10] Sonar, A. (2024). Socio-Economic Condition of Tribal Population of Majhua Busty, Jalpaiguri District, WB. *EPRA International Journal of Research and Development*, 9(1), 220–225. https://doi.org/10.36713/epra2016

ANC and PNC Services Received by Tribal Mothers from Community Health Workers (CHWs): A Study in Mayurbhanj District, Odisha

Sabita Soren[1] **and Sibabrata Das**[2]

ABSTRACT: Mothers' Survival and well-being are central to a nation's broader socioeconomic development. To promote maternal health and improve the quality of life of pregnant mothers within the developmental goals of UNICEF, the Government of India launched the National Rural Health Mission (NRHM) in 2005, with the mission to improve the availability of health care facilities for pregnant mothers, especially the vulnerable sections in the community and to improve their access to quality health care. Under NRHM, a new cadre of Community Health workers (CHWs) called Accredited Social Health Activists (ASHAs) were introduced, and they serve as a link between the government, healthcare delivery systems, and pregnant women. Among the various responsibilities, CHWs are expected to provide certain basic services to women during pregnancy, delivery and post-delivery period. This study has been conducted in tribal-dominated Mayurbhanj district of Odisha state to identify the services received by tribal women from CHWs during their pregnancy to 42 days after childbirth and the perceptions of these women about CHWs services. Data was collected from 200 tribal mothers of the Khunta block of Mayurbhanj district. The result shows that maternal and child health services delivery definitely improved after the inception of CHWs in rural areas. About 81% of tribal women get proper services regarding Antenatal care, advice on pregnancy care,

[1] Ph.D Research Scholar, Department of Applied Geography, Ravenshaw University/Assistant Professor, F.M University, Odisha, India.

[2] Professor, Department of Applied Geography, Ravenshaw University, Cuttack, Odisha, India.

pregnancy complications, diet instructions during pregnancy and post-delivery, etc. Tribal women who are getting help regarding JSY benefits are around 87%. Still, the overall service provided by the CHWs is not adequate, as only 75% per cent of tribal mothers are coming out with positive perceptions regarding the services provided by the CHWs.

Keywords: *CHWs, Maternal Health Services, Tribal Mother, Perceptions.*

1. Introduction

The health status of the tribal people and other marginalized groups is very poor in many parts of the country. The maternal mortality and infant mortality among the tribal groups are comparatively more significant than the non-tribal population. Most rural people are deprived of basic health facilities compared to those who live in urban areas, as healthcare facilities are mainly concentrated in urban centres. To address this issue, the Ministry of Health and Family Welfare (MoHFW) launched the National Rural Health Mission (NRHM) in 2005 to provide basic healthcare facilities to rural dwellers, especially the tribals who live in inaccessible parts of the country. National Rural Health (NRHM) of the Ministry of Health and Family Welfare (MoHFW) began a mission in the year 2005 with the introduction of Community Health Workers (CHWs) designated as Accredited Social Health Activists (ASHAs) to connect marginal communities to the healthcare system at village level. CHWs are the trained local women who act as health educators and health promoters in their communities. The CHWs are mainly involved in facilitating Ante Natal Care (ANC) services to pregnant women right from the onset to the six months of Child delivery, along with the immunization process of the child. In June 2005, NRHM was established in Odisha to enhance the availability and accessibility of high-quality healthcare for people across the state with a focus on low human development and health indicator regions, especially tribal concentrated districts, with emphasis on women and child health. CHWs first came in action in 2006 in 18 high-focus states—out of ten were very high-focus states (Bihar, Jharkhand, Madhya Pradesh, Chhattisgarh, Himachal Pradesh, Jammu and Kashmir, Uttar Pradesh, Uttaranchal, Odisha, and

Rajasthan) and 8 high-focus northeastern states (Arunachal Pradesh, Manipur, Assam, Nagaland, Meghalaya, Tripura, Mizoram, and Sikkim). Odisha is moving ahead in the healthcare sector, but still, it has not achieved the required status in case of utilizing maternal healthcare services. Mayurbhanj district has the lowest in case of availing full ANC services among the other 30 districts. The Percentage of Institutional deliveries is even lower than the state's average. This could be possible because of the significant number of tribal populations in the study district. Odisha has 13 tribal districts where the tribals share more than half of the district's total population. Among them, Mayurbhanj district alone has 51 tribal groups and shares 58% of the district's total population. The tribal population is more susceptible to a variety of health issues that increase the rates of infectious diseases, maternal and newborn mortality, and other communicable diseases. In this connection, the current study has been carried out to analyze ANC and PNC services that the tribal women received from Community Health Workers in the Mayurbhanj district. The Main objectives of the study are to enquiry about the ANC and PNC services received by the tribal women from CHWs in Khunta Block of Mayurbhanj district of Od and to Study the perception and level of satisfaction of the tribal mothers about the services received from CHWs.

2. Methodology

2.1 *Study Design*

This descriptive study aims to investigate whether the maternity services from pregnancy to post-childbirth are received properly from CHWs and the level of satisfaction of these tribal mothers in getting the services from CHWs.

- **Study population**: Tribal women from 15–49 age groups.
- **Target population**: Tribal mother who has baby of one year old.
- **Sampling**: Based on the concentration of tribal population, Khunta block have been selected purposively for the primary study. Two hundred mothers who have kids not less than one year have been selected for collecting the data.

2.2 *Data Collection and Methods*

This was a cross-sectional, community-based study. Both qualitative and quantitative methods were used for data collection. Interview schedules, in-depth interviews, and focus group discussions were used to collect data. The collected data were analyzed using descriptive statistical methods such as frequency and percentage.

2.3 *Study Area Map*

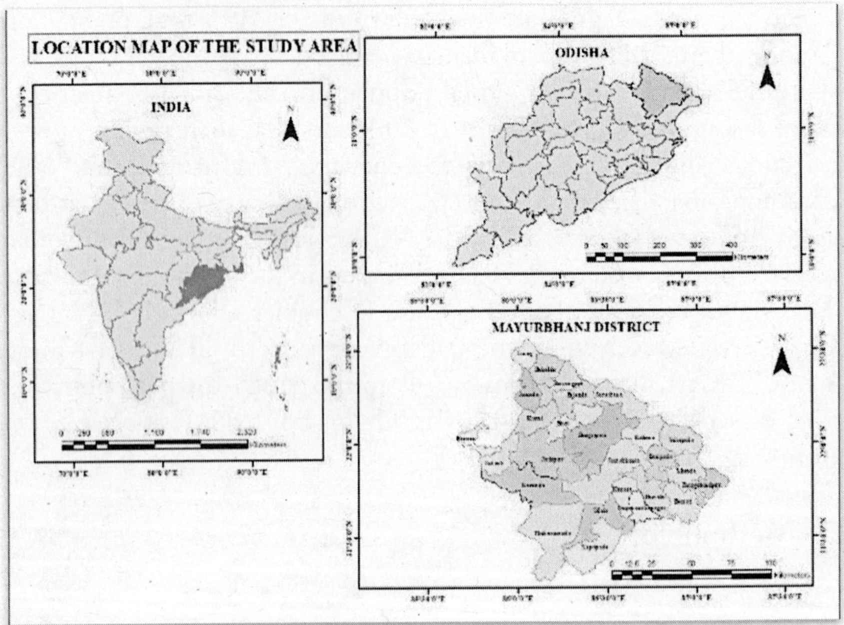

3. Results and Discussion

3.1 *Socio-Economic Information about the Respondents.*

Socio-economic factors play a significant role in determining utilization of maternal health care services in India.

Sandals are the dominant tribes in the Mayurbhanj district. The above table and diagram reveal that the study block has five major tribe populations. The majority of the respondents belong to the Santal tribe (55%). Next to them, 14% of mothers are from the Munda tribe. Others include Kolha (11.5%), Bhumij (11%) and

Table 1: Distribution of Respondents by Tribes

Sl. No.	*Com munity*	*No. of respondents*	*Percentage*
1.	Santal	110	55
2.	Munda	28	14
3.	Kolha	23	11.5
4.	Bhumij	22	11
5.	Bathudi	17	8.5
	Total	**200**	**100**

Bathudi (8.5%). A mother's age is one of the key variables that affect how much risk a mother experiences during her pregnancy and childbirth. Young pregnancy (i.e., ≤ 19 years old) and late pregnancy (i.e., ≥ 35 years old) carry certain risks for both the mother and the child. The above table shows that almost half of the respondents are in the 20–23 age group, whereas a significant percentage (26%) of respondents are in the teenage group, which is 16 to 19 years old. Only 8 respondents came under the 32–35 age group, which was having their second or third issue in the last year. It is understood that the level of education can influence a woman to obtain healthcare facilities from the service provider efficiently. The tribal population of the Mayurbhanj district is less literate than other caste people. It is clear from the above table that nearly 43% of tribal women have no education. Around 27% of women had access to primary education, 25% to high school, and only 11 of the 200 women had completed their intermediate studies. Source of income is a significant factor in accessing health care services better. Data from Table 4 depicts that there is a diversity of sources of income for the respondents. Half of the tribal mothers' family income comes from agriculture and allied activity, followed by daily wage labour (20.5%), industrial workers (13.5%), Business (9.5%), and only 6% of respondents have their source of income from government jobs.

3.2 *ANC and PNC Services Received from CHWs*

Community Health Workers are trained local women who act as health educators and health promoters at the village level. The CHWs are mainly involved in facilitating Ante Natal Care (ANC) services to pregnant women right from the onset to the six months of Child delivery, along with the immunization process of the child. The tribal mothers have received Maternal Health (MNH) care services like a number of ANC and PNC visit, accompanied by CHWs during child delivery, getting advice regarding balance diet during pregnancy and in postpartum phase, warning sign of pregnancy, motivation for institutional delivery and also take help in getting Janani Suraksha Yojna (JSY) benefits.

CHWs have made visits between three to seven times throughout the pregnancy, childbirth and postpartum period. About one-third of the total mothers (32.5%) have received attention around four times during the visit of CHWs. Most of the visits are done in the last trimester of pregnancy, and just after childbirth, as during those phases of time, it becomes difficult for a mother to go outside.

Table 2: Service Received from CHWs during Pregnancy

Sl. No.	*Services*	*No. of Respondents*	*Percentage*
1.	Helped in registration of pregnancy	144	72
2.	Informed the expected date of delivery	169	84.5
3.	Helped in receiving at least four ANC check up	168	84
4.	Helped in getting TT injections	194	97
5.	Provided/helped in getting IFA tablets	190	95
6.	Explained the importance of balanced diet	93	46.5
7.	Helped in getting nutrition supplement from Anganwadi	172	86
8.	Motivated to attend monthly village health and nutrition day	167	83.5
9.	Informed about the warning signs during pregnancy	154	77
10.	Motivated for hospital delivery	161	80.5

According to the figure given in table 6, CHWs assisted to more than 95% of tribal mothers to get Tetanus and IFA tablets. About 80% of the respondents were motivated to deliver in a health facility. More than 80% of moms expressed motivation to participate in the monthly VHND. Merely 46.2% of women get consultation on a balanced diet during pregnancy.

Table 3: Service Received during Child Delivery

Sl. No.	*Services*	*No. of Respondents*	*Percentage*
1.	Arranged vehicle to reach the health institution	138	69
2.	Accompanied the mother to the health institution	158	79
3.	Arranged blood	53	26.5
4.	Visited the mother at hospital and helped	144	72

Table 7 offers information regarding the services provided by CHWs to tribal moms during their delivery. CHWs arranged transportation for 69% of mothers to the health facility. About 158 mothers said that CHWs have accompanied them to the hospital and offered assistance. As many of them are ignorant about healthcare delivery system, CHWs make them help in arranging blood for 26.5% of mothers during delivery.

Table 4: Services Received during Post-natal Period

Sl. No.	*Services*	*No. of Respondents*	*Percentage*
1.	Visited the mother and baby at home	186	93
2.	Counselled for early initiation of breast feeding	123	61.5
3.	Explained the importance of balanced diet	108	54
4.	Explained the importance of personal hygiene	156	78
5.	Motivated to adopt suitable family planning method	182	91

From the above Table 8 it is evident that during the postnatal period CHWs make sure to visit almost all mothers and newly born children. 93% of both mother and child were looked after by the health workers. A huge number (182) of respondents were motivated to adopt a suitable family planning method. Mostly the newly mothers (61%) were Counselled for early initiation of breastfeeding.

3.3 *Janani Suraksha Yojna (JSY)*

Janani Suraksha Yojana (JSY) is a safe motherhood intervention under the National Rural Health Mission (NRHM) being implemented with the objective of reducing maternal and neo-natal mortality by promoting institutional delivery among poor pregnant women. JSY is a 100% centrally sponsored scheme and it integrates cash assistance with delivery and post-delivery care (JSY. GoI, 2006). Community health workers play a vital role in rolling out this program. About 87% of tribal mothers get help both in enrolling and filling up JSY form. Only 7 mothers did not get any help regarding the JSY benefits from the community health workers due to some inconveniences from their side.

3.4 *Perception and Level of Satisfaction of the Tribal Mothers about the Services Provided by CHWs*

Table 10 makes it evident that the majority of those surveyed (78%) are highly satisfied with the service provided by CHWs. They felt the services available during their most recent pregnancy and delivery were very helpful, and 19.5% thought it was barely helpful. CHWs services were reported as being ineffective by five mothers.

5. Conclusion

Based on the aforementioned findings, it can be said that the tribal mothers' recent pregnancies services from CHWs were somewhat sufficient to meet their demands for maternal health care. Despite the high illiteracy among the tribal mothers, they are not deprived of getting all the ANC and PNC services along with JSY benefits. This could have been possible only because of the timely intervention of CHWs in the field. During the survey, around 69% of the mothers believed that the CHWs were doing a very good job, while 30% of mothers felt improvising was necessary for CHW's services. However, some of the tribal mothers experienced that the CHWs' post-natal and delivery services fell short of what they experienced during their pregnancy.

The Community health workers (ASHAs and Anganwadi Workers) are front-line health workers. They are the bridge between the community and the Healthcare service system. They are the 'ray of hope' for many women, especially those in the marginalised section. More effort should be given to empower the CHWs to bring a change in the field of Maternal and child healthcare delivery systems.

Bibliography

[1] Registrar General of India (2011). Census of India. New Delhi: Census Commissioner; 2011. https://www.censusindia.co.in/district/rayagada-district-odisha-396

[2] International Institute for Population Sciences (IIPS) and ICF. National Family Health Survey (NFHS-5), 2019–21. Odisha. http://rchiips.org/NFHS/NFHS-4Reports/Odisha.pdf.

[3] International Institute for Population Sciences (IIPS) and ICF. National Family Health Survey (NFHS-5), 2019–21. Odisha./Mayurbhanj Dist. http://rchiips.org/NFHS/NFHS-4Reports/Odisha.pdf.

[4] Janani Suraksha Yojana (2006). Govt. of India; Ministry of Health and Family Welfare New Delhi

[5] Roy, S. and Sahu, B. (2013). Can ASHA be the ray of hope for providing MCH services in Odisha, India? Exploring through a Qualitative study. Journal of Global Health Care Systems

[6] Saprii, L., Richards, E., Kokho, P. *et al.* Community health workers in rural India: analysing the opportunities and challenges Accredited Social Health Activists (ASHAs) face in realising their multiple roles. *Hum Resour Health* 13, 95 (2015).https://doi.org/10.1186/s12960-015-0094-

[7] Paul, P. and Chouhan, P. (2020). Socio-demographic factors influencing utilization of maternal health care services in India.

[8] Joseph, J. and Celine, A. (2018). Maternal Health Services Received by Tribal Women from ASHAs (Accredited Social Health Activists) in Wayanad District, Kerala. Indian Journal of Research, PARIPEX

[9] Gupta, A. and Khan, S. (2024). Importance of Community Health Workers for Maternal Health Care Management. Public Health Rev. 2024 Feb 22.

[10] Pande, B. (2020). Are health workers effective in tribal part? Results from evaluation survey of health workers from tribal community.

Indian Indigenous Tribal Population Sustainable Development and Associated with Their Problems

Bishnu Barman[1], Sankar Biswas[2] and Tamal Basu Roy[3]

ABSTRACT: A tribe is a group of people who share a common religion, history, language, or culture. Each tribe is unique and will often have its practices, many of which differ from other tribes. There are different tribal regions in India based on physical characteristics and other aspects of life. Most of the tribal people live in hill stations and naturally isolated areas but some of them come in contact with modern culture and move to cities for work, if development projects are conducted in their areas, people will study their lifestyles and now the government is trying. During cultivation, they have been cheated by many so-called civilized people who have grabbed their land instead of helping them. Unlike their counterparts, they have largely retained their traditions and customs as a socially distinct community. Tribes have attracted more and more scholars to study them. In developing societies, instead of encouraging indigenous farmers to adopt input-intensive agriculture, closer interaction with the natural and physical environment and cultural adaptations are environmentally friendly and more sustainable, resulting in indigenous-specific local knowledge. They followed unsustainable methods then came into contact with modern civilization and adopted unsustainable capital-intensive practices in agriculture resulting in debt problems. The current approach of government, non-governmental

---

[1] Research Scholar, Department of Geography, Raiganj University, and SACT, Department of Geography, Dinhata College, Cooch Behar, West Bengal, India. E-mail: bishnugeomanbu@gmail.com

[2] Research scholar, Department of Geography and Applied Geography, University of North Bengal, Darjeeling, West Bengal, India.
E-mail: sankarbiswas.cob@gmail.com

[3] Assistant Professor, Department of Geography, Raiganj University, Raiganj, West Bengal, India. E-mail: [3]raiganjgeo@gmail.com

organizations, and research institutes is again teaching and reviving sustainable organic practices to tribal people to increase their income.

Keywords: Tribal Problems, Sustainable Tribal Development, Organic Practices of Farming.

1. Introduction

According to the 2011 Census, the Scheduled Tribes account for 104 million representing 8.6% of the country's population. These Scheduled Tribes are spread throughout the country largely in forest and hilly regions.

The essential characteristics of these communities are:

- Primitive Traits
- Geographical isolation
- Distinct culture
- Shy of contact with the community at large
- Economically backward

The term "tribe" though a regular word in most of the scholastic dimensions of today's world, astonishingly hasn't found a universal definition to date even after years of study and research. The problem is not a lack of dedication or interest, but the world is so diverse and dynamic to accommodate dissimilar sets of human populations into one Mold. For example, the tribes call themselves by names that associate them with their land and surroundings; they declare themselves to be the first inhabitants of their land, or the "first human beings". This assertion though falls short in the constitutional framework of defining the tribes based on their socio-economic status in comparison to the other sub-populations of the country. The Indian Constitution defines them under the constitutional term, "the Scheduled Tribes", which serves the purpose of designating certain communities, where membership is acquired by birth, for the benefits that the government provides them with the explicit aim of bringing them at par with the other communities of the country. Article 366(35) of the Constitution of India states that the Scheduled Tribes are those communities that are scheduled by Article 332 of the Constitution. But this definition is again contradicted by the field study approach of the sociological, anthropological, and historical scholars along with the different NGOs working with the tribes, who try to define "tribes" through certain measure-able characteristics, some of which are:

1. Group having a territorial affiliation
2. Segmental solidarity (socially and structurally similar)
3. No surplus generation
4. Importance of family and kinship relations (recognition of identity through clan and lineage)
5. Use of simple technology
6. Resilient to change
7. Endogamous
8. Economic interdependence
9. No specialization of function
10. Common language/dialect
11. Recognize social distance with the other tribes and castes
12. Follow tribal traditions, beliefs and customs

2. The Factors Affecting the Tribal Development

2.1 *Urbanization and Industrialization*

The tribal communities being autonomous are highly dependent upon natural resources around them to sustain their life in the harshest zones of the world. Apart from satisfying the basic requirements of these communities, these zones are also rich in industrial and mineral resources which are turned into economic gains through several governmental and non-governmental industrial projects. During the British period, the first wake of industrialization in the tribal areas started in Chotanagpur with the exploitation of a coal mining industry in Jharia in Bokaro and Karanpura coal fields in Dhanbad district in 1857, also the establishment of the Tata Iron and Steel Factory in Jamshedpur in Singhbhum district in 1907. They try to imitate their culture by changing their lifestyle and spending exorbitantly on urban markers which is beyond their capacity. Some of the major transformations noticed are:

- Changes in lifestyle including dressing, modes of entertainment, food, etc.
- No regulation on the expenditure because of a lack of education and awareness about savings
- Agriculture-based economy turning to a market economy
- Poverty leading to indebtedness
- Disintegration of joint families into nuclear families
- Loss of land
- Introduction to the outside world and technology
- Displacement and migration
- Rehabilitation problems.

2.2 *Socio-Cultural Factors*

Like the effects on the other social extents of India, the tribes have also changed in terms of their structure and function, though this change is slow and mostly because of circumstances rather than acceptance.

The tribal structure which is supposed to be simple and rigid, has observed penetrance of some external elements into their lifestyle which is shifting them more towards a civilized yet complex society. In the Indian sub-continent, due to already existing diversity, there are different compartments of society like religion, economy, power, politics, etc. which span through the "other cultures" to locate where they could be attuned with their community. One such shift is through religion, which finds more potent followers among the socially marginalized tribals, by building contacts with them. This may be induced by force by capturing their area or by acceptance via increasing trade and infiltration into their domains. The tribal communities are more susceptible to religious conversions because of either ostracism by their community members or lack of literacy and inability to make alert decisions. For, in the Chhotanagpur Region, most of the Kharias took to Christianity and were able to gain educational opportunities through the Christian missionaries. They were the ones who were aware of the stipends, scholarships, and reservations provided to them, which they readily accepted and consequently made their way to the urban areas. Such tribals on migration got socially isolated from their brethren in the rural areas and developed a new way of living. So, the differentials created in this manner diverged one tribe into two parts. Similarly, in one region if the members of a tribe convert to two or more religious sects, there is a socio-cultural barrier created between them which restricts their interaction and creates tension.

2.3 *Forest Policy and Tribals*

Forest policies are the governmental inputs to safeguard the interests and protection of the tribes and their natural habitats from over-exploitation. Because of different developmental levels of different tribes, their dependency on their natural surroundings varies. Research on the same points out that Birhors (PTG) is almost 90% dependent on the forests, whereas this percentage among the Malers (hill cultivators) and other communities like Mundas, Oraons, Hos, etc is 60% and 45% respectively. Keeping this in mind, a concrete and uniform policy for all the regions and tribes seems insuperable. As every tribe and its requirements vary, owing to its social, educational, occupational, and survival needs, specific policies are required to be framed and implemented at different regional levels.

Before the 19th century, the tribals enjoyed absolute rights over their areas, but when in 1894 the first National Policy on Forest was formulated, the commercial exploitation of the resources started with the state controlling most of its affairs leading to tribal revolts. This exploitation changed to the developmental terms named "industrialization and urbanization" when independence was achieved, again restricting tribal rights. The New Forest Policy of 1952, recognized 6 vital needs that focused on national development based on deriving resources from the forest and limiting its access to the people including the tribals by levying a grazing fee. The state governments introduced some resettlement and rehabilitation schemes for the displaced nomads by arranging tribal colonies with pucca houses and settled occupation bases, the tribals were inclined to abandon them and return to their old habitats.

2.4 *Their Conservatism and Reluctance to Change*

The tribes being the cultures developed in isolation have devised their way of living confining themselves to their own set of cultures, dialects, people, communities, and regions. Because of this, they incline their people, area, and resources and an element of reluctance, mistrust, and non-dependence towards any alien agency penetrating them. This element has intensified over time because of the establishment of industries, frauds by money lenders and traders, and unfocused and weak government policies.

Even if the government tries to bring some developmental programs and policies to their area, they tend to be rejected and stalled. Many of the governmental policies framed lacked understanding of this relationship between the tribes and their lands, which created problems both for the tribes and the officials deployed at their place to monitor the developmental programs and raged tribal revolts.

3. The Problems of Tribal Development

3.1 *Land-Alienation*

Tribes and their territory are considered inseparable in terms of their emotional and ancestral attachment to it. Their land is not only their inhabitation area but also their identity, source of livelihood, and responsibility inherited through years of tradition. Any external interference or intrusion has witnessed resistance in the form of tribal revolts and failure of governmental schemes or programs related to the development of the tribes. One such example is from the Chowra island of Nicobar Archipelago when the local tribes demolished the water reservoir constructed by PWD as soon as the officials left. They reasoned the act by stating that the construction would have caused disease and death on the island.

The problem of land alienation of the tribes in India started with the advent of British Rule when they appointed the non-tribals as Zamindars in the tribal areas for tax collection, who in turn further recruited the non-tribals for agricultural production in the areas. Later activities like commercial exploitation of forest resources for timber, minerals, water, etc. increased traders' access to the area leading to the concept of "private/individual property" rather than the use of land as a "communal property" by tribals. After independence, because of urbanization and industrialization an explosive use of tribal lands started for mining industries, hydel projects, thermal projects, etc. This led to the uprooting of tribals from their land, when non-monitoring of their rehabilitation and inadequate compensation added to their difficulties, and illiteracy and lack of skills made their life miserable in novel lands. This affected the trust of the tribals in the socio-political system framing diverse governmental programs and leading to revolts and resistance from them.

The major problem areas lying around the problem of land alienation include:

- Failure of non-tribal planners to understand the special relationship between the tribals and their land.
- The nature of dispossession of the tribals from their land: political motive, economic motive, religious motive, etc.
- Increased chances of exploitation of tribals by the traders and money lenders.
- Loss of tribal rights over their land through changes in the forest policy.
- Inadequate amount of compensation for their land given to tribals.
- Displacement and migration issues.
- Rehabilitation problem
- Ineffective machinery and measures for implementation of legislation and prevention of alienation.
- Faulty preparation of the record of rights.
- Recruitment of the tribal laborers into cruel working conditions.
- Social implications of different patterns of legislation.

3.2 *Indebtedness*

The issue of indebtedness among the tribals of India is in escalation as noticed through a sample survey conducted by the Planning Commission which reports that between 1975 and 1983, the indebtedness increased from 14.47% to 33.77%, with the debt liability per household increasing from •419 (1975–76) to •819 (1982–83). According to the 1961 Census conducted over 78 tribal villages of different states, it was seen that more than 50% of the households in 30 villages surveyed were very highly indebted, whereas only below 5% of households in 1 village were deficient in indebtedness (Vidyarthi, 1976:441)

The main reasons for indebtedness can be listed as:

- Poor income
- Ignorance of equitable price system
- Extravagant expenditure on large-scale social celebrations, festivals, and occasions like marriages, birth, and death
- Adherence to the panchayat decisions regarding fines for fear of ex-communication
- The entire population is not covered
- The extent of the practice in different states is unknown
- The word bonded labor has not been well-defined
- Lack of machinery to enforce these orders
- Cases of bonded labor not reported mostly because of their socio-economic background and lack of knowledge
- Financial Constraints for the developmental projects

3.4 *Poor Literacy and Education*

An important index of development is the estimate of the literacy and education level of an area. It imparts social cognition and the ability to comprehend their social, political, and cultural environment better. It is a catalyst for social upliftment promoting the importance of health, nutrition, savings, employment, hygiene, and personal and community growth. As per the 2001 Census, the literacy rate among the Scheduled tribes was recorded as 47.10% with the females of the tribes of Bihar accounting for the lowest 15.54%. The data shows that the literacy rate among the STs was lowest in Bihar (28.17%) and the highest in Mizoram (89.34%). Even among the tribes of India, the dispersion of literacy is not uniform. For example, In Bihar, the Oraons and Mundas are educated but the Birhors, Asurs, and many other numerically small tribal groups are the least educated.

Over the years, illiteracy and lack of education have proved to be the major cause of most of the tribal problems including land alienation, indebtedness, exploitation by money lenders, unemployment, etc. The major issues felt with the non-attainment of the literacy level in tribal areas include:

- Remoteness of the schools and institutions
- Poor livelihood means
- Inadequate facility and quality of schools
- Language and cultural barriers
- Unavailability and unwillingness of teachers to teach in remote and tribal areas
- Lack of vocational training
- The schedule and vacations of schools don't match the period of important tribal festivals

3.5 *Unemployment*

The major reasons for unemployment among the tribals of India is illiteracy, addiction to alcohol, and several other social and cultural factors. Though the government has provided them with reservations and provisions against discrimination, most of the reserved seats remain vacant because of a lack of eligibility for the position or unawareness among the tribals.

3.6 *Displacement and Rehabilitation*

The rapid establishment of industries and modern infrastructure requires land and resources which are generally sought from the forest areas. These being the inhabitation areas of the tribals, are disturbed by such a penetration, making the tribals leave their land and hence identity to a new place where they do not know the people and resources and their illiteracy and lack of skills adds to their obstructions. With the declaration of the second five-year plan by Pt. Jawaharlal Nehru, the need for the establishment of industries to gain self-sufficiency was realized. So, big industries like Heavy Engineering Corporation in Ranchi, Bokaro Steel City in Bihar, Durgapur Steel Plant in West Bengal, Bhilai Steel Plant in Madhya Pradesh, and Rourkela Steel Plant in Orissa were started. These are majorly the tribal-occupied areas that led to their uprooting from their natural habitat without adequate compensation, failure of their resettlement, discouragement of shifting cultivation and nomadism by the government, and preference to the settled subsistence mode like agriculture. According to L.P. Vidyarthi, because of ignorance of the '*Nature-Man-Spirit Complex*', the tribals revolt, and many of the governmental projects are discarded or kept on hold leading to the stalling of a large amount of funds.

3.7 *Health, Nutrition and Hygiene*

One of the major problems among the tribals is the one created by them and the lack of effective research and policies- i.e., lack of health, nutrition, and hygiene. The major reasons for the poor health among the tribals include:

- Lack of personal hygiene and sanitation
- Tobacco and alcohol consumption from an early age
- Early marriage
- Absence of effective waste disposal
- Lack of family planning. Early childbirth
- Lack of ventilation in the living place (overcrowding and congestion)
- Paucity of clean drinking water
- Lack of immunization and medical facilities
- Illiteracy and lack of awareness
- Superstitions
- Low consumption of important dietary products like meat, fish, egg, milk etc.

The problem is manifested in different forms like malnutrition, frequent abortions, and fatal microbial and pest diseases leading to low life expectancy among the tribals.

3.8 *Other Problems*

The other problems as L.P. Vidyarthi pointed are at the level of polity, implementation, and recruitment and training of personnel. The reasons for poor impact can be listed as:

- Lack of special attention to tribal and scheduled areas despite constitutional provisions.
- Inadequate allotment of funds in both general and special sectors to cover all aspects of tribal development.
- Lack of coordination and integration between the sectorial programs and departments both at the Centre and State level.

- Ineffective personnel policy of the government, e.g., the high transfer rate of monitoring professionals, inadequate incentives, lack of specialized training in tribal cultures, and lack of social service spirit in them.
- Lack of scientific planning and research.
- Politicization of the tribal issues and failure on the part of tribal societies to erect dedicated and enlightened social representatives.

4. Approach, Plans, and Programs for Tribal Development in India

Plans for tribal development should be such as to empower tribal communities to decide about their development based on their needs and priorities, including the protection of their distinct identities. Tribal sub-plans by the government have failed to achieve their objectives due to a lack of community participation, transparency, and accountability since it was implemented in 1974–75.

4.1 *Approaches to Tribal Welfare*

The isolation of tribal had led them to live in the subsistence stage. The term tribal welfare is used to cover an all-round development of the tribal people as a weaker section of the Indian population. Central and State Governments are working to improve the social, economic political, and other conditions of the tribal people. Two types of efforts for their welfare are seen (i) Reform Approach and (ii) Administrative Approach.

According to Mazumdar (1960) reform approach should be initiated among the tribal by firstly understanding the tribal dynamics. The reform approach can work out only when it is important and tribal leadership is developed. In the administrative approach general programs for tribal development have been launched whereas each tribal area has different problems and settings, needing different approaches. Thus, Welfare Programs should be suitably adjusted to the requirements of each area. S.C. Dube (1960) outlines four main approaches to tribal problems (i) the social service approach, (ii) the political approach (iii) the religions approach, and (iv)the anthropological approach. In the social service approach, voluntary social agencies show a humanitarian approach in the tribal areas in their cultural frame. In independent India, different all-India tribal conferences are indirectly uniting tribal people. In religious approach conversion of tribal people and the anthropological approach call for understanding the tribal and then chalking out the tribal welfare programs. Anthropologists believe in the ultimate integration of the tribes into the mainstream of Indian life (Vidyarthi L.P. and Rai Binay Kumar (2000).

4.2 *Welfare Schemes for Schedule Tribes*

In the Eighth Schedule of the constitution a list of tribes was incorporated in 1977 it contained names of 527 tribes. It's a constitutional obligation to provide tribal people with reservations and protect them from discrimination.

Constitutional Safeguards

- Article 15(A) for the educational advancement of the scheduled tribe's provision of reservation of seats, relaxation in marks in admission, scholarship, etc.
- Article 46: The education and economic interests of SC and ST are safeguarded and protected from social injustice and exploitation.
- Article 330 and 332: Reservation of seats in Lok Sabha and State Vidhan Sabhas for SC and ST.
- Article 339(1): The President may at any time appoint a Commission to report on the administration of the Scheduled Area and the Welfare of the Scheduled Caste and Tribes in the state.

5. Sustainability and Tribal Welfare

Innovative sustainable means should be adopted to increase the income of the tribal people. A drip irrigation prototype was developed in Jharkhand to provide small and marginal farmers with sustainable income and livelihood has helped farmers with innovative technology best suited to vegetable cultivation on small and marginal holdings. Initially demonstrated in five districts of Jharkhand is now being extended across the state by the Rural Development Department. It has been developed in Jharkhand as part of a livelihood generation project supported by UNDP which strengthens the state government's capacity to implement livelihood programs in the state. In Jharkhand population is mostly tribal facing a high level of poverty. Since 2009 UNDP in partnership with the state government of Jharkhand has been helping it to effectively deliver livelihood schemes and programs. In areas of acute water shortage, multiple cropping being practiced after introducing drip irrigation is almost doubling their farm income (www.in.undp.org>home>success stories) Wadi model for sustainable livelihoods has been tried and tested in tribal areas of India. Abhijeet Mohanty, Kieran Robson, and Rosie Clarkson have tried to see how it is working in Koraput district in Odisha. In Daswantpur block in Koraput traditionally tribal communities were practicing shifting cultivation of subsistence crops like millets and pulses supplemented by a collection of forest fruits, roots honey, etc. Over-exploitation of the forests has reduced soil fertility thus threatening the well-being of the tribal community which draws livelihood from agriculture and forest pushing them to be bonded and migrant labor, their debt burden has increased and they are exploiting forest produce for income.

The Wadi project is one of the integrated tribal development initiatives of NABARD which supports various welfare projects for Scheduled Tribes in the country under the Tribes Development Fund. Wadi means orchard. Any marginal farmer not having more than 5 acres of land can be a beneficiary covering one acre for the project to reduce the risks of climatic, biological and marketing. On each acre, fruit trees like cashews, mangoes, litchis, etc. are planted with the crops. The Wadi project aims to strengthen the agrarian livelihoods of the tribal households and increase food and nutritional security. The basic features are economic upliftment of the farmers through sustainable agriculture, social empowerment, improvement in quality of life including health, and women empowerment in tribal-dominated areas of the country. It looks into land use planning, soil and water harvesting, and improved farming through ago-forestry practices. NABARD sanctioned a Wadi Project in 37 villages covering 1116 tribal families of Dasmantpur block. Firstly, an exposure visit for tribal farmers was organized and gained experience in Gujarat where Wadi plantations were initiated during the 1980s. Water and soil conservation is practiced through the earth and stone bunding platform, trenches and ring basis, ring wells, check dams and diesel pump sets reducing water flow controlling erosion and ground water levels improved increasing crop intensity. Fruit trees were planted and fencing was done in "H" type to protect their cattle. For optimal use of land and meeting short-term requirements inter-cropping was practiced to cultivate a range of crops like grams, millets, and vegetables providing rich nutritional food and surplus supplements for their income. Organic farming is practiced Verme-compost pits are constructed cow dung and goat droppings are used for composting. Organic produce is grown as it reduces dependency on chemical fertilizers and improves soil fertility. Neem cake and cow urine are used to prevent termite bacterial and fungicide attacks. This naturally boosted production. Udyan Vikas Samiti (UVS) is formed to ensure better aftercare activities and marketing. It is helping in providing capacity building and skill upgradation training on orchard development, income generation, and resource mobilization. All UVS was helped to open their respective bank accounts for smooth and transparent fund flow 157 landless households were especially focused on providing support for animal husbandry, a multipurpose utility shop, a tailoring unit, a vegetable vending unit, and a cycle repair shop. This has reduced distress migration by 30 percent. Their income is now about 8,000 to 10,000 per annum from WADI. Wayanad in Kerala has a high percentage of tribal population and options for livelihood are restricted as this is not an industrialized area. Things become more difficult for landless especially from tribal communities due to their dependency on daily wages as agricultural workers and local bio-resources. M.S. Swaminathan Research Foundation (MSSRF) is focusing on such communities to improve their livelihood options.

Boosting the agricultural sector was important as the economy of Wayanad is predominantly agrarian. The farmers were using inorganic methods of cultivation and were replacing food crops with cash crops. Thus, organic cultivation methods and technologies of stability and sustainability which will increase the productivity of small farms are promoted. For improving new income generation avenues of tribal/rural farmers' appropriate agro-techniques for on-farm value addition to agricultural products, by-products, and wastes for greater economic returns are implemented. Capacities of individual farmers and farmer's groups were exposed to various composting techniques, new cultivation practices, increased usage of manure, screening of bio-pesticide plants, and preparation of bio-pesticides. Azolla, spawn mushrooms, and vermin-compost production are adopted for income generation. Training is imparted to prepare panchagavya – a traditional plant tonic for organic farming, 'Trichoderma' a bio-control agent, and vermin compost for market production.

They are also taught to utilize soil kits for testing soil pH and NPK values advantage of biogas plants, the relevance of effective microorganisms, the importance and scope of medicinal plants for income generation and Primary Health Care, marketing and efficiency of organic manures, poultry and animal husbandry. The livelihood programs are implemented through Self Help Groups and they are based upon the local bio-resources and their value addition and cultivation of medicinal plants for enhanced income.

6. Conclusion

Tribes have their way of living in forests, and hills their practices and knowledge are invaluable, and sustainable which is observed when research is done on their mode of living. We should not think that we are very developed and they are backward it's just a perception when we look from the point of view of the modern development concept of the West. After adopting the Green Revolution and experiencing its ill effects after so many decades, especially on health and its unsustainability we are talking about the Second Green Revolution which is based on more organic and sustainable means. It is seen that traditional farming practices followed earlier in rural areas and tribal pouches were practicing more sustainable means and now we are carrying out projects to teach sustainable practices to them. The lifestyle they were living was environmentally friendly, self-reliant and sustainable with no adverse impact on climate but by coming in contact with so-called more civilized people their life was disturbed and they faced problems of land alienation, indebtedness bonded labor, immigration, education, and health problems. In independent India, there are constitutional provisions, welfare schemes for Scheduled Tribes institutional financial support, central government, state government, and NGOs trying to train them to cope with their problems, integrate them into mainstream development, and safeguard them from exploitation by spreading health, educational and infrastructural facilities. They are being helped to adopt sustainable means and increase their incomes preserving their cultural, and traditional beauty.

The focus of tribal development is ensuring an enabling ecosystem of equal opportunities for education, health, and livelihood and promoting sustainable development of the tribal community preserving the unique identities and culture of these communities. In India, more than 500 tribal groups reside possessing separate ethnic situations and cultural traits and it is their identity. They need to be inclusive part of mainstream development yet preservation and sensitivity towards their socio-cultural identity need to be addressed. The large projects of commercial development and modernization such as the construction big power projects, and mining construction of large dams lead to the displacement of tribal as they are not skilled or educated enough to get jobs in these projects on the other hand the forest land on which their livelihood depends is also disturbed increasing their misery. Thus, their economic base has been reduced due to the exploitation of natural forest resources. Both the government and voluntary sectors have emphasized tribal development with the approach of project formulation and timely effective implementation of the development projects and the sustainability issue has not received much attention.

References

[1] Dube, S.C. (1960). Approaches to Tribal Problems in Indian Anthropology in Action, Ranchi.

[2] Vidyarthi, L.P. and Rai, Binay Kumar. "The Tribal culture of India" (2000). Concept Publishing Company, New Delhi.

[3] Sahyatindra Singh Sisodia, D.C. (2004). Tribal issues in India. Madhya Pradesh Institute of Social Science Research, Ujjain Published.

[4] Prakash Chandra Mehta (ed.), (2000). Tribal Development in 20th Century, Siva Publishers and Distributors, Udaipur.

[5] Kumar Anil K. "Local Knowledge and Agricultural Sustainability A case study of Pradhan Tribe in Adilabad District" Centre for Economic and Social Studies Hyderabad (Working Paper No. 81) January 2010. www.cess.ac.in) cess home.

[6] Dholni, S.P. and Singh, R.S.P. "Indian Anthropology and Tribal Culture" (1996) Piyush Publications, Delhi).

[7] Jain, P.C. (1999). Planned Development Among Tribals, Prem Rawat for Rawat Publications, New Delhi.

[8] Bakshi, S.R. and Kiran, Bala (2000). Social and Economic Development of Scheduled Tribes, Deep and Deep Publications Pvt. Ltd., New Delhi.

[9] Mazumdar, D.N. (1960) "Adivasi aur Unki Samasayen" in Bihar ke Adivasi, Patna Book Centre pp 180–196.

Literacy Differentials and Educational Development of Manipur: A District Level Analysis

Khamnam Michael Meitei[1] and Biswajit Das[2]

ABSTRACT: Literacy is the ability to read, write and comprehend simple sentences. The development of a society is very much dependent on how much of its population are literate. Higher literacy rate contributes to higher capability, productivity, income and esteemed living. In 2011, Manipur has a high literacy rate of 76.94% which is higher than that of India i.e. 74.04%. Although there is a huge gap between various sections of population like General, SC and ST; between male and female literacies, and rural and urban literacies as well as huge spatial variations among the districts mostly in terms of educational development. The present paper is an attempt to analyse the spatial patterns of literacy differentials of General, SC and ST populations and spatial patterns of differential indices in terms of male-female and rural-urban literacies using Differential Index and Choropleth Mapping and to explain these spatial patterns with a set of explanatory variables using Pearson's Correlation and finally assess the Composite Index of Educational Development in the state. Imphal West District excels in literacy rates across all demographic groups, including SC and ST, thanks to improved educational facilities. Senapati District, with challenging topography and inadequate infrastructure, faces the lowest literacy rates. Per capita Income, Urbanization Rate, Density of School are positively related; while Poverty Index, Population Growth and Proportion of Child Population are negatively related to Literacy/Female Literacy Rate. Churachandpur and Ukhrul exhibit negligible literacy disparities, while Bishnupur faces significant differences; understanding these variations is crucial for

---

[1] Corresponding Author's, Research Scholar, Department of Geography, Manipur University, India. E-mail: michaelkhamnam@manipuruniv.ac.in

[2] Assistant Professor, Department of Geography, Manipur University, India.

targeted interventions. Hill Districts encounter infrastructure challenges and limited educational opportunities. Valley Districts benefit from better facilities and increased opportunities.

Keywords: *Literacy Rate, Literacy Differential, Differential Index, Educational Development.*

1. Introduction

Literacy, in simple terms, is the ability to read and write. The United Nations defines literacy as the ability to read and write a short statement about their daily lives. The UNESCO defines literacy as the ability to identify, understand, interpret, create, communicate, and compute using printed and written materials. Census of India, 2011 defines a literate as a person age 7 years and above who can both read and write with understanding in any language; a person who can only read but cannot write is not literate; it is not necessary that to be considered as literate, a person should have received any formal education or passed any minimum educational standard; and literacy could also have been achieved through adult literacy classes or through any non-formal educational system.

Literacy is vital for achieving multiple Sustainable Development Goals (SDGs), primarily Goal 4: Quality Education, which seeks inclusive and equitable education for all. Without literacy, accessing education becomes challenging, hindering knowledge acquisition and societal participation. Additionally, literacy intersects with Goal 5: Gender Equality, where it empowers women and girls to engage actively in their communities and economies. Moreover, literacy fosters Goal 10: Reduced Inequalities by bridging socio-economic gaps and promoting social inclusion. It also contributes to Goal 11: Sustainable Cities and Communities by enhancing access to information and civic engagement. Lastly, literacy supports Goal 16: Peace, Justice, and Strong Institutions by enabling individuals to uphold democratic principles and prevent conflicts, ultimately promoting peaceful and inclusive societies.

Literacy reflects the socio-economic and cultural setup of a nation, an ethnic group or a community. It influences and determines qualitatively and quantitatively not only the human resources but also other population attributes like fertility, mortality, age of marriage and economic participation of a population ultimately, aiming towards welfare of the society (Sawant and Lewis, 2004). Higher literacy rate contributes to higher capability and productivity, greater income and esteemed living. A study by World Bank (2013) says that educating women is not a charity, it is good economics and if developing nations are to be abolish poverty, they should educated their women. The development of a society is very much dependent on how much of its population are literate.

Although there is significant improvement in literacy rate since Independence in India, there are regional disparity in the state level (Kumar & Kumar, 2012). There is also regional disparity in the district level. This shows that there is not only difference in level of literacy in state level but it also differs within state. There is also differential in literacy in various groups like; male-female, rural-urban. In 2011, Manipur has a high literacy rate of 76.94% which is higher than the India's literacy rate i.e. 74.04%; although there is a huge gap between male and female literacies, rural and urban literacies, and as well as huge spatial variations among the districts mostly in terms of educational development.

2. Methodology

2.1 *Study Area*

Manipur, one of the states situated in the North Eastern Region of India, is an isolated hill-girt state stretching between 92°58′23.422" East to 94°43′35.553" East longitudes and 23°49′45.530" North to 25°42′1.456" North latitudes. The State has international border with Burma (Myanmar) to the south-east and border with the adjacent states of Nagaland on the north, Cachar District of Assam on the west and Chin Hills (Myanmar) and Mizoram on the south and the south-west and Surma Tract and upper Chindwin of Myanmar (Burma) on the East. Manipur has a geographical area of 22, 327 km^2. 90% of the total geographical area of the state i.e. 20, 089 km^2 is covered by hills, the remaining area is a small valley covering only 2, 238 km^2 and accounting for only one-tenth of the total area of the state. The population of Manipur as per 2011 census was 28.56 lakhs comprising 14.39 lakhs of males and 14.17 lakhs of females. The population growth rate (decadal) of Manipur in 2011 is 24.50% as against all India growth rate of 17.70%. The literacy rate has increased from 70.50% in 2001 to 76.94% in 2011. Among the males, it has increased from 80.30% in 2001 to 83.58% in 2011, whereas among females, it has increased from 60.50% in 2001 to 70.26% in 2011.

2.2 *Materials*

The study is primarily based on the secondary data obtained from the Census of India, 2011. The data of literacy rates for the General, SC and ST populations as well as for the totals, males, females, and population residing in rural and urban areas at the district level has been collected from the Census of India (2011). The data on the number of schools is obtained from Unified District Information System for Education Plus (UDISE+). Per capita Income is provided by Directorate of Economics and Statistics, Government of Manipur and Poverty Index is taken from the academic work of Malini Nair *et al.* (2013).

2.3 *Methods*

In order to explain spatial patterns of literacy rate with a set of explanatory variables, correlation test is conducted using Pearson co-relation method in IBM SPSS Statistics 20. The selected independent variables used in the study are Per capita Income, Urbanization Rate, Density of School, Poverty Index, Population Growth and Proportion of Child Population.

To analyse the spatial patterns of literacy differentials, the following formula of differential index as used by Krishan and Shayam has been used in the present analysis.

$$DI = \frac{x2 - x1}{T}$$

Where, DI = Differential Index

x_2 =Literacy Percentage of Males, Urban population

x_1= Literacy Percentage of Females, Rural population

T = Literacy Percentage of total population

As on 1st March 2021, the projected population of Manipur is 3165 thousands as per Population Projections for India and States

2011–2036 (published by Report of the Technical Group on Population Projections, July, 2020). Based on knowledge of the projected population at the state level for any future year, the estimation of the population at the sub-state level such as a district can be obtained by ratio method. In this method it is assumed that the ratio of the population of a district to the total population of the state follows the same trend as observed in the recent past and projected into the future to estimate the district population. Regression uses a mathematical equation of straight line to predict the value of dependent variable based on the independent variable. The Literacy Rate of 2021 is predicted by Regression Method.

For finding out the district level of educational development in the state, Composite Index have been calculated by using the following formula:

$$\text{C.I.} = \frac{x1 \times \bar{x}/\sigma + x2 \times \bar{x}/\sigma + x3 \times \bar{x}/\sigma + x4 \times \bar{x}/\sigma + x5 \times \bar{x}/\sigma + \cdots + xn \times \bar{x}/\sigma}{w1 + w2 + w3 + w4 + w5 + \cdots + wn}$$

Where, C.I. = Composite Index

$x_1, x_2, x_3, \ldots, x_n$ are the selected variables (indicators)

$\bar{x}$ = Mean value of the district and

σ = Standard deviation of each indicator

The composite indices of all districts have been calculated in taking the state average as 100. So, the disparity in the level of educational development in Manipur state is expressed as:

$$\text{Composite Indices} = \frac{\text{Composite Index of any Block}}{\text{Average Composite Index}} \times 100$$

Various statistical methods are used for the calculation of data. After calculating the data, Choropleth mapping techniques are used by using standard deviation as the basis of break points for mapping maps of literacy rate, literacy differential indices and composite index of educational development of the state using GIS platform ArcGIS 14.

3. Objectives of the Study

1. To analyze the spatial patterns of literacy differentials of General, SC and ST populations and to explain correlational association between explanatory variables and literacy rate.

2. To analyze the spatial patterns of differential indices in terms of male-female and rural-urban literacies.
3. To analyze the spatial patterns of educational development in the state.

4. Results and Discussions

4.1 *Spatial Patterns of Literacy Differentials of General, SC and ST Populations*

The Census of India, 2011 provides a comprehensive overview of the nation's literacy, documenting a collective literacy rate of 74.04%. However, the state of Manipur distinguishes itself with a literacy rate of 76.94%, surpassing the national average. Table 1 offers a detailed breakdown of literacy rates within Manipur, categorizing the data by General population, Scheduled Castes (SC), and Scheduled Tribes (ST) at the district level.

Table 1: District wise Literacy Rates of General, SC and ST Populations

State/District	*General LR*	*SC LR*	*ST LR*
Manipur	76.94	76.09	72.58
Imphal East	81.95	70.33	86.68
Imphal West	86.08	81.15	89.78
Bishnupur	75.85	68.09	75.57
Thoubal	74.47	81.25	83.20
Ukhrul	81.35	71.30	81.17
Senapati	63.60	58.13	62.74
Tamenglong	70.05	61.90	69.51
Chandel	71.11	66.94	69.73
Churachandpur	82.78	72.91	82.75

Source: Census of India, 2011.
LR-Literacy Rate, SC-Scheduled Castes & ST-Scheduled Tribes.

Within the array of Manipur's districts, Imphal West is distinguished by its highest literacy rate of 86.08% indicating a robust educational infrastructure. Conversely, Senapati district exhibits a literacy rate of 63.50%, underscoring the persistent educational challenges in the district. Utilizing Standard Deviation, valued at 7.30, as an analytical tool, we systematically classify the districts into four literacy rate categories: 'Very Low', 'Low', 'Moderate', and 'High'. This classification not only facilitates a nuanced understanding of the literacy distribution but also serves as a narrative framework for examining the literacy development across Manipur. In the domain of literacy, Imphal West stands as a paragon within the 'High' category, exemplifying literacy prowess. Conversely, Senapati languishes in the 'Very Low' category, underscoring a profound need for educational advancement. The 'Low' category comprises a tapestry of districts—Tamenglong, Chandel, Thoubal, and Bishnupur—each narrating its distinct journey toward literacy. In parallel, Ukhrul, Imphal East, and

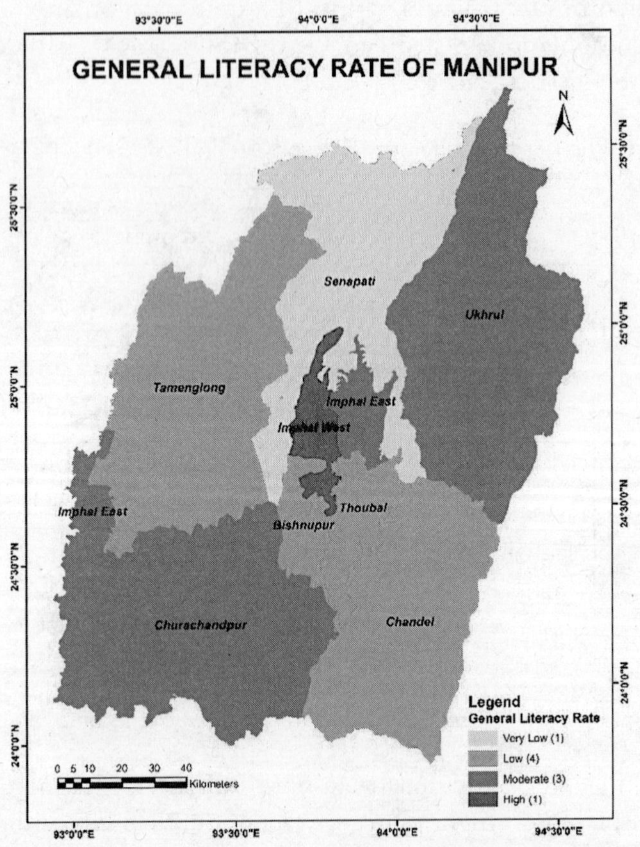

Churachandpur occupy the 'Moderate' category, indicative of consistent, optimistic advancement. The General Literacy Rate of Manipur reveals a continuum of literacy levels across the four central valley districts, ranging from 'Low' to 'High'. This contrasts with the surrounding five hill districts, which collectively delineate a literacy landscape as diverse as the region's topography, extending from 'Very Low' to 'Moderate'. The southeastern part of the state, which encompasses the districts of Thoubal, Bishnupur, and Chandel, all fall within the low category of literacy rate.

In Manipur's educational milieu, the Scheduled Castes (SC) demographic serves as a beacon for the transformative impact of education, evidenced by a literacy rate of 76.09%. This statistic is nearly congruent with the General literacy rate, symbolizing a collective commitment to educational attainment. Employing the analytical tool of Standard Deviation, we delineate distinct socio-economic strata within this group. Thoubal and Imphal West districts shine as exemplars within the 'High' literacy category, illuminating the path of educational enlightenment. In stark contrast, the districts of Senapati and Tamenglong are categorized as 'Very Low', akin to latent seeds awaiting the invigorating essence of erudition to germinate. This stratification embodies a narrative steeped in resilience and resolve, chronicling the communal odyssey towards the enlightenment of literacy.

In the context of Manipur's demographic literacy rates, the Scheduled Tribes (ST) population exhibits a literacy rate of 72.58%. This figure is notably lower than both the General literacy rate and that of the Scheduled Castes (SC) population. A district-wise classification of the ST population, based on literacy rates and employing Standard Deviation as a methodological tool, reveals a stark disparity. The Senapati district is categorized within the 'Very Low' literacy group, while the Imphal West district is distinguished by its placement in the 'High' literacy group. This dichotomy underscores the varying degrees of educational attainment among the ST population across different districts.

From Table 2, Imphal West possesses a relatively superior literacy rate across all demographic categories, including SC and ST, attributable to enhanced educational facilities and opportunities. The notable literacy rate among the SC population in Thoubal can be ascribed to greater educational engagement and the high enrollment rates in the Kakching area, predominantly inhabited by the SC community. Conversely, the Senapati district exhibits the lowest literacy rates across all populations, a consequence of its challenging topography and the absence of fundamental infrastructure, such as road networks and educational institutions. Tamenglong and Chandel districts exhibit literacy rates that are comparable to Senapati, reflecting similar developmental challenges.

Table 2: Category Wise Literacy Differentials of General, SC & ST Populations

(In order of Literacy Rate)

Category	*General Literacy Rate*	*SC Literacy Rate*	*ST Literacy Rate*
Very Low	Senapati	Senapati, Tamenglong,	Senapati
Low	Tamenglong, Chandel, Thoubal, Bishnupur	Chandel, Bishnupur	Tamenglong, Chandel, Bishnupur,
Moderate	Ukhrul, Imphal East, Churachandpur	Imphal East, Ukhrul, Churachandpur	Ukhrul, Churachandpur, Thoubal, Imphal East
High	Imphal West	Imphal West, Thoubal	Imphal West

Source: Compiled by author from Table 1.

4.2 *Correlational Association between Explanatory Variables and Literacy Rate*

Table 3 presents a hypothetical framework illustrating the relationship between explanatory variables and literacy rate. These variables comprise Per Capita Income, Urbanization Rate, School Density, Poverty Index, Population Growth Rate, and the Proportion of the Child Population. They are subjected to Pearson's correlation test to assess the strength and direction of their association with literacy rates.

Table 3: Model of Literacy

Variables	*Proximate Determination Factor*	*Relationship*
Income	Increase Educational Opportunity	Direct
Urbanization	Increase Educational Infrastructure	Direct
School Density	Increase Educational Accessibility	Direct
Poverty Index	Decrease Educational Affordability	Inverse
Population Growth	Decrease Per capita Educational Investment	Inverse
Child Population	Decrease Female Enrollment due to Child Care	Inverse

4.2.1 *The Relationship between Per Capita Income and Literacy Rate*

The interplay between per capita income and literacy rates is a subject of extensive empirical research, revealing a complex yet discernible pattern. Numerous studies have consistently demonstrated a positive relationship between these two indicators, suggesting that higher educational attainment tends to coincide with increased income levels, and conversely, higher income levels contribute to better educational outcomes. A notable example is the research conducted by Psacharopoulos and Patrinos in 2018, which utilized cross-country data to uncover a robust positive correlation between national literacy rates and per capita income. Building upon this foundation, the current study examines the correlation between per capita income and literacy rates across various districts, unveiling a significant positive influence with a correlation coefficient of $r = 0.488$. This finding underscores the mutual reinforcement of economic prosperity and educational advancement, highlighting the pivotal role of literacy in driving socioeconomic development.

4.2.2 *The Interrelation between Urbanization and Literacy Rates*

The nexus between urbanization and literacy rates has been the focus of numerous scholarly inquiries, which have predominantly identified a positive correlation. This body of research posits that urban centers are typically characterized by elevated literacy rates in comparison to rural locales. A UNICEF study from 2018 corroborates this view, revealing that children in urban settings generally benefit from superior access to educational resources, culminating in higher literacy rates, especially within the context of developing nations. Furthering this discourse, Som and Mishra (2014) argue that urbanization fosters the enhancement of fundamental amenities, inclusive of educational institutions, thereby facilitating the literacy and education of children. The current study lends weight to these findings, presenting evidence of a positive moderate correlation between urbanization and literacy, quantified by a correlation coefficient of $r = 0.596$. This suggests that urban development is a significant contributor to the advancement of literacy, reflecting the critical role of urban growth in educational progress.

4.2.3 *The Correlation between School Density and Literacy Rates*

The relationship between the density of educational institutions and literacy rates has been extensively explored in scholarly research, revealing a generally positive but variable association. This variance is particularly evident across different regions and demographic groups. For instance, UNESCO's 2019 study highlighted that areas with a higher concentration of schools typically report superior literacy rates. This trend is especially pronounced in rural regions where educational facilities are scarce. In alignment with these findings, Hanushek and colleagues (2013) have demonstrated that augmenting the number of schools in traditionally underserved communities can markedly enhance literacy levels and overall educational achievement. The current study contributes to this body of evidence by presenting a correlation analysis that indicates a positive effect of school density on literacy rates, denoted by a correlation coefficient of $r = 0.363$. This underscores the significance of school accessibility in promoting literacy and suggests that educational infrastructure development can be a key driver of literacy enhancement.

4.2.4 *The Correlation between the Poverty Index and Literacy Rates*

A plethora of research has established poverty as a formidable obstacle to accessing education and achieving literacy. Individuals from impoverished households often exhibit literacy levels inferior to those from more affluent backgrounds. The World Bank's 2018 study elucidates this disparity, illustrating a pronounced link between poverty and diminished literacy rates, alongside a lack of quality educational opportunities, especially within marginalized communities in developing nations. An extensive array of Indian research endeavors—spanning from Panchmukhi (1991) to Dholakia (2003)—has endeavored to demonstrate that economic deprivation plays a critical role in the observed deficiencies in literacy rates and educational attainment across various population segments. The current study draws upon the Poverty Index data from Nair, Malini., *et al.* (2013), revealing a starkly negative correlation with literacy rates, as evidenced by a correlation coefficient of $r = -0.886$. This compelling negative relationship accentuates the profound impact of economic status on literacy development.

Table 4: District Wise Explanatory Variables of Literacy Rate of Manipur

STATE/ District	*Per capita Income* (Rs.)*	*Urbanization Rate (%)*	*School Density^ (per km²)*	*Poverty Index@*	*Population Growth (%)*	*Proportion of Child Population (%)*
MANIPUR	18547	29.21	0.207	---	24.50	13.14
Imphal East	15144	40.17	0.870	0.5690	15.51	13.14
Imphal West	29494	62.33	1.037	0.1065	16.56	11.95
Bishnupur	19946	36.86	0.609	1.6811	13.93	13.19
Thoubal	15948	35.85	9.315	1.4260	15.94	14.34
Ukhrul	17078	14.78	0.085	1.7909	30.70	13.27
Senapati	13691	01.56	0.270	3.1730	68.94	13.22
Tamenglong	18131	13.77	0.094	3.7005	26.15	13.73
Chandel	15015	11.68	0.115	3.1056	21.85	11.92
Churachandpur	14107	6.70	0.133	0.8900	20.29	13.66
Correlation, r	0.488	0.596	0.363	–0.886	–0.664	–0.221

Source: * Directorate of Economics & Statistics, Government of Manipur, ^ Computed by author,
@ Nair, Malini. *et al.* (2013) and Remaining data from Census of India, 2011.

4.2.5 *The Correlation between Population Growth and Literacy Rates*

The interrelation between population growth and literacy rates has been extensively documented, with a predominant focus on the negative correlation observed in various settings. Seminal works by Birdsall and Kelley (1992), as well as Bloom and Canning (2000), have identified that elevated rates of population growth are often linked to diminished investments in education and, consequently, lower literacy rates. This trend is particularly acute in low-income nations. Complementing these findings, Deininger and Squire (1996) have shed light on the detrimental impacts of rapid population expansion on educational quality, manifesting in reduced governmental spending on education and the prevalence of overcrowded learning environments. The analysis conducted in the current study aligns with these perspectives, revealing a moderate negative correlation between population growth and literacy rates, with a correlation coefficient of $r = -0.664$. This underscores the complex challenges posed by population dynamics on the pursuit of educational advancement.

4.2.6 *The Correlation between Child Population Proportion and Female Literacy*

In India, the vast majority of women shoulder the primary responsebility for domestic duties, which traditionally encompass child-rearing and elder care within the family unit. As the number of children per household escalates, the resultant increase in domestic obligations significantly curtails the time women can dedicate to self-improvement activities, including education. This dynamic often leads to a rise in female illiteracy rates concurrent with the growth in the proportion of children within families. The findings of the current study illuminate this phenomenon, revealing a weak negative correlation between the proportion of the child population and female literacy, as indicated by a correlation coefficient of $r = -0.221$. This suggests that the demographic composition of families, particularly the number of dependents, can have a discernible impact on the educational attainment of women.

4.3 *Spatial Pattern of Differential Indices of Male-Female and Rural-Urban Literacies*

Table 5 presents a detailed breakdown of the literacy rates in Manipur, disaggregated by gender and locale. It includes the male and female literacy rates, alongside the literacy rates for rural and urban areas. Additionally, the table provides calculated indices for the male-female literacy gap and the rural-urban literacy disparity across the districts of Manipur.

Table 5: District Wise Literacy Differential Indices of Manipur

State/District	*Male LR*	*Female LR*	*M/F DI**	*Rural LR*	*Urban LR*	*R/U DI**
MANIPUR	83.58	70.26	0.173	73.40	85.38	0.156
Imphal East	88.77	75.32	0.164	78.39	87.12	0.107
Imphal West	92.24	80.17	0.140	82.16	88.40	0.072
Bishnupur	85.11	66.68	0.243	29.37	79.64	0.663
Thoubal	85.00	64.09	0.281	71.20	80.25	0.122
Ukhrul	85.52	76.95	0.105	80.03	88.92	0.109
Senapati	69.21	57.67	0.181	63.27	85.12	0.344
Tamenglong	76.09	63.69	0.177	67.36	86.95	0.280
Chandel	77.78	63.96	0.194	71.06	71.47	0.006
Churachandpur	86.97	78.50	0.102	82.34	88.65	0.076

Source: Census of India, 2011 and * Computed by author.
M/F-Male/Female, R/U-Rural/Urban & DI-Differential Index.

4.3.1 *Spatial Patterns of Differential Index of Male and Female Literacy*

The state of Manipur exhibits a Male-Female Literacy Differential Index of 0.173. This index measures the disparity in literacy rates between genders across the state. A closer examination of district-level data reveals that Churachandpur district has the smallest differential index at 0.102, marginally lower than Ukhrul's 0.105. Conversely, Thoubal district exhibits the largest disparity with an index of 0.281, followed by Bishnupur at 0.243. To categorize the districts based on the extent of literacy disparity, we employ the standard deviation method, dividing them into four classifications: Very Low, Low,

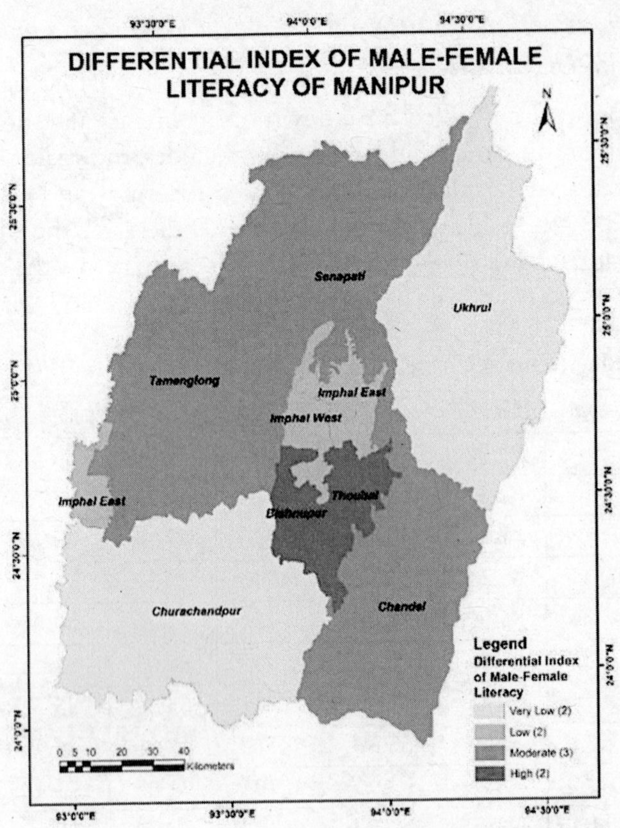

Moderate, and High. Under this scheme, Churachandpur and Ukhrul fall into the Very Low category, while Imphal West and Imphal East are categorized as Low. The districts of Tamenglong, Senapati, and Chandel are placed in the Moderate category. Lastly, Bishnupur and Thoubal are classified as High, indicating significant literacy disparities as illustrated in the Differential Index of Male-Female Literacy in Manipur. An interesting pattern emerges when comparing valley and hill districts. Valley districts are predominantly classified as either Low or High, whereas hill districts are typically Very Low or Moderate. Specifically, the northern (Imphal West and Imphal East) and southern (Bishnupur and Thoubal) parts of the Imphal valley are categorized as Low and High, respectively. Meanwhile, the north-western region of the state, comprising Senapati and Tamenglong, falls within the Moderate category.

4.3.2 *Spatial Patterns of Differential Index of Rural and Urban Literacy*

In Manipur, the Rural-Urban Literacy Differential Index stands at 0.156, signifying the variance between rural and urban literacy rates. Within this index, Chandel district boasts the narrowest gap at 0.006, followed by Imphal West with 0.072. In stark contrast, Bishnupur district exhibits the widest gap, with an index value of 0.663. Employing the standard deviation as a classification tool, districts are sorted into four distinct categories: Very Low, Low, Moderate, and High. Notably, Chandel, Imphal West, Churachandpur, Imphal East, Ukhrul, and Thoubal districts fall into the Very Low category,

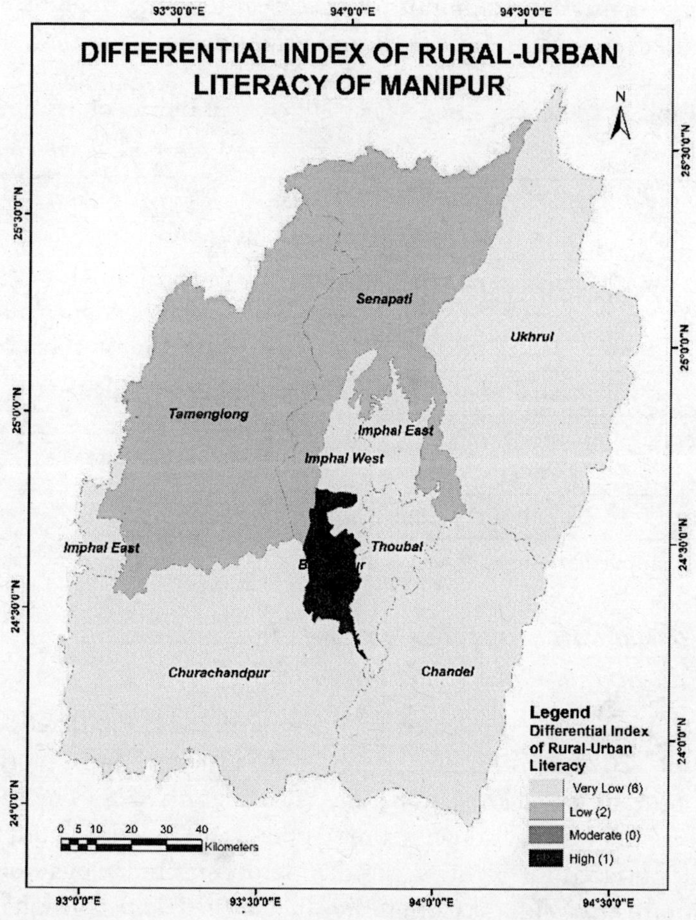

indicating minimal literacy disparities. This is a positive indication, as these districts collectively span over half of the state's area, extending diagonally from the southeast corner, as illustrated in the Differential Index of Rural-Urban Literacy of Manipur. Tamenglong and Senapati districts are categorized as Low, reflecting modest literacy gaps. Interestingly, no district falls within the Moderate category. Meanwhile, Bishnupur stands alone in the High category, pointing to significant rural-urban literacy disparities.

Table 6 reveals that Churachandpur and Ukhrul districts exhibit negligible disparities in both gender and rural-urban literacy, placing them in the Very Low category. This trend of minimal literacy differentials is also observed in Imphal East and Imphal West districts. In stark contrast, Bishnupur district registers the highest literacy differentials in both indices, indicating significant disparities.

Table 6: Category Wise Literacy Differential Indices of Manipur

(In order of Differential Index)

Category	*Differential Index of Male and Female Literacies*	*Differential Index of Rural and Urban Literacies*
Very Low	Churachandpur, Ukhrul	Chandel, Imphal West, Churachandpur, Imphal East, Ukhrul, Thoubal
Low	Imphal West, Imphal East	Tamenglong, Senapati
Moderate	Tamenglong, Senapati, Chandel	
High	Bishnupur, Thoubal	Bishnupur

Source: Compiled by author from Table 5.

4.4 *Spatial Patterns of the Composite Index of the Educational Development in the State*

Table 7 presents the Projected Population of 2021, Predicted Literacy Rate of 2021, Computed Composite Index, and Normalized Composite Index of Educational Development of 2021. The data used for computation is drawn from Appendix 1, which outlines the variables utilized for constructing the Composite Index of Educational Development. With a Composite Index of 109.05, Imphal West exhibits the highest level of educational development. Following closely, Imphal East boasts a Composite Index of 108.73, indicating a similarly strong educational profile. In contrast, Pherzawl District has the lowest Composite Index at 87.42, signifying a relatively lower level of educational development. Senapati District follows closely with a Composite Index of 88.07. To classify districts based on their educational development, we have applied standard deviation as the basis for defining breakpoints. Consequently, the districts are categorized into four classes: Very Low, Low, Moderate, and High.

Table 7: District Wise Composite Index of Educational Development of Manipur, 2021

Districts	*Population*[@]	*Literacy Rate#*	*Composite Index**	*Normalized CI^*
Imphal East	421190	87.02	34.21	108.73
Imphal West	535018	89.27	34.31	109.05
Bishnupur	238710	82.63	33.17	105.42
Thoubal	297022	81.36	32.53	103.40
Kakching	136311	82.53	33.11	105.24
Jiribam	44976	82.36	33.37	106.08
Ukhrul	162764	86.19	32.06	101.91
Kamjong	50837	86.25	29.06	92.38
Senapati	457234	70.08	27.71	88.07
Kangpokpi	213494	81.52	30.47	96.85
Tamenglong	119045	78.68	29.35	93.29
Noney	38874	79.41	32.24	102.49
Chandel	92704	81.50	31.08	98.79
Tengnoupal	63621	76.76	29.57	93.98
Churachandpur	255118	87.40	33.63	106.90
Pherzawl	38081	85.78	27.50	87.42

Source: Computed by author.

[@] Projected Population by Ratio Method, # Predicted Literacy Rate by Regression Method.

* Computed using Variables in Appendix 1 & ^ Normalized District Average Composite Index as 100.

The Composite Index of Educational Development sheds light on the educational landscape across Manipur's districts. Notably, three districts—Pherzawl, Senapati, and Kamjong—exhibit a very low level of educational development (with Composite Indices ranging from 85.64 to 92.82). With a Composite Index of 87.42, Pherzawl ranks as the least developed district in the entire state of Manipur. This index indicates that Pherzawl lags behind the district average by 12.56%. The primary contributors to this educational disparity are the district's alarmingly low number of schools: Only 129 schools exist in Pherzawl, compared to the district average of 289 schools. Specifically, there are 71 primary schools, 35 upper primary schools, 20 secondary schools, and 2 higher secondary schools. Most concerning is the absence of any colleges within Pherzawl, further exacerbating its educational backwardness. Like Pherzawl, Kamjong also lacks a college. Consequently, Kamjong falls within the same very low category of educational development. In summary, addressing the educational infrastructure deficit—particularly the scarcity of schools and absence of colleges—is crucial for uplifting these districts and ensuring equitable educational opportunities.

The districts of Tamenglong, Tengnoupal, Kangpokpi, and Chandel exhibit a low level of educational development. Their Composite Indices fall within the range of 92.82 to 100.00. Notably, these districts are situated in the north-western and south-eastern parts of Manipur. This observation underscores the need for targeted interventions to uplift educational infrastructure and opportunities in these regions. By addressing the specific challenges faced by these districts, we can work towards fostering equitable development in terms of education.

The moderate level of educational development (with Composite Indices ranging from 100.00 to 107.18) is observed in seven districts within Manipur. These districts include Ukhrul, Noney, Thoubal, Kakching, Bishnupur, Jiribam and Churachandpur. This category predominantly occupies the southern part of the Imphal valley and its adjoining southwest districts. Notably, 43.75% of all Manipur districts fall within this moderate level of educational development. Efforts to strengthen educational infrastructure and promote equitable opportunities in these districts are crucial for further progress.

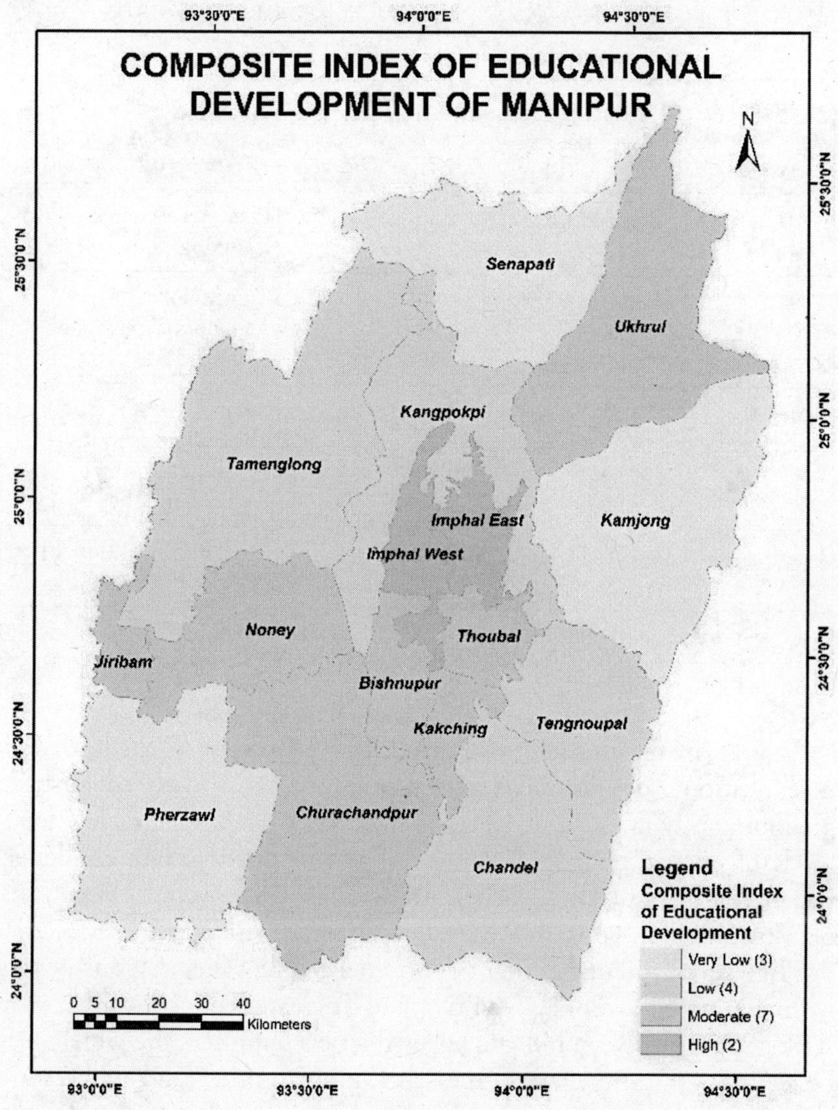

The high level of educational development, characterized by Composite Indices ranging from 107.18 to 114.36, is prominently observed in two districts: Imphal East and Imphal West. These districts share the northern part of the Imphal valley. Efforts to sustain and further enhance educational quality in these districts are crucial for continued progress.

Table 8: Category wise Level of Educational Development of Manipur, 2021

Category of Educational Development	*Composite Index Value*	*No. of Districts*	*Percentage of Districts*	*Name of the Districts (in order of composite index)*
Very Low	85.64–92.82	3	18.75	Pherzawl, Senapati & Kamjong
Low	92.82–100.00	4	25.00	Tamenglong, Tengnoupal, Kangpokpi & Chandel
Moderate	100.00–107.18	7	43.75	Ukhrul, Noney, Thoubal, Kakching, Bishnupur, Jiribam & Churachandpur
High	107.18–114.36	2	12.5	Imphal East & Imphal West
	Total	16	100.00	

Compiled from Table 7.

Based on the preceding discussions, we observe distinct patterns in educational development across Manipur's districts: Hill districts predominantly fall into the categories of Very Low, Low, or Moderate levels of educational development. The hill districts face challenges related to infrastructure, access to schools, and overall educational opportunities. In contrast, the valley districts exhibit either Moderate or High levels of educational development. The valley regions benefit from better educational facilities and increased opportunities. The stark contrast between hill and valley districts reinforces the widely held belief that educational resources and opportunities tend to be more abundant in the valley areas. As we continue our efforts to bridge this gap, understanding these regional disparities is crucial for informed policy decisions and targeted interventions.

5. Conclusions

Imphal West District demonstrates a superior literacy rate across all demographic groups, including SC and ST, owing to improved educational facilities and opportunities. The notable literacy rate among the SC population in Thoubal can be attributed to active educational engagement and high enrollment rates in the Kakching area, predominantly inhabited by the SC community. In contrast, Senapati District faces the lowest literacy rates, primarily due to its challenging topography and the lack of essential infrastructure, such as road networks and educational institutions. Tamenglong and Chandel Districts exhibit literacy rates comparable to Senapati, reflecting similar developmental challenges. A Pearson correlation analysis is performed using six selected explanatory independent variables in relation to the Literacy Rate. Per capita Income (r = 0.488), Urbanization Rate (r = 0.596), Density of School (r = 0.363) are positively related; while Poverty Index (r = –0.886), Population Growth (r = –0.664) and Proportion of Child Population (r = –0.221) are negatively related to Literacy/Female Literacy Rate. Churachandpur and Ukhrul Districts exhibit negligible disparities in both gender and rural-urban literacy and placed in the Very Low category. Imphal East and Imphal West Districts also observe minimal literacy differentials and trend align with the Very Low category. Bishnupur District registers the highest literacy differentials in both indices and indicates significant disparities and understanding these variations is crucial for targeted interventions.

The study observes distinct patterns in educational development across Manipur's districts. Hill Districts (Very Low, Low, or Moderate levels): Face challenges related to infrastructure and access to schools. Educational opportunities are comparatively limited. Valley Districts (Moderate or High levels): Benefit from better educational facilities and increased opportunities. The widely held belief that valley areas have more abundant educational resources is reinforced. Understanding these regional disparities is crucial for informed policy decisions and targeted interventions.

References

[1] Birdsall, N. and Kelley, A.C. (1992). Population Growth and Global Warming. *The Journal of Economic Perspectives*, 6(3), 169–192.

[2] Bloom, D.E. and Canning, D. (2000). The Health and Wealth of Nations. *Science*, 287(5456), 1207–1209.

[3] Census of India, 2011.

[4] Deininger, K. and Squire, L. (1996). A New Data Set Measuring Income Inequality. *The World Bank Economic Review,* 10(3), 565–591.

[5] Hanushek, E.A., Schwerdt, G., Wiederhold, S. and Woessmann, L. (2013). Returns to skills around the world: Evidence from PIAAC. *European Economic Review*, 66, 247–260.

[6] Jhariya, G.P. and Jain, C.K. (2014). Pattern and Differential of Literacy in Madhya Pradesh. IOSR Journal of Humanities and Social Science (IOSR-JHSS), 19(9), Ver. I, 77–84. e-ISSN: 2279–0837, p-ISSN: 2279–0845.

[7] Krishan, G. and Shayam, M. (1978). Regional Aspects of Urban-Rural Differentials in Literacy in India. *The Journal of Developing Areas,* 13(1), 11–22.

[8] Kumar, M. and Kumar, V. (2012). Spatial Pattern and Differential in Literacy: A District Level Analysis of Haryana, 2011. *International Journal of Advanced Research in Management and Social Sciences,* 1(6), ISSN: 2278-6236.

[9] Nair, M., Ravindranath, N.H., Sharma, N., Kattumuri, R. and Munshi, M. (2013). Poverty index as a tool for adaptation intervention to climate change in northeast India. *Climate and Development*, 5(1), 14–32. DOI: 10.1080/17565529.2012.751337

[10] Population Projections for India and States 2011–2036, Report of the Technical Group on Population Projections, July, 2020.

[11] Psacharopoulos, G. and Patrinos, H.A. (2018). Returns to investment in education: A decennial review of the global literature. *Education Economics*, 26(5), 445–458.

[12] Sawant, M.N. and Lewis, C. (2004). Literacy in Goa: A Spatio-Temporal Review. *The Goa Geographers,* 2(2), 32–41.

[13] Som, K.S. and Mishra, R.P. (2014). Literacy and Their Differential in West Bengal. *International Journal of Science and Research (IJSR),* 3(6), ISSN (Online): 2319–7064.

[14] UNESCO (2019). Global Education Monitoring Report 2019: Migration, displacement and education. Paris: UNESCO.

[15] UNICEF (2018). State of the World's Children 2018: Children in a Digital World. New York: UNICEF.

[16] World Bank. (2018). World Development Report 2018: Learning to Realize Education's Promise. Washington, DC: World Bank.

[17] Yadav, S. (2023). Spatial Patterns of Literacy Differentials in Ajmer District (2011): A Tehsil Level Analysis. *International Journal of Development Research*, 13(03), 62148–62152.

[18] Yadav, S., Khan, Z. and Sharma, D.K. (2021). Spatial Patterns of Literacy in Rajasthan. International Journal of Innovative Research in Science, *Engineering and Technology (IJIRSET),* 10(9), DOI:10.5680/IJIRSET.2021.1009006, e-ISSN: 2319-8753, p-ISSN: 2347–6710.

SECTION-D

Tourism and Sustainable Development

Understanding the Role of Ecotourism and Its Contribution to Sustainable Development

Gobinda C. Roy[1] and Anirban Pandey[2]

ABSTRACT: An indispensable constituent of each nation's economy is tourism. A novel idea in the tourist industry, ecotourism offers an alternative route to environmental preservation while falling under the purview of sustainable development. Ecotourism holds incredible promise for both environmental preservation and economic growth in poor nations. It preserves and promotes the local cultures in the areas it operates in while providing accommodations and entertainment for tourists in a way that is as little of a disruption to the environment as possible. The phrase has recently gained much popularity, particularly in emerging nations. To put it simply, it refers to managing tourism and nature conservation in a way that preserves a subtle balance between the demands of ecology and tourism on the one hand and the requirements of the local communities on the other, including jobs, innovative skills, and income generating employment, and improved status for women. It is more than just a tourism idea. It entails preserving the environment and cultural legacy and elevating bio-cultural diversity, community engrossment through better employment opportunities and local capacity building to combat poverty, a focus on environmental cognizance, and life-changing experiences. Ecotourism may benefit the destination's economy, society, and ecology by fostering employment growth, escalating investment

---

[1] Assistant Professor, Dinhata College, Department of Zoology, CoochBehar, West Bengal-736135, India. E-mail: gobindar82@gmail.com

[2] Assistant Professor, A.B.N. Seal College, Department of Zoology, Cooch Behar, West Bengal-736101, India.

prospects, and safeguarding the natural resources areas, culture, and environment.

Keywords: Ecotourism, Environment, Sustainable Development.

1. Introduction

A nation's economy depends heavily on tourism. Compared to tourism alone, ecotourism is a broader notion. An effective tactic for promoting conservation and generating revenue for the local populations in and around protected areas is ecotourism. It can support local jobs, community ownership, and sustainable protected area management by a) creating income that can be utilized to manage protected areas, b) creating jobs locally, and c) encouraging economic growth[1]. Conservationists have pushed ecotourism as a crucial instrument for protecting the environment and advancing the interests of native populations [2]. Ecotourism has helped achieve the twin objectives of resource conservation and poverty alleviation in many world regions [3]. Locals who continue to participate in a range of tourism-related activities have many job options thanks to the promotion of ecotourism. By encouraging local and indigenous populations in host nations and visitors to maintain and appreciate the natural and cultural legacy, ecotourism significantly increases the potential for biodiversity conservation, protection, and sustainable use of natural regions. In both theory and practice, ecotourism has evolved to combine environmental development and conservation [4].

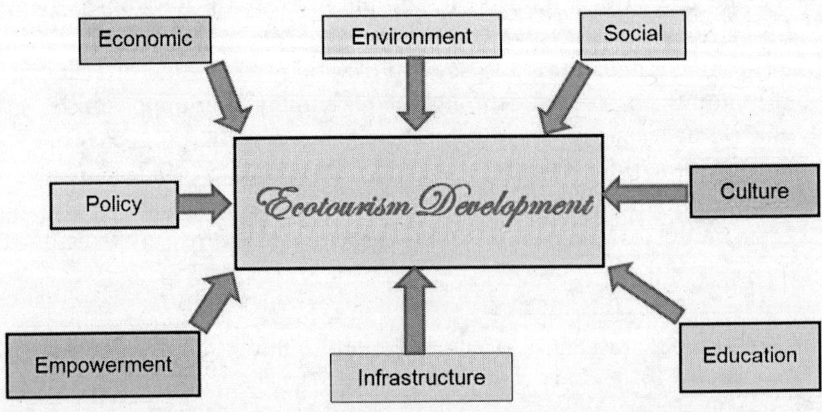

Figure 1: Ecotourism Development Model

2. Economic Role of Ecotourism

Ecotourism strongly encourages the relationship between livelihood pursuits and conservation. It is recognized as a technique to improve local residents' quality of life in the vicinity of protected areas. Ecotourism, or the development of tourism in protected areas, offers an alternative to exploiting natural resources [5]. Financial rewards are essential for protecting the environment [6]. Ecotourism is, therefore, designed to preserve biodiversity by giving the people living in and around protected areas a means of making a living. The strategy is thoroughly discussed in the following section.

3. Jobs and Revenue from Ecotourism

With the prospect of jobs, new business possibilities, and skill development, ecotourism is being embraced by many rural areas as a possible economic savior [7]. In tropical and underdeveloped nations, ecotourism is viewed by several indigenous people as a way to improve living conditions and open up new revenue streams [8]. Local people can increase the stability of their livelihood by developing small businesses and creating better access to tourists through well-organized ecotourism [9;10]. The growth of ecotourism will generate jobs in tourism-related businesses, including dining establishments, gift stores, and food. Additionally, eco-lodges, campgrounds, homestays, restaurants, transportation, and guiding services directly assist the local economy [11; 12].

4. Development of Production System

Because of the increasing amount of items that visitors consume, the growth of ecotourism has occasionally resulted in the development of production systems for commodities and services related to tourism, such as local handicrafts, agriculture, and services. Those with a livelihood connected to ecotourism and who answered the survey felt that the growth of their livelihood is where ecotourism has the most significant positive effect. People began to engage in ecotourism activities instead of fishing or using non-timber wood since it paid better [1].

Employees in ecotourism destinations will purchase consumer products with the extra money they get from occupations connected to ecotourism. The demand for these products will rise, adding jobs. Ecotourism's positive effects on the local economy and job market have contributed significantly to the relative prosperity of the communities it has affected [13; 14].

5. Importance of Ecotourism in Society and Culture

By raising the socio-economic and political status of the locals, ecotourism promotes respect for human rights and diverse cultures while also empowering the community. Positive attitudes toward conservation are fostered by indirect incentives such as better infrastructure, health facilities, awareness, and education, which result from the growth of the tourism industry [14].

6. Role of Ecotourism in Empowerment

Ecotourism empowers local populations through its advantages to the economy, society, politics, and psychology. Consistent financial benefits from jobs in the formal or informal sector and company ventures give the community economic leverage. It makes it possible for people to coexist peacefully, which promotes social empowerment. Political empowerment results from involvement in decision-making processes, but psychological power relates to community members' sense of self-worth, which may be raised by outside acknowledgement and appreciation of the unique cultural, natural, and traditional resources and knowledge [14].

7. Effects of Ecotourism on the Environment

Ecotourism is a sustainable option for the commercial use of natural resources [15; 16]. The exploitation of environmental resources can be substituted by ecotourism or tourist development in protected regions [16; 17]. To ensure the sustainable use of finite natural resources, ecotourism policies primarily focus on implementing green growth strategies within the tourism industry. Managing natural resources makes sense when biodiversity is used as a revenue-producing asset.

8. Conclusion

Ecotourism must be centred on the environment rather than business. The economy alone will cause issues if it is the primary focus. When tourist expansion surpasses the natural capacity of the ecosystem, catastrophic consequences may ensue. Crowded conditions and inappropriate behaviour may result in harm to natural attractions. Resort and hotel construction may contribute to deforestation and environmental deterioration. These operations can potentially harm the delicate ecology and native animals by producing trash, pollution, and non-biodegradable garbage. Properly executed ecotourism represents a significant economic and educational endeavour. In addition to strengthening public support for conservation, it has the potential to educate the general public about the value and vulnerability of these ecosystems. It also encourages the non-consumptive usage of wilderness areas to help the nearby populations who depend on these delicate environments. Travelling to natural locations provides a reprieve from the pollution of big cities and an escape from the highly stressed artificial environment. When individuals have a personal connection to nature, it fosters an awareness of environmental issues and a sense of personal responsibility for protecting it. This increases the number of environmentally conscious tourists. It instils respect for these little-known cultures by highlighting the local and tribal ones. Not only does ecotourism provide jobs, but it also helps the local community financially and gives them more authority. In a developing nation like India, ecotourism offers several prospects for addressing environmental concerns, strengthening indigenous communities, creating jobs, and promoting sustainable growth.

References

[1] Jalani, J.O. (2012). Local people's perception on the impacts and importance of ecotourism in Sabang, Palawan, Philippines. *Procedia-Social and Behavioral Sciences*, 57, 247–254.

[2] Stronza, A. (2007). The economic promise of ecotourism for conservation. *Journal of Ecotourism*, 6(3), 210–230.

[3] Surendran, A. and Sekar, C. (2011). A comparative analysis on the socio-economic welfare of dependents of the Anamalai Tiger Reserve

(ATR) in India. *Margin: The Journal of Applied Economic Research,* 5(3), 361–379.

[4] Gray, N. (2003). Unpacking the baggage of ecotourism: nature, science and local participation. *Great Lakes Geographer*, 9(2), 113–123.

[5] Nyuapane, G.P. and Poudel, S. (2011). Linkages among biodiversity, livelihood and tourism. *Annals of Tourism Research*, 38(4), 1344–1366.

[6] Wunder, S. (2000). Ecotourism and economic incentives—an empirical approach. *Ecological Economics*, 32(3), 465–479 (www.ecotourism.org.).

[7] Scheyvens, R. (2007). Exploring the tourism-poverty nexus. In C.M. Hall (Ed.), Pro-poor tourism: Who benefits? Perspectives on tourism and poverty reduction (pp. 121–144). Clevedon, England: Channel View.

[8] Stronza, A. (2007). The economic promise of ecotourism for conservation. *Journal of Ecotourism*, 6(3), 210–221.

[9] Ashley, C. (2002). Methodology for pro-poor tourism case studies.

[10] Goodwin, H. (2002). Local community involvement in tourism around national parks: *Opportunities and constraints. Current Issues in Tourism*, 5(3–4), 338–360.

[11] Mustika, P.L.K., Birtles, A., Welters, R. and Marsh, H. (2012). The economic influence of community based dolphin watching on a local economy in a developing country: *Implications for conservation. Ecological Economics,* 79, 11–20.

[12] Reimer, J.K. (Kila) and Walter, P. (2013). How do you know it when you see it? Community-based ecotourism in the Cardamom Mountains of south-western Cambodia. *Tourism Management*, 34, 122–132.

[13] Seetanah, B. (2011). Assessing the dynamic economic impact of tourism for island economies. *Annals of Tourism Research,* 38(1), 291–308.

[14] Taylor, J.E., Hardner, J. and Stewart, M. (2006). Ecotourism and economic growth in the Galapagos: An island economy-wide analysis. Working paper no. 06–001. Davis: Department of Agricultural and Resource Economics University of California.

[15] Nyuapane, G.P. and Poudel, S. (2011). Linkages among biodiversity, livelihood and tourism. *Annals of Tourism Research,* 38(4), 1344–1366.

[16] Li, W. (2004). Environmental management indicators for ecotourism in China's nature reserves: A case study in Tianmushan Nature Reserve. *Tourism Management*, 25(5), 559–564.

[17] Wood, M.E. (2002). Ecotourism: principles, practices and policies for sustainability. *United Nations Publication.*

Tourism and Sustainability in Hill Areas of India

Sima Biswas[1]

ABSTRACT: Hills are one of nature's most beautiful gifts, and they have ecological and aesthetic significance. They are the natural biosphere reserve full of natural resources. Hill stations are located at a higher elevation than nearby planes or valleys. Most of these stations are characterised by a dynamic ecosystem. Since ancient times, Religious and spiritual tourism have been an important part of the tourism industry. At present, most of the hill stations are overcrowded for tourism, and to combat it, unplanned tourism has raised the problem of land use, environmental pollution, infrastructural stress, transport and service-related stress, which ultimately leads to the change of climate. The detrimental effect of tourism development can lead to the destruction of environmental resources. To promote tourism, which is an important source of foreign currency, earning conservation of hill area resources is necessary. Now, the prime goal of developing countries is to achieve the UN sustainable development Goals (SDGs). The three pillars of Sustainable Development—Economic, Social, and Environmental aspects must be taken into consideration without compromising the needs for future generations. Tourism and sustainable development can be the balancing factor for the conservation of the environment. So, intensive planning and design are of utmost importance to the development of the hill area.

Keywords: Hill-area, Sustainable Development, Tourism, Conservation, Natural Resources.

1. Introduction

Hills, often regarded as paradise on earth, are significant in relation to aesthetics, environment and economic growth of the

[1] Assistant Professor Department of Botany, Vidyasagar College for Women 39, Sankar Ghosh Lane, Kolkata-06, India. E-mail: biswas.sima1412@gmail.com

concerned area, state or country. Though the hill areas are rich in natural resources, they remained poverty-driven because of unscientific planning and lower-order development for a long time. For the increasing pressure of anthropological activities associated with tourism development, the environment and ecology of hill areas are under threat. Most of the hill states are working with different policies and programmes to promote their state as attractive tourist destinations within and outside the country. So the increased influx of tourists and the associated unplanned infrastructural development has put the environment, biodiversity, ecosystem and culture of hill areas at risk (Gupta, 2022). Modern facilities and transportation have made remote mountain areas accessible to visitors. Along with the natural and scenic beauty, the tribal life, ethnic culture, folk traditions and the innumerable religious shrines of the Himalayan region and the foothill regions attract tourists to such centres. So, for the unbalanced tourist pressure, the acute problem of land use and infrastructural stress arises. At this point, effective management for sustainable development is required as a future strategic option (Saraswati and Ram, 2017). Darjeeling district of West Bengal has a number of tourist spots and attractions that are breathtakingly beautiful. For the influx of tourists, all the hill towns are overcrowded. To accommodate tourist construction of new buildings in an unplanned way is putting the concerned land area under stress. Moreover, poor coordination between different sectors, such as tourism, PWD, Darjeeling improvement fund, district administration, and municipality, has led to demand for sustainable tourism development (Bhutia, 2015). Matheran Hill Station of Mumbai metropolitan city is under threat in terms of ecology and environment due to the growing developmental pressure (Latkar, n.d). The eastern Himalayan tourist hotspot Sikkim has high tourist potential but it is vulnerable too. So, sustainable tourism development is the prime need to address social inequalities, insecurities, and communities' empowerment besides the protection of natural resources and the ecosystem (Chakraborty and Ghosal, 2024). Bhutan has imposed a sustainable development fee of $200 per day for travellers, of which a part goes toward environmental protection (Raawat, Sahu, Singh and Mishra, 2022). So, my review work aims to identify issues of sustainability through some case studies and planning for sustainable development related to tourism.

2. Issues of Sustainability/Case Study

In case of sustainability issues in hill towns of India the problems or issues have been identified are as follows:

According to Pushpalata Garg and Harsimran Kaur.

2.1 *Slope Instability*

Himalayan hill towns like Nainital faces the most important problem of Hill instability in terms of sustainability. The stability of the town is being affected by civic structures, different types of discontinuities and neotectonic activity. Hill slopes stability are disturbed by the natural factors like area gradient, intrinsic geologic structure and lithology, hydrology as well as cloudburst, heavy rainfall and seismic activities and the human activities like unplanned construction or development, inefficient drainage, accelerated soil erosion, slope failure, landslides, cutting and filling of slopes for road and constructions.

2.2 *Disturbance in Natural Drainage Pattern*

Drainage, which plays a vital role for the stability of hill slopes have changed for unplanned development of buildings, cuttings of hills leading to flash floods, water logging, landslides, soil erosions. Constructed wall retaining without sufficient weeping holes affects natural drainage system. Cutting of slopes generates huge amount of debris which also affects stability of slopes.

2.3 *Inaccessibility*

In mountain areas steep slope, higher altitude, terrain conditions, seasonal hazards lead to less economic growth and inconvenience. To combat this road construction are taken into consideration. For the natural hill terrain linear pattern of development occurs and the new residential areas are being developed away from the central areas which results in longer distance to access the town centres. Commercial activities carried out along the roads causes traffic bottleneck which puts enormous pressure on road network.

2.4 *Housing, Infrastructure and Community Facilities*

To fulfil the need of tourist, infrastructural and community facilities which are essential creates pressure on existing infrastructure facilities like water supply, sewage collection and disposal. Most of the hill towns are facing the problem of poor water quality and shortage of water supply. In the public places garbage can be seen littered over the roads and other areas. Furthermore, no effort to recycle the wastage causes the blockage of drain, visual pollution, air pollution leading to an unhealthy condition. Health facilities are also inadequate in most of the hill areas and if it is available in some areas the emergency facility is absent.

2.5 *Tourism and Heritage sites Preservation*

Himalayan tourist spots are mainly known for pilgrimage tourism and sightseeing. Other activities like trekking, mountaineering, winter sports are also the prime attraction for some tourist. Kedarnath, Badrinath, Gangotri, Yamunatri are some important pilgrimage site in Himalayan region and Mussoorie, Rishikesh, Nainital, Almora, Ranikhet etc. are some other important tourist spots which are very popular. Government's aim to promote tourism and socio economic growth has raised the influx of tourist. But the lack of proper regulatory mechanism and management for controlling the tourist are causing disturbances in ecosystem. Carrying capacities which is very important for any ecosystem or area are also being compromised.

There are many valuable natural heritage sites in hill areas. The pressure of extensive tourism is damaging the sites or leading to the abolition of these sites. Unauthorized encroachment is another reason in destroying the important public spaces and heritage sites.

Pallavi Latkar in "Spatial Planning Concepts for The Sustainable Development of Hill Stations" mentioned.

Matheran Malangad ridge of Matheran hill area of Mumbai receives rainfall up to 2500–3500 mm per year. The western slope originating rivers drain into Arabian sea through Panvel creek which is the major source of water to all farm land and the eastern slope which forms the catchment of Ulhas river finally joins the Arabian sea. Catchment of Dhavir river is formed by the southern part. Boundary of Matheran Malan gad region, Patal ganga river is the source of water supply of to Navi Mumbai. So the change in vegetation and forest cover which is the principal character of this area will affect the water supply.

At present for the increased tourist pressure formation of recreational areas, landscape gardening, paving intensive use of forested area the area is vulnerable to destruction and degradation.

2.6 *Carrying Capacities*

Hill areas possess lower carrying capacities but are now densely populated with multi-storied buildings. The increased pressure of tourism disrupting the carrying capacity leading to stress on land area and ecological sensitiveness (D'souza and Pandia, 2020).

3. Practices and Policies for Sustainable Development

According to the article published in "Vernacular practices: as a basis for formulating building regulations for hill areas" by Ashwani Kumar and Pushpalata, 2013

For the planning and design of new buildings traditional or vernacular settlements characteristics is important.

3.1 *Ground Coverage*

Traditional or Vernacular buildings have small footprints and low built to open ratio in comparison to the contemporary buildings in hilly areas. This can minimise the impact of new development. In vernacular building the open space between buildings can be used for growing vegetation to reduce the detrimental impact of land stress.

3.2 *Earth Quake Resistant Constructions and Safety Regulations*

In hill regions in planning and designing of buildings safety against natural calamities is most serious issue. Suitable vernacular practices can be applied for the construction and design of earthquake resistant buildings. Materials used in traditional building can be made fire resistant and more durable as witnessed in Pehalgam hotel Srinagar. Dhajji wall, kath kuni, koti - banal, wooden buildings proved good during previous earthquake (Rautela and Joshi, 2008). Locally available renewable materials along with new construction technology should be made compulsory through building regulations.

3.3 *Slope Stabilization and Protection*

In contemporary practices concrete retaining walls used to protect slope affect the aesthetic value. Natural materials and modern technique in the protection of slope will protect the aesthetic value and will look better. For the stabilisation and protection of slopes materials like stone, bamboo, tree branches, thatch, pine leaves like natural materials which are already used in some area can be used in place of contemporary practices where concrete walls are used for the retaining of slopes for the improvement of visual quality.

3.4 *Aesthetic and Façade Design Regulations*

Modern buildings have facades made up of contemporary materials look dull and appear as visual blight in magnificent hill settings (Pushpalata and Kumar, 2009). Traditional hill settlements carrying building facades built with natural elements, decorative treatment can be adopted to improve aesthetic value. Building regulations need to modified to use traditional forms, pattern and decorative elements.

3.5 *Space Standard and Norms*

In the National Building Code 2005 new building designing and formulation regulation in hill settlements, space standard and norms are specified but those are not conductive in hill regions for the different geo-environment characteristics of hill areas. In case of vernacular buildings floor to ceiling height varies from 2.40m to 2.70m, door height is considered as 1.80m above floor level whereas in contemporary buildings floor to ceiling height is usually 3.0m and door height is 2.10m. In case of window to floor area ratio existing norms is higher than the traditional system. Space area norms of traditional building forms should be considered in hill areas.

3.6 *Site Selection*

In site selection also the basis should be the traditional settlements system for the new constructions. To have adequate solar exposure new development should be in southern slope and on leeward side for the protection from cold winds. New development must be developed on stable ground and flatter terrain to become less prone to the hill area hazards like landslide and cloudburst. Proximity of surface water source has to be considered also.

3.7 *Minimal Disturbance to Natural Environment and Contextual Development*

Constructions should be eco-friendly to minimise the disturbance on environment. Kapoor and Bansal (2023) suggested

3.8 *Geo-design based Process*

Geographic information system help in providing ecological map area. For the development in hill area site understanding, site analysis and site synthesis were the main three stages for the planning in traditional system. To design properly proposed geodesign based process will fill the gap found in Creative Problem Solving (CPS) based process. Active stakeholders input and evaluation are also included in the mentioned process. Three cycles of the process; delineate the planning context, define the planning method, and execute the defined method are based on conventional planning and will have positive impact on the site or environment.

"A study on best practices in sustainable tourism in Sikkim" by Dipankar Karmakar (2022) suggested

3.9 *Eco-tourism*

In Sikkim Eco tourism was started in the year 1995–96 with trainings, awareness, changed regulations to adapt to the mountain terrains. The involvement of village tourism activities has enhanced the concept of ecotourism. Sikkim Ecotourism Policy (2011) has provided the policy guidelines to all the stakeholders. The aim of ecotourism is to conserve the nature, cultural revival, economic development and diversification. So if the fundamental principles; nature friendly, ecologically sustainable, environmentally educative, economically beneficial to the local people are implemented properly then the sustainability issues of tourism would be solved.

According to Jit Kumar Gupta (2022) in "Sustainable Development of Hill Areas- Issues and Options":

- European and Swiss Model
- Regional approach
- Development without destructions

Jit kumar Gupta (2023) in "Leveraging Tourism for Promoting Sustainable Development of Hill states":

- Promoting sustainable, Responsible and Inclusive tourism
- Promoting Digitalization
- Promoting Ek Bharat Shrestha Bharat
- Green Tourism (National Tourism Policy, 2022)

4. Conclusion

Sustainable tourism creates balance between environmental, economic and socio cultural aspects of tourism. To achieve this goal constant support, monitoring system, quality leadership and proper govt. policies are important. The ecosystem characteristics should be given importance to the planners to mitigate the damage we have already done. Participation of legitimate stake holders in the sustainable development model for hill stations is very important. Safety measures against natural calamities should be considered in the new development. Formation of building regulations according to the topography of the area and its environmental hazards should be adopted. Vernacular practices should be adopted and formulated in building regulations. As the hill areas have a fragile ecology so the duty of us should be to maintain the environment and ecological balance.

References

[1] Bhardwaj, A. and Gupta, A. (2022) Tourism Sustainability in Hilly Regions—A Review for Shimla.

[2] Bhutia, S. (2015). Sustainable Tourism development in Darjeeling Hills of West Bengal, India: Issues and Challenges.

[3] Chakraborty, P. and Ghosal S. (2024) Environment Development: An eco-social exploration in mountains through stakeholders' perspective.

[4] Gupta, J.K. (2022). Promoting Sustainable Development of Hill Areas- Issues and Options Gupta J K. (2023). Leveraging Tourism for

promoting Sustainable development of Hill States Garg P and Kaur H. (2020). Sustainability Issues in Context of Indian Hill Towns,

[5] Kapoor, N. and Bansal, V.K. (2023). Planning at Site-Level in Hill Regions Using Geo design-Based Approach,

[6] Karmakar, D. (2022) A study on Best Practices in Sustainable Tourism in Sikkim,

[7] Kumar, A and Pushpalata (2013). Vernacular practices: as a basis for formulating building regulations for hill areas,

[8] Latkar, P. Spatial Planning Concepts for the Sustainable Development of Hill Stations,

[9] Rawat, K.S., Sahu, S.R., Singh, S.K. and Mishra, A.K. (2022). Cloudburst analysis in the district, Himalayan Region, 2021,

[10] Saraswati and Ram (2013). Hill Tourism and Sustainable development of the Destinations: A situation analysis of Kumaon Region of Uttarakhand.

SECTION-E

Environmental Quality and Sustainable Development

Household Air Pollution and Its Impact on Health: Problem and Solution

Pasang Tshering Dukpa[1] and Neetu Chettri

ABSTRACT: Household air pollution (HAP) refers to indoor air contamination resulting from cooking, heating, lighting, and other household activities. It is a pressing global health issue that disproportionately affects populations in low- and middle-income countries, particularly rural areas. HAP arises from the Combustion Combustion of solid fuels such as biomass (wood, crop residues, dung), coal, and kerosene for cooking, heating, and lighting purposes in poorly ventilated indoor environments. As a result, indoor air quality is often compromised, exposing individuals to a complex mixture of pollutants that can profoundly affect health. Exposure to HAP has been linked to a wide range of adverse health outcomes, including acute respiratory infections, chronic obstructive pulmonary disease (COPD), lung cancer, cardiovascular diseases, adverse pregnancy outcomes, and low birth weight.

Keywords: Household Air Pollution, Indoor Air Quality, Health Impacts, Respiratory Diseases, Cardiovascular Diseases, Adverse Pregnancy Outcomes, Low Birth Weight.

1. Introduction

Indoor air pollution (also known as household air pollution) is a condition where the concentration of air pollutants increases in and around a building or structure, high enough to harm people and the ecosystem in general.

[1] Assistant Professor, Department of Physiology, Acharya Brojendra Nath Seal College, Cooch Behar–736101. E-mail: pasangmac@gmail.com

[2] Assistant Professor, Department of Education, Acharya Brojendra Nath Seal College, Cooch Behar-736101. E-mail: nchettri1823@gmail.com

Air pollution can originate indoors. Activities such as cooking, heating and lighting using obscure fuels such as firewood, coal, animal dung and kerosene [1]. The incomplete Combustion Combustion of these fuels produces carbon monoxide, nitrogen oxides and sulfur oxides [2]. Other indoor activities, such as the use of pesticides, insecticides, air conditioners and cigarette smoke, can also contribute to a large proportion of indoor particulate matter [3]. Particulate matter is a complex mixture of dust, soot, smoke and airborne liquid droplets, which can be inhaled in small amounts. Exposure to indoor air pollutants causes sensitive people to inhale these pollutants and activate up to 15 sensory functions. Nerve receptors in the respiratory system result in a reflex mechanism [4]. Pollutants with a diameter of fewer than 5 micrometres can enter the alveoli, crossing the physiological and mechanical barriers of the respiratory tract [5]. When inhaled and\distal airway receptors, pollutants cause acute respiratory infection\most commonly pneumonia in young children and aggravate asthma, chronic\lung diseases and cancer in adults [6].

Although air pollution is becoming a global problem affecting Overall sectors of the world's population, indoor air pollution is particularly dangerous for the health of poor and developing countries [7]. Subpopulation groups such as infants, women, the elderly, people with chronic illnesses, and urban dwellers who spend much of their time indoors are at greater risk than the general population [8].

2. Status of Household Air Pollution in India

The main sources of household air pollution are Combustion Combustion, building materials and bioaerosols.[9] Although radon, asbestos, pesticides, heavy metals, volatile organic compounds and environmental tobacco smoke are important household air pollutants in developed countries, biomass fuel from combustion products is increasing. Indoor air pollution is most common in developing countries. Of the 0.2 billion people in India who use fuel for cooking, 49% use firewood; 8.9% cow dung cake; 1.5% coal, lignite or charcoal; 2.9% kerosene; 28.6% liquefied petroleum gas (LPG); 0.1% electricity; 0.4% biogas; and 0.5% other resources. [10] The products of incomplete combustion combustion of biomass fuels include suspended particles, carbon oxide, polyaromatic hydrocarbons, polyorganic substances, formaldehyde, etc., which have harmful effects on health. Sulfur, arsenic and fluoride oxides are produced when coal is burned. Additives such as aldehydes and volatile and semi-volatile organic substances are produced from resins, waxes, polishing materials, cosmetics and binders. Finally, biological pollutants such as dust mites, moulds, pollen and pathogens from standing water, mattresses, carpets and humidifiers excessively pollute indoor air.[11]

A study on particulate matter inhalation found that particulate matter concentrations ranged from 500 to 2, 000 mg/m^3 in homes during the cooking of the used biomass. Average 24-hour exposure ranged between 82 ± 39 mg/m3 for those using clean fuel and 231 ± 109 mg/m^3 for those using biofuel for cooking. [12] Carbon monoxide levels in indoor air from manure, wood, coal, kerosene, and LPG are 144, respectively. 156, 94, 108 and 14 mg/m3. Indoor total polyaromatic hydrocarbons from manure, wood, coal, kerosene and LPG were 3.56, 2.01, 0.55, 0.23 and 0.13 mg/m^3 air. [13] Average levels of formaldehyde were 670, 652, 109, 812 and 109 mg/m^3. for fertilizer, wood, coal, kerosene and LPG.[14]

3. Effects of Household Air Pollution on Health

An estimated 2 million premature deaths occur annually as a result of indoor air pollution; 44% of these deaths are attributable to pneumonia, 54% to chronic obstructive pulmonary disease (COPD), and 2% to lung cancer. [15] Since women and younger children spend the most time at home, they are the most affected populations. [15] Respiratory disorders, such as acute respiratory tract infections [16] and COPD, [17] poor prenatal outcomes, such as low birth weight [18], stillbirths, and cancers of the nasopharynx, larynx, and lung [19], and leukaemia are the morbidities linked to indoor air pollution. Formaldehyde has a variety of detrimental impacts on health, including bronchitis, acute irritation, decreased vital capacity, and carcinogenicity via lung cancer and leukaemia.[20, 21]

Research on the impact of wood smoke on cardiovascular health is still in its early stages of development. According to a Guatemalan study, using an upgraded chimney stove to reduce wood smoke exposure reduced blood pressure systolic by 3.7 mmHg (95% confidence interval (CI): –8.1, 0.6) and diastolic by 3.0 mmHg (95%

CI: –5.7, –0.4) [22]. In a different study, ST-segment depression was found to have decreased following stove intervention (odds ratio (OR) 0.26, 95% confidence interval (CI): 0.08, 0.90).[23]

Household air pollutants have a potentially harmful effect on one's health. [24] Particulates lead to exacerbations of COPD and cause chronic bronchitis, respiratory infections, and other conditions. Sulfur dioxide and nitrogen dioxide aggravate asthma and causes wheezing. Nitrogen dioxide also impairs lung function and increases the risk of respiratory infections. Another etiological role of sulfur dioxide is in the aggravation of cardiovascular disease and COPD. Exposure to carbon monoxide raises the chance of adverse perinatal outcomes, such as low birth weight and perinatal mortality. Biomass smoke, particularly metal ions and polycyclic aromatics contributes to cataract formation. Polycyclic aromatic hydrocarbons cause malignancies in the larynx, nasopharynx, mouth, and lungs.[24]

Numerous Indian studies have documented the detrimental consequences of indoor air pollution. In an extensive case-control analysis, solid-fuel consumption significantly increased the number of child deaths between the ages of one and four years, the girl child mortality was more than boy child caused by exposure to solid fuel (prevalence ratio for boys: 1.30, 95% CI: 1.08–1.56; for girls: 1.33, 95% CI: 1.12–1.58). The usage of solid fuel was also linked to nonfatal pneumonia (prevalence ratio 1.94; 95% CI: 1.13–3.33) and 1.54 in boys and 1.35 in girls.[25] Even after adjusting for other risk variables, the use of fuel other than LPG was substantially linked to acute lower respiratory tract infections (adjusted OR = 4·73, 95% CI: 1.67–13.45). Among children with acute lower respiratory infections, pneumonia accounted for 24.8%, and severe pneumonia accounted for 45.5%.[26]

In Ladakh, due to harsh cold and limited ventilation, inmates are exposed to high concentrations of soot, resulting in morbidities similar to pneumoconiosis.[27, 28] Using biomass fuel resulted in a longer nasal mucociliary clearance time (765.8 ± 378.16 s) compared to clean fuel users (545.4 ± 215.55 s) and a lower peak expiratory flow rate (319.3 l/min) compared to clean fuel users (371.7 l/min).[29] There was a significant correlation seen between the usage of biomass as cooking fuel and a high prevalence of active tuberculosis (OR = 3.56,

95% CI: 2.82–4.50). Even after examining the prevalence individually for men (OR = 2.46) and women (OR = 2.74), as well as for urban (OR = 2.29) and rural areas (OR = 2.65), it remained high and significant for individuals using biomass as cooking fuel. Cooking smoke has been accountable for 51% of the prevalence of active TB in those aged 20 and older. [30]

A study on older individuals (≥60 years) found that households utilizing biomass fuels had a greater prevalence of asthma compared to those using cleaner fuels (OR = 1.59; 95% CI: 1.30–1.94). Cooking smoke's effect on asthma was found to be more in women compared to men (OR = 1.83; 95% CI: 1.32–2.53). [31] The prevalence of COPD was found to be greater among biomass fuel users than among clean fuel users, according to study results from southern India (OR: 1.24; 95% CI: 0.36–6.64). Additionally, it was discovered that women who spent more than two hours a day cooking had a prevalence that was twice as high. [32]

Carcinogens such as formaldehyde and polyaromatic hydrocarbons are present in biomass fuels. According to a case-control study on women diagnosed with lung cancer, exposure to biomass fuels is another factor that contributes to the development of lung cancer in addition to tobacco use. Exposure to biomass fuel was linked to an increased risk of lung cancer in nonsmoking women (OR 3.04, 95% CI: 1.1–8.38). Even when other variables like smoking and passive smoking were taken into account, there was still a substantial correlation between lung cancer and biomass fuel exposure. [33]

4. Control Measures

Studies conducted in India have provided sufficient evidence that household air pollution is a cause of rising morbidity and mortality, indicating the need for immediate intervention. Financial, cultural, and societal considerations all play a role in how people make decisions regarding cooking and energy.[34] The following is a list of suggested measures that could be adopted to address the threat of indoor air pollution:

4.1 *Public Awareness*

Raising people's knowledge of the problem and the grave danger indoor air pollution poses to their health and welfare is one of the most crucial measures in the prevention of indoor air pollution. Education would benefit an individual in discovering various approaches to lower exposure through improved kitchen management at home. In addition, people should be made aware of the benefits of switching from direct combustion of biomass fuel to cleaner alternative energy sources. Politicians, bureaucrats, and the general public must all be involved in order to guarantee their commitment and raise public knowledge of the detrimental impacts of indoor air pollution on health.

4.2 *Modification in the Pattern of Fuel Use*

The utilization of fuel is contingent upon an individual's habits, accessibility, and, primarily, cost. Currently, the majority of low-income families rely solely on direct Combustion Combustion of biomass fuels for their cooking needs because it is the cheapest and most convenient option available to them; however, this could be changed by encouraging the use of cleaner energy sources such as gobar gas, which uses cow dung to produce gas for cooking.

3.3 *Changes in the Design of the Cooking Stove*

Stoves that are fuel-efficient, smokeless, and provide an exit (such as a chimney) for interior pollutants should replace conventional, smoky, and leaky cooking stoves. One excellent example is the one created by the Ministry of New and Renewable Energy's National Biomass Cookstoves Initiative as part of a Special Project on Cookstoves in 2009–2010. The main goal of this initiative was to increase the availability of clean and efficient energy for the nation's poorer and energy-deficient regions.[35]

3.4 *Improving Ventilation*

Proper ventilation should be considered while building a home; in cases where ventilation is inadequate, strategies such as installing a window above the stove and creating cross ventilation through doors should be considered.

3.5 *Global Initiative and Intersectoral Coordination*

Controlling household air pollution requires coordinated efforts from several sectors that deal with housing, rural development, energy, health, and the environment.

4. Conclusion

Despite the fact that there is evidence linking India's rising levels of household air pollution to higher rates of morbidity and mortality, more research is still required to determine the exposure levels of indoor pollutants and to bolster the data supporting their links to conditions like cancer, tuberculosis, cataracts, asthma, and cardiovascular health. Additionally, the need of the hour is for efficient interventions, ranging from education, altering fuel patterns, and properly designed homes and stoves to a dedicated and determined intersectoral collaboration towards the promotion of public health

References

[1] C.C. Attribution-noncommercialsharealike and C.C. By-nc-sa. Compendium of WHO and other UN guidance on health and environment Chapter 2. Air pollution, Vol. 2022, pp. 0–28, 2022.

[2] Colome & Samet. Indoor Air Pollution: An Introduction for Health Professionals. 1995.

[3] Salvador, S. and Salvador, E. Overview of Particle Air Pollution Air Quality Communication Workshop. San Salvador. 2012.

[4] Van Tran, V., Park, D. and Lee, Y. Indoor Air Pollution, Related Human Diseases, and Recent Trends in the Control and Improvement of Indoor Air Quality. *International Journal of Environmental Research and Public Health*. 2020. pp. 1–27. DOI: 10.3390/ijerph17082927

[5] Sheet, F.. Criteria Pollutants: Particulate Matter (PM 2.5/PM 10). 2012:3–5.

[6] Repace, J.L., Ott, W.R., Klepeis, N.E. Indoor air pollution from cigar smoke. Smoking and Tobacco ControlMonograph No. 9. 1996;i(9).

[7] Krupnova, T.G. *et al.* Elemental Composition of PM 2. 5 and PM 10 and Health Risks Assessment in the Industrial Districts of Chelyabinsk. Russia: South Ural Region; 2021.

[8] Warwick, H. and Doig, A. Smoke—the Killer in the Kitchen: Indoor Air Pollution in Developing Countries. *Journal of children.*

[9] Indoor air pollution in India—a major environmental and public health concern. *ICMR Bulletin 2001*; 31:1–9. Available from: http://www.icmr.nic.in/bumay01.pdf [Last accessed on 2013 Mar 10].

[10] Houselisting and Housing Census Data Highlights—2011. Available from: http://www.censusindia.gov.in/2011census/hlo/ hlo_highlights.html [Last accessed on 2013 Mar 16].

[11] Zhang, J., Smith, K.R. Indoor air pollution: A global health concern. Br Med Bull 2003; 68: 209–25.

[12] Balakrishnan, K., Sankar, S., Parikh, J., Padmavathi, R., Srividya, K., Venugopal, V., *et al.* Daily average exposures to respirable particulate matter from combustion of biomass fuels in rural households of southern India. *Environ Health Perspect* 2002; 110:1069–75.

[13] Patel, T.S. and Aryan, C.V. Indoor air quality: Problems and perspectives. In: Shukla PR, editor. Energy Strategies and Greenhouse Gas Mitigation. 1st ed. New Delhi: Allied Publishers Limited; 1997, p. 72.

[14] Raiyani, C.V., Jana, J.P., Desai, N.M., Shah, S.H., Shah, P.G. and Kashyap, S.K. Assessment of indoor exposure to polycyclic aromatic hydrocarbons for urban poor using various types of cooking fuels. Bull *Environ Contam Toxicol,* 1993; 50:757–63.

[15] Indoor air pollution and health. Available from http://www.who.int/mediacentre/factsheets/fs292/en [Last accessed on 2013Mar 20].

[16] Dherani, M., Pope, D., Mascarenhas, M., Smith, K.R., Weber, M. and Bruce, N. Indoor air pollution from unprocessed solid fuel use and pneumonia risk in children aged under five years: A systematic review and meta-analysis. *Bull World Health Organ*, 2008; 86: 390–8C.

[17] Kurmi, O.P., Semple, S., Simkhada, P., Smith, W.C. and Ayres, J.G. COPD and chronic bronchitis risk of indoor air pollution from solid fuel: A systematic review and meta-analysis. Thorax 2010; 65: 221–8.

[18] Pope, D.P., Mishra, V., Thompson, L., Siddiqui, A.R., Rehfuess, E.A., Weber, M., *et al.* Risk of low birth weight and stillbirth associated with indoor air pollution from solid fuel use in developing countries. *Epidemiol Rev 2010*; 32:70–81.

[19] Sapkota, A., Gajalakshmi, V., Jetly, D.H., Roychowdhury, S., Dikshit, R.P., Brennan, P., *et al.* Indoor air pollution from solid fuels and risk of hypopharyngeal/laryngeal and lung cancers: A multicentric case control study from India. *Int J Epidemiol 2008*; 37: 321–8.

[20] Blair A, Saracci R, Stewart PA, Hayes RB, Shy C. Epidemiologic evidence of the relationship between formaldehyde exposure and cancer. *Scand J Work Environ Health* 1990; 16: 381–93.

[21] Acheson, E.D., Barnes, H.R., Gardner, M.J., Osmond, C., Pannet, B., Taylor, C.P.. Formaldehyde process workers and lung cancer. Lancet 1984;1: 1066–7.

[22] McCracken, J.P., Smith, K.R., Díaz, A., Mittleman, M.A. and Schwartz, J. Chimney stove intervention to reduce long-term wood smoke exposure lowers blood pressure among Guatemalan women. *Environ Health Perspect* 2007; 115: 996–1001.

[23] McCracken, J.P., Smith, K.R., Stone, P., Díaz, A., Arana, B. and Schwartz, J. Intervention to lower household wood smoke exposure in Guatemala reduces ST-segment depression on electrocardiograms. *Environ Health Perspect* 2011; 119: 1562–8.

[24] Bruce, N., Perez-Padilla, R. and Albalak, R. Indoor air pollution in developing countries: A major environmental and public health challenge. *Bull World Health Organ* 2000;78: 1078 92.

[25] Bassani, D.G., Jha, P., Dhingra, N. and Kumar, R.. Child mortality fromsolid-fuel use in India: A nationally-representative case-control study. *BMC Public Health 2010*; 10: 491.

[26] Ramesh Bhat, Y., Manjunath, N., Sanjay, D. and Dhanya, Y. Association of indoor air pollution with acute lower respiratory tract infections in children under 5 years of age. *Paediatr Int Child Health* 2012;32:132–5.

[27] Norboo, T., Yahya, M., Bruce, N.G., Heady, J.A. and Ball, K.P. Domestic pollution and respiratory illness in a Himalayan village. *Int J Epidemiol* 1991; 20: 749–57.

[28] Norboo, T., Angchuk, P.T., Yahya, M., Kamat, S.R., Pooley, F.D., Corrin, B., *et al.* Silicosis in a Himalayan village population: Role of environmental dust. Thorax 1991; 46: 341–3.

[29] Priscilla, J., Padmavathi, R., Ghosh, S., Paul, P., Ramadoss, S., Balakrishnan, K., *et al.* Evaluation of mucociliary clearance among women using biomass and clean fuel in a periurban area of Chennai: A preliminary study. *Lung India 2011*; 28:30–3.

[30] Mishra, V.K., Retherford, R.D. and Smith, K.R. Biomass cooking fuels and prevalence of tuberculosis in India. *Int J Infect Dis 1999;* 3:119–29.

[31] Mishra, V. Effect of indoor air pollution from biomass combustion on prevalence of asthma in the elderly. *Environ Health Perspect 2003;* 111:71–8.

[32] Johnson, P., Balakrishnan, K., Ramaswamy, P., Ghosh, S., Sadhasivam, M., Abirami, O., *et al.* Prevalence of chronic obstructive pulmonary disease in rural women of Tamilnadu: Implications for refining disease burden assessments attributable to household biomass combustion. *Global Health Action 2011;* 4:7226.

[33] Behera, D., Balamugesh, T. Indoor air pollution as a risk factor for lung cancer in women. *J Assoc Physicians India* 2005; 53:190–2.

[34] Global Alliance for Clean Cookstoves. Available from: http://www.cleancookstoves.org/resources/reports-andresearch/? country=IN [Last accessed on 2013 Apr 11].

[35] National Biomass Cookstoves Programme (NBCP). Ministry of New and Renewable Energy. Available from: http://mnre.gov.in/schemes/decentralizedsystems/national-biomass-cookstovesinitiative/ [Last accessed on 2013 Apr 11].

Effect of Arsenic Polluted Environment of South 24 Parganas on the Human Systems of Local Residents

Arindam Bhattacharyya[1]

ABSTRACT: Arsenic is the major environmental pollutant whose exposure occurs through environmental, occupational & medicinal sources. The contaminated drinking water is the main source of exposure. Such exposure for a longer period leads to ill effect on several organ systems of the human body. The main affected countries of this arsenic exposure are India, Bangladesh, China, Taiwan, Thailand, Chile, Argentina & Romania. In India West Bengal is the worst affected state. The district South 24 Parganas of West Bengal is affected most by the arsenic exposure.Different studies revealed that the extent of arsenic contamination in the ground water of South 24 parganas is very much alarming. Nearly 12 blocks of the district are worst affected due to its high level of arsenic content in ground water. Water samples collected from tube wells in the affected places contained arsenic above the normal level i.e. 10 microgram per litter which is specified by World Health Organization.

Keywords: *Arsenic, Arsenic Pollution, Arsenicosis, Arsenic Poisoning, Hyperkeratosis, Hyper Pigmentation, Ground Water.*

1. Introduction

Arsenic is a naturally occurring semi-metallic element widely distributed in the Earth's Crust. It is not a metal, but it has some of the properties of a metal, so arsenic is a metalloid. Arsenic can exist in many different chemical forms in combination with other elements. There are two general forms of arsenic: organic & inorganic. Inorganic

---

[1] Department of Physiology, Sonarpur Mahavidyalaya.
E-mail: arindambhattacharya1971@gmail.com

arsenic exists in four primary chemical forms, which are known as valency or oxidation states. Arsenic occurs in large quantities in the earth's crust. It is present in multiple minerals but occurs in trace quantities in rocks, water, soil & air. Nearly 33% of atmospheric arsenic is derived from natural sources like volcanoes & the remaining 67% occurs through artificial sources. High levels of arsenic can be found in drinking water, collected from deeply drilled wells, and a natural phenomenon where groundwater has been contaminated by minerals dissolving from rocks and soils. The major industrial processes that cause anthropogenic arsenic contamination of air, soils and water in the environment are the mining & smelting of non-ferrous metals and the burning of fossil fuels. Pesticides containing arsenic have also contaminated large areas of agricultural land. Among Himalayan Rivers, the Ganga river system is well known for its erosive activities throughout the evolution of the Himalayas. It forms alluvial deposition around its course. The finding of elevated levels of arsenic in the Gangetic belt is supported by the river's erosive and alluvial-forming nature. Arsenic naturally occurs in the sediments all over Asia and is a problem in areas dominated by Holocene & organic-rich sediments. Human exposure to elevated levels of inorganic arsenic occurs mainly through the consumption of arsenic-contaminated groundwater, food prepared with this contaminated water and food crops irrigated with high arsenic water resources. According to the provisional guidelines of the WHO, in view of scientific uncertainties surrounding the risk assessment for arsenic carcinogenicity, arsenic in drinking water up to the level of 10 micrograms per litter is decided to be a permissible limit.

It is estimated that, in the entire world, about 300 million populations are exposed to arsenic poisoning in groundwater. The most significant number of people in the world affected by chronic arsenic toxicity is due to the drinking of arsenic-contaminated groundwater in Bangladesh, India & China. Inorganic arsenic is naturally present at high levels in the groundwater of a number of countries, such as Argentina, Chile, Mexico, the United States of America, China, India and Bangladesh. In Bangladesh, approximately half of the total population is at risk of drinking arsenic-contaminated water from tubewells and groundwater hand pumps. Approximately higher levels of arsenic contamination in the drinking water from several 100 ppb to over 1 ppm have been observed in several countries like Argentina, Bangladesh, Chile, India, Mexico, Thailand & Taiwan. Arsenic contamination was first reported in India in Punjab, Haryana, Himachal Pradesh & Uttar Pradesh. Thereafter, in 1984, groundwater arsenic contamination was identified in the lower Ganga plain of West Bengal. Furthermore, arsenic groundwater contamination was reported in Bangladesh, the lower plain area (Terai) of Nepal, Bihar (middle Ganga plain), Uttar Pradesh (Lying in the middle & upper Ganga plain), Jharkhand & Assam.There are more than 25% of domestic wells presented in alluvial aquifers of West Bengal carry arsenic in drinking water beyond the permissible limit of WHO, 1993, 2017 (0.01 mg/L). West Bengal lies within the Ganga-Brahmaputra delta basin and has high contamination of arsenic (<0.05 mg/ml), mainly in groundwater. West Bengal can be divided into three arsenic-prone zones, i.e. highly affected areas cover the eastern side of the Bhagirathi River, mildly affected areas include the northern part of the Bhagirthi River, and the Unaffected region carries the western part of the state.In India, Arsenic concentration in groundwater was first reported in West Bengal in 1978, and it includes 79 blocks in 8 districts among 26 districts where arsenic concentration in groundwater exceeded 50 micrograms/L. According to Das, 2015, this problem is expanding rapidly, and in 2006, almost 3235 villages were affected, including North 24 Parganas, South 24 Parganas, Nadia Murshidabad& Burdwan, Howrah & Hooghly and Malda districts. The severely affected districts are Murshidabad, Malda, Nadia, North & Soiuth 24 Parganas, Burdwan, Howrah & Hooghly. The values of arsenic-contaminated groundwater of the affected districts are tabulated here.

Districts	*Permissible Limit (BSI) Arsenic in mg/L*
South 24 Parganas	0.06–3.20
North 24 Parganas	0.06–1.28
Maldah	0.05–1.434
Nadia	0.05–1.00
Murshidabad	0.05–0.90

Districts	*Permissible Limit (BSI) Arsenic in mg/L*
Burdwan	0.10–0.50
Howrah	0.09
Hooghly	0.6

2. Methodology

To identify the situation of South 24 Pargana district, the Arsenic conditions of different parts of South 24 Pargana district are considered. Specifically, the groundwater conditions of different parts of South 24 Pargana district, specifically the different parts of Baruipur and Sonarpur blocks, are considered. The groundwater Arsenic levels are measured in different parts of these two blocks and try to identify the main health problems.

3. Result

There are multiple studies organized by different institutions that clearly show the dangerous condition of South 24 parganas due to arsenic exposure. My Study clearly revealed that the extent of arsenic contamination in the groundwater of South 24 Parganas is very much alarming. Nearly 12 blocks of the district are worst affected due to its high level of arsenic content in groundwater. Water samples collected from tube wells in the affected places contained arsenic above the average level, i.e. 10 micrograms per litre, which WHO specifies. The main problem related to arsenic exposure is the use of deep tube wells for water supply in the Ganges delta, causing serious arsenic poisoning to the maximum number of people. Baruipur & Sonarpur block of South 24 Parganas are worst affected, where the arsenic concentration is very high in these two blocks. Arsenic concentration in tube wells was divided into 6 types. The first two divisions are safe for drinking purposes, and the other four are above the permissible limit and unsafe for human consumption. In Baruipur, 88 per cent and Sonarpur, almost 97% of tube wells contain water that is not harmful to the human body, according to WHO & BIS. Baruipur and Sonarpur contain arsenic concentrations of more than 1 mg/L. In Baruipur, the maximum concentration is 256 times and in Sonarpur it is 272 times greater than the permissible limit of WHO. The following table illustrates the actual situation.

Distribution of Arsenic Concentration in Baruipur & Sonarpur Block

Name of the Blocks	*Percent of Tube Wells having Arsenic Concentration in mg/L*						*Maximum Arsenic Concentration*
	0	0.01–0.05	0.06–0.1	0.11–0.5	0.5–1.00	1.1–3.00	
Baruipur	80.78	7.34	2.18	8.35	1.17	0.15	2.56
Sonarpur	48.9	47.73	1.29	0.38	0.25	1.12	2.72

Other than the Baruipur and Sonarpur block, Arsenic content of groundwater has been found to be beyond the permissible limit of 0.05 ppm in a number of localized patches in a sporadic manner in 7 blocks Bhangar I, Bhangar II, Jaynagar I, Bishnupur I & II, Magrahat II and Budge Budge II in this district. (ATSDR 2007)

3.1 *Health Effects on South 24 Parganas Districts Local Residents*

Sonarpur & Baruipur have been categorized as a highly arsenic-affected region where 0.3 mg/L of arsenic is found in many parts of the blocks (Chakraborti *et al.* 2009). Infants are exposed to arsenic when they start taking formula milk or semisolid food made up of arsenic-contaminated water. Physiology & behavioural patterns impact the exposure to arsenic in children. The symptoms of arsenic poisoning are more or less similar in the child & adult populations. skin lesions are considered the main diagnostic criteria for arsenicosis. Long-term consumption of arsenic-contaminated water can cause hyperkeratinization on the palms and feet, Keratinized warts, hyperpigmentation on skin, and numbness in hands and feet.

In an epidemiological study carried out in the district of south 24 Parganas, 493 (11.6%) out of 4216 participants exposed to arsenic were found to have chronic lung diseases. Many people in this district have arsenical skin lesions such as melanosis, leucomelanosis, keratosis, hyperkeratosis, dorsum, non-pitting oedema, gangrene, and skin cancer. More information is coming from this district where the arsenic patients have Cancer of the bladder & lungs.

4. Discussion

Arsenic has widespread effects on human systems. Multiple organs & systems are affected by arsenic. The effects of arsenic on Human systems are-The gastrointestinal systems are affected most due to arsenic exposure. The gastrointestinal effects of arsenic are generally the result of ingestion. GI effects are seen acutely after arsenic ingestion and less often after inhalation or dermal absorption. The main effects are extensive inflammation & necrosis of the mucosa and sub-mucosa of the stomach and intestine, which may occur and progress to perforation of the gut wall. Hemorrhagic gastroenteritis may develop with bloody diarrhoea. Acute arsenic toxicity may be associated with hepatic necrosis with elevated liver enzyme levels. Chronic arsenic ingestion may lead to cirrhotic portal hypertension (ATSDR 2007, Datta 1976). Chronic high level of arsenic exposure leads to hepatic angiosarcoma, a rare form of liver Cancer (Popper *et al.,* 1978; Zaldiver *et al.,* 1981; ATSDR 2007) Arsenic has great effects on the renal system. The systemic toxicity occurring in severe arsenic poisoning may include acute tubular necrosis with acute renal failure. Chronic renal insufficiency from cortical necrosis has also been reported. Glomerular damage can result in proteinuria. Arsenic gas is more nephrotoxic than arsenic. However, both can cause acute tubular necrosis (Giberson *et al.,* 1976). Both acute and chronic exposure to high levels of arsenic may result in a wide range of adverse cardiovascular effects. There is a minimal strength of association between chronic arsenic exposure and peripheral vascular disease, Hypertension and Cardiovascular disease (ARC 2004). Acute arsenic poisoning may cause both diffuse capillary leakage and cardiomyopathy, resulting in shock. This also causes hypotension due to vasodilation. Other reports of arsenic poisoning have resulted in peripheral vascular disease rather than congestive heart failure (Engel *et al.,* 1994). Hypertension has been reported with long-term exposure to arsenic (Chen *et al.,* 1995). Arsenic ingestion affects the cardio-vascular system, altering myocardial depolarization and causing cardiac arrhythmias and hypertension in some populations (Guha 2003).

Gangrene of the extremities, known as “Blackfoot disease”, has been reported with drinking arsenic-contaminated well water. Pathologically, Blackfoot disease was due to arteriosclerotic or thromboanginits obliterans. After the water supply was changed, the vascular & cardiovascular mortality reversed. (Pi *et al.,* 2005; Chang *et al.,* 2004) Persons with black foot disease also had a higher incidence of arsenic induced skin Cancers. Arsenic has great effects on Nervous system also. Arsenic may cause encephalopathy at high acute doses (72 mg AS/Kg/day) [Uede& Furukawa 2003; Vantroyen *et al.,* 2004, ATSDR 2007]. Arsenic poisoning can cause peripheral neuropathy. The lesion is a sensory-motor axonopathy. In high levels of arsenic exposures, the onset of neuropathy may occur after 7 to 14 days with intense-muscle cramps, muscle tenderness, numbness, paresthesia & spontaneous pain (Bleecker 2007). Sensory effects are also very evident, particularly painful dysesthesia that occurs earlier and may predominate in moderate poisoning. At the same time, ascending weakness and paralysis may be apparent in more severe poisoning.The dermal effects due to arsenic poisoning are the most significant. Pigment changes & palm plantar hyperkeratosis are characteristic of chronic arsenic exposure. Benign arsenical keratoses may progress to malignancy. Delayed effects of acute or chronic exposure may be seen as Mee's line in nails. The skin lesions occurring most frequently in arsenic-exposed humans are- Hyperkeratosis, Hyperpigmentation and skin cancer. Patchy hyperpigmentation may be found anywhere on the body due to chronic exposure to arsenic. This patchy hyper-pigmentation occurs particularly on the axillae, eyelids, Neck, groin, and nipples. In severe cases, the pigmentation extends broadly over the chest, back & abdomen. Pigment changes have been observed in populations consuming drinking water containing 400 ppb or more arsenic. Arsenical hyperkeratosis occurs in palms & soles.

Inhalation of high concentrations of arsenic compounds produces irritation of the respiratory mucosa. Lung cancers are also identified due to chronic arsenic exposure. Hematopoietic & Hematologic effects are also very significant in chronic & acute arsenic exposure. Bone marrow depression may result from acute or chronic arsenic intoxication. Anaemia and leucopenia are common in chronic arsenic toxicity and are often accompanied by thrombocytopenia & mild eosinophilia. This anaemia may be normocytic or macrocytic, and basophilic. According to NRC & Arc, there is a suggestive association between chronic arsenic exposure and immune suppression (NRC

2000; IARC 2004). Acute intoxication with arsenic gas can cause fulminant intravascular hemolysis.

Due to arsenic exposure, increased frequency of spontaneous abortions and congenital malformations are identified. It clearly shows that arsenic is a reproductive toxicant and a teratogen (Shalat 1996). So the, arsenic exposure has a great effect on the reproductive system.The carcinogenicity of arsenic in humans has been established. In humans, chronic arsenic ingestion may cause cancers of the bladder, kidney, Liver, Liver, Lung, Prostate & Skin (ATSDR 2007).

5. Conclusion

From the above discussion, it is quite clear that the groundwater contamination of arsenic in South 24 Parganas is very alarming and present in very dangerous conditions. This high arsenic-containing water intake causes multiple health problems in this district. So we should have to be aware of this growing problem in the South 24 Parganas. Installation of deep tube wells greater than 1000 feet to avoid arsenic-contaminated shallow aquifers where suitable arsenic-safe deep aquifers are available to produce water of acceptable quality for a water supply and installation of the arsenic treatment plant is not the only solution. Unnecessary boredom should be avoided, and local residents should spread awareness about the bad effects of arsenic-contaminated water. It is also an essential solution to this problem.

References

[1] Agency for Toxic Substances and Disease Registry (ATSDR) (2007) Report on 'Toxicological profile for Arsenic' published by U.S. Department of Health and Human Services, Public Health Services, Washington, DC, USA. https://www.atsdr.cdc.gov/toxprofiles/tp2.pdf, accessed on 12.09.2019

[2] Bhattacharya, P., Jacks, G., Frisbie, S.H., Smith, E., Naidu, R. and Sarkar, B. (2002). 'Arsenic in the environment: a global perspective'. In: Sarkar, B. (Ed.), *Heavy Metals in the Environment. Marcel Dekker*, New York, pp. 47–215.

[3] Bureau of Indian Standards (2012). Indian Standard Drinking water-Specification, http://cgwb.gov.in/Documents/WQ-standards.pdf, accessed on 10.09.2019.

[4] Census data of India (2011). http://censusindia.gov.in/2011census/dchb/ 1917_PART B_DCHB_SOUTH%20TWENTY%20FOUR%20PARGANAS.pdf, accessed on 18.09.2019

[5] Chakraborti, D., Das, B., Rahman, M.M., Chowdhury, U.K., Biswas, B., Goswami, A.B., Nayak, B., Pal, A., Sengupta, M.K., Ahamed, S., Hossain, A., Basu, G., Roychowdhury, T. and Das, D. (2009). 'Status of groundwater arsenic contamination in the state of West Bengal, India: A 20-year study report'. *Molecular Nutrition and Food Research*, 53 (5), pp. 542–551.

[6] Chaudhuri, P., Aitch, P. and Dutta, A. (2019). 'Identification of Arsenic Hazard Locations and Impact on Children—A Case Study on Baruipur Block, South 24 Parganas, West Bengal' in Pal, I., Meding, J.V., Shrestha, S. and Gajendran, T. (ed.), *An Interdisciplinary Approach for Disaster Resilience and Sustainability,* Springer Nature, Singapore, pp. 427–450.

[7] Das, A. and Roy, R. (2013). 'Socio-Economic Fallout of Arsenicosis in West Bengal: A Case Study in Murshidabad District', *Journal of the Indian Society of Agricultural Statistics,* 67(2), pp. 273–285.

[8] Guha Majumder, D.N. (2000). 'Diagnosis and treatment of chronic arsenic poisoning,' in United Nations Synthesis Report on Arsenic in Drinking Water, WHO, Geneva, Switzerland.

[9] Guha Mazumder, D.N. and Dasgupta, U.B. (2011). 'Chronic arsenic toxicity: Studies in West Bengal, India', *Kaohsiung Journal of Medical Sciences,* 27, pp. 360–370.

[10] Huy, T.B., Tuyet-Hanh, T.T., Johnston, R. and Nguyen-Viet, H. (2014). 'Assessing Health Risk due to Exposure to Arsenic in Drinking Water in Hanam Province, Vietnam', *International Journal of Environmental Research and Public Health*, 11(8), pp. 7575– 7591.

[11] Kumar, R. and Mandar, B. (2018). 'GIS based study on groundwater quality of Sikar district, Rajasthan', *Journal of Global Resources*, 4 (01), pp. 81–88.

[12] Mori, S., Lowenstein, E.J. and Steffen, C. (2018). 'The Largest Mass Poisoning in History: Arsenic Contamination of Well Water in Bangladesh', *SKINmed* 16(4): pp. 265–267

[13] Patel, U.B. and Teli, B. L. (2019). 'Population and urban sprawl in Lucknow city: problems & prospects', *Journal of Global Resources,* 5 (01), pp. 01–12.

[14] PHED Portal (2015). Public Health Engineering Department, Accessed on 25.3.2017

[15] Routh, J. and Hjelmquist, P. (2011) 'Distribution of arsenic and its mobility in shallow aquifer sediments from Ambikanagar, West Bengal, India', *Applied Geochemistry* 26, pp. 505–515.

[16] Singh, S.K. and Ghosh, A.K. (2012). 'Health Risk Assessment Due to Groundwater Arsenic Contamination: Children Are at High Risk', *Human and Ecological Risk Assessment,* 18(4), pp. 751–766.

[17] USEPA (U.S. Environmental Protection Agency) (1996). Proposed guidelines for carcinogen risk assessment. Notice, Federal Register 61(79): 17959–18011, https://cfpub.epa. gov/ncea/raf/pdfs/propcra_1996.pdf, accessed on 19.9.2019.

[18] World Health Organization (2011). Guidelines for Drinking water Quality, 4, pp. 315.

[10] World Health Organization (2018). https://www.who.int/news-room/fact-sheets/detail/ arsenic. Accessed on 19.09.2019.

[2-] www.who.int/news-room/fact-sheets/detail/arsenic,2018 accessed on 25.06.2019.

[21] Cebrian, M.E., Albores, A., Aguilar, M. and Blakely, E. Chronic arsenic poisoning in the north of Mexico. *Hum Toxicol* 1983; 2:121E33.

[22] Ahmad, S.A., Bandaranayake, D., Khan, A.W., Hadi, S.A., Uddein, G. and Halim, M.A. Arsenic contamination in ground water and arsenicosis in Bangladesh. *Int J Environ Health Res.* 1997; 7: 271E6.

[23] Morris, J.S., Schmid, M., Newman, S. and Scheuer, P.J., Path MRC, Sherlock S. Arsenic and noncirrhotic portal hypertension. *Gastroentero-logy,* 1974; 66:86E94.

[24] Szuler, I.M., Williams, C.N., Hindmarsh, J.T. and Park-Dinesoy, H. Massive variceal hemorrhage secondary to presinusoidal portal hypertension due to arsenic poisoning. *Can Med Assoc J.* 1979; 120:168E71.

[25] Nevens, F., Fevery, J., Van Streenbergen, W., Sciot, R., Desmet, V. and De Groote, J. Arsenic and non-cirrhotic portal hypertension: a report of eight cases. *J. Hepatol* 1990; 11:80E5.

[26] Franklin, M., Bean, W. and Harden, R.C. Fowler's solution as an etiologic agent in cirrhosis. *Am J Med Sci.* 1950; 219:589E96.

[27] Rosenberg, H.G. Systemic arterial disease and chronic arsenicism in infants. *Arch Pathol* 1974; 97:360E5.

[28] Santra, A., Gupta, J.D., De, B.K., Roy, B. and Guha Mazumder, D.N. Hepatic manifestations in chronic arsenic toxicity. *Indian J Gastroenterol,* 1999; 18:152E5.

[29] Saha, K.C. Melanokeratosis from arsenic contaminated tube well water. Indian J Dermatol 1984; 29:37E46.

[30] Tseng, W.P., Chu, Hm, How, S.W., Fong, J.M., Lin, C.S. and Yeh, S. Prevalence of skin cancer in an endemic area of chronic arsenicism in Taiwan. *J Natl Cancer Inst,* 1968; 40: 453E63.

[31] Engel, R.R. and Smith, A.H. Arsenic in drinking water and mortality from vascular disease: an ecological analysis in 30 counties in the United States. *Arch Environ Health* 1994; 49:418E27.

[32] Chen, C.J., Hsueh, Y.M., Lai, M.S., Shyu, M.P., Chen, S.Y., Wu, M.M., *et al.* Increased prevalence of hypertension and long-term arsenic exposure. *Hypertension,* 1995; 25:53E60.

[33] Rahman, M., Tondel, M., Ahmad, S.A., Chowdhury, I.A., Faruquee, M.H., Axelson, O. Hypertension and arsenic exposure in Bangladesh. *Hypertension,* 1999; 33:74E8.

[34] Chen, C.J., Chiou, H.Y., Chiang, M.H., Lin, L.J. and Tai, T.Y. Dose-response relationship between ischemic heart disease mortality and long-term arsenic exposure. *ArterioscleThrombVascBiol,* 1996; 16:504E10.

[35] Hotta, N. Clinical aspects of chronic arsenic poisoning due to environmental and occupational pollution in and around a small refining spot. *Nippon Taishitsugaku Zasshi* [Jpn J. Const Med] 1989; 53:49E70 [in Japanese].

[36] Kilburn, K.H. Neurobehavioral impairment from long-term residential arsenic exposure. In: Abernathy CO, Calderon RL, Chappell WR, editors. Arsenic exposure and health effects. London, UK: Chapman & Hall; 1997. p. 159E77. 14.

[37] Guha Mazumder, D.N., Gupta, J.D., Santra, A., Pal, A., Ghose, A., Sarkar, S., *et al.* Non cancer effects of chronic arsenicosis with special reference to liver damage. In: InAbernathy CO, Calderon RL, Chappell WR, editors. Arsenic exposure and health effect. London, *UK: Chapman & Hall*; 1997. p. 112E23.

[38] Mukherjee, S.C., Rahman, M.M., Chowdhury, U.K., Sengupta, M.K., Lodh, D., Chanda, C.R., *et al.* Neuropathy in arsenic toxicity from groundwater arsenic contamination in West Bengal, *India. J. Environ Sci. Health A.,* 2003; 38:165E83.

[39] Hindmarsh, J.T., McLetchine, O.R., Heffernan, L.P.M. and Hayne, O.A., Ellenberger HAA, McCurdy RR, *et al.* Electromyographic abnormalities in chronic environmental arsenicalism. *J Anal Toxicol.,* 1977; 11:270E6.

[40] Chen, C.J., Chiou, H.Y., Huang, W.I., Chen, S.Y., Hsueh, Y.M., Tseng, C.H., *et al.* Systemic non-carcinogenic effects and developmental toxicity of inorganic arsenic. In: Abernathy CO,

Calderon RL, Chappell WR, editors. Arsenic exposure and health effects. London, *UK: Chapman & Hall;* 1997. p. 124E34. 11.

[41] NRC (National Research Council). Arsenic in drinking water. Washington, DC: *National Academic Press;* 1999. 27E82.

[42] Harrington, J.M., Middaugh, J.P., Morse, D.L. and Housworth, J. A survey of a population exposed to high concentrations of arsenic in well water in Fairbanks, Alaska. *Am J Epidemiol,* 1978; 108: 377E85.

[43] Southwick, J.W., Western, A.E. and Beck, M.M. An epidemiological study of arsenic in drinking water in Millard County, Utah. In: Lederer W, Fensterheim R, editors. Arsenic: industrial, biomedical, environmental perspectives. *New York: Van Nostrand Reinhold;* 1983. p. 210E25.

[45] Lai, M.S., Hsueh, Y.M., Chen, C.J., Shyu, M.P., Chen, S.Y., Kuo, T.L., *et al.* Ingested inorganic arsenic and prevalence of diabetes mellitus. *Am J Epidemiol,* 1994; 139:484E92.

[46] Rahman, M., Tondel, M., Ahmad, S.A. and Axelson, O. Diabetes mellitus associated with arsenic exposure in Bangladesh. *Am J Epidemiol,* 1998; 148:198E203.

[48] von Ehrenstein, O.S., Guha Mazumder, D.N., Smith, M.H., Ghosh, N., Yuan, Y., Windham, G., *et al.* Pregnancy outcomes, infant mortality and arsenic in drinking water in West Bengal, India. *Am J Epidemiol,* 2006; 163:662E9.

[49] Hopenhyne-Rich, C., Browning, S., Hertz-Picciotto, I., Ferreccio, C., Peralta, C. and Gibb, H. Chronic arsenic exposure and risk of infant mortality in two areas in Chile. *Environ Health Perspect 2000;* 108:667E73.

[50] Milton, A.H., Smith, W., Rahman, B., Hasan, Z., Kulsum, U., Dear, K., *et al.* Chronic arsenic exposure and adverse pregnancy outcomes in Bangladesh. *Epidemiology* 2005; 16:82E6.

[51] Ahmad, S.A., Sayed, M.H.S.U., Barua, S., Khan, M.H., Faruquee, M., Jalil, A., *et al.* Arsenic in drinking water and pregnancy outcomes. *Environ Health Perspect,* 2001; 109:629E31.

[52] Rahman, A., Vahter, M., Ekstrom, E.C., Rahman, M., Mustafa, A.H.G., Wahed, M.A., *et al.* Association of arsenic exposure during pregnancy with fetal loss and infant death: a cohort study in Bangladesh. *Am J Epidemiol,* 2007; 165:1389E96.

[53] Guha Mazumder, D.N., Gupta, J.D., Chakraborty, A.K., Chatterjee, A., Das, D. and Chakraborti, D. Environmental pollution and chronic arsenicosis in south Calcutta. *Bull World Health Organ,* 1992; 70:481E5.

[54] Chowdhury, T.R., Mandal, B.K., Samanta, G., Basu, G.K., Chowdhury, P.P., Chanda, C.R., *et al.* Arsenic in groundwater in six districts of West Bengal, India: the biggest arsenic calamity in the world: the status report up to August, 1995. In: Abernathy CO, Calderon RL, Chappell WR, editors. Arsenic exposure and health effects. London, UK: Chapman & Hall; 1997. p. 93E111.

[55] Saha, K.C. Saha's grading of arsenicosis progression and treatment. In: Chappell WR, Abernathy CO, Calderon RL, Thomas DJ, editors. Arsenic exposure and health effects V. Oxford, UK: Elsevier Science; 2003. p. 391E414.

[56] Warner, M.L., Moor, L.E., Smith, M.T., Kalman, D.A., Fanning, E. and Smith, A.H. Increased micronuclei in exfoliated bladder cells of individuals who chronically ingest arsenic contaminated water in Nevada. *Cancer Epidemiol Biomarkers Prev,* 1994; 3: 583E90.

[57] Gonsbatt, M.E., Vega, L., Salazar, A.M., Montero, R., Guzman, P., Blasm J., *et al.* Cytogenetic effects in human exposure to arsenic. *Mutat Res.* 1997; 386:219E28.

Harmonizing Environmental Health Based on Air Pollution with Sustainable Progress: The Siliguri Imperative

Jagriti Nandi[1] and Sova Rani Das[2]

ABSTRACT: Poor air quality remains a significant concern in urban areas worldwide, including Siliguri. This study employs the Exceedance Factor (EF) method to evaluate the air quality of Siliguri based on average annual concentrations of pollutants, including NO2, SO2, PM2.5, and PM10. Results indicate that PM2.5 and PM10 are the primary pollutants posing a severe threat to the city. PM2.5 levels ranged from moderate to high pollution, while PM10 levels fell within the high to critical pollution range. NO2 and SO2 concentrations were found to be moderate to low. Trend analysis reveals fluctuating concentrations of pollutants, with PM10 consistently exceeding national standards and PM2.5 nearing violation of standards. Conversely, NO2 and SO2 levels remain below national standards. The study categorizes Siliguri's air quality into clean air and polluted periods, with winter months exhibiting skewed concentrations leading to smog episodes. The findings underscore the urgent need for attention to mitigate air pollution in Siliguri. Suggestions for improving air quality are also discussed. The findings underscore the urgent need for attention to mitigate air pollution in Siliguri. Suggestions for improving air quality include measures such as transitioning to alternative fuels like compressed natural gas (CNG) and electric vehicles, implementing real-time air monitoring stations at various locations, mandating stricter emissions standards for vehicles, and enhancing solid waste

[1] Ph.D Research Scholar, Department of Geography and Applied Geography, University of North Bengal, India. E-mail: jagritinandi.jn@gmail.com

[2] Ph.D Research Scholar, Department of Geography and Applied Geography, University of North Bengal, India. E-mail: ranisovadas@gmail.com

management practices. Public awareness campaigns emphasizing the importance of using public transportation, carpooling, and reducing vehicle emissions can also play a crucial role in improving air quality and public health in Siliguri.

Keywords: *Air Quality, Mitigate, Public Health, Sustainability.*

1. Introduction

Despite significant advancements in the prevention and management of air pollution in recent years, it remains a significant environmental health concern globally. Particularly in many third-world countries, including India, air pollution often exceeds the maximum limits recommended by the World Health Organization (WHO). Rapid urbanization and industrialization have exacerbated this issue, with automobile emissions being a major contributor, accounting for about 60% of air pollution in Indian cities. The rapid growth of motor vehicles has led to traffic congestion, increased air pollution, and noise problems. Notably, the transportation sector is responsible for a substantial portion of nitrogen oxide (NOx) and carbon monoxide (CO) emissions. Air pollution has been rightly characterized as a significant threat to human health, affecting individuals of all ages and genders. According to the UN Environment Programme, an estimated 1.1 billion people worldwide suffer from respiratory issues due to poor air quality. Medical research has shown that air particle concentrations have various detrimental effects on human health, particularly on the cardiovascular and respiratory systems. This study aims to investigate the air quality conditions and potential threats to the expanding city of Siliguri by employing the Exceedance Factor (EF) method. By utilizing this method, the study identifies pollutants posing significant risks that need urgent mitigation measures to prevent Siliguri from becoming a severely polluted city. Additionally, trend analysis of various pollutants, with a focus on PM10 and PM2.5, highlights the dominant concerns for the city. The study also utilizes the Air Quality Index (AQI) method to assess the current ambient air quality in Siliguri. Interestingly, the AQI reveals distinct seasonal variations in air quality, categorizing the city into periods of clean air and polluted air. Further examination of PM10 and PM2.5 concentrations for the year 2019 elucidates seasonal variations and underscores their significance as pollutants of concern. Given the scarcity of studies on ambient air quality in Siliguri, this research fills an important gap by examining available literature and data. The study objectives include assessing air quality status and pollution levels, analyzing pollutant concentrations and trends from 2014 to 2018, evaluating present air quality using AQI, and identifying current trends in PM2.5 and PM10 concentrations.

2. Study Area

Siliguri serves as the gateway to Northeast India and is experiencing rapid growth, driven by robust trade and commerce activities. The municipality of Siliguri was chosen as the study area for its strategic location and significant economic activities. It covers an area of 41.9 sq. km and has a population of over 500, 000. The selection was based on several factors, including its role as a trade and commerce hub, tourist destination, centre of population growth, employment nucleus, and crucial supply point for the entire Northeast region. The city's strategic location has earned it the monikers "gateway" of Northeast India due to its connectivity between the north-eastern states and the rest of India. Situated at the base of the Himalayas, Siliguri spans across two districts, Darjeeling, and Jalpaiguri, within the state of West Bengal. Its coordinates lie at approximately 26°43'N and 88°26'E. The city is traversed by the trans-boundary river Mahananda, which flows through its heart. However, despite its economic significance and strategic location, Siliguri faces challenges such as massive traffic congestion, which contributes significantly to air pollution and disturbs the ambient air quality of the city. These factors make Siliguri an ideal study area for assessing air quality and understanding the dynamics of air pollution in a rapidly growing urban centre with diverse economic activities.

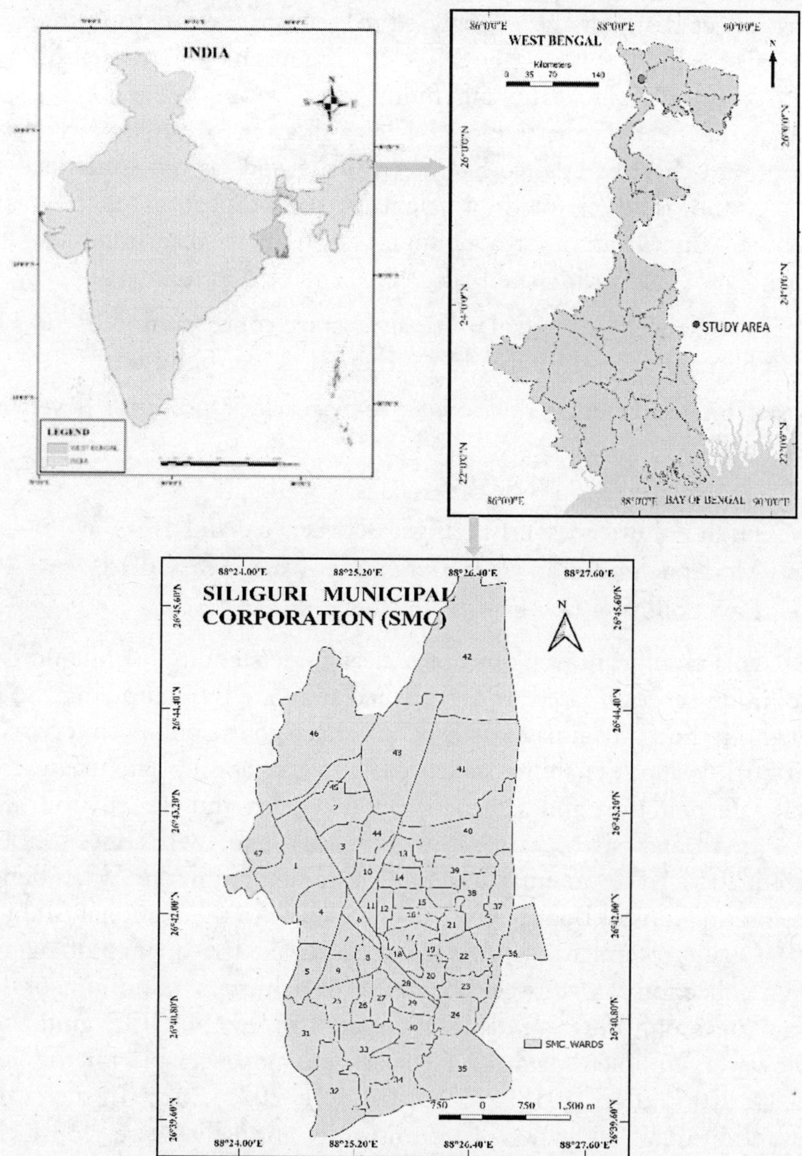

3. Data and Methodology

Siliguri's air quality assessment was conducted utilizing data obtained from the Central Pollution Control Board (CPCB) and the West Bengal Pollution Control Board (WBPCB). The available information was collected and analyzed analyzed to evaluate the pollution intensity and air quality status in the region. It's important to note that Siliguri has only one automatic air monitoring station at ward no. 32, Babupara, near Tinbatti more. The evaluation of air quality status employed the Exceedance Factor (EF) method, as recommended by the CPCB. The EF method calculates the proportion of the yearly average concentration of a pollutant to its particular standard. The formula for calculating the Exceedance Factor is as follows:

Exceedance Factor (EF) = (Yearly average concentration of the pollutant)/(Yearly standard for that particular pollutant)

Based on the calculated Exceedance Factor, air pollution levels are classified into four categories:

- Critical pollution (C): EF exceeds 1.5
- High pollution (H): EF ranges between 1.0 and 1.5
- Moderate pollution (M): EF ranges between 0.5 and 1.0
- Low pollution (L): EF is below 0.5

This classification allows for a clear understanding of Siliguri's air pollution severity based on established standards. By applying the EF method, the study aims to provide insights into the pollution levels and air quality status, enabling stakeholders to take appropriate measures to mitigate pollution and safeguard public health and the environment. For trend analysis of various air pollutants and their concentrations from 2014 to 2, manual data was obtained from the West Bengal Pollution Control Board (WBPCB), adhering to the National Ambient Air Quality Standards (NAAQS). The targeted frequency of manual data collection was bi-weekly, aiming to achieve a minimum of 104 days of monitoring annually as prescribed by NAAQS guidelines. However, complete data for 104 days was not available for the years 2014, 2015, 2016, 2018, 2019, 20202021, 2022, 2023. In such cases, an additional 40 days of monitoring annually were considered sufficient for data evaluation. The manual dataset from WBPCB for the years 2014 to 2023 comprised data collected twice a day per week, resulting in 102 days for 2013, 99 days for 2015, 103 days for 2016, 104 days for 2017, 103 days for 2018, 102 days for 2019, 98 days for 2020, 103 days for 2021, 98 days for 2022 and 103 days for 2023 respectively. This dataset was used to analyze analyze trends in air pollutant concentrations over the specified period. To assess the present air quality scenario in Siliguri for the year 2023, Air Quality Index (AQI) data was obtained from the automatic station in Siliguri. This data was presented through a master table, utilizing utilizing different colours to indicate the health impact and pollution level for ease of understanding. The master table provided a clear picture of the present air quality in Siliguri for the year 2023. Daily mean average data of 24 hours was collected and analysed from the AQI bulletin issued by the Central Pollution Control Board (CPCB) to prepare this master table. Additionally, trend lines were constructed to understand the trends of PM2.5 and PM10. These trend lines were based on data collected from the automatic station thrice a month at regular intervals during the first, second, and third weeks of each month. The trend lines illustrated sudden peaks, particularly during the winter months, providing insights into seasonal variations in PM2.5 and PM10 concentrations.

3.1 *Air Quality Index (AQI)*

The Air Quality Index (AQI) serves as a tool to communicate air quality conditions to the public in a simple and understandable manner. It transforms complex air quality data from various pollutants into a single value classification and corresponding colour scheme.

Currently, there are six categories of AQI, each associated with specific colours indicating their impact on human health. These categories include Good, Satisfactory, Moderately polluted, Poor, Very Poor, and Severe. The AQI is determined based on the Indian National Air Quality Standards established by the Central Pollution Control Board (CPCB). These standards consider twelve pollutants, including nitrogen dioxide (NO2), carbon monoxide (CO), sulfur dioxide (SO2), PM2.5, PM10 (particulate matter smaller than 2.5 microns and 10 microns), ozone (O_3), lead (Pb), ammonia (NH3), benzene (C6H6), pyrene (BaP), arsenic (As), and nickel (Ni). Among these pollutants, the primary eight have both short-term (1, 8, and 12 hours) and annual standards, except for carbon monoxide and ozone. The remaining four pollutants have only annual standards. However, not all pollutants may be monitored at every location. Generally, AQI is calculated only if data for at least three pollutants are available, including either $PM_{2.5}$ or PM_{10}. Otherwise, AQI analysis is not feasible. Additionally, a minimum of 16 hours of data is required to calculate the sub-index for each pollutant. Overall, AQI provides a simplified assessment of air quality, enabling the public to understand and respond to current air pollution levels effectively.

Table 1: Air Pollution Level and Annual Concentration of Various Pollutant

	NO_2			*PM_{10}*			*$PM_{2.5}$*			*SO_2*		
Year	*Annual Average*	*Value of E.F**	*Air Quality***	*Annual Average*	*Value of E.F**	*Air Quality***	*Annual Average*	*Value of E.F**	*Air Quality***	*Annual Average*	*Value of E.F**	*Air Quality***
2014	23	0.6	M	117	1.95	C	NA	NA	NA	6	0.1	L
2015	18	0.5	M	87	1.45	H	NA	NA	NA	3	0.06	L
2016	20	0.5	M	83	1.38	H	38	0.95	M	2	0.04	L
2017	18	0.5	M	59	0.98	M	22	0.55	M	2	0.04	L
2018	17	0.4	L	73	1.21	H	37	0.93	M	2	0.04	L
2019	28	0.7	M	68	1.13	H	26	0.65	M	6	0.1	L
2020	35	0.8	M	78	1.3	H	38	0.95	M	7	0.14	L
2021	35	0.8	M	110	1.83	C	60	1.50	H	9	0.18	L
2022	34	0.9	M	110	1.83	C	62	1.55	C	9	0.18	L
2023	24	0.6	M	74	1.23	H	43	1.07	H	5	0.1	L

Source: Calculated from WBPCB data.

NAAQS (annually): SO_2-50 $\mu g/m^3$; NO_2-40 $\mu g/m^3$; PM_{10}-60 $\mu g/m^3$; $PM_{2.5}$-40 $\mu g/m^3$; (all are standard values for yearly average exceeding these standards values consequence in bad air quality)

*Note:** Value of Exceedance factors. **Air Quality (L=Low Pollution, M= Moderate Pollution, H=High Pollution, C= Critical).NA=Data not available.

The assessment of air quality and pollution levels in Siliguri using the Exceedance Factor (EF) method revealed several noteworthy findings, as summarized in Table 1 and Figure 1

- Sulfur dioxide (SO_2) levels were consistently low throughout the years studied, indicating a minimal impact on air quality from this pollutant.

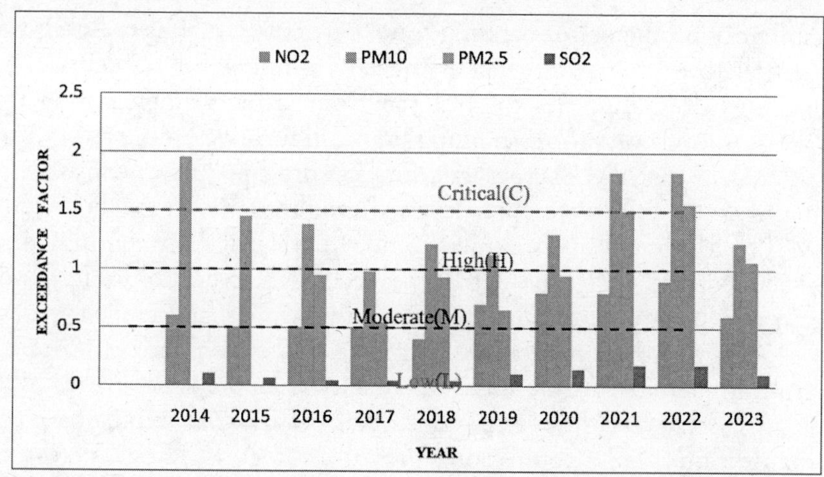

Figure 1: Pollution Level of Siliguri based on Exceedance Factor

- Nitrogen dioxide (NO_2) concentrations showed a moderate level from 2014 to 2023, but decreasing to a low level in 2018. The average pollution level from NO_2 remained moderate in Siliguri. The Exceedance values for NO_2 ranged from 0.5 to 0.6 in consecutive years from 2014 to 2023, indicating a moderate level, except for 2018.
- Data for PM2.5 was unavailable for 2014 and 2015. However, from 2016 to 2023, significant concentrations of PM2.5 were observed in the city, ranging from moderate to high levels. The Exceedance values for PM2.5 ranged from 0.6 to 0.95 in consecutive year 2016 to 2020, indicating a moderate level. But exceedance value is critical in 2021to 2022 and high in 2023. This indicates a likelihood of surpassing moderate limits and reaching high or critical values in the near future.
- PM10 levels were consistently severe throughout the years, ranging from critical to high levels from 2014 to 2023 except 2017. PM10 emerges as a primary concern for the city due to its potential to cause severe damage to the respiratory system and health complications.

Overall, it is evident that PM2.5 and PM10 are significant pollutants in Siliguri, requiring immediate action to mitigate their impact. The ambient air quality in Siliguri is precarious, posing severe threats to public health, particularly in terms of cardiovascular and respiratory problems. Addressing these particulate matter pollutants is essential to ensure a healthier living environment for residents. The diagram below illustrates the findings from Table 1, highlighting the pollution levels of various pollutants in Siliguri over successive years. It is evident that PM10 emerges as the foremost pollutant, consistently ranging from critical to high levels throughout the years. Following PM10, PM2.5 exhibits a similar trend, fluctuating between high and moderate levels, with a potential to exceed high to critical limits if not addressed promptly. Similarly, NO_2 shows a moderate level in recent years, but without intervention, it may escalate to high levels, posing significant hazards to the city's air quality. On the other hand, SO2 remains relatively low and controlled. With the rapid pace of urbanization and population growth, Siliguri faces increasing challenges, exacerbated by a rising number of vehicles contributing to congestion in the city. Emissions from diesel-run city autos are identified as a primary contributor to the city's pollution levels. Additionally, extensive construction activities, including road construction and multi-storey buildings, further add to the pollution burden in the city.

Overall, the combustion from vehicles and construction activities serve as major sources of PM2.5 and PM10 pollution in Siliguri. Addressing these sources of pollution is crucial to mitigate the deteriorating air quality and safeguard public health in the city.

Mitigation Measures for Sustainable Development

- Because of the small shape of the city, walking and cycling can help minimize traffic, congestion, and vehicle-emitted smoke.
- Restrictive parking regulations and lesser roads would also compel residents to refrain from driving their own cars.
- Enhancing public transportation, including its speed, comfort, and regularity. So that people utilize public transportation more often than they drive their own cars, reducing the number of automobiles on the road.

4. Conclusion

The study aimed to assess the concentration of major ambient air pollutants and their trends in Siliguri city, providing insights into the present condition of ambient air quality through the Air Quality Index (AQI). The concentrations and trends of sulfur dioxide (SO_2) and nitrogen dioxide (NO_2) in Siliguri's ambient air were found to be below the standards set by the National Ambient Air Quality Standards (NAAQS). However, the concentration of particulate matter PM10 was observed to exceed the acceptable limits set by NAAQS. Although PM2.5 was currently considered a moderate pollutant under the acceptable limit, it is anticipated to violate the national standard soon. The AQI study of 2023 revealed that air quality deteriorated during winter seasons, leading to serious health issues such as breathing problems, headaches, and irritation of eyes, exacerbated by frequent smog episodes. The inferior air quality and high concentration of PM10 and PM2.5 in Siliguri can be attributed to emissions from vehicles, especially diesel-run city autos. Immediate measures such as introducing alternative fuels like compressed natural gas (CNG) and electric vehicles are necessary to mitigate pollution levels. Additionally, setting up real-time air monitoring stations at various locations in the city, mandating the transition from Bharat Stage 4 to Bharat Stage 6 engines for two and three-wheelers, and enforcing short-term validity Pollution under Control (PUC) certificates can help curb particulate matter emissions. Furthermore, reducing dust particle emissions from construction sites, upgrading public transport systems, and implement-ting advanced solid waste management methods are essential steps towards improving air quality in Siliguri.

Public awareness campaigns emphasizing the importance of using public transport, cycling, carpooling, and regular vehicle maintenance are crucial for achieving long-term improvements in air quality. Overall, concerted efforts from both governmental and societal levels are necessary to make Siliguri a better place in terms of air quality and public health.

References

[1] Bedi, J.P, Dhaka, P., Vijay, D., Aulakh, R.S., Gill, J.P.S. (2020), "Assessment of air quality changes in the four metropolitan cities of India during COVID-19 pandemic lockdown", Aerosol Air Quality Res., 20(10), 2062–2070. https://doi.org/10.4209/aaqr.2020.05.0209.

[2] Bera, B., Bhattacharjee, S., Shit, P.K., Sengupta, N., Saha, S. (2020), "Significant impacts of COVID-19 lockdown on urban air pollution in

Kolkata (India) and amelioration of environmental health" Environ. Dev Sustain, 23(5), 6913–6940. https://doi.org/10.1007/s10668-020-00898-5

[3] Biswal, A., Singh, T., Singh, V., Ravindra, K., Mor, S. (2020), "COVID-19 lockdown and its impact on tropospheric NO2 concentrations over India using satellite-based data", Heliyon, 6(9), e04764. https://doi.org/10.1016/j.heliyon.2020.e04764.

[4] Biswas, K., Chatterjee, A., Chakraborty, J. (2020), "Comparison of air pollutants between Kolkata and siliguri, India, and its relationship to temperature change", J. Geovisual. Spatial Anal., 4(2), 1–15. https://doi.org/10.1007/s41651-020-00065-4.

[5] Biswas, K., Chatterjee, A., Chakraborty, J. (2020), "Comparison of air pollutants between Kolkata and siliguri, India, and its relationship to temperature change", J. Geovisual. Spatial Anal., 4(2), 1–15. https://doi.org/10.1007/s41651-020-00065-4.

[6] Census of India (2011), District data handbook Kolkata; Directorate of Census operations, West Bengal, India. https://censusindia.gov.in

[7] Das, R., Khezri, B., Srivastava, B., Datta, S., Sikdar, P.K., Webster, R.D., Wang, X. (2015), "Trace element composition of PM2.5 and PM10 from Kolkata—a heavily polluted Indian metropolis", Atmos Pollut. Res., 6(5), 742–750. https://doi.org/10.5094/APR.2015.083.

[8] Garg, A., Kumar, A., Gupta, N.C. (2020), "Impact of lockdown on ambient air quality in COVID-19 affected hotspot cities of India: Need to readdress air pollution mitigation policies" Environ Claims J., 33(1), 65–76. https://doi.org/10.1080/10406026.2020.1822615.

[9] Ghosh, P., Ghosh, R., Chakraborty, B. (2020), "COVID-19 in India: State wise analysis and prediction", JMIR Public Health Surveill., 6(3), e20341. https://doi.org/10.2196/20341.

[10] Gomez, K.A. and Gomez, A.A. (1984), Statistical Procedures for Agricultural Research, John Wiley and Sons, New York, USA.

[11] Government of India (2011), Road Transport Year Book (2007–2009), Transport Research Wing, Ministry of Road Transport and Highways, Government of India, New Delhi, India.

[12] Government of India (2019), Road Transport Year Book (2016–2017), Transport Research Wing, Ministry of Road Transport and Highways, Government of India, New Delhi, India.

[13] India State-Level Disease Burden Initiative Air Pollution Collaborators (2020) "Health and economic impact 143 Rajib Majumder of air pollution in the states of India: The global burden of disease study 2019", Lancet Planetary Health, 5(1), e25–e38. https://doi.org/10.1016/S2542-5196(20)30298-9.

[14] IQAir (2019), IQAir World Air Quality Report (Region & City PM2.5 Ranking, 2019; IQAir Group, Goldach, Switzerland. www.iqair.com

[15] NAAQS (2009), Revised National Ambient Air Quality Standard, Notification; Central Pollution Control Board, India. https://cpcb.nic.in. NAQI-CPCB (2020), Live Air Quality - Data of Monitoring Stations, Central Pollutions Control Board, Ministry of Environment, Forest and Climat Change, Government of India.

Assessing Air Pollution Management in the Context of the UN Sustainable Development Goals: A Comprehensive Review

Keshab Mondal[1]

ABSTRACT: This paper conducts an in-depth evaluation of the origins and consequences of air pollution and its control from the United Nations Sustainable Development Goals (SDGs) perspective. Utilising a review of existing literature and expert evaluations, it explores how air pollution impedes the achievement of the SDGs and examines the positive role that air quality management can play. This analysis addresses each goal and provides a comprehensive view of the 17 interconnected objectives. While the main goals of the SDG framework do not explicitly mention air quality and pollution management, these issues are implicitly linked to various specific targets and indicators. The study finds that air pollution is a significant obstacle to reaching all the individual SDGs. In contrast, initiatives to improve air quality are considered facilitators for achieving eight goals and offer additional advantages for the remaining nine. The critical need to tackle air pollution to ensure sustainable progress and the benefits of maintaining clean air for achieving the SDGs are emphasised.

Keywords: Air Pollution Control, Air Quality Enhancement, UN Sustainable Development Goals.

1. Introduction

This document delves into the origins and effects of air pollution from the viewpoint of human needs, aligning its discussion with the framework of the United Nations Sustainable Development

[1] Assistant Professor, Department of Geography, Cooch Behar College, West Bengal, India. E-mail: mondalkeshab83@gmail.com

Goals (SDGs). The SDGs, which the UN General Assembly established in September 2015 and which became operational on January 1, 2016, provide a thorough roadmap for international, regional, and local organisations in their pursuit of a sustainable future through 17 overarching goals and 169 specific targets that are inclusive, transformative, and interconnected. These goals collectively address human progress's complex challenges, providing strategies to meet various human needs. According to the United Nations Development Programme (UNDP), the SDGs aim to achieve global desires for peace, prosperity, well-being, and the preservation of the environment. Additionally, they emphasise the importance of environmental management, promoting a shift from merely adhering to fundamental standards to a more comprehensive strategy that sustainably meets various human needs. This notion is consistent with the Brundtland Commission's original vision for sustainable development.

The United Nations initiative, known as the Sustainable Development Goals (SDGs), represents the conclusion of a thorough process that involved all 193 member nations and a more prominent global civil society. As a successor to the Millennium Development Goals (MDGs), the SDGs serve as a collective commitment towards fostering a sustainable growth trajectory up to 2030. These goals encompass a broad spectrum of concerns spanning environmental, economic, and social realms, including but not limited to poverty alleviation, health improvement, advancing education, gender equality, ensuring access to clean water and sustainable energy, promoting economic growth and employment, fostering innovation, reducing inequalities, building sustainable cities and communities, encouraging responsible consumption and production, addressing climate change, preserving aquatic and terrestrial life, enhancing peace, justice, and the strength of institutions, and nurturing global partnerships. While critics dismiss the SDGs as overly romantic or too encompassing, they represent a unified vision for progress achieved through collaborative efforts under the United Nations' guidance. This vision not only aims for broad-based sustainability but also emphasises the interconnectedness of these goals. Everard and Longhurst stress the importance of viewing the SDGs as a closely linked framework, suggesting that focusing too narrowly on individual goals could potentially jeopardise others, as exemplified by how prioritising service enhancement without considering environmental impacts could harm ecosystems vital for food security and disease prevention.

This manuscript evaluates how air pollution is an obstacle to realising the Sustainable Development Goals (SDGs) and explores how effective air quality management can contribute to advancing these goals. The analysis delves into the overarching objectives and specific subsidiary targets, highlighting the importance of a holistic approach to the 17 goals. It posits that air pollution is fundamentally at odds with the principles of sustainable development, arguing for the necessity of incorporating air quality management within the SDG agenda. Despite the critical importance of air quality and pollution control, these issues still need to be explicitly addressed across the broad spectrum of the SDG framework. However, they are implicated in specific objectives related to health (SDG 3), urban areas (SDG 11), and sustainable consumption and production practices (SDG 12). Air pollution is identified as a significant concern within each of these goals. The SDGs serve as milestones for sustainable development and a lens through which to examine and overcome challenges, including air pollution, that hinder goal achievement. Conversely, they also highlight the potential pathways to expedite the fulfilment of these objectives. According to Lode *et al.*, the SDGs offer a pivotal opportunity to combat air pollution worldwide, emphasising its critical impact on public health.

Considering the adverse effects of substandard air quality on public health and its impact on achieving sustainable development goals, Everard and colleagues acknowledge the essential nature of air as a communal resource. Consequently, access to clean air should be considered a fundamental human right. The need for improved management of air pollution is becoming increasingly critical across countries at all economic levels, each affected differently by the quality of their air. The World Health Organisation's Global Urban Ambient Air Pollution Database reveals that over 80% of urban dwellers in areas where air pollution is tracked are subjected to air quality levels that fall below WHO's recommended standards. With the rise of air pollution in cities, there's an escalated risk of cardiovascular diseases, lung cancer, and both chronic and acute respiratory conditions such as asthma among residents. The WHO has identified air pollution as the most significant environmental threat to health globally, with estimates suggesting that ambient air pollution results in approximately 4.2 million premature deaths annually.

2. Methodology

An evaluation of air pollution's current effects on each of the 17 Sustainable Development Goals (SDGs) has been conducted, utilising both existing literature and insights from subject matter experts. This evaluation includes an analysis of how air pollution control can contribute to achieving the objectives set for 2030. Both direct and indirect effects of air pollution on the goals have been identified, and the potential benefits of current and improved air pollution control measures for each goal have been explored. Given the interconnected nature of the SDGs, it's critical to understand that actions taken to address air pollution about any single goal can have systemic implications across the entire suite of goals. A modified Delphi method was employed to conduct this comprehensive analysis, gathering a group of experts with backgrounds in air pollution and the SDGs. This group engaged in a rigorous iterative process, encompassing four rounds of dialogue that involved sharing information, challenging viewpoints, resolving disagreements, and ultimately reaching a consensus on the impact of air pollution and the role of air quality management in the findings and discussions.

Table 1: Allocation of SDGs to Primary Categories

Category	*SDGs*
Economic	1 (No Poverty), 8 (Decent Work and Economic Growth), 9 (Industry, Innovation, and Infrastructure), 10 (Reduced Inequalities), 12 (Responsible Consumption and Production)
Social	2 (Zero Hunger), 3 (Good Health and Well-being), 4 (Quality Education), 5 (Gender Equality), 11 (Sustainable Cities and Communities), and 16 (Peace, Justice and Strong Institutions)
Environmental	6 (Clean Water and Sanitation), 7 (Affordable and Clean Energy), 13 (Climate Action), 14 (Life Below Water), and 15 (Life on Land)
Cross-Cutting	17 (Partnerships for the Goals)

Note: SDG 17 is considered a cross-cutting goal as it emphasises partnerships crucial for achieving all other SDGs and, thus, spans across all categories.

3. Results and Discussion

To streamline the reporting process, the Sustainable Development Goals (SDGs) have been categorised into three distinct groups: economic-focused goals, social-focused goals, and environmental-focused goals. This classification mirrors the innovative methodology the Stockholm Resilience Centre introduced for analysing food systems within the SDG framework. SDG 17, which emphasises partnerships for the goals, spans all categories and is, therefore, analysed independently.

3.1 *Economic Subset of SDGs*

SDG 1 targets eradicating poverty in all its manifestations across countries at varying economic levels. Individuals living in poverty are disproportionately affected by air pollution despite typically contributing less to pollution levels compared to wealthier populations. Environments plagued by pollution deter economic investments, hindering the establishment of new businesses and creating job opportunities that could help lift communities out of poverty. Families with lower incomes are particularly vulnerable to the effects of air pollution, often lacking the means to mitigate their exposure. Poverty also amplifies the health risks associated with air pollution, affecting the severity and duration of symptoms and limiting access to healthcare and medications. Addressing air pollution reduces these health risks and supports food security by protecting crops from harmful pollutants, a vital component in the fight against poverty. Furthermore, improving air quality can make regions more appealing for investment and local economic development, leading to healthcare savings and increased productivity by decreasing work absences due to illness. Thus, initiatives focused on air quality management can offer significant advantages towards achieving this goal. SDG 2 focuses on eliminating hunger by ensuring access to sufficient and nutritious food for all. Air pollution significantly undermines food security by compromising crop production by depositing harmful substances such as nitrogen compounds, ozone, and sulphur oxides. These pollutants are known to decrease agricultural yields, threatening food. These effects have a disproportionately negative impact on vulnerable groups, such as those who are sick, undernourished, or economically disabled Additionally, nitrogen pollutants frequently accelerate the process of eutrophication in water bodies, which can reduce fish populations and exacerbate food scarcity. food scarcity. Agricultural methods that involve burning crop residues also contribute to air pollution, affecting nearby crop health and increasing health risks for agrarian workers. By targeting emissions reductions and minimising harmful exposures, initiatives aimed at improving air quality directly contribute to food security. These efforts are crucial in combating local and cross-border pollution challenges, thereby supporting the achievement of SDG 2. SDG 3 aims to promote well-being and ensure healthy lives for all ages, recognising the profound threat air pollution poses to health, particularly affecting the respiratory and cardiovascular systems, with growing evidence of its impact over a person's lifetime. Vulnerable populations, including the elderly, those with preexisting health conditions, and young children, face the greatest danger from conventional air pollutants. Recent studies indicate potential links between air pollution and neurological conditions such as dementia, as well as epigenetic disorders. Pregnant women are also notably susceptible, with their exposure potentially harming the developing fetus, leading to lower birth weights, decreased birth rates, and higher infant mortality rates. Furthermore, air pollution can deter people from engaging in physical activities. By reducing emissions and curtailing exposure to harmful pollutants, the health risks can be significantly mitigated. Such targeted measures can help address national and global pollution exposure disparities. Ultimately, initiatives to improve air quality are crucial for enhancing public health and decreasing healthcare costs associated with pollution. Efforts in air quality management align directly with the objectives of SDG 3. SDG 4 emphasises the importance of ensuring inclusive and equitable education, noting how air pollution can impair children's neurological and cognitive growth. Indirectly, air pollution exacerbates food insecurity and poverty, both of which can diminish the effectiveness of educational programmes. Smog may cause schools to close temporarily in areas with high pollution levels. Reducing emissions and limiting harmful exposures can protect learners, particularly children, ensuring they can fully benefit from education without interruptions. Enhancing air quality can lead to fewer educational disruptions due to health issues or school shutdowns, supporting this SDG. SDG 5 focuses on achieving gender equality and empowering all women and girls. Women in low- and middle-income nations face more significant risks from indoor air pollution, primarily due to traditional cooking methods. The World Health Organisation reports that nearly 3 billion people use polluting open fires or rudimentary stoves with kerosene, biomass, or coal, leading to approximately 3.8 million premature deaths annually from related diseases. Improving cooking practices can enhance indoor air quality and health, benefiting women and aligning with this SDG's objectives. SDG 7 ties directly to clean and affordable energy. While cheaper, traditional energy sources like wood and coal generate significant air pollution. In developing regions, burning waste for heating and cooking, such as in Delhi, contributes to primary unregulated emissions. Pollution can also impair the efficiency of renewable energy installations, like solar panels affected by smog or dust. Transitioning to renewable energy presents a viable solution, offering substantial health benefits by minimising pollutant exposure. Achieving energy access, efficiency, and renewable energy targets can indirectly address air pollution. This underscores the need for sustainable energy policies to experience the dual advantages of cleaner energy and reduced air pollution emissions. Addressing air quality issues thus supports the achievement of these SDGs.

SDG 11 aims to create sustainable cities and communities where air pollution significantly impacts urban appeal, particularly in large cities. Exposure to various pollutants compromises urban residents' health, affecting mortality and morbidity rates. High levels of air pollution can discourage outdoor activities and infrastructure development for active transportation, which is essential for sustainable urban development. Initiatives to make cities more livable and strategies to cut emissions can lower the risk of harmful exposure, thereby improving public health outcomes. Programmes targeting emission reductions can also boost demand for and foster the creation of infrastructure that supports active travel. Moreover, enhancing air quality can promote physical activity and decrease sedentary lifestyles by reducing vehicle reliance. Efforts to pursue this SDG can counteract local and cross-border air pollution, offering additional benefits. SDG 16 focuses on promoting peace, justice, and strong institutions, noting how air pollution can exacerbate climate change and reduce access to vital resources, potentially sparking conflicts over resources like food and water at both local and international levels. This scenario could increase the number of environmental refugees, as seen when citizens in China sought refuge in less polluted areas, reminiscent of historical patterns in Western Europe and North America, where socio-economic status influenced residential areas relative to pollution levels. Addressing emissions from fossil fuel combustion can alleviate the risk of resource-based conflicts. Through improved resource efficiency and reduced consumption, emission levels can be lowered. Addressing this SDG necessitates robust environmental governance and active civil society participation to ensure policies prioritise ecological justice and practical regulatory frameworks are established and enforced to enhance air quality. Such actions, crucial across all income levels, will mitigate air pollution and address environmental inequalities, bringing additional advantages to this goal.

3.3 *Environmental Subset of SDGs*

SDG 11 is dedicated to fostering sustainable cities and communities, highlighting the detrimental effects of air pollution on the desirability of urban environments, especially in densely populated areas. The exposure of city dwellers to pollutants can lead to increased health issues, affecting life expectancy and quality of life. Pollution discourages public spaces, and implementing active transport solutions is critical for eco-friendly urban living. Enhancing urban environments and reducing emissions can decrease exposure risks, improving overall health indicators. Initiatives focused on lowering emissions can also encourage the development of infrastructure conducive to active transportation, contributing to reduced dependency on motor vehicles. Actions supporting this goal will address local and international air pollution challenges. SDG 16 underscores the importance of fostering peace, justice, and effective institutions, observing that air pollution contributes to climate change and may limit access to essential resources, potentially leading to conflicts over food and water. This dynamic has historically led to the movement of populations seeking cleaner environments, as observed with migration patterns within

China and between different regions in the West. Strategies to lower emissions from the combustion of fossil fuels can mitigate these conflicts. Enhanced efficiency and reduced consumption contribute to lowering pollution levels. Commitment to this goal requires strong governance and community involvement to ensure environmental justice and the implementation of effective air quality regulations. These efforts are vital for all nations to reduce air pollution and its inequalities. SDG 6, aimed at ensuring the availability and sustainable management of water and sanitation for all, notes the direct influence of air pollution. The deposition of acidic substances in the air can deteriorate water quality. Additionally, actions to improve sanitation may generate bioaerosols and odours from waste treatment facilities and indirect emissions from energy used in these processes. Initiatives to cut emissions will positively affect water bodies, enhancing water quality for drinking, recreation, and food production. SDG 13, which calls for urgent action to combat climate change and its impacts, recognises the significant role of air pollution emitted through the combustion of fossil fuels across various sectors. Mitigating these emissions is crucial for reducing the adverse effects on natural ecosystems and human societies. Climate change can alter energy needs and affect the patterns of secondary pollutants, necessitating actions that can help manage climate change and air pollution. SDG 14 focuses on conserving life below water. It highlights how air pollution threatens aquatic ecosystems through acidification and eutrophication from various sources. Reducing emissions can alleviate these threats, safeguarding marine and freshwater ecosystems for future generations. SDG 15 concentrates on life on land, acknowledging how air pollution directly affects plant life through contamination and changes in the deposition of pollutants. Actions to improve air quality benefit terrestrial ecosystems and contribute to the broader objectives of combating air pollution on a global scale.

3.4 *Partnerships for the Goals*

SDG 17 highlights the challenge of often slow or ineffective institutional responses to recognised risks, including those related to air pollution and climate change, both nationally and internationally. The absence of robust partnerships at various levels—local, national, and global—hampers cohesive policy development and diminishes public engagement on these critical issues. Partnerships, ranging from international organisations like the UN to regional entities such as the EU and national and local levels, are essential for raising awareness, prioritising actions, implementing emission control strategies, and promoting behaviour shifts. Collaborative efforts, particularly at the city level, are crucial for educating the public about the adverse effects of fossil fuel use across different sectors, including transportation and residential, and the broader implications for global climate change. There is a concern that without inclusive and sustainable approaches to economic growth, as exemplified by SDG 8, efforts may not fully harness the potential benefits of collaborative work in air pollution management. Effective partnerships are crucial to mitigating both local and cross-border pollution challenges. Thus, actively managing air quality through collaborative efforts aligns with the objective of SDG 17, serving as a practical example of partnership success.

Table 2: Impact Analysis Outcomes

	SDG	*Direct Impact of Air Pollution*	*Co-benefits of Air Quality Management*
1.	No Poverty	Increased health expenses burden the poor	Economic savings could support anti-poverty programmes
2.	Zero Hunger	Reduced crop yields affecting food security	Improved crop productivity enhances food security
3.	Good Health and Well-being	Health risks from pollution exposure	Reduced healthcare costs and improved public health
4.	Quality Education	Cognitive impacts from pollution exposure	Fewer school absences, enhanced learning environments
5.	Gender Equality	Women and girls are disproportionately affected by indoor pollution	Enhanced well-being and empowerment through cleaner environments
6.	Clean Water and Sanitation	Pollution runoff affects water quality	Improved water resources management and access

	SDG	*Direct Impact of Air Pollution*	*Co-benefits of Air Quality Management*
7.	Affordable and Clean Energy	Dependence on polluting energy sources	Transitioning to clean energy reduces emissions
8.	Decent Work and Economic Growth	Pollution can deter investment and job creation	Healthier work environments can boost productivity
9.	Industry, Innovation, and Infrastructure	Pollution as a byproduct of industrial activity	Cleaner technologies can drive innovation and sustainability
10.	Reduced Inequalities	Vulnerable populations are more exposed to pollution	Equity in health and well-being through improved air quality
11.	Sustainable Cities and Communities	Polluted cities are less livable and attractive	Enhanced urban livability and sustainability
12.	Responsible Consumption and Production	Waste contributes to air pollution	Sustainable practices reduce emissions and waste
13.	Climate Action	Air pollutants contribute to climate change	Mitigation efforts can address both air quality and climate change
14.	Life Below Water	Airborne pollutants deposited in water bodies	Protection of aquatic ecosystems through reduced emissions
15.	Life on Land	Pollution affects soil and terrestrial biodiversity	Restoration of natural habitats and biodiversity
16.	Peace, Justice, and Strong Institutions	Pollution can exacerbate resource conflicts	Strengthened governance and cooperation on environmental issues
17.	Partnerships for the Goals	Fragmented efforts to tackle air pollution	Integrated approaches enhance efficacy and outreach

4. Conclusions

This comprehensive overview explores the critical role of air pollution as an obstacle to achieving the Sustainable Development Goals (SDGs) and the transformative potential of enhanced air quality management. Echoing the sentiments of Lode and colleagues, the 2030 Agenda is sometimes criticised for being an advisory framework without stringent enforcement mechanisms. Despite this, it stands as the universally agreed-upon roadmap towards sustainability. Notably, no SDG explicitly addresses air pollution and its direct management. Yet, this analysis has demonstrated that air pollution intersects with every goal, suggesting that its absence as a standalone issue may not be as problematic as initially perceived. This presents an opportunity for a holistic approach to tackling air pollution within the SDG framework.

Further investigation is needed to understand how policies can holistically address these goals and how specific objectives can incorporate air quality improvement measures into their action plans. Pursuing the global SDGs should not sideline the critical issue of air pollution. The SDGs play a crucial role in reaffirming the World Commission on Environment and Development's (WCED) original vision of sustainable development, which has seen its focus diluted over time due to various implementations. Recognising air pollution as a significant barrier to sustainable development and acknowledging the positive impact of clean air on achieving the SDGs is essential for moving forward.

References

[1] Almorza, D., Longhurst, J.W.S., Brebbia, C.A. & Barnes, J.H. (eds), Air Pollution XXV. WIT Transactions on Ecology and the Environment, vol. 211, WIT Press: Southampton and Boston, 2017.

[2] Brebbia, C.A., Longhurst, J.W.S., Marco, E. & Booth, C. (eds), Sustainable Development and Planning IX. WIT Transactions on Ecology and the Environment, vol. 226, WIT Press: Southampton and Boston, 2017.

[3] Elder, M. & Zusman, E., Strengthening the Linkages Between Air Pollution and the Sustainable Development Goals. Policy Brief 35. Institute for Global Environmental Strategies, 2017.

[4] European Environment Agency, Air quality in Europe—2017 report, EEA Report No 13/2017, Copenhagen, 2017.

[5] Everard, M. and Longhurst, J.W.S., Reasserting the importance of human needs to reclaim sustainable development's 'lost half'. Science of the Total Environment, 621, pp. 1243–1254, 2018.

[6] Everard, M. *et al.*, Air as a Common Good. Environmental Science & Policy, 33, pp. 354–368, 2013.

[7] Lode, B., Schonberger, P. and Toussaint, P.: Clean air for all by 2030? Air quality in the 2030 agenda and international law. Review of European, Comparative and International Environmental Law, 25(1), pp. 27–38, 2016.

[8] Longhurst, J.W.S., Brebbia, C.A. & Barnes, J.H. (eds), Air Pollution XXIV. WIT Transactions on Ecology and the Environment, vol. 207, WIT Press: Southampton and Boston, 2016.

[9] Longhurst, J.W.S., Capilla, C., Brebbia, C.A. & Barnes, J. (eds), Air Pollution XXIII. WIT Transactions on Ecology and the Environment, WIT Press: Southampton and Boston, 2015.

[10] Longhurst, J.W.S. & Brebbia, C.A. (eds), Air Pollution XXII. WIT Transactions on Ecology and the Environment, WIT Press: Southampton and Boston, 2014.

[11] UNICEF, Clear Air for Children. The Impact of Air Pollution on Children, United Nations Children's Fund: New York, 2016.

[12] United Nations Development Programme (2015). Consensus Reached on New Sustainable Development Agenda to be Adopted by World Leaders in September, UNDP, Online. http://www.undp.org/content/undp/en/home/presscenter/pressreleases/2015/08/02/consensus-reached-on-new-sustainable-development-agenda-to-be-adopted-by-world-leaders-in-september.html. Accessed on: May 20, 2018.

[13] United Nations, Sustainable Development Goals, United Nations, New York, 2015, online. https://sustainabledevelopment.un.org/?menu=1300. Accessed on: May 18, 2018.

[14] WCED, Our Common Future, Oxford University Press, Oxford, 1987.

[15] WHO, Ambient Air Pollution, A Global Assessment of Exposure and Disease Burden, WHO: Geneva, 2016.

[16] WHO, Ambient (outdoor) air quality and health, 2018, Online. http://www.who.int/news-room/fact-sheets/detail/ambient-(outdoor)-air-quality-and-health. Accessed on: 23 May 2018.

[17] WHO, Global Urban Ambient Air Pollution Database, 2016, Online. http://www.who.int/phe/health_topics/outdoorair/databases/cities/en/. Accessed on: 23 May 2018.

[17] WHO, Household Air Pollution and Health, WHO: Geneva, 2018, Online. http://www.who.int/news-room/fact-sheets/detail/household-air-pollution-and-health. Accessed on: 23 May 2018.

[18] WHO, World Health Statistics 2016: Monitoring Health for the SDGs,

An Overview of the Toxicological Impact of Cadmium (Cd) on the Physiological Status of Fishes

Somnath Kundu[1] and Tapan Sarkar[2]

ABSTRACT: The presence of elevated levels of cadmium (Cd) in the environment poses a significant threat to the sustainable development of the aquaculture industry and hampers the progress of the food processing sector. Investigation of the distribution and harmful effects of Cd in fish, as well as its potential impacts on human health, holds considerable importance. Numerous studies have demonstrated that the accumulation and distribution of Cd in fish are biologically specific, leading to tissue variations and severe damage to tissue structure, function, antioxidant defence systems, reproductive regulatory mechanisms, and immune systems. Exposure to Cd results in changes at physiological, biochemical, enzymatic, molecular, and gene expression levels, which vary depending on the concentration and duration of exposure. These alterations are closely linked to the target sites of Cd action within fish tissues, indicating that the toxic effects of Cd across multiple tissues, systems, and levels.

Keywords: *Cadmium (Cd), Fish Physiology, Toxicology, Enzymatic Impact.*

1. Introduction

In recent decades, the contamination of freshwater by different substances has become a major concern. Heavy metal pollution of natural aquatic systems is frequently caused by human activities like industrial and household garbage. Cadmium pollution in rivers and

---

[1] Assistant Professor, Department of Zoology, Tufanganj Mahavidyalaya, Tufanganj-736160, WB, India. E-mail: Somnath782@gmail.com

[2] Assistant Professor, Department of Zoology, Raiganj University, Raiganj-733134, WB, India.

lakes is primarily caused by urban industrial waste, which causes the element to build up in aquatic organisms all the way up the food chain. Since cadmium is harmful and takes a long time to leave animal bodies, it is a severe hazard to both fish and mammals. In living things, especially in organs like fish liver and kidneys, cadmium tends to accumulate quickly and cause pathogenic and structural abnormalities (Mekkawy *et al.*, 2010). Investigations show that the kidneys and liver are the main organs that suffer from sub-chronic cadmium poisoning, whilst fish gills and kidney tubules are the main organs impacted by acute poisoning. Since they can't get away from aquatic pollutants, fish are a good way to measure the health of an ecosystem as they can accumulate toxins in the food chain. Heavy metals have been shown to interfere with physiological and biochemical processes in tissues and blood, based on investigations on a variety of fish species. The negative consequences of heavy metals, such as bioaccumulation, have been well-researched and documented. Since heavy metals may advance up the human food chain, their accumulation in aquatic organisms especially fish presents a chronic concern that needs continuous monitoring and surveillance (Afzaal *et al.*, 2022).

1.1 *Cadmium Accumulation Effects*

Studies illustrate that through using the advantage of similarities to calcium ions (Ca2+), cadmium (Cd) may get into cells through calcium ion channels. Although the diameters of Cd2+ and Ca2+ are similar, Cd2+ possesses a greater affinity for the anion binding sites that exist in calcium ion channels, making it possible for the ion to competitively hinder the active flow of Ca2+ inside cells. Once within the cell, Cd2+ interferes with physiological functions associated with Ca2+. For instance, it interferes with Ca2+ outflow by competing with it for binding sites on Ca2+-ATPase, that enhances intracellular Ca2+ levels. Moreover, Cd2+ can interact with calmodulin (CaM) in place of Ca2+, stimulating related enzymes directly or activating CaM-dependent kinases, that could disrupt intracellular Ca2+ related signalling (Belyaeva *et al.*, 2004). Furthermore, Cd2+ has the ability to remove Ca2+ from binding sites on cellular components such as microtubules. Furthermore, Cd2+ has the capacity to shift Ca2+ form binding locations on cellular components including actin, microtubules, and microfilaments. The following may lead to disruptions to tight and gap junctions between cells, compromise the integrity of the cytoskeleton, and subsequently impact basic cellular operation (Bagur & Hajnóczky, 2017).

1.2 *Approaches Determining Cadmium Detection*

The percentage of cadmium (Cd) in organisms can typically be determined via an array of approaches, each having benefits and drawbacks on its own. The majority of Cd in nature exists in an ionic form. But once within fish, the majority of Cd ions quickly create organic combinations with metallothionein, and a smaller proportion builds coordination compounds with proteins, nucleosides, as well as other substances via ionic bonds within the organism. At the present time, inductively coupled plasma (ICP) and atomic absorption spectroscopy (AAS) are among the most common techniques for detecting Cd in fish. ICP covers inductively coupled plasma-mass spectrometry (ICP-MS) and inductively coupled plasma optical emission spectrometry (ICP-OES), while AAS includes methods like flame atomic absorption spectrometry (FAAS) and graphite furnace atomic absorption spectrometry (GFAAS). Cadmium (Cd) quantification is widely assisted utilizing graphite furnace atomic absorption spectrometry (GFAAS), that is highly sought after for its exceptionally high sensitivity, narrow detectable limit, and minimal specimen requirements (Chen *et al.*, 2023). In various fishes the concentration that affects physiological integrity varies. Lethal concentrations of Cd on various fish species are summarized below (Table 1).

Table 1: Lethal Concentrations of Cd on Various Fish Species

Fish Species	*LC50 (Median lethal Concentration)*	*Time*	*Reference*
Labeo rohita	89.5 mg/L	96 hours	(Dutta & Kaviraj, 2001)
Cyprinus carpio	0.20 μM	96 hours	(Delahaut *et al.*, 2020)
Poecilia reticulata	0.17 mg/L	96 hours	(Shuhaimi-Othman *et al.*, 2013)
Oreochromis niloticus	14.8 mg/L	96 hours	(Annune *et al.*, 1994)

Fish Species	*LC50 (Median lethal Concentration)*	*Time*	*Reference*
Clarias gariepinus	10.85 mg/L	96 hours	(Annune *et al.*, 1994)
Oncorhynchus mykiss	8 µg/L	96 hours	(Jurgelėnė *et al.*, 2019)
Danio rerio	25 µg/L	9 days	(Renieri *et al.*, 2017)
Trichogaster fasciata	49.5 mg/L	96 hours	(Roy *et al.*, 2022)

2. Effects of Cadmium Accumulation in Fish

2.1 *Cadmium Toxicity and Structural Damage to Fish Tissues*

Fish that are exposed to cadmium (Cd) for extended periods of time may have pathological damage to their organs or tissues, which may result in necrosis or inflammation. Fish gills are the main location of Cd absorption during breathing in water. Cd ions are first accumulated in surface cells and then go to other organs or tissues through the bloodstream. As a result, Cd has harmful effects on the tissue structure of fish gills, causing necrosis, apoptosis, inflammation, and other negative outcomes.

The ability of the gills to control osmotic pressure and ion transport is compromised by changes in gill cell structure brought on by Cd ion stress in water. Research conducted on *Lates calcarifer* subjected to 20.12 mg/L Cd during 48 hours showed gill tissue aneurysm lesions, which developed into clear pathological alterations. Higher Cd exposure cause more severe pathological changes in gill tissue, such as cell growth, gill lamellae deformation, aneurysm formation, cell shedding, and oxidative damage like mitochondrial vacuolization and swelling (Thophon *et al.*, 2003).

2.2 *Cadmium Toxicity and Changes in Blood Plasma Parameters*

In a study on Nile tilapia, increasing cadmium levels in fish diet causes serum creatinine, glutamic-pyruvic transaminase (GPT), and aspartate aminotransferase (AST) levels to increase significantly and albumin and serum total protein concentrations to decrease. In a similar study on carp revealed that cadmium poisoning disrupted renal tubule reabsorption, increasing the excretion of calcium and phosphorus in urine and lowering serum levels of these elements. Furthermore, it has been discovered that cadmium harms renal tubules, prevents vitamin D from activating, and has detrimental effects on the metabolism of calcium and phosphorus. Aminotransferases are generally found in small amounts in serum and in greater abundance in tissues such as the liver, kidneys, heart muscle, and bones. However, these enzymes may reach the circulation and raise serum transaminase activity when organs, especially the liver and kidneys, are injured or diseased (Fırat & Kargın, 2009). Consequently, increases in serum glutamic oxaloacetic transaminase (GOT) and GPT activity may be a sign of poisoning or pathological changes. Different haematological parameters are also influenced by Cd toxicity (Table 2).

Table 2: Haematological Effect of Cd on Different Fish Species

Experimental Fish Species	*Dose of Cd Exposure (mg/L)*	*Duration of Exposure (Hours*/ Days#)*	*Changes in Haematological Parameters*	*Quantitative Alteration Against Control (%)*	*Reference*
Oreochromis niloticus	1.68	10#	Hb concentration decreases. Total RBC count decreases. PCV value decreases.	↓ 11.83 ↓ 3.29 ↓ 1.56	(Al-Asgah *et al.*, 2015)
Heteropneustes fossilis	2.07	7#	Hb concentration decreases. Total RBC count decreases. PCV value decreases. Total WBC count increases.	↓ 21.29 ↓ 32.9 ↓ 1.76 ↑ 6.98	(Mekkawy *et al.*, 2010)
Cyprinus carpio	92.5	15#	Hb concentration decreases. Total RBC count decreases. PCV value decreases. Total WBC count increases.	↓ 10.71 ↓ 18.79 ↓ 2.03 ↑ 29.58	(Ali *et al.*, 2018)
Labeo rohita	0.5	30#	Hb concentration decreases. Total RBC count decreases. PCV value decreases. Total WBC count increases.	↓ 18.86 ↓ 50 ↓ 0.17 ↑ 3.88	(Abdul Latif, 2012)

Experimental Fish Species	*Dose of Cd Exposure (mg/L)*	*Duration of Exposure (Hours*/ Days#)*	*Changes in Haematological Parameters*	*Quantitative Alteration Against Control (%)*	*Reference*
Clarias batrachus	13.8	30#	Hb concentration decreases. Total RBC count decreases. PCV value decreases. Total WBC count decreases.	↓ 30.76 ↓ 35.14 ↓ 2.39 ↓ 3.12	(Narra, 2017)
Clarias gariepinus	2	21#	Hb concentration decreases. Total RBC count decreases. PCV value decreases. Total WBC count decreases.	↓ 10.46 ↓ 6.77 ↓ 1.7 ↓ 4.15	(Ajani, 2012)
Catla catla	4.5	96*	Hb concentration decreases. Total RBC count decreases. PCV value decreases. Total WBC count increases.	↓ 24.3 ↓ 25.52 ↓ 6.7 ↑ 4.15	(Naz *et al.*, 2020)

2.3 *Cadmium Toxicity Impacts Fish Development and Endocrine System*

Fish reproductive systems are significantly compromised by prolonged exposure to cadmium (Cd). Long-term exposure to Cd results in substantial harm to the ovarian or sperm tissue's cellular structure and function, which reduces the ability to reproduce, incompletely develops embryos, and significantly retards the growth and development of young fish. A number of endocrine hormones are affected by Cd, including those that are associated with the hypothalamic-pituitary-gonadal (HPG) axis. According to a study, *Oncorhynchus mykiss* exposed to Cd, a marked suppression of the expression of the estrogen receptor in the gonads resulted in a disturbance of downstream pathways, which in turn caused aberrant development of the egg, irregular production of yolks, and finally, failure to reproduce (Bernhoft, 2013). In addition, exposure to cadmium can cause aberrant gonadotropin secretion, an imbalance in the oestrogen hormone, and a decrease in the ability to procreate.

Furthermore, as demonstrated in Mullet and Guppies, whose progeny numbers and survival rates dropped under Cd stress, Cd inhibits sterol synthesis, which in turn alters the blood levels of sex hormones in fish. At high doses, cadmium can also inhibit sperm motility and quantity and harm the genesis and maturation of germ cells (Massányi *et al.*, 2020). Cd induced immunological disruption is summarized below (Table 3).

Table 3: Cadmium Toxicity and Immune Disruption in Fish

Fish	*Toxic impact of Cd on Immunological System*	*Reference*
Ictalurus melas	Considerable suppression of lymphocyte proliferation.	(Liu *et al.*, 2022)
Yellow catfish	Blockage of the functions of liver acid phosphatase, alkaline phosphatase, and lysozyme.	
Zebrafish larvae	Increases neutrophil proliferation, which results in their accumulation in inflammatory sites in the liver tissue.	
Juvenile channel catfish	Chronic exposure impacts growth, survival, cellular stress, and glucose metabolism.	

2.4 *Cadmium Toxicity and Disruption in Energy Metabolism System in Fish*

Energy metabolism is essential to an organism's ability to grow and survive because it powers a number of biological functions, including immunological response, development, proliferation, and regulation of osmotic pressure. Research has indicated that exposure to Cd causes a drop in blood Ca2+ content, which inhibits the action of Ca2+-ATPase. This may be because free radicals can disrupt the structure of ATPase and cause oxidative damage to amino acids. Fish energy metabolism is impacted by cadmium, which also damages mitochondria, the main site of energy metabolism. In *Silurus meridionalis*, exposure to cadmium has been observed to cause substantial damage to the structure and function of the mitochondria, which lowers enzyme activity and the energy used by the liver for metabolism (Liu *et al.*, 2021). In addition, cadmium interacts with the expression of important mitochondrial genes and impairs respiratory regulation and oxidative phosphorylation efficiency in the mitochondria of *Oncorhynchus mykiss* (Branca *et al.*, 2020).

2.5 *Mechanism of the Toxic Effects of Cadmium on Fish*

When fish are stressed by cadmium (Cd), more reactive oxygen species (ROS) and reactive nitrogen species (RNS) than they can naturally scavenge build up in their bodies, which sets off a cascade of oxidative damaging responses. The main way that cadmium poisoning affects fish is through oxidative stress brought on by reactive oxygen species (ROS). This can lead to pathogenic changes in the long run, as well as structural changes in biological macromolecules like DNA and proteins. Furthermore, ROS can start the lipid peroxidation of unsaturated fatty acids in the cell membrane, which results in the production of malondialdehyde (MDA) and structural damage to the membrane. Enzymes on the cell membrane that control cell division, proliferation, and apoptosis may become dysfunctional as a result of the combined effects of these variables (Jomova *et al.*, 2023).

3. Conclusion

This study gives a broad overview of the biological build-up and harmful consequences of cadmium (Cd) in fish, including the latest findings on the effects of Cd on blood plasma parameters, reproduce-tive, immune system, tissue structure, and physiological metabolism. The goal is to protect aquatic ecosystems and life, minimizing the effects of Cd pollution in aquatic habitats, and guide the production of safe aquatic goods. The focus is on understanding fish toxicity to Cd and identifying future research objectives in this area. Research on the toxicological effects and mechanisms of various forms of Cd on fish is essential to fully assess ecological risks, environmental quality standards, and put mitigation measures to reduce the pollution caused by Cd in aquatic environments. Furthermore, more research is necessary to understand the mechanisms underlying the harmful effects of Cd, particularly when combined with other heavy metals.

References

[1] Abdul Latif (2012, April 24). Effect of cadmium chloride and ascorbic acid exposure on the vital organs of freshwater Cyprinid, Labeo rohita. *African Journal of Biotechnology*, 11(33). https://doi.org/10.5897/ajb12.118

[2] Afzaal, M., Hameed, S., Liaqat, I., Ali Khan, A.A., abdul Manan, H., Shahid, R. and Altaf, M. (2022, April 20). Heavy metals contamination in water, sediments and fish of freshwater ecosystems in Pakistan. *Water* Practice and Technology, 17(5), 1253–1272. https://doi.org/10.2166/wpt.2022.039

[3] Ajani, F. (2012, January 10). Hematological Changes of the African Catfish Clarias gariepinus (Burchell, 1822) Juveniles Induced by Diuron. *British Biotechnology Journal, 2*(4), 247–256. https://doi.org/10.9734/bbj/2012/2119

[4] Al-Asgah, N.A., Abdel-Warith, A.W.A., Younis, E.S.M. and Allam, H.Y. (2015, September). Haematological and biochemical parameters and tissue accumulations of cadmium in Oreochromis niloticus exposed to various concentrations of cadmium chloride. *Saudi Journal of Biological Sciences, 22*(5), 543–550. https://doi.org/10.1016/j.sjbs.2015.01.00

[5] Ali, A.J., Akbar, N.J., Kumar, M.A., Vijayakumar, S. and John, B.A. (2018, January 1). Effect of Cadmium Chloride on the Haematological Profiles of the Freshwater Ornamental Fish, Cyprinus Carpio Koi (Linnaeus, 1758). *Journal CleanWAS*, 10–15. https://doi.org/10.26480/jcleanwas.02.2018.10.15

[6] Annune, P.A., Ebele, S.O. and Oladimeji, A.A. (1994, August). Acute toxicity of cadmium to juveniles ofClarias gariepinus(Teugels) and Oreochromis niloticus(Trewavas). *Journal of Environmental Science and Health. Part A: Environmental Science and Engineering and Toxicology, 29*(7), 1357–1365. https://doi.org/10.1080/10934529409376116

[7] Bagur, R. and Hajnóczky, G. (2017, June). Intracellular Ca2+ Sensing: Its Role in Calcium Homeostasis and Signaling. *Molecular Cell, 66*(6), 780–788. https://doi.org/10.1016/j.molcel.2017.05.028

[8] Belyaeva, E.A., Glazunov, V.V. and Korotkov, S.M. (2004, December). Cd2+ versus Ca2+-produced mitochondrial membrane permeabilization: a proposed direct participation of respiratory complexes I and III. *Chemico-Biological Interactions, 150*(3), 253–270. https://doi.org/10.1016/j.cbi.2004.09.019

[9] Bernhoft, R.A. (2013). Cadmium Toxicity and Treatment. *The Scientific World Journal, 2013*, 1–7. https://doi.org/10.1155/2013/394652

[10] Branca, J.J.V., Pacini, A., Gulisano, M., Taddei, N., Fiorillo, C. and Becatti, M. (2020, November 30). Cadmium-Induced Cytotoxicity: Effects on Mitochondrial Electron Transport Chain. *Frontiers in Cell and Developmental Biology, 8.* https://doi.org/10.3389/fcell.2020.604377

[11] Chen, K., Mou, P., Zhu, A., Chen, P., Chen, J., Gao, G., Wang, X., Feng, X. and Yu, C. (2023, July 31). A comparative study of different methods for the determination of cadmium in various tissues of ramie (Boehmeria nivea L.). *Environmental Monitoring and Assessment, 195*(8). https://doi.org/10.1007/s10661-023-11601-2

[12] Delahaut, V., Rašković, B., Salvado, M.S., Bervoets, L., Blust, R. and De Boeck, G. (2020, April 9). Toxicity and bioaccumulation of Cadmium, Copper and Zinc in a direct comparison at equitoxic concentrations in common carp (Cyprinus carpio) juveniles. *PLOS* ONE, 15(4), e0220485. https://doi.org/10.1371/journal.pone.0220485

[13] Dutta, T.K. and Kaviraj, A. (2001, March). Acute toxicity of cadmium to fish Labeo rohita and copepod Diaptomus forbesi pre-exposed to CaO and KMnO4. *Chemosphere, 42*(8), 955–958. https://doi.org/10.1016/s0045-6535(00)00166-1

[14] Fırat, Z. and Kargın, F. (2009, June 2). Individual and Combined Effects of Heavy Metals on Serum Biochemistry of Nile Tilapia Oreochromis niloticus. *Archives of Environmental Contamination and Toxicology, 58*(1), 151–157. https://doi.org/10.1007/s00244-009-9344-5

[15] Jomova, K., Raptova, R., Alomar, S.Y., Alwasel, S.H., Nepovimova, E., Kuca, K. and Valko, M. (2023, August 19). Reactive oxygen species, toxicity, oxidative stress, and antioxidants: chronic diseases and aging. *Archives of Toxicology, 97*(10), 2499–2574. https://doi.org/10.1007/s00204-023-03562-9

[16] Jurgelėnė, I., Stankevičiūtė, M., Kazlauskienė, N., Baršienė, J., Jokšas, K. and Markuckas, A. (2019, August 22). Toxicological Potential of Cadmium Impact on Rainbow Trout (Oncorhynchus mykiss) in Early Development. *Bulletin of Environmental Contamination and Toxicology, 103*(4), 544–550. https://doi.org/10.1007/s00128-019-02694-y

[17] Liu, W., Qiu, H., Yan, Y. and Xie, X. (2021, August 29). Acute Cd Toxicity, Metal Accumulation, and Ion Loss in Southern Catfish (Silurus meridionalis Chen). Toxics, 9(9), 202. https://doi.org/10.3390/toxics9090202

[18] Liu, Y., Chen, Q., Li, Y., Bi, L., Jin, L. and Peng, R. (2022, October 19). Toxic Effects of Cadmium on Fish. *Toxics, 10*(10), 622. https://doi.org/10.3390/toxics10100622

[19] Massányi, P., Massányi, M., Madeddu, R., Stawarz, R. and Lukáč, N. (2020, October 29). Effects of Cadmium, Lead, and Mercury on the Structure and Function of Reproductive Organs. *Toxics*, *8*(4), 94. https://doi.org/10.3390/toxics8040094

[20] Mekkawy, I.A.A., Mahmoud, U.M., Wassif, E.T. and Naguib, M. (2010, July 13). Effects of cadmium on some haematological and biochemical characteristics of Oreochromis niloticus (Linnaeus, 1758) dietary supplemented with tomato paste and vitamin E. *Fish Physiology and Biochemistry*, *37*(1), 71–84. https://doi.org/10.1007/s10695-010-9418-3

[21] Narra, M.R. (2017, February). Haematological and immune upshots in Clarias batrachus exposed to dimethoate and defying response of dietary ascorbic acid. *Chemosphere*, *168*, 988–995. https://doi.org/10.1016/j.chemosphere.2016.10.112

[22] Naz, S., Hussain, R., Ullah, Q., Chatha, A.M.M., Shaheen, A. and Khan, R.U. (2020, September 30). Toxic effect of some heavy metals on hematology and histopathology of major carp (Catla catla). *Environmental Science and Pollution Research*, *28*(6), 6533–6539. https://doi.org/10.1007/s11356-020-10980-0

[23] Renieri, E.A., Sfakianakis, D.G., Alegakis, A.A., Safenkova, I.V., Buha, A., Matović, V., Tzardi, M., Dzantiev, B.B., Divanach, P., Kentouri, M. and Tsatsakis, A.M. (2017, August). Nonlinear responses to waterborne cadmium exposure in zebrafish. An in vivo study. *Environmental Research*, *157*, 173–181. https://doi.org/10.1016/j.envres.2017.05.021

[24] Roy, S., Karmakar, D. and Pal, S. (2022, May 12). Acute Toxicity Bioassay and Determination of LC50 of Cadmium Chloride in Trichogaster (Colisa) fasciata. *Applied Biochemistry and Biotechnology*, *194*(9), 3890–3900. https://doi.org/10.1007/s12010-022-03953-1

[25] Shuhaimi-Othman, M., Yakub, N., Ramle, N.A. and Abas, A. (2013, January 9). Comparative toxicity of eight metals on freshwater fish.

Toxicology and Industrial Health, *31*(9), 773–782. https://doi.org/10.1177/0748233712472519

[26] Thophon, S., Kruatrachue, M., Upatham, E., Pokethitiyook, P., Sahaphong, S. and Jaritkhuan, S. (2003, March). Histopathological alterations of white seabass, Lates calcarifer, in acute and subchronic cadmium exposure. *Environmental Pollution*, *121*(3), 307–320. https://doi.org/10.1016/s0269-7491(02)00270-1

People's Perception Towards Solid Waste Management and Sustainable Development: A Geographical Study of Falakata Municipality, Alipurduar, West Bengal

Sudarshan Das[1]

ABSTRACT: Municipal Solid Waste Management (MSWM) is a growing problem in our country. The size of the problem and the lack of sustainable solutions are causing pollution and health problems. Solid waste management has become a daunting task for municipalities and district authorities, who seem to lack the capacity and supply to deal with the growing waste situation. The key to sustainable development is finding ways to reduce the amount of solid waste that is produced. This is an essential municipal function to provide efficient service to keep the cities and towns clean. This paper was examined the peoples' perceptions and attitudes towards municipal solid waste management and sustainable development in Falakata Municipality of Alipurduar District of West Bengal. Falakata municipality is formed in the year of 2021 covering 55, 039 populations. The study is based on both primary and secondary data collected from households and municipal offices using a survey questionnaire and in-depth interviews. It was found that about 88.24% of respondents are willing to pay for a better collection system of waste and recycling

Keywords: Perception, Solid Waste Management, Sustainable Development, Alipurduar.

---

[1] State Aided College Teacher-I, Department of Geography, Falakata College. E-mail: sudarshandas.10029@gmail.com

1. Introduction

Solid waste is an international term used to describe useless and unwanted products in solid form arising from domestic, trade, commercial, agricultural, industrial, and mining activities as well as public services (Bhuiyan, 2010). Municipal solid waste consists of organic (fruits and vegetables) and inorganic (plastics, paper, glass, etc.), which are used in medical, industrial, Radioactive and agricultural wastes. But in Asia, household waste, human excreta, and agricultural, industrial, and hospital waste are collectively called municipal solid waste (Kaseva & Mbuligwe, 2005). Thus, waste originating from Asian cities is considered more hazardous than that from European countries (Cointreau, 2006). Solid waste management (SWM) is usually considered as a major environmental problem, especially in big cities. Still, until now its generation is unavoidable and highly neglected in most developing countries because it was not a big problem. Still, it has become a big problem and concept widely known to municipal authorities worldwide (Batool & Chaudhary, 2009). Similarly, bad People's consumption patterns, high standard of living, exploitation of resources and institutional framework are among the major issues related to waste management and pose serious threats to health and the environment that need to be addressed efficiently and effectively from industry to domestic sector (Sharholy *et al.*, 2008). Integrated Solid Waste Management (ISWM) is recommended as the most effective way to manage solid waste problems (Kasseva & Mbuligwe, 2000). Developed countries have many success stories as they implement their projects quite well using different waste management techniques like segregation, composting and recycling (Chowdhury, 2009). In contrast, developing countries struggled to copy these schemes without making meaningful efforts and adapting them to their state requirements as they had fewer resources, education, skills, and financial and technical capacity to meet the needs (Asase *et al.*, 2009). Municipal Solid Waste Management (MSWM) is a growing problem in our country. The size of the problem and the lack of sustainable solutions are causing pollution and health problems (Sharholy *et al.*, 2). Solid waste management has become a daunting task for municipalities and district authorities, who seem to lack the capacity and supply to deal with the growing waste situation (Gowda *et al.*, 2014). The key to sustainable development is finding ways to reduce the amount of solid waste produced. This is an essential municipal function to provide efficient service to keep the cities and towns clean (Ferronato *et al.*, 2017). According to the States of India's Environment report (2023), MSW generation in India is estimated to be around 150, 000 tons per day (TDP). The main practices of SWM are primary and only secondary collection of solid waste. However, using this waste collection means only 60% of the generated waste is collected, and about 90% is disposed of in open spaces. The remaining unconsolidated waste is thrown in empty plots, roads and roadsides, where it accumulates over time, causing various diseases and destroying the aesthetic beauty of nature (Gowda *et al.*, 2014).

2. Location of the Study Area

Alipurduar is one of the newly formed districts of West Bengal. The district has an area of 3, 010 sq. km. It consists of Alipurduar municipality, Falakata municipality and six community development blocks: Madarihat–Birpara, Alipurduar–I, Alipurduar–II, Falakata, Kalchini and Kumargram. Geographically the district lies in between

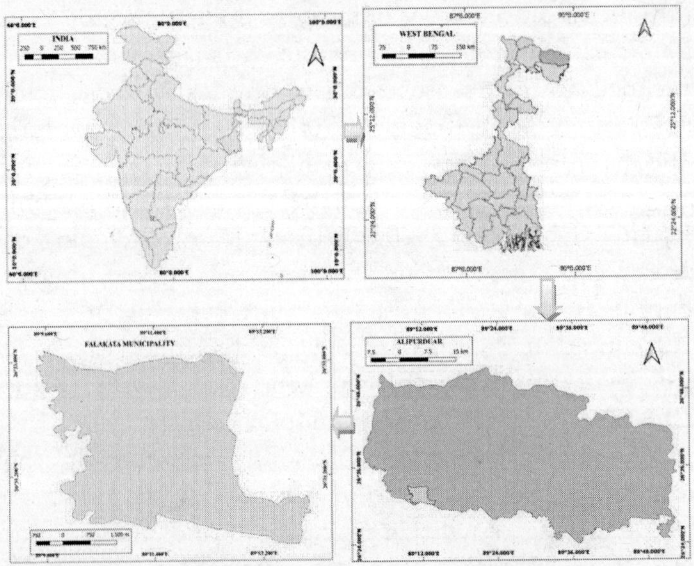

Figure 1: Location of the Study Area

26.4°N to 26.83°N and 89°E to 89.9°E. Alipurduar district has a population of 1, 491, 250, of which 1, 183, 704 are rural and 307, 456 are urban. Scheduled Castes and Scheduled Tribes make up 456, 706 (30.62%) and 382, 112 (25.62%) of the population respectively (Census of India, 2011).

In 2021, Falakata municipality was formed covering Falakata-I & II panchayats and parts of Parengerpar and Guabarnagar panchayats of Falakata block. Population of Falakata Municipality is *55, 039* people. The total number of households is 13502. 51% of the population is male and 49% is female. Falakata has a literacy rate of 86.01%, which is higher than the all-India literacy rate of 59.5%: male literacy is 89.48%, and female literacy is 82.42% (Census of India, 2011). The main objectives of the study are to highlight the basic profile of the study area and find out the association between volume of solid waste and socio-economic factors.

3. Methodology

The present study is based on the primary and secondary sources of data. A study was designed to examine people's perceptions towards waste management and sustainable development in Falakata Municipality. A semi-structured questionnaire was used to survey the socio-economic status of the respondents, their consumption patterns, perceptions and attitudes towards solid waste management and sustainable development. Data were collected through face-to-face interviews from respondents above 18 years of age old by simple random sampling. To test the validity and accuracy of the questionnaire, a pilot study was conducted in Falakata Municipality. Descriptive statistics (Frequency, percentage etc) has been used to analyse people's perception of solid waste management. Pearson Chi-Square has been applied to know the association between solid waste volume and socio-economic factors.

4. Result and Discussion

4.1 *General Profile of the Respondent*

Majority of the respondents were male with 61.76% and remaining 38.25% were female. Surprisingly 23.53% respondents were illiterate.

19.12% of respondents had educational qualification up to primary school. The proportion of respondents up to higher secondary was 30.88%. Only 10 respondents found to be graduates. Only 7.35% of the respondents have been found to have post graduation and above. Most of the respondents belong to 30–39 and 60 and above age group with same proportion (26.47 percent), followed by second prominent age group 40–49 years old, with 23..53 percent proportion. Third prominent age group was 50–59 years old with 14.71 percent. Only 8.82 per cent of respondents belong to the most young age groups, i.e. 20–29. Most of the households have the less than 5 members with 58.82 percent. Only 41.18 percent of households were found 5 and above members.

4.2 *Solid Waste Management of Falakata Municipality*

4.2.1 *Knowledge about Solid Waste Management*

The study area shows that most people know about solid waste management. About 83.76% of people heard about solid waste management, and 16.14% of people have no knowledge about solid waste management.

4.2.2 *Source of Acquiring Knowledge about Solid Waste*

In the study area, 51.47% of respondents acquiring knowledge about solid Waste from Television (TV), 26.47% of respondents from public meetings, 14.71% people came to know from through school and 7.35% people came to know from poster.

4.3 *Waste Generation at the Household Level*

4.3.1 *Food Waste Generation at Household Level (In Gram/Day)*

In the study area, it was found that 18.60% households generated less than 50 grams of food waste everyday, 39.53% households generated 50–100 grams of food waste per day, 27.91% household generated 100–150 grams and 13.95% household generated above 150 grams food waste every day.

4.3.2 *Paper Waste Generation at Household Level (In Gram/Day)*

Paper waste means newspapers, magazines, cardboard, and any other form of paper that is free of contaminated matter and capable of being recycled. In the study area, it is found that 23.81% of households produced less than 50 grams of paper waste per day, 39.68% of households produced 50–100 grams, 25.40% of households produced 100–150 grams, and 11.11% of households produced above 150 grams of others Waste per day.

4.3.3 *Plastic Waste Generation at Household Level (in gram/day)*

Plastic Waste is the accumulation of plastic objects (example – plastic bottles and much more) in the earth's environment that adversely affects wildlife, wildlife habitat and humans. The study showed that 22.64% of households generated less than 50 grams of plastic Waste every day, 43.40% of households generated 50–100 grams of plastic Waste per day, 20.75% of households generated 100–150 grams and 13.21% of households generated above 150 grams of plastic Waste every day.

4.3.4 *Others Waste Generation at Household Level (in gram/day)*

In the study area, it is found that 47.27% of households produced less than 50 grams of others waste per day, 23.64% household produced 50–100 grams, 18.18% household produced 100–150 grams and 10.91% household produced above 150 grams others waste per day.

4.4 *Association between Volume of Solid Waste and Socio-economic Factors*

Pearson chi-square was applied to identify the association between waste generation and the socio-economic status of the respondents. The results showed that the number of household members and the amount of solid Waste generated were positively correlated as the amount of Waste generated increased as the number of household members increased. The p-value of Waste (0.243) showed that no association was found between education and the amount of Waste generated. Although, it was generally assumed that a well-educated household generates less Waste on a daily basis. Conversely, the results obtained show the opposite trend in these study areas, as the volume of waste generation in high-income households is quite higher than that of lower-income households.

4.5 *Perception and Attitude of the Respondent Regarding Use of Shopping Bag to the Marketplace:*

It was observed that nowadays, people are becoming more concerned about pollution caused due the usage of plastic bags and their degradation than in the past, but, still, they were using plastic bags for shopping. The current study was also depicted the same results 78.17% of the respondents use plastic bags for carrying shopping materials, 18.61% people have cotton bags taken from their market whereas only 3.22% people used to bring reusable cotton bags from their homes.

4.6 *Attitudes of People Towards Solid Waste Collection Container*

Figure 9 shows that people had different attitudes towards keeping Waste outside their homes in different containers and boxes etc. In the study area 7.35% households collect Waste in carton, 11.76% in old bucket, 13.24% in tin or can, 44.12% in waste dustbin and 23.53% in plastic bag.

4.7 *Willingness to Pay (WTP) for Better Collection System of Waste and Recycling*

The study shows that 88.24% people pay for better collection of Waste and 11.76% pay for better collection of garbage. The majority of the respondents showed a positive attitude towards willingness to pay (WTP) for recycling their waste products, as shown in Figure 9, because people were informed that these practices are very important in resource conservation, sustainable development, economic opportunities, and reduction in waste disposal issues. Education had a positive effect on WTP for recycling as (p-value = 0.003) showed that well-educated people were more aware of the benefits of recycling. Therefore, a well-educated public can ensure the success of the WTP program's implementation. Turan *et al.* (2008) also mentioned the importance of public participation and awareness for better waste management.

4.8 *Problem for Long-Distance Dumping Side*

A landfill site, also known as a tip, dump, rubbish dump, garbage dump, or dumping ground is a site for the disposal of waste materials.86.76% of the people in the study area have no problem with the distance to the primary dumping side and 13.24% of the people in the study area have problem with the distance to the primary dumping side.

4.9 *Availability of Sufficient Community Bins*

Community bins mean a bin having a separate compartment for depositing bio degradable and non biodegradable Waste by households in a particular locality in consolation with the waste management committee. 19.12% of households in the study area had community bins and 80.88% did not have a community bin system.

4.10 *Perception about Disposal of Solid Waste*

Male's and female's perceptions of solid waste disposal were not the same as male were more concerned about segregation and recycling than female. The following perception about the disposal of solid Waste has been studied-

4.11 *Solid Waste is Disposed Directly in the Nearby Drain or Stream*

In the study area it was observed that 19.12% of household waste is always dumped directly in the nearby drain or stream. 27.94% and 29.41% of household frequently and sometimes disposed of their Waste directly in the nearby drain or stream. 10.29% household rarely disposed their solid Waste directly in the nearby drain or stream and 13.24% household never waste is directly disposed directly in the nearby drain or stream.

4.12 *Waste is Directly Disposed on the Road or Vacant Land*

The study showed that 22.06% households always waste are directly disposed on the road or vacant land. 16.18% and 20.59% of households frequently and sometimes Waste is directly disposed of on the road or vacant land. 22.06% household rarely and 19.12%

household never disposed their Waste directly on the road or vacant land.

4.13 *Waste as Composed or Manure*

The study found that 29.94% of households always used Waste as compost or manure. 22.06% and 16.18% household frequently and sometimes used Waste as compost or manure. 17.65% of households rarely and 16.18% of households never used Waste as compost or manure.

4.14 *Burn or Dispose Plastic Material and Polythene Bags along with Household Waste*

The study showed that 36.76% households always burn or dispose plastic materials and polythene bags along with household waste. 13.24% of households frequently and 19.12% of households sometimes burned or disposed of plastic materials and polythene bags along with household waste. 22.06% of households rarely and 08.82% of households never burned or disposed of plastic materials and polythene bags along with household waste.

4.15 *Burn or Dispose of Waste Paper Materials and Newspapers along with Household Waste*

In the study, it was found that 23.53% household always burn or dispose waste paper materials and newspapers along with household waste. 36.76% of households frequently and 14.715% of households sometimes burn or dispose of waste paper materials and newspapers along with household waste. 13.24% household rarely and 11.76% never burn or dispose waste paper materials and newspapers along with household waste.

4.16 *Perception about Sustainable Development*

In the study area 67.23% respondent have knowledge about sustainable development and 32.77% respondent have not knowledge about sustainable development. About 73.73% respondent said that solid waste management has impact on sustainable development and

26.27% respondent said opposite. 75.37% respondent mention that Solid Waste Management (SWM) should be developed in Falakata Municipality for sustainable development and 24.63% respondent said that SWM should not be developed in the study area for sustainable development.

Table 1: Perception about Disposal of Solid Waste

Statement	*Always*	*Frequently*	*Sometimes*	*Rarely*	*Never*
Solid waste generated is disposed directly in the nearby drain or stream	13 (19.12%)	19 (27.94%)	20 (29.41%)	07 (10.29%)	09 (13.24%)
Waste is directly disposed on the road or vacant land	15 (22.06%)	11 (16.18%)	14 (20.59%)	15 (22.06%)	13 (19.12%)
use of waste as composed or manure	19 (29.94%)	15 (22.06%)	11 (16.18%)	12 (17.65%)	11 (16.18%)
Do you burn or disposed plastic material and polythene bags along with household waste	25 (36.76%)	09 (13.24%)	13 (19.12%)	15 (22.06%)	06 (08.82%)
Do you burn dispose waste paper materials and news papers along with household waste	16 (23.53%)	25 (36.76%)	10 (14.71%)	09 (13.24%)	08 (11.76%)

Source: Field survey, 2023.

5. Conclusion

The current study thus revealed that the attitude and participation of local community towards SWM is very important for the successful implementation of any waste alleviation program and Integrated Solid Waste Management (ISWM). Education about solid waste Management should start from school level in the form of cartoon painting that will be helpful to understand the problem effectively. Inadequate SWM is associated with poor public health, and is a major problem affecting environmental quality and sustainable development of the municipality. Effective community involvement in SWM requires promoting positive public attitudes. Public awareness campaigns through print, electronic and social media should encourage people to refrain from littering and follow proper waste disposal practices. Improper SWM also results in water pollution and unhealthy air in cities. Therefore, for sustainable development, the government should take initiative and work jointly with other public and private sectors as well as municipal authorities to implement segregation strategies that will be conducive to effective recycling.

References

[1] Kasseva, M.E. and Mbuligwe, S.E. (2000). Ramifications of solid waste disposal site relocation in urban areas of developing countries: A case study in Tanzania. *Resources, conservation and recycling, 28*(1–2), 147–161.

[2] Kaseva, M.E. and Mbuligwe, S.E. (2005). Appraisal of solid waste collection following private sector involvement in Dar es Salaam city, Tanzania. *Habitat international, 29*(2), 353–366.

[3] Cointreau, S. (2006). Occupational and environmental health issues of solid waste management: special emphasis on middle-and lower-income countries. *Urban papers, 2.*

[4] Jin, J., Wang, Z. and Ran, S. (2006). Solid waste management in Macao: practices and challenges. *Waste management, 26*(9), 1045–1051.

[5] Kasapoğlu, A. and Turan, F. (2008). Attitude-behaviour relationship in environmental education: a case study from Turkey. *International Journal of Environmental Studies, 65*(2), 219–231.

[6] Sharholy, M., Ahmad, K., Mahmood, G. and Trivedi, R.C. (2008). Municipal solid waste management in Indian cities–A review. *Waste management, 28*(2), 459–467.

[7] Zhen-Shan, L., Lei, Y., Xiao-Yan, Q. and Yu-Mei, S. (2009). Municipal solid waste management in Beijing City. *Waste management, 29*(9), 2596–2599.

[8] Batool, S.A. and Ch, M.N. (2009). Municipal solid waste management in Lahore city district, Pakistan. *Waste management, 29*(6), 1971–1981.

[9] Chowdhury, M. (2009). Searching quality data for municipal solid waste planning. *Waste management, 29*(8), 2240–2247.

[10] Asase, M., Yanful, E.K., Mensah, M., Stanford, J. and Amponsah, S. (2009). Comparison of municipal solid waste management systems in Canada and Ghana: A case study of the cities of London, Ontario, and Kumasi, Ghana. *Waste management, 29*(10), 2779–2786.

[11] Bhuiyan, S.H. (2010). A crisis in governance: Urban solid waste management in Bangladesh. *Habitat international, 34*(1), 125–133.

[12] Gowda, K., Sridhara, M.V. and Chandrashekar, M.N. (2014). Planning strategies for municipal solid waste management in the city of Hassan, Karnataka. *International Journal of Innovative Technology and Research, 2*(3), 948–958.

[13] Haider, A., Amber, A., Ammara, S., Mahrukh, K.S. and Aisha, B. (2015). Knowledge, perception and attitude of common people towards solid waste management-A case study of Lahore, Pakistan. *International Research Journal of Environment Sciences, 4*(3), 100–107.

[14] Pujara, Y., Pathak, P., Sharma, A. and Govani, J. (2019). Review on Indian Municipal Solid Waste Management practices for reduction of environmental impacts to achieve sustainable development goals. *Journal of environmental management, 248*, 109238.

SECTION-F

Sustainable Management Practice

Designing Sustainable Supramolecular Gels for Self-delivery Application

Rumana Parveen[1]

ABSTRACT: A new bioconjugate derived from a non-steroidal-anti-inflammatory drug (NSAID) namely ibuprofen has been synthesised by amidation with biogenic molecules *i.e.* 5–aminoisophthlic acid with the aim of converting the nongelator NSAID ibuprofen into a sustainable supramolecular hydogelator for plausible drug delivery application. The synthesized bioconjugate showed gelation ability with green solvent water: DMF (95:5). The gel was characterized by table top rheology as well as dynamic rheology. Entangled fibrous morphology of the gel network was observed for under HR-TEM microscopy. Additionally, the biocompatibility of the gelator bio conjugate was assessed using a methyl thiazolyl diphenyl tetrazolium bromide (MTT) assay in mouse macrophage RAW 264.7 cells, confirming its suitability for biomedical applications. Finally, the anti-inflammatory response (PGE_2 assay) comparable to the parent ibuprofen drug; retaining its therapeutic effectivity. The synthesis of a bioconjugate derived from ibuprofen, a non-steroidal anti-inflammatory drug (NSAID), represents an innovative approach to transform ibuprofen into a supramolecular gelator for potential drug delivery applications.

Keywords: *Anti-inflammatory; SAFiNs; Supramolecular Gels; Drug Delivery.*

1. Introduction

Low molecular weight gelators (LMWGs)[1–5] are compounds with molecular weights typically below 3000 that possess the ability to form gels in a wide range of organic and aqueous solvents. Various

---

[1] Assistant Professor, Department of Chemistry, Dinhata College, Dinhata-736135, India. E-mail: rumanaparveeniacs@gmail.com

studies (microscopy, X-ray diffraction etc.) indicate that the gelator molecules form 1D network which further entangled through various weak intermolecular forces such as hydrogen bonding, π-π stacking, van der Waals interactions, hydrophobic interactions, charge-transfer interactions *etc.* to form 3D network structure (self-assembled fibrillar networks or SAFiNs)[6] within which the solvent molecules are immobilized resulting in a gel. LMWG based supramolecular gels, have gained significant attention in recent years due to their diverse potential applications across various fields such as optics/photonics,[7] sensors,[8] cosmetics,[9] structure directing agents,[10] conservation of art,[11] catalysis,[12] bio-medical applications,[13–16] etc. Recently, supramolecular gels are being explored as controlled drug delivery systems.[17, 18] Converting drug molecules into sustainable supramolecular gels *i.e.* environment friendly hydrogel formulation has been intensified because of various drawbacks associated with conventional drug delivery system where delivery vehicle is needed. However, this conventional drug delivery system has some basic limitations such as synthetic limitation of carrier molecule, loading drug molecule and its sustain release, cytotoxicity of the carrier molecule[19] *etc.* Whereas, self delivery[20] is an alternative option where drug molecule is modified into a supramolecular rather hydrogel in such a way that the drug may be effectively delivered to the affected site without the help of a carrier molecule following an environment friendly process. The motif of this present study is to develop supramolecular hydrogel for self-delivery applications displaying anti-inflammatory effects. For this purpose, we choose ibuprofen: well-known nongelator NSAID which is a well-known painkiller for the treatment of patients with acute or chronic inflammatory diseases. However, poor water solubility,[21] and hence lower bioavailability are the major problems associated with NSAIDs; in order to get efficient therapeutic effects, high dose is required which further causes various adverse side effects such as renal problem, gastrointestinal problems, cardiovascular attacks etc.[22] All these adverse effects can be avoided by converting the drug molecule into supramolecular hydrogel in a self-delivery fashion. Recently, scientefic community have been employed to develop various NSAIDs based supramolecular gels for self-delivery applications via various covalent modifications. Kim and co-workers reported enzyme-triggered release of ibuprofen from corresponding peptide based hydrogel.[23] Xu *et al.* synthesized D-amino acids conjugated NSAID-naproxen based hydrogels in a self-drug delivery fashion.[24]

In the present study, the basic objective was to convert drug molecule into sustainable supramolecular gel *i.e.* environment friendly hydrogel. In this context, it is worth mentioning that, sustainability of a gel depends on holistic assessment of its lifecycle; including use of non-toxic starting materials as well as aqueous medium as gelling solvent, environmental friendly production processes, environment friendly applications, and ease of bio-degradation etc. Herein, we have reported the synthesis and characterization of bioconjugate based hydrogelator in a self-delivery fashion using a environmental friendly production processes as shown in **Scheme 1**. The boiconjugate gelator showed excellent *in vitro* biocompatibility as well as retains its anti-inflamatory activity comparable with mother ibuprofen drug.

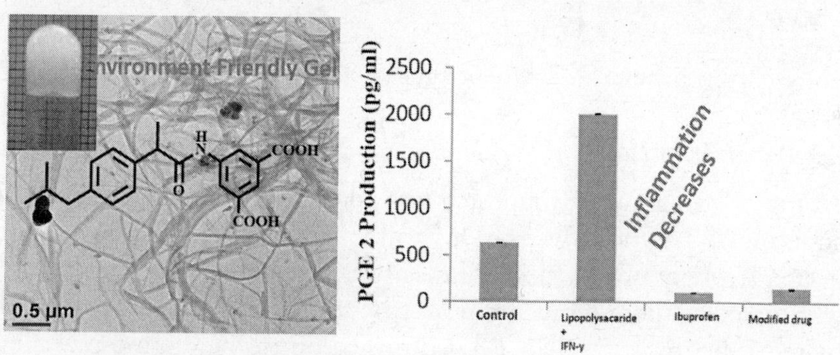

Scheme 1: Schematic Diagram of Environment Friendly Hydrogel of Modified Ibuprofen Bioconjugate Demonstrating to be Useful in Vitro Inflammation Treatment

2. Results and Discussions

2.1 *Synthesis*

In order to synthesize the bioconjugate, a time effective easy synthetic pathway has been utilized. 425 µL oxalyl chloride was added to a solution of 5 mmol (1030 mg) of ibuprofen in 50 ml dry DCM followed by few drops of DMF at room temperature. The mixture was then stirred for 6 hours. The solution was evaporated and a yellow mass was obtained. Next, the yellow mass in dry DCM was added dropwise to a solution of 5-amino isophthalic acid (906 mg, 5 mmol) dissolved in 30 ml dry THF and the mixture was stirred for 1 hour at r.t. The mixture was refluxed for 6 hours. The solvent was evaporated and a cream coloured solid was obtained (Yield: 80%). which was further characterized by Mass and IR spectroscopy.

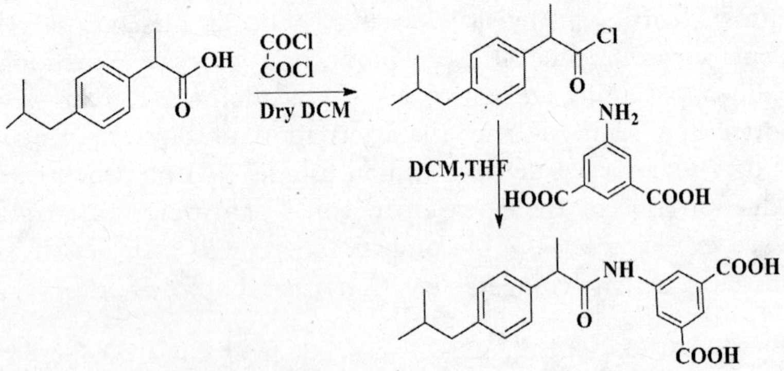

Scheme 2: Synthetic Procedure of Bioconjugate

2.2 Gel Formation

10 mg of bioconjugate ibuprofen was taken in a test tube followed by addition of 1.5 ml of water- DMF mixture (95:5). This solution was heated strongly until a clear solution was obtained. Next the solution was cooled at room temperature. Hydrogel was formed and confirmed by test tube inversion. The gel was turned out to be thermo-reversible with a minimum gelator concentration (MGC) of 1.5 wt% and gel dissociation temperature (T_{Gel}) was 56°C. T_{Gel} of these gels were determined following dropping ball method using different gelator concentrations. In a typical this experiment, a glass ball weighing 450 mg was placed on a 0.5 ml hydrogel taken in a test tube. The test tube was then immersed in an oil bath and heated gradually. The temperature at which the ball touches the bottom of the test tube was recorded as T_{Gel}. T_{Gel} vs concentration plot further revealed that with increasing concentration of gelator, Tgel value gradually increased; therefore, various non covalent interactions, such as hydrogen bonding, π–π stacking, C-H··· π interactions etc. plays crucial roles for gel network formation. (Figure 1)

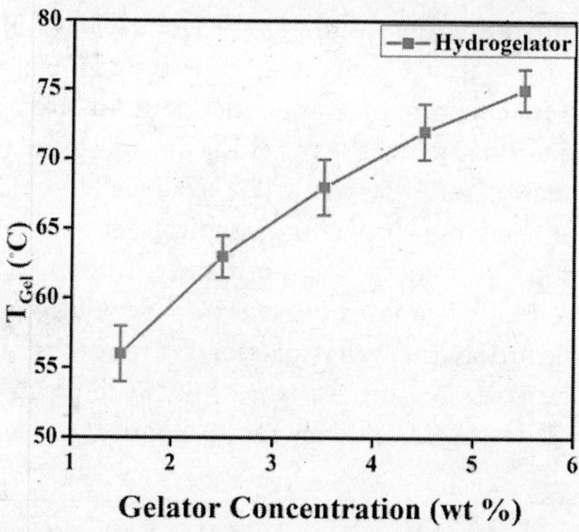

Figure 1: T_{gel} *vs* [gelator] (wt % w/v) Plot for Gel

In order to check the insight view of the gel network, HRTEM analysis of the hydrogel was performed. In a typical experiment, TEM samples were prepared by drop casting very dilute solution of gelator on a carbon-coated Cu (300 mesh) TEM grid. The grid was then dried under vacuum for overnight and subjected to record TEM images. Entangled fibrous gel network was observed in this experiment (Figure 2).

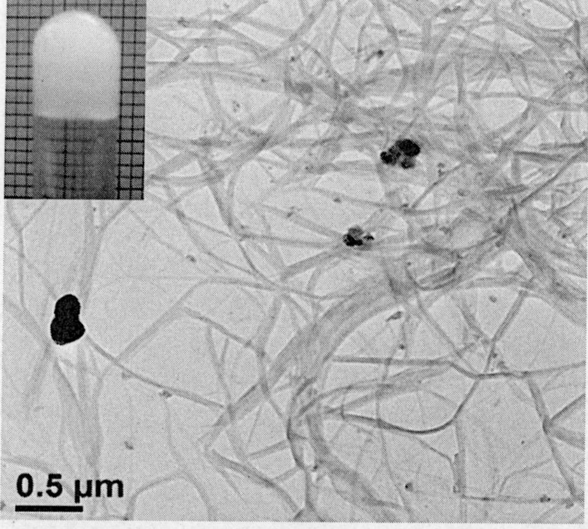

Figure 2: TEM Morphology of the Gel Network

Visco-elastic properties of the hydrogel (1.5 wt%) were further characterized by various dynamic rehological experiments. First amplitude sweep experiment was carried out in order to determine their LVE (linear viscoelastic) range. Elastic modulus (G') of the gel gradually decreased and after critical a strain it fell below the viscous modulus (G"): therefore displaying a typical gel like behaviour. Then frequency sweep experiment was performed under a constant strain 0.1% as suggested by amplitude sweep. The hydrogel displayed its visco-elastic nature as the value of storage modulus (G') was much higher than the corresponding loss modulus (G") and was frequency invariant over the entire frequency range (Figure 3).

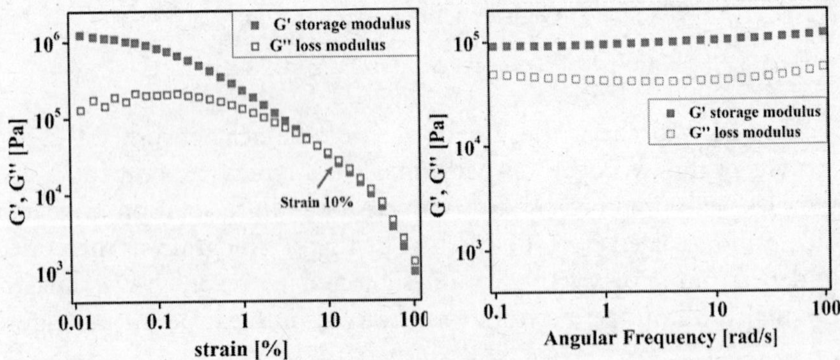

Figure 3: Rheological Responses of the 1.5 wt % (w/v) Hydrogel a) Strain Sweep and b) Frequency Sweep Experiment at Constant Strain of 0.1 % at 25°C

2.3 *Biological Studies*

Cytotoxicity of the Gelator by MTT Assay

After successfully converting ibuprofen into hydrogelator, it was very meaningful to examine whether the gelator having self- delivery capability or not. For this purpose, we decided to evaluate the cytotoxicity of this bioconjugate by MTT assay. The gelator bioconjugate molecule and mother ibuprofen drug were investigated in variuos concentrations using a standard protocol[25] for 72 hour at 37°C in RAW 264.7 macrophage cell line.This experiment clearly revealed that the gelator were biocompatible up to 1 mM comparable to mother drug ibuprofen(IC_{50} = 0.5 mM). In a close inspection, it was revealed that the IC_{50} value for the hydrogelator was found to be 1 mM where ~ 62% of cells survives even after charging the dose. (Figure 4).

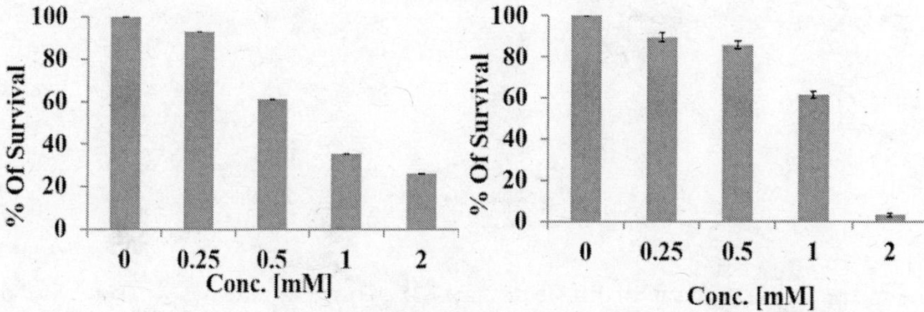

Figure 4: MTT Assay of Parent NSAID Ibuprofen and its Bioconjugate in Mouse Macrophage RAW 264.7 Cells for 72 Hours

Evaluation of anti-inflammatory activity of hydrogelator by PGE_2 assay:

After converting the nongelator ibuprofen drug into sustainable hydrogel by enviornment friendly green pathway in a self-delivery fashion, it was very meaningful to check whether the bioconjugate displays anti-inflammatory activity or not? For this purpose, PGE_2 assay was performed following a published protocol[26] using RAW 264.7 cell line. In a typical experiment, lipopolysaccharid (LPS) and interferon-gamma (IFN-γ) were added gradually inorder to obtain maximum inflammation to the cell, monitered by PGE_2 formation in the cell media. Then the cells were treated with bioconjugate as well as mother ibuprofen drug. Control experiment was also performed without addition of any external materials. After 24 hours, it was observed that PGE_2 level was 634 pg/ml in control experiment(no LPS and IFN-γ) whereas for LPS and IFN-γ inflmmated cells it as 2012 pg/mL which was further reduced to 107 pg/mL and 147 pg/mL for ibuprofen and bioconjugate treated cells. This suggests that the bioconjugate not only serves as a supramolecular hydrogelator but also retains the therapeutic effectiveness of ibuprofen, making it a promising candidate for localized drug delivery in inflammatory conditions.

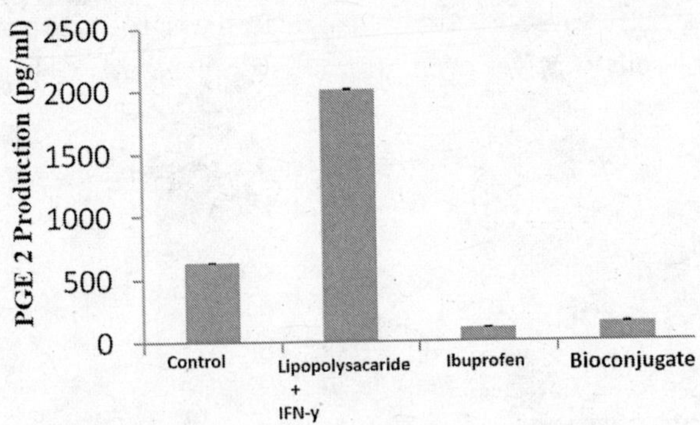

Figure 5: PGE_2 Assay of Ibuprofen and Bioconjugate in RAW 264.7 Cells

3. Conclusion

The present study deals with the design, synthesise and characterization of a new bioconjugate derived from NSAID-ibuprofen by conjugating it with 5-amino isophthalic acid following a very easy synthetic pathway. The bioconjugate was capable of gelling in green solvent water-DMF mixture (95:5). Microscopic studies of the gel demosnstarted the fibrous gel like entangled morphology and rheological experiments clearly indicated the visco-elastic (gel) nature of the hydrogel. The gelator bioconjugate showed comparable biocompatibility evaluated by MTT assay in mouse macrophase RAW 264.7 cells. One of the significant findings is the retention of the anti-inflammatory properties of ibuprofen in the bioconjugate, as demonstrated by the comparable response in prostaglandin PGE2 assay to that of the parent drug. The bioconjugate not only serves as a sustainable supramolecular gelator but also retains its drug activity; behaving as a good candidate for drug delivery in inflammatory conditions.Overall, this bioconjugate-derived supramolecular gel represents a promising approach for developing advanced drug delivery systems with comparable therapeutic efficacy and patient compliance.

Experimental Section

- **Materials:** All the chemicals including ibuprofen, 5-amino isophthalic acid etc. were purchased from Sigma Aldrich and used without further purification. Analytical reagent (AR) grade solvents were purchased from local market.

- **Methods:** FT-IR spectra of the compounds were carried out using Shimadzu FT-IR 8300 instrument. Transmission Electron Microscopy (TEM) images were recorded using a JEOL instrument with 300 mesh copper TEM grid. Rheological experiments were carried out using SDT Q series advanced rheometer AR 2000. MTT and PGE_2 assay were performed using a multi plate ELISA reader (Varioskan Flash Elisa Reader, Thermo Fisher).
- **MTT assay:** Raw cells were cultured in High Glucose DMEM (Dulbecco's modified Eagle's medium) media containing 10% fetal bovine serum (FBS) and 1% penicillin and streptomycin in a humidified incubator at 37°C and 5% CO_2. Then approximately 0.6× 10^4 cells were seeded in each well of a 96 well plate and kept it at humidified incubator for 24 hours. The cells were then charged with various concentrations (upto 2 mM) of mother drug ibuprofen, bioconjugate and DMEM alone and kept it at 37°C for 72 hours. Next, 100 μg of MTT (3-(4, 5-Dimethylthiazol-2-yl) -2, 5 -diphenyltetrazolium bromide) was added to each well and kept it for 2 hours. Thereafter, 100 μL DMSO was added to each well and shaked it for 20 minutes. Formazon was produced form the mitochondrial reductase of living cells, which was then dissolved in DMSO and formed purple coloured solution. The absorbance of this purple coloured solution was then recorded using a multiplate ELISA reader at 570 nm. The percentage of live cells present in hydrogelator was determined by considering the DMEM-treated (control) experiment as 100%.
- **PGE_2 assay:** In a typical experiment, approximately 1 × 10^6 cells/well (Raw 264.7) were seeded in a six well plate for 24 hours. 1 ml of DMEM was taken (control) in one well whereas the rest of the wells were treated with 1 μg/mL lipopolysaccharid (LPS) and 100 ng/ml interferon-gamma (IFN-γ) in order to obtain maximum inflammation. Out of these LPS/IFN-γ treated wells one well was treated with ibuprofen (0.5 mM) and another was treated with 0.5 mM concentration of hydrogelator in such a way that the total volume in each of the wells remains 1 ml. After 24 hours, the amount of PGE_2 produced in the culture medium was

determined using a Prostaglandin E_2 EIA kit-monoclonal (Cayman Chemicals, MI).

Characterization Data

Physico-chemical Data: FT-IR (NEAT): 3301 (s, amide N-H stretch), 1736 (b, acid C = O stretch), 1660 (amide C=O stretch) cm^{-1}. **(Figure S1) HR-MS, ESI (MeOH) m/z (100%):** calculated for $[C_{21}H_{23}NO_5 + 2H]^+$ is 371.16. Found 371.

Supporting Information

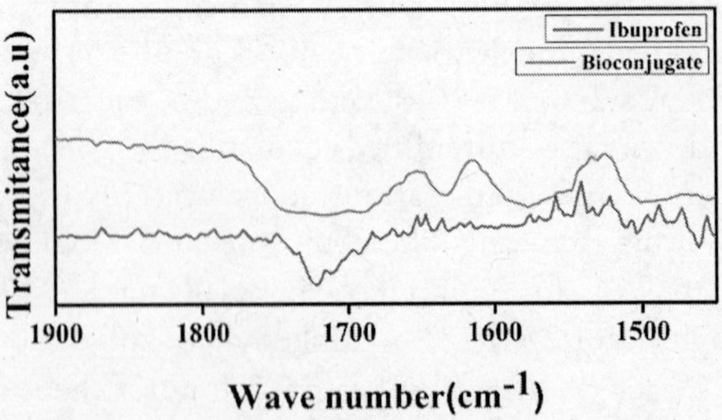

Figure S1: FT-IR Spectra of Ibuprofen and Bioconjugate

Acknowledgements

R.P. thanks WBDSTBT, West Bengal for financial support (Sanctioned G.O. No. 1362(Sanc.)/STBT-11012(25)/43/2021-ST SEC. dt: 21.03.2022) for the financial assitanship.

References

[1] Terech, P. and Weiss, R.G., *Chem. Rev.*, 1997, 97, 3133–3159.

[2] Suzuki, M. and Hanabusa, K., *Chem. Soc. Rev.*, 2009, 38, 967–975.

[3] Piepenbrock, M.-O.M., Lloyd, G.O., Clarke, N. and Steed, J.W., *Chem. Rev.*, 2010, 110, 1960–2004.

[4] Weiss, R.G. and Terech, P., Eds. *Molecular Gels: Materials with Self-Assembled Fibrillar Networks*, Springer: Dordrecht, The Netherlands, 2005.

[5] Tomasini and Castellucci, N., *Chem. Soc. Rev.*, 2013, 42, 156–172.

[6] George, M. and Weiss, R.G., *Acc. Chem. Res.*, 2006, 39, 489–497.

[7] Prasanthkumar, S., Ghosh, S., Nair, V.C., Saeki, A., Seki, S. and Ajayaghosh, A., *Angew. Chem. Int. Ed.* 2015, 54, 946–950.

[8] Ikeda, M., Fukuda, K., Tanida, T., Yoshii, T. and Hamachi, I., *Chem. Commun.* 2012, 48, 2716–2718.

[9] Wynne, A., Whitefield, M., Dixon, A.J. and Anderson, S., *J. Dermatol. Treat.* 2002, 13, 61–66.

[10] Basit, H., Pal, A., Sen, S. and Bhattacharya, S., *Chem. - Eur. J.* 2008, 14, 6534–6545.

[11] Carretti, E., Bonini, M., Dei, L., Berrie, B.H., Angelova, L.V., Baglioni, P. and Weiss, R.G., *Acc. Chem. Res.* 2010, 43, 751–760.

[12] Escuder, B., Rodrıguez-Llansola, F. and Miravet, J.F., *New J. Chem.* 2010, 34, 1044–1054.

[13] Wang, Q., Yang, Z., Zhang, X., Xiao, X., Chang, C.K. and Xu, B., *Angew. Chem. Int. Ed.* 2007, 46, 4285–4289.

[14] Jayawarna, V., Ali, M., Jowitt, T.A., Miller, A.F., Saiani, A., Gough, J.E. and Ulijn, R.V., *Adv. Mater.* 2006, 18, 611–614.

[15] Khademhosseini, A. and Langer, R., *Biomaterials* 2007, 28, 5087–5092.

[16] van Bommel, K.J.C., Stuart, M.C.A., Feringa, B.L. and van Esch, J., *Org.Biomol.Chem.* 2005, 3, 2917–2920.

[17] Pires, R.A., Abul-Haija, Y.M., Costa, D.S., Novoa-Carballal, R., Reis, R.L., Ulijn, R.V. and Pashkuleva, I., *J. Am. Chem. Soc.* 2015, 137, 576–579.

[18] Majumder, J., Deb, J., Das, M.R., Jana, S.S. and Dastidar, P., *Chem. Commun.,* 2014, 50, 1671–1674.

[19] Webber, M.J., Matson, J.B., Tamboli, V.K. and Stupp, S.I., *Biomaterials* 2012, 33, 6823–6832.

[20] Uhrich, K.E., Cannizzaro, S.M., Langer, R.S. and Shakesheff, K.M., *Chem. Rev.,* 1999, 99, 3181–3198

[21] Du, X., Zhou, J. and Xu, B., *Chem. Asian J.* 2014, 9, 1446–1472.

[22] Lee, B.J. and Lee, J.R., *Arch. Pharm. Res.,* 1995, 18, 22–26.

[23] Silverstein, F.E., Faich, G., Goldstein, J.L., Simon, L.S., Pincus, T., Whelton, A., Makuch, R., Eisen, G., Agarwal, N.M., Stenson, W.F., Burr, A.M., Zhao, W.W., Kent, J.D., Lefkowith, J.B., Verburg, K.M. and Geis, G.S., *J. Am. Med. Assoc.,* 2000, 284, 1247–1255.

[24] Bhuniya, S., Seo, Y.J. and Kim, B.H., *Tetrahedron Lett.,* 2006, 47, 7153–7156.

[25] Li, J., Kuang, Y., Gao, Y., Du, X., Shi, J. and Xu, B., *J. Am. Chem. Soc.,* 2013, 135, 542–545.

[29] Wang, Q.-S., Xiang, Y., Cui, Y.-L., Lin, K.-M. and Zhang, X.-F., *PLoS ONE* 2012, 7, 1–11.

[30] Heiss, E., Herhaus, C., Klimo, K., Bartsch, H. and Gerhäuser, C., *J. Biol. Chem.* 2001, **276**, 32008–32015.

Heritagization of Cooch Behar Town from a Critical Perspective

Partha Das*, Roshan Mahato** and Sourav Adhikary***

ABSTRACT: In one way history is a narration of earlier events in its present day context. Identification and declaration of heritage properties of historical and cultural importance in a region, is much of a present day phenomena. Authorities, embarking on this task, are supposed to perform a neat groundwork. They need to go through available literature, to meet and consult with local people and particularly the academicians and to physically visit each and every potential heritage spots therein. Centuries' old town of Cooch Behar has recently been declared a heritage town by the Government of West Bengal and a list of heritage spots of the place has been released accordingly. The present study observes this heritagization process from a critical perspective. An attempt has been made to classify and map these properties according to their physical conditions and occupancy and to critically examine their historical importance etc. Responsible authorities, academicians and activists involved with this ongoing heritagization process have been consulted to understand the nature and progress of the ongoing process, opportunities arising out of it and the flaws or obstacles, if any, associated with it.

Keywords: Heritage, Cooch Behar Town, Preservation, Opportunities, Critical Evaluation.

---

*Corresponding Author, Assistant Professor, Dept. of Geography, Acharya Brojendra Nath Seal College, Cooch Behar. E-mail: parthapranab@gmail.com; https://orcid.org/0000-0002-6124-8689

**Student, PG Dept. of Geography and Applied Geography, University of North Bengal, Siliguri. E-mail: roshan9474569801@gmail.com

***Student, PG Dept. of Geography, Sikkim University, Gangtok. E-mail: adhikarysourav569@gmail.com

1. Introduction

In mid-2017, the Chief Minister of West Bengal revealed the proposal to offer heritage status to the centuries old towns of Cooch Behar and Nabadwip[1]. Following this the West Bengal Heritage Commission (W.B.H.C.) notified that it "intends to declare the Cooch Behar town as a place of heritage buildings/temples/precincts/ sites etc." on 5th of July, 2019, in notification no. 79/N-1/WBHC/ 2008–09[2]. Then in August, 2019 both the towns were officially declared as heritage towns with a proposed list of 155 heritage sites in Cooch Behar[3]. However, irrespective of this declaration, the Cooch Behar district and its namesake headquarter have already been famous for their history and heritage. Before independence Cooch Behar was a princely state in subsidiary alliance initially with the East India Company since 1773 (Paul, 2018) and later with British India Government till 1947. Such a rich history of any place invariably results in presence of heritage sites across its geographical extension. So Cooch Behar possessing such a storied past must delve into preservation of its heritage.

Protection and conservation of heritage sites of a country used to be a national concern till the early 20th century. Initial attempts to build up an international consensus on preservation of heritage dates back to the Athens Conference on the restoration of heritage buildings in 1931 and publication of the Athens Charter at the fourth assembly of the International Congress on Modern Architecture in 1933. The first Congress of Architects and Technicians of Historic Monuments in Paris (1957) recommended all member states of UNESCO to join the International Centre for the Study of the Preservation and Restoration of Cultural Property (ICCROM)[4]. Their second Congress

---

[1] As reported by the Millennium Post on 27.06.2017 which is available in the following URL: https://www.millenniumpost.in/kolkata/kolkata-249369

[2] The notification is available with West Bengal Heritage Commission website accessible through the following URL: https://wbhc.in/files/contents/coochbehar_heritage_place_list.pdf

[3] As reported by the India Blooms on 16.08.2019 which is available in the following URL: https://www.indiablooms.com/news-details/N/53757/nabadwip-and-cooch-behar-given-heritage-status-by-west-bengal-government.html

[4] As stated in the website of International Council on Monuments and Sites (ICOMOS) which is available in the following URL: https://www.icomos.org/en/about-icomos/mission-and-vision/history?start=1

in Venice (1964) resulted in the adoption of International Charter for the Conservation and Restoration of Monuments and Sites or the Venice Charter and in the creation of International Council on Monuments and Sites (ICOMOS). UNESCO in its Paris General Conference (1972) adopted the convention concerning the Protection of the World Cultural and Natural Heritage to promote cooperation among nations to protect heritage around the world. It had the five strategic objectives of strengthening credibility of the World Heritage List, ensuring effective conservation of World Heritage Properties, promoting the development of effective capacity building measures, increasing public awareness through communication and enhancing the role of communities in the implementation of World Heritage Convention.

The protection of heritage sites in India is overseen by the Archaeological Survey of India (ASI) functioning under the Ministry of Culture. Article 49 of Indian Constitution makes it obligatory for the state to protect every monument or place or object of artistic or historic interest from spoliation, disfigurement, destruction, removal, disposal or export. The country's earliest attempts to protect and preserve heritage date back to the British period. The Ancient Monument Preservation Act (1904), the Antiques Export Control Act (1947) are few examples of those initiatives. The Ancient and Historical Monuments and Archaeological Sites and Remains Act (1951), the Ancient Monuments and Archaeological Sites and Remains Act (1958) and the Antiques and Art Treasures Act (1972) are independent India's initiatives in this regard (Patel, 2017). The aforementioned act in 1958 states that "Ancient Monument means any structure, erection or monument, or any tumulus or place of interest, or any cave, rock structure, inscription or monolith, which is historical, archaeological or artistic interest and which has been in existence for not less than 100 years and includes- remains of an ancient monument and the means of access to, and convenient inspection or, an ancient monument". On the contrary heritage can be cultural and natural or tangible and intangible. Tangible heritages both cultural and natural have a physical presence; e.g. geological heritage sites like Ramgarh crater in Rajasthan or built heritages like Taj Mahal in Uttar Pradesh. Intangible heritages, mostly cultural, include traditions or living expressions inherited from our ancestors and passed on to our descendants; e.g. indigenous knowledge, festivities, oral traditions, performing arts, social practices and rituals etc. These often have tangible objects, artefacts or places associated with them. Throughout the world preservation of tangible heritage has been given more importance than the intangible ones (Munjeri, 2004) and India is no different. Ministry of Urban Development, Govt. of India, in January 2015, has launched the scheme called HRIDAY (Heritage City Development and Augmentation Yojana). It has identified twelve (12) heritage cities in the country and aims to "preserve and revitalize soul of the heritage city to reflect the city's unique character.., to undertake strategic and planned development of heritage cities aiming at improvement in overall quality of life.. retaining the city's cultural identity" (Ministry of Urban Development, Govt. of India, 2015). After no urban centre from West Bengal could make it to the list, the state government in the same year announced the town of Bishnupur to be its first heritage city[5]. The laurel came to Cooch Behar and Nabadwip after a couple of years.

The Superintendent of Census Operations 1951, Ashok Mitra has identified ten (10) principal ancient monuments in the Cooch Behar district (Census of India, 1951). ASI has recognized and protects two (2) monuments there, namely- Cooch Behar Palace and Gosanimari *Rajpat* site. In addition the state government protects three (3) more heritage sites. Following the declaration of the entire Cooch Behar town as a heritage town, a team from Indian Institute of Technology (I.I.T.), Kharagpur has visited and have identified a total of 155 heritage sites across it[6]. It included natural objects like water bodies to cultural objects like palaces and temples, offices and private residences etc. The objective is the preservation and protection of heritage properties in and around the town.

This current work is an attempt to investigate the physical conditions, occupancy and historical importance of the heritage sites

[5] As reported in The Times of India on 20.05.2015 which is available in the following URL: https://timesofindia.indiatimes.com/west-bengal/wb-plans-first-heritage-city-in-bishnupur/articleshow/47353625.cms

[6] As reported in The Telegraph online on 08.08.2019 which is available in the following URL: https://www.telegraphindia.com/west-bengal/panel-suggests-heritage-tag-for-nabadwip-and-cooch-behar/cid/1696458

thus enlisted, to understand the nature and progress of the heritagization process and to identify the flaws involved and the opportunities arising out of this.

2. Literature Review

Cambridge Dictionary defines heritage as "features belonging to the culture of a particular society, such as traditions, languages, or buildings that were created in the past and still have historical importance". Again heritage has been defined as "a version of the past received through objects and display, representations and engagements, spectacular locations and events, memories and commemorations, and the preparation of places for cultural purposes and consumption" (Waterton & Watson, 2015). It is often considered as a value-laden concept (Lowenthal, 1998). Tunbridge and Ashworth mention that "the present selects an inheritance from an imagined past for current use and decides what should be passed on to an imagined future" (Tunbridge & Ashworth, 1996). Thus heritage is not only about history; rather it is produced in the present in relation to our current experience (Salazar & Zhu, 2015). It creates and strengthens social relations, values and a meaning about people's past and present (ibid). It provides ample opportunities for different ways of seeing and valuing the past (Boniface & Fowler, 1993). The scope of heritage has expanded over time and is no longer considered to be a static set of objects with fixed meaning (Torre, 2013). Now it is a social process through which "any human artefact can be deliberately invested with memorial function" (Choay, 2001). The significance of a heritage place is determined by the values that are attributed to it (Pearce, 2000). Heritage conservation is "a complex and continual process that involves determinations about what constitutes heritage, how it is used, cared for, interpreted, and so on, by whom and for whom. It has also become evident that decisions about what to conserve and how to conserve are largely defined by cultural contexts, societal trends, political and economic forces—which themselves continue to change" (Avrami, Randall, & Torre, 2000). A holistic and systematic assessment of maintenance approaches in heritage sites is there (Al-Sakkaf, El-Zahab, Abdelkader, & Alfalah, 2021). There are works attempting to introduce the complex relations among culture, heritage, geography, tourism and economy (Bujdoso, *et al.*, 2015).

Now a work has discussed different bottlenecks of heritage conservation in India like- limited number of heritage structures in the custody of national and state agencies, inadequacy of quality trained manpower, lack of convergence between modern-day engineering education and traditional knowledge of construction materials and practices and man-made vandalism, pollution etc. (Menon, 2014) There is addressal of the issue of little attention to the rehabilitation and conservation of old inner-city areas and historic monuments in the developing countries (Steinberg, 1996). Most of the historical areas in Indian cities are found to be neglected in the process of urban development and growth and undergoing rapid decline due to lack of appropriate policies, legal frame-works, funding and awareness etc. (Indian National Trust for Arts & Cultural Heritage, 2015) So a working group has been formed under the NITI Aayog in June 2019 with the objectives to examine the management of heritage structures and sites, to bring in institutional changes for improved heritage management, ways and means to involve the private sector and local communities in the process and possibilities of enhancing tourism and employment through heritage management (NITI Aayog, 2020). The issue of urban heritage preservation has taken wind across the world in the 21st century.

There is work on revitalizing urban heritage in old Baghdad city and the significance of preserving such historical places to promote socio-economic and sustainability aspects (Al-Saffar, 2018). A review of successful urban heritage conservation strategies in India has examined the different approaches taken in Mumbai inner city, in Nizamuddin Basti, New Delhi and in Jaipur, Rajasthan (Kadian & Nirmala, 2019). A study conducted in Surat, India shows how heritage is disappearing at an alarming rate with rapid urban growth in face of increasing housing demand of an ever-growing urban population (Udeaja, *et al.*, 2020). Government plays a dual role of conserving urban heritage and promoting development and this makes balancing the urban conservation-development relationship a dynamic process (Zhang, Edelenbos, & Gianoli, 2024). A recent study in India tries to identify and prioritise the factors needed to be considered for an urban heritage conservation project from the perspective of experts that can be further evaluated from the perspective of stakeholders (Huq & Puthuvayi, 2024). Research on heritage in West Bengal has been inadequate so far and researches on heritage preservation are only a handful and mostly limited to the Kolkata metropolis and its surroundings. An article has discussed the role of cost-benefit analysis in heritage building conservation with reference to Kolkata Municipal Corporation (Sen R. K., 2015). Another work on Kolkata analyses the change in settlement pattern over the years and its effect in the diminishing nature of heritage (Deo, Swain, & Das, 2022). Yet another work assesses the potential damage factor to the famous St. Paul's Cathedral of the city (Basu, *et al.*, 2021). Bente Wolf has studied the local perspectives of colonial heritage buildings, popular history and cultural identity of the Dutch trading hub Serampore, an hour drive from Kolkata (Wolff, 2020). Such works are almost missing for rest of the state and existing works mostly deal with heritage from the perspective of tourism or the perspective of archaeology and historical significance. There is analysis of cultural heritage tourism in West Bengal (Ahamed, 2017). While a study has introduced us to various heritage sites in Birbhum district and their heritage tourism potentialities (Barman, 2013), another has highlighted the issues of cultural crisis and deteriorating heritage among folk cultures in *Jangal Mahal* (Chatterjee & Dwivedi, 2023). Yet another study has discussed about the archaeological findings from north Bengal and how the museums there, are inadequate for their conservation (Sarker, 2019). An article has introduced us to different historical places in Cooch Behar and their tourism potential (Sarkar, 2014). There is a book on the cultural heritage of North Bengal with special focus on *Bhawaiya* song from the district (Adhikary, 2023). So, a comprehensive study on heritage of the district is unavailable and it remains relevant to study the ongoing heritagization process in Cooch Behar town.

3. Study Area

The erstwhile princely state of Cooch Behar joined the Indian Union on 12th September, 1949 and turned into a district of West Bengal on 1st January, 1950 (Paul, 2018). This remote district, found in the north-east corner of the state, shares its eastern boundary with Indian state of Assam and its southern boundary with independent nation of

Bangladesh. Apart from its rich colonial history, mention of this region can be found in antiquity. Hindu mythology describes Cooch Behar as a part of ancient kingdom of *Pragjyotisha-* and evidences show it to be a part of *Kamrupa-* in the ancient Indian history (Census of India, 2011). Her highness Maharani Sunity Devi of Cooch Behar has referred to a myth describing the place as 'earthly home' of lord Shiva (Devee, 1921). During the 15th century the region used to be governed by *Khen* kings from their capital in *Kamatapur* or present day Gosanimari in the Dinhata-I C. D. Block of the district (Roy, 2018). Later in 1510 a new *Koch* dynasty came in power and ruled it till independence. Following a treaty of subsidiary alliance in 1773, the state of Cooch Behar lost its sovereignty to British East India Company. Census 1901 reports a population of 566974 in this princely state out of which only 14060 people were living in the four (4) municipal towns of Cooch Behar, Dinhata, Mathabhanga and Haldibari existing back then (Dutt, 1903). Among these, the town of Cooch Behar (26°19'N, 89°27'E) has acted as the capital of the kingdom for most of its existence and now it serves as the district-headquarter. It is located on the left bank of river Torsa, the principal stream of the district, and is bounded on its eastern flank by an abandoned channel of the same river called *Buri* or *Mora* Torsa. Presently the town is connected with rest of the country via National Highway 31 and also by Northeast Frontier Railway through New Cooch Behar railway station. It experiences a hot and humid climate.

The proper development and growth of this town actually started in the last quarter of the 19th century. Before that the town consisted of "mat huts…few public buildings of any note" (Hunter, 1876). Settlement *Naib Ahilkar* of the princely state Harendra Narayan Chaudhuri writes that "the town of Cooch Behar was full of jungle…With the establishment of a municipality in 1885–86; arrangements were made for a proper conservancy" (Chaudhuri, 1903). Now the town consists of twenty (20) wards, a railway station, an airport and a wide network of roadways. Census 2011 reported a population of 77935 in the Cooch Behar municipality[7].

---

[7] As available in the official website of Cooch Behar District Administration and accessible through the following URL: http://coochbehar.nic.in/htmfiles/population_total.html

This town is also famous as '*Dighi-r Shohor*' (City of Lakes) for its numerous tanks or lakes among which *Sagar Dighi*, excavated by King Harendranarayan in 1807, is the largest. Famous among other lakes are *Bairagi Dighi* opposite *Madan Mohan* Temple and *Lal Dighi* opposite *Bhabanigunj* Market. These three lakes along with most of the other existing lakes in the town have been enlisted as heritage sites by the W.B.H.C. There are ample monuments and heritage places too, that boast rich history of their own. Probably the most popular among them are the Royal Palace and *Madan Mohan* Temple, both built during the reign of king Nripendra Narayan, in 1889 and 1890 respectively (Das B., 1985). The Royal Palace is undertaken by the ASI and both the places fall within the recently prepared heritage list by the W.B.H.C. Other famous historical sites in the town include Jenkins School for Boys, Cooch Behar Municipality building, Artizan School, State Library, Cooch Behar State Press, *Sunity* Academy for girls, Victoria College or A B N Seal College and *Narendra Narayan* Park etc.; all established in the end 19th century. So it is clear that Cooch Behar town deserves the heritage tag it has received after around seventy years of its joining with the Indian Union. The present study involves a thorough survey of those heritage properties and a detail inspection of the ongoing heritagization process from a critical perspective.

4. Objectives

The study aims to evaluate the ongoing process of heritagization. To do so, it becomes obligatory to visit each of the sites to understand their historical importance and to inspect their physical conditions and current occupancy etc. Accordingly heritage mapping of the town is planned to be attempted. The study further intends to examine the affair in progress from a critical perspective. It attempts to find the flaws involved so that responsible authorities can act duly. It also hopes to suggest the opportunities for Cooch Behar town arising out of this heritagization process.

5. Methods Applied

Such an attempt to evaluate the ongoing heritagization demands a detailed background check, thorough ground work and conversation with the different stakeholders etc. The work started with conceptualization and topic selection followed by review of existing literature. After the identification of the research problem and chalking out the research objectives, field surveys and personal interviews were ensued. The findings were verified with further literature review and expert opinions. The drafting and mapping of the manuscript came last.

Review of literature has aided in the initial concept building purpose. From newspaper articles to government notifications, from the British era gazetteers to the history of the princely state and from the global practices of heritage preservation to the relevance of the same in the local context etc., all kinds of literatures have been consulted. Next a municipality map of Cooch Behar town has been collected from the municipality website. Initially 155 spots were proposed as heritages, but now only 151 remain on the list. All such places, except the *Nilkuthi* Site and King's Hanger falling within restricted zones, have been personally visited and their physical conditions and occupancy status have been carefully recorded. At the same time their co-ordinates have been collected using Garmin eTtrex 10 GPS receiver for the purpose of heritage mapping. The location of each spot has been verified with the people in the neighbourhood and the local historians so that no error is committed in their identification. Next comes the turn of consultation with every stakeholder. Officially the heritage committee, in charge of looking over the entire procedure, consists of 26 members with 2 more patrons selected from local political representatives. Along with different government executives the *Sabhadhipati* of Cooch Behar *Zilla Parishad*, the Chairman and Vice-chairman of Cooch Behar Municipality, a representative from the erstwhile royal family, a local historian, two representatives from Cooch Behar Panchanan Barma University and A B N Seal College respectively and few more local academicians are included in that committee. From among the twenty six, only 6 (six) have shared their thoughts with the authors. Apart from these policy makers, stakeholders are also those whose properties have been enlisted as heritages, the neighbourhood people and every concerned citizen of the town of Cooch Behar taking interest in the process. The current survey interviewed members from all such families whose properties have been enlisted as heritages, people from neighbourhood around such heritage sites along with the enthusiasts from among the citizen, although only a handful in number. This entire survey has been conducted between November, 2023 and February, 2024. Literature review also continued simultaneously to validate the information received. MS Office and GIS software have been used for mapping and drafting.

6. Findings

6.1 *The Issue with Identification of Heritage*

When the proposed heritage list was published, it raised many an eyebrows in Cooch Behar. For a town spreading across just 8.29 sq. km[8], 155 heritage spots is supposed to put up some questions. Even the heritage committee members and local experts have their difference of opinion regarding the presence of so many sites in the list. The principal issue of contention has been the historicity of many places enlisted. Inclusion of many sites like- Additional District Magistrate Bungalow and Ram Krishna Math, established after 1950, has created ambiguity around the selection process. It is also reported that many deserving historical spots have been left out[9]. This issue also cropped up during the conversation with the heritage committee members and local experts. All forty-five (45) water bodies in the town have been included in the list, while three (3) of them are reported to be dug up post-independence. It is not clear why sites like *Nilkuthi* or residence of Ahsanullah Ahmed, not existing anymore, are there in the list.

Many current occupants of private properties have shared that they have not been properly intimated about inclusion in the heritage list. From the preliminary list, serial 104 *Dev Bakshi Bari* has already been removed after the same was appealed from the present family members. Few other current occupants of such private properties have informed that they have applied for similar exclusion. On the

---

[8] As available in the official website of Cooch Behar Municipality and accessible through the following URL: https://coochbeharmunicipality.com/history.php

[9] As reported in the daily *Uttarbanga Sambad* on page 1, dated January 3, 2024

other hand, places like serial 22 *Ananda Bhaban*, serial 89 Old Military Mosque and serial 94 New Cinema have been excluded from the list between September and October, 2023. Now 151 sites remain on the list. Both *Ananda Bhaban* and Old Military Mosque are century old structures from the *Raj* era, apt for preservation as heritage properties. New Cinema, too with its unique architecture and history, deserve to remain as heritage.

All these confusions have their origins in two facts. Firstly it has been too late to declare Cooch Behar as a heritage town as many of the places with past lineages have either been lost (*Nilkuthi*) or have been transformed into modern usages. Secondly preparation of the heritage properties list lacked the proper involvement of local stakeholders. Conversation with committee members and local academicians clearly revealed that though the local heritage committee was formed way back in 2017, they were not adequately involved during the survey work by the team of I.I.T., Kharagpur. For the acceptance and success of any project, it is necessary to involve the local community in the planning, implementation, monitoring and evaluation (Dwivedi & Dwivedi, 2012). So far the heritagization process in Cooch Behar has remained more a bureaucratic affair, lacking community participation.

6.2 *Distribution and Classification of Heritage Properties*

Irrespective of the debate on the list of heritages, it is important to observe the nature of distribution of these 151 properties across the town. The maximum numbers of heritage (22 each) sites are reported from ward 17 and 19, followed by ward 18 (20 sites). Whereas the minimum, only a single site, are recorded from wards 3 and 5 and no heritage site is present within wards 11, 12 and 14. Wards 2, 10 and 15 host a couple of heritage sites each, whereas ward 1 has three (3) sites. Wards 6 and 13 have five (5) sites within their boundaries. Wards 4, 7 and 16 include six (6), seven (7) and eight (8) heritage properties respectively. Again one can spot thirteen (13), fourteen (14) and eighteen (18) heritages in wards 8, 9 and 20 respectively.

Now one of the important concerns with heritage properties is their nature of occupancy and current usage. Among the currently enlisted sites in the town, many are under government undertaking, many are religious places mostly running under the Debuttor Trust Board of the district, many water bodies in both public and private occupancy and some private properties. Now among the forty-five (45) water bodies enlisted, few fall within premises of complexes with another heritage structure. Rest of the thirty-four (34) water bodies has found separate mention in the heritage list. Similarly twenty (20) religious places and fourteen (14) properties under private or society occupancy (e.g. Cooch Behar Club) are there in the list. Remaining eighty-three (83) sites are found to be under government or public undertaking during the survey. See Figure 1a.

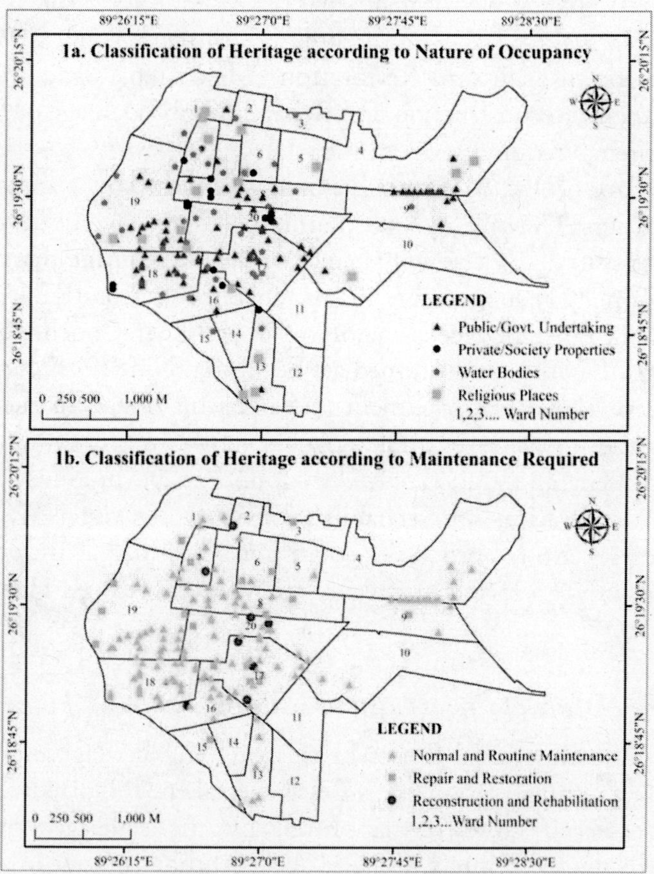

Figure 1: Heritage Map of Cooch Behar Town by a. Nature of Occupancy and b. Maintenance Required

Source: Prepared by Authors.

Another concern in relation to heritage properties is their maintenance which makes the assessment of physical conditions of the sites very important. Visual inspection is an important method of such assessment. It involves recording with the use of photographs, taking notes on architectural and structural components along with informed judgement on the defects or flaws observed (Noor, Mei, Ibrahim, Sarbini, Osman, & Khiyon, 2019). Again expert opinion plays a key role in absence of in-depth study requiring official and owner permission. Following Maintenance Action method attempted by Zuraidi *et al.*, heritage sites in Cooch Behar town can be classified into three (3) categories of maintenance (Zuraidi, Rahman, & Akasah, 2018)- Normal and Routine maintenance (need minor servicing or repair work), Repair and Restoration (Major repair and restoration required) and Reconstruction and Rehabilitation (Damage or Defect in the elements require serious attention). For example—the Cooch Behar palace or *Madan Mohan* Temple is found to be well maintained and another 117 similarly well maintained sites have been identified during the survey. These only need normal and routine maintenance. Twenty-one (21) sites require major repair and restoration, e.g. places like Heritage arcade needs major repair work or Cooch Behar Fish Seed Firm Dighi 3 needs immediate de-silting. Nine (9) sites are found in ruins or under encroachment and need major reconstruction and rehabilitation. Take example of the *Bou Dighi,* found under encroachment and the *Top Khana*, found to be in ruins; requiring serious reformation and rehabilitation. Among the 151, physical condition of two (2) properties could not be verified as they are either lost (*Nilkuthi*) or located within restricted zone (King's Hanger). See Figure 1b.

6.3 *The Nature of Preservation Measures Taken*

The most controversial aspect of this ongoing heritagization process has been the preservation measures undertaken. Reportedly a budget of Rupees 110 crore was approved by the state government to transform the town into a heritage one[10]. Authors are not in a position

[10] As reported by the Millennium Post on 24.05.2023 which is available in the following URL: https://www.millenniumpost.in/bengal/work-underway-to-turn-

to comment if the amount is ample or not, what is desired is its proper utilization.

The focus of heritagization has so far remained on the grand mansions, famous spots like *Sagar Dighi* or *Madan Mohan* Temle. Reconstruction and beautification work in such places are going on in full swing. A heritage gate, costing a sum of 1.4 crore rupees, has been built at the entrance of the town[11]. On the other hand dilapidated structures, like- *Bani Bhaban* or *Top Khana* have not even received the official heritage notice board till now.

There is lack of coordination between the district administration and members of heritage committee. There are reports of highhandedness from the end of decision makers; meetings of the heritage committee are often irregular[12] and inconclusive. From the selection of heritage sites to the execution of repair and restoration work, opinions of the committee members and local academicians have mostly remained unheard.

Preservation measures taken have often ignored local sentiments and people's participation. There are complaints that in the name of renovation, administration is actually causing harm to heritage. During the beautification work around the *Sagar Dighi* and *Bairagi Dighi*, historical *ghats* have been demolished and reconstructed afterwards without paying any attention to their historical value or the local emotions associated with them[13]. Whereas water bodies like *Chandan Dighi* and *Shiv Bari Dighi* etc. remain either encroached or silted and often hidden from public view by illegal occupation around the lakeside. Locales complain that even after repeated appeals, no decisive measures have been taken so far to recover and rejuvenate these.

Restoration work, where undertaken, have often been limited to beautification only. The heritage main building of A B N Seal College has been recently painted without repairing the damages

cooch-behar-into-heritage-town-519806#:~:text=The%20process%20to%20transform%20Cooch, budget%20of%20Rs%20110%20crore.

[11] As reported in the daily *Uttarbanga Sambad* on page 9, dated May 15, 2023.

[12] As reported in the daily *Uttarbanga Sambad* on page 9, dated February 20, 2024.

[13] As reported in the daily *Uttarbanga Sambad* on page 13, dated January 20, 2024.

following heritage standards. Most of these age old heritage structures consist of lime based architecture and should be lime-washed during painting. But it is observed that plastic based paints are being used for the purpose which is not suitable for heritage structures.

The main hurdle in this entire process has been the issue of preservation of private properties. So far, neither any separate guidelines nor any separate budget for their restoration and rehabilitation have been released. Most of such properties, like *Bhattacharya Bari* in ward 7 or *Roy Bari* in ward 20 are found in dilapidated conditions and need urgent repair[14]. But the onus for the same remains on existing occupants and the heritage law prohibits them from any major reconstruction. Strict implementation of the heritage laws also remain wanting in this regard. For example—during the survey one such private heritage house in ward 13 or another in ward 18 are found to have either been partly or fully reconstructed, dismantling the heritage property.

Another drawback has been the failure of administration to generate awareness about heritagization, among local people. Though no opinion survey could be conducted, one of the limitations of this current research, but common people in general is not well informed about what is happening in their town. Neither their opinion and wisdom have been taken into account nor have they been instructed about how to treat their heritage. So issues continue to crop up; like-illegal construction and encroachment inside heritage properties, polluting heritage sites and defacing the heritage foundation stones and memorials etc.

Finally the heritagization process is found to be progressing at a sluggish pace. After more than four (4) years of its official announcement, the district administration revealed their plan of completing work of an estimated Rupees 30 crore before Rasmela 2023[15], less than one-third of the total work budget. Announcements

---

[14] As reported in the daily *Uttarbanga Sambad* on page 1, dated February 10, 2023.

[15] As reported in The Telegraph online on 06.11.2023 which is available in the following URL: https://www.telegraphindia.com/west-bengal/cooch-behar-aims-to-finish-beautification-projects-worth-rs-30-crore-before-raas-utsav/cid/1977916

were made to free the footpaths from illegal encroachment[16] or to build roadside rest shade for passengers in line of heritage of Cooch Behar[17] and many more. But their realizations are still awaited.

7. Opportunities Arising Out of Heritagization of Cooch Behar Town

Heritage is not only about preservation of the past artefacts, not a static object rather a dynamic concept. Heritage is what we inherit; it is about creating an identity. The heritage properties in Cooch Behar provide the town its unique appeal; make it distinct from any other. Heritage is not only about conservation, it also has consumption values offering a distinct avenue of recreation.

Apart from such subjective values, the ongoing heritagization leads the town on road to beautification and infrastructural development. With the government financial aids, it is awaiting a revamp in terms of improved road condition, street lighting and sewage system etc. The beautification work is evidently going on and it desirably invites more tourist arrival in this old town from the pre-British era. Increased tourist arrival is sure to improve the local economy in terms of employment generation, revenue collection and eradication of poverty etc. So there should be concerted efforts, co-ordination among government machinery and private players and citizens forums like NGOs to make the town more tourist-friendly.

Existing tourist information centres are hardly of any help with no readily available data on tourist arrival in the town (Das & Biswas, 2023). Most of the heritage spots remain unknown to even a resident of the town. Important heritage properties should be promoted so that locales get aware of their prestigious past and tourists find some added interests in visiting the town. In this regard efforts of Cooch Behar Archive, a local non-profit organisation, are really appreciable. They organize regular heritage walks, seminars to increase awareness. If such initiatives could be jointly organized along with the government offices and private establishments like hotels, tourists could also take part. If light and sound show, depicting the royal

---

[16] As reported in the daily *Uttarbanga Sambad* on page 1, dated May 27, 2023.
[17] As reported in the daily *Uttarbanga Sambad* on page 15, dated April 30, 2023.

history of Cooch Behar, could be displayed in places like the Cooch Behar palace or *Baro Debi Bari*, with ample space for a large audience, it would draw both citizens of the town and tourist alike. Similarly if cultural events could be organised in heritage premises like what we see in *Princep Ghat*, Kolkata or in Red Fort, Delhi; it would surely elevate the appeal of the town. The three day long 11th Rashtriya Sanskriti Mahotsav, organized between 14th and 16th February, 2021 at the Cooch Behar palace premises, had drawn huge crowd from all over North Bengal, is an example.

The town lacks any certified tourist guide, in absence of which Toto drivers are acting as ones[18]. Local unemployed youths could be engaged in line of *Monument Mitra* scheme of central government's *Adopt a Heritage* Program (Ministry of Tourism, Govt. of India, 2020). They on one hand would secure safety and cleanliness of the unprotected sites, and again can answer to tourists' queries. They could be properly trained by the *Incredible India Tourist Facilitator* (IITF) Certification Programme launched by the Tourism Ministry of central government and turn out as well-trained and professional tourist facilitators (Ministry of Tourism, Govt. of India, 2020). Thus heritagization also plays a key role in job creation and boost local economy.

8. Critical Evaluation

Heritage is not only about memories, not only about inheritance from the past, rather about what we pass on to our next generation and sources of pride across all generations. Thus the historicity is not the only measure of identifying a heritage. If it is worth preserving, providing the place with any kind of uniqueness, then it should be conserved as heritage. So if the experts believe that 151 sites in the town need preservation, then it is welcome to declare all such as heritage. The cultural, social and economic benefits of the heritage have already been discussed. Sparing all, at least it promotes tourism and thus acts as the driver of urban economy. Hence heritagization of Cooch Behar town is a welcome move from the state government.

---

[18] As reported in the daily *Uttarbanga Sambad* on page 13, dated June 4, 2023.

But the responsible authorities should take note that heritage preservation cannot be done only at policy level and should be encouraged at individual and community levels. People's participation in the heritagization process is necessary for its success. They should be aware of why it is important to preserve heritage and should take pride in the same. They need to be motivated to appreciate their heritage and only then they would take interest in their protection. Again preservation of heritage is a serious affair and needs to be led by a team of experts. Heritage, particularly the ancient monuments in any place are generally made of locally available materials. They were built keeping in mind the local climatic conditions and they possess sustainable architecture. Hence they are considered as environment friendly establishments and their conservation work should be done using traditional materials and methods.

Another issue with heritagization of Cooch Behar town has been its failure to incorporate the intangible cultural heritages therein. The existing list includes only tangible ones and thus do not offer a total picture on heritage of the town. For example, *Rash Mela* Ground is not just the heritage; the fair it organizes for a fortnight from *Guru Purnima* every year is the real heritage of the town. Similarly Gunjabari is famous for the week long *Rath Yatra* fair organized around it. The fair along with the place is the real heritage of Cooch Behar. The administration should take measures to preserve such intangible cultural heritages in their traditional form. The local, traditional items sold in such fairs and their makers should be supported to carry on their craft.

Lastly it would be ideal to expand the periphery of heritage across Cooch Behar district. The rich history, which invites the heritagization of the town, is spread all over the district. Jagaddipendra Narayan Hospital at Khagrabari, Nripendra Narayan Memorial Library at Mathabhanga, P V N Library and Dak Bungalow at Haldibari are few of such heritage structures worthy of preservation (Das T. C., 2018). Artefacts and monuments, from the era of *Koch* kingdom and even older than that, are found in different corners of the region. Take example of Gosanimari *Rajpat*, the citadel of earlier *Khen* kings or the Baneswar *Shiva* Temple, mentioned in *Puranas*. There are many religious places of archaeological value around the district which deserve preservation (Roy, 2018); e.g. Siddhanath Shiva Temple at Dhaluabari, Madhupur Dham at Rajarhat, Madan Mohan Temple at Tufanganj and Mathabhanga, Hujur Saheb-r Darga at Haldibari etc. Again Handicrafts of Cooch Behar district, namely- preparation from Sital Pati (*Schumannianthus dichotomus*) works in Cooch Behar I and II and Tufanganj I and II C. D. blocks is worthy of preservation as heritage. Among the intangible cultural heritages, *Bhawaiya* song of Cooch Behar is well renowned. Other folk arts like *BishHari Pala* and *Kushan Gan*, to name a few, are unique cultural identities of the district (Saha, 2018). Such intangible cultural heritages should also be incorporated in heritagization process. Only then the process would turn into effective and holistic in nature and could serve its true purpose.

References

[1] Adhikary, M.C. (2023). The Cultural Heritage of North Bengal: A Reflection on Bhawaiya. Abhijeet Publications.

[2] Ahamed, M. (2017). Cultural Heritage Tourism- An Analysis with special reference to West Bengal, India. International Journal on Recent Trends in Business and Tourism, 1(4), 55–62.

[3] Al-Saffar, M. (2018). Urban Heritage and Conservation in the Historic Centre of Baghdad. International Journal of Heritage Architecture, 2(1), 23–36.

[4] Al-Sakkaf, A., El-Zahab, S., Abdelkader, E.M. and Alfalah, G. (2021, June). A Holistic and Systematic Assessment of Maintenance Approaches in Heritage Sites. Wseas Transactions on Systems and CONTROL, 335–350.

[5] Avrami, E., Randall, M. and Torre, M.D. (2000). Values and Heritage Conservation Research Report. Los Angeles: The Getty Conservation Institute.

[6] Barman, K. C. (2013). Heritage Tourism sites in Birbhum District of West Bengal: Its Present Condition and Potentialities. Periodic Research, II(I), 210–215.

[7] Basu, C., Bhattacharyya, S., Chaudhuri, A., Akhtar, S., Chatterjee, A., Thakur, B., et al. (2021). Assessment of Potential Damage Factor: A Case Study of St. Paul's Cathedral, Kolkata. Journal of Heritage Management, 6(1), 53–68.

[8] Boniface, P. and Fowler, P. (1993). Heritage and Tourism in The Global Village. London: Routledge.

[9] Bujdoso, Z., David, L., Tozser, A., Kovacs, G., Major-Kathi, V., Uakhitova, G., *et al.* (2015). Basis of Heritagization and cultural tourism development. Procedia- Social and Behavioural Sciences, 188, 307–315.

[10] Census of India (2011). District Census Handbook: Koch Bihar. Directorate of Census Operations, West Bengal.

[11] Census of India (1951). District Handbooks: Cooch Behar. Calcutta-9: Sree Saraswaty Press Ltd.

[12] Chatterjee, B. and Dwivedi, A. (2023). Cultural Crisis, Deteriorating Heritage, and Placemaking: A Study of Rural West Bengal, India. Space and Culture, India, 11(3), 56–68.

[13] Chaudhuri, H.N. (1903). The Cooch Behar State and its Land Revenue Settlement. The Cooch Behar State Press.

[14] Choay, F. (2001). The Invention of The Historic Monument. New York: Cambridge University Press.

[15] Das, B. (1985). Kochbihar. In B. Das (Ed.), Uttar Banga-r Purakirti (pp. 101–102). Kolkata: Nath Publishing.

[16] Das, P. and Biswas, P.C. (2023, June). An appraisal of the scope of domestic tourism in Dooars foothills tourist circuit in the post-pandemic scenario. Conscientia, XI.

[17] Das, T.C. (2018). Aitihya-r Nidarshan Samagra Jela Hure. In P.R. Saha (Ed.), Coochbehar (2 ed., pp. 216–256). Jalpaiguri: Ekhon Dooars.

[18] Deo, B.S., Swain, S.S. and Das, S. (2022). Impact of Surrounding Settlements on the Heritage Area- A Case of the Elite Street, Kolkata. Journal of Emerging Technologies and Innovative Research, 9(8).

[19] Devee, S. (1921). The Autobiography of an Indian Princess. London: John Murray.

[20] Dutt, C.D. (1903). Introduction. In H. N. Chaudhuri, The Cooch Behar State and its Land Revenue Settlements (pp. XXV-XXXV). Cooch Behar State Press.

[21] Dwivedi, P. and Dwivedi, A. (2012). Public Community Participation Model for Renewable Energy Projects in India. World Renewable Energy Forum Conference. Denver: National Renewable Energy Laboratory (NREL).

[22] Hunter, W.W. (1876). A Statistical Account of Bengal; Volume X: Darjiling, Jalpaiguri & State of Kuch Behar. London: Trubner & Co.

[23] Huq, S.A. and Puthuvayi, B. (2024). Assessing the performance of urban heritage conservation projects—influencing factors, aspects and priority weights. Built Heritage, 8.

[24] Indian National Trust for Arts & Cultural Heritage (2015). Urban Heritage in Indian Cities. New Delhi: National Institute of Urban Affairs.

[25] Kadian, A. and Nirmala. (2019). Review of successful strategies of Urban Heritage Conservation. Journal of Emerging Technologies and Innovative Research, 6(5), 158–163.

[26] Lowenthal, D. (1998). The Heritage Crusade and the Spoils of History. Cambridge: Cambridge University Press.

[27] Menon, A. (2014). Heritage Conservation in India: Challenges and New Paradigms. In F. Pena and M. Chavez (Ed.), Proceedings of the SAHC2014—9th International Conference on Structural Analysis of Historical Constructions. Mexico City.

[28] Ministry of Tourism, Govt. of India. (2020, November 25). https://tourism.gov.in/schemes-and-guidelines/guidelines/guidelines-incredible-india-tourist-facilitator-iitf. Retrieved March 12, 2021, from https://tourism.gov.in/: https://tourism.gov.in/sites/default/files/2020-08/IITFC%20Guidelines.pdf

[29] Ministry of Tourism, Govt. of India. (2020, March). https://tourism.gov.in/schemes-and-guidelines/schemes. Retrieved March 2021, from https://tourism.gov.in/: https://tourism.gov.in/sites/default/files/2020-08/adopt%20a%20Heritage%20Project%20Guidelines.pdf

[30] Ministry of Urban Development, Govt. of India. (2015, January). www.mohua.gov.in. Retrieved April 2024, from https://mohua.gov.in/upload/uploadfiles/files/GuidelinesHRIDAY.pdf

[31] Munjeri, D. (2004). Tangible and Intangible Heritage: from difference to convergence. Museum International, 56(1–2), 12–20.

[32] NITI Aayog. (2020). Improving Heritage Management in India. New Delhi: Govt. of India.

[33] Noor, S.M., Mei, C.S., Ibrahim, I.S., Sarbini, N.N., Osman, M.H. and Khiyon, N.A. (2019). Heritage building condition assessment: a case study from Johor Bahru, Malaysia. IOP Conference Series: Earth and Environmental Science, 220.

[34] Paul, N.N. (2018). Kochbiharer Rajkahini. In P. R. Saha (Ed.), Kochbihar (2 ed., pp. 9–20). Jalpaiguri: Ekhon Dooars.

[35] Patel, E. (2017). Conservation of Heritage Sites in India. International Journal of Engineering and Advanced Technology, 6(5), 275–278.

[36] Pearce, S. (2000). The Making of Cultural Heritage. In E. Avrami, R. Mason and M. d. Torre (Eds.), Values and Heritage Conservation Research Report (pp. 59–64). Los Angeles: The Getty Conservation Institute.

[37] Roy, S.K. (2018). Dhormiyo Chetanamoy Protnokshetra Kochbihar. In Cooch Behar (pp. 45–76). Jalpaiguri: Ekhon Dooars.

[38] Saha, A.K. (2018). Cooch Behar-r Lokgan. In P.R. Saha (Ed.), Coochbehar (2 ed., pp. 21–30). Jalpaiguri: Ekhon Dooars.

[39] Salazar, N. B. and Zhu, Y. (2015). Heritage and Tourism. In L. Meskell (Ed.), Global Heritage: A Reader (pp. 240–258). Wiley Blackwell.

[40] Sarkar, B.C. (2014). Nature of Tourism in Koch Bihar district: A study of Recreation geography. Journal of Geo-Environment Observer, 45–51.

[41] Sarker, A. (2019). Art Heritage from northern Bengal: A multi-fragmented narrative in twenty-first century eastern Indian archaeology. Kolkata: 5th Indian Social Sciences and Humanities Congress.

[42] Sen, R.K. (2015). Cost Benefit Analysis and Heritage Buildings Conservations, special reference to Kolkata Municipal Corporation. International Journal of Advanced Research, 3(7), 1418–1423.

[43] Steinberg, F. (1996). Conservation and rehabilitation of urban heritage in developing countries. Habitat International, 20(3), 463–475.

[44] Torre, M.D. (2013). Values and Heritage Conservation. Heritage & Society, 155–166.

[45] Tunbridge, J.E. and Ashworth, G.J. (1996). Dissonant Heritage: The Management of the Past as a Resource in Conflict. Chichester: Wiley.

[46] Udeaja, C., Trillo, C., Awuah, K.G., Makore, B.C., Patel, D.A., Mansuri, L.E., *et al.* (2020). Urban Heritage Conservation and Rapid Urbanization: Insights from Surat, India. Sustainability, 12(6).

[47] Waterton, E. and Watson, S. (2015). Heritage as a Focus of Research: Past, Present and New Directions. In E. Waterton and S. Watson (Eds.), The Palgrave Handbook of Contemporary Heritage Research (pp. 1–17). London: Palgrave Macmillan.

[48] Wolff, B. (2020). Restoring the glory of Serampore. Colonial heritage, popular history and identity during rapid urban development in West Bengal. International Journal of Heritage Studies, 27(8), 777–791.

[49] Zhang, X., Edelenbos, J. and Gianoli, A. (2024). Balancing urban conservation and (re)development: tracing policy layering in the Mainland of China (1906–2023). Policy Studies, 1–21.

[50] Zuraidi, S.F., Rahman, M.A. and Akasah, Z.A. (2018). The Development of Condition Assessment for Heritage Building. International Conference on Civil and Environmental Engineering, 65.

Sustainable Resource Management: An Overview

S.K. Rafikul Alam[1]

ABSTRACT: The term Sustainable Resource Management (SRM) refers to developing and implementing methods and solutions for using and protecting resources such as water, energy and raw materials, as well as treating waste streams and waters. The demand for raw materials and energy is increasing rapidly worldwide, causing scarcity and increases in the volatility of raw material prices since many resources remain renewable. Additionally, the progressive pollution of soil, air, water and other resources with harmful emissions is threatening sustainable development in many parts of the world. The SRM working groups analyse and address such challenges. It helps us to develop environmentally and socially compatible resources and waste management methods, encourages the sustainable use of water resources through comprehensive water and drainage basin management and develops strategies to avoid waste streams or to reuse/recycle material flows and energy using cleaner production (CP) and Industrial Symbiosis (IS) approaches. In this paper, besides the above-stated approach, other approaches that are associated with SRM are also explained. Different methods and tools that are used for sustainable resource management are also included in this paper.

Keywords: Sustainable, Management, Corporate Social Responsibility (CSR), Cleaner production (CP), Industrial Symbiosis (IS).

1. Introduction

Sustainable Resource Management is a combination of three important words that obey the vital meaning in this respect. The word Sustainable refers to the ability to maintain or support a process continuously over time. In business and policy contexts, sustainability

[1] Assistant Professor of Commerce, Dinhata College. E-mail: rafikulg.p@gmail.com

seeks to prevent the depletion of natural or physical resources so that they will remain available for the long term. In this context, Resource refers to natural resources, which are defined as the resources that exist on the planet independent of human actions. These resources are found in the environment and are developed without the intervention of humans. The last word is management, which plays a crucial role because, through management, resources can be conserved or used in an efficient and effective way, keeping in mind future generations. SRM means managing resources with the future in mind. It is defined as the application of sustainable practices by managing resources in a way that will benefit current and future generations. Simply put, it means managing resources in a way that ensures resources are not depleted to the point where it will affect future generations. Natural resources are vital for sustaining life on the planet. Therefore, effective Management is required to maintain ecological balance and meet human needs. The Management of resources includes a complex system of policies, practices, and strategies that are applied to ensure sustainable use.

2. Objectives of the Paper

Aims and objectives of this paper are:

1. Discuss about the overview of different approaches of SRM.
2. Highlighting the key concept and emerging trends of SRM.
3. Explain the Methods and Tools of SRM.
4. Benefits and Challenges associated with SRM.

3. Approaches and Emerging Trends of SRM

3.1 *Integrated Natural Resources Management (INRM)*

INRM is a holistic approach that recognizes the interconnectedness of various natural resources and their social, economic, and environmental dimensions. It strengthens the need for collaborative decision-making and integrated planning across sectors. INRM integrates scientific knowledge with local knowledge and involves stakeholders at different levels to achieve sustainable resource use (Campbell *et al.*, 2009).

3.2 *Participatory Approaches in Natural Resources Management*

Participatory approaches involve involving local communities, stakeholders, and indigenous knowledge in decision-making processes. Such approaches bring up social inclusion, enhance local ownership, and promote sustainable resource management (Reed, 2008). Participatory methods, such as participatory mapping and community-based monitoring, has been successfully applied in various natural resource contexts (Danielsen *et al.*, 2009; Chambers *et al.*, 2014).

3.3 *Corporate Social Responsibility towards SRM*

Corporate Social Responsibility (CSR), usually refers to a company's commitment to practice environmental and social sustainability and to be good stewards of the environment and the social landscape in which they operate. Approaches to sustainability and CSR vary according to industry. Some companies and economists reject the idea of CSR because it implies an obligation to society and future generations beyond those contained in the binding legal requirement of business. However, most companies now follow the some notion of CSR. Some companies invest in CSR as reputation management or to sustain the probability of a company and some invest in CSR out of a sense of moral obligation to society.

3.4 *Adaptive Management*

Adaptive management is a globally recognized approach that acknowledges the uncertainty and complexity innate in natural resource systems. This frequent process involves monitoring, experimentation, and learning from management actions to improve decision-making over time (Walters, 1986). Adaptive management promotes flexibility and elasticity in resource management and is applicable in both global contexts and specific cases like India, where ecosystems are dynamic and face various challenges, it is crucial in addressing natural resource challenges.

3.5 *Ecosystem Services and Natural Capital*

The concept of ecosystem services and natural capital has gained significant attention in natural resource management. Ecosystem services refer to the benefits that people obtain from ecosystems, such as clean water, pollination, and climate regulation. Natural capital represents the stock of natural resources and ecological infrastructure that provide these services. Valuing ecosystem services and natural capital enables decision-makers to incorporate their worth into policy and investment decisions, promoting sustainable resource management (Costanza *et al.*, 1997).

3.6 *Community-Based Natural Resources Management (CBNRM)*

Community-Based Natural Resources Management involves local communities in the management and conservation of natural resources. This approach recognizes the importance of local knowledge, traditional practices, and community empowerment in achieving sustainable resource use. CBNRM fosters a sense of ownership and responsibility, leading to improved resource stewardship.

3.7 *Biodiversity Conservation*

The country has established a network of protected areas, including national parks, wildlife reserves, and conservation areas. India's Biodiversity Strategy and Action Plan aims to conserve and sustainably manage biodiversity, enhance ecosystem services, and promote community participation. However, issues such as habitat degradation, illegal wildlife trade, and climate change impact pose challenges to biodiversity conservation (Department of National Parks and Wildlife Conservation, 2014).

3.8 *Water Resources Management*

Hydropower generation, agriculture, and drinking water supply all depend on the efficient management of water resources. The Water Resources Strategy focuses on integrated water resources management, emphasizing the equitable allocation of water, watershed management, and climate change adaptation.

3.9 *Renewable Energy*

Access to clean energy is a catalyst for sustainable development. In underserved and remote communities, the lack of reliable energy sources hampers progress in education, healthcare and economic activities. Clean energy solutions, such as solar power and wind energy, offer a sustainable and environmentally friendly alternative, unlocking opportunities for growth and development. Clean energy is not just about providing electricity; it's about empowering communities, fostering sustainable development and creating a path to a brighter future.

3.10 *Circular Economy*

Circular economy is a new production and consumption model that ensures sustainable growth over time. With the circular economy, we can drive the optimization of resources, reduce the consumption of raw materials, and recover waste by recycling or giving it a second life as a new product. The aim of the circular economy is therefore to make the most of the material resources available to us by applying three basic principles: reduce, reuse and recycle. In this way, the life cycle of products is extended, waste is used and a more efficient and sustainable production model is established over time. The idea arises from imitating nature, where everything has value and everything is used, where waste becomes a new resource. In this way, the balance between progress and sustainability is maintained.

4. Methods and Tools of SRM

4.1 *Cost Benefit Analysis (CBA)*

CBA used to compare the costs and benefits of various sustainability issues and sectors, such as energy, water, waste, transport, agriculture, or health. For instance, it can evaluate the advantages of renewable energy sources versus fossil fuels, assess the costs of water conservation measures versus water supply projects, analyze the benefits of waste reduction versus land filling or incineration, estimate the costs and benefits of public transport versus private vehicles, calculate the advantages of organic farming versus conventional farming, and calculate the benefits of health promotion versus disease treatment. CBA can help make decisions that consider economic, social, and environmental factors in order to maximize net benefits for those involved now and in the future.

4.2 *Industrial Ecology*

Industrial ecology (IE) is the study of material and energy flows through industrial systems. The global industrial economy can be modeled as a network of industrial processes that extract resources from the Earth and transform those resources into by-products, products and services which can be bought and sold to meet the needs of humanity. Industrial ecology seeks to quantify the material flows and document the industrial processes that make modern society function. Industrial ecologists are often concerned with the impacts that industrial activities have on the environment, with use of the planet's supply of natural resources, and with problems of waste disposal. Industrial ecology is a young but growing multidisciplinary field of research which combines aspects of engineering, economics, sociology, toxicology and the natural sciences.

4.3 *Life Cycle Assessment (LCA)*

One of the most common methodologies for quantifying sustainability is **life cycle assessment** (LCA). An LCA is a systematic analysis of environmental impact over the course of the entire life cycle of a product, material, process, or other measurable activity. LCA models the environmental implications of the many interacting systems that make up industrial production. When accurately performed, it can provide valuable data that decision-makers can use in support of sustainability initiatives. Read on for a basic introduction to LCA: What it is, how one is performed, and why it helps businesses, policymakers, and consumers make decisions that are more informed when it comes to supporting sustainability.

4.4 *Material Flow Analysis (MFA)*

Materials flow analysis, discussed in Chapter 3, is a quantitative procedure for determining the flow of materials and energy through the economy. It uses input/output methodologies, including both material and economic information. It captures the mass balances in an economy where inputs (extractions + imports) equal outputs (consumption + exports + accumulation + wastes). It too is based on the laws of thermodynamics. MFA asks whether the flow of materials is sustainable in terms of the environmental burden it creates. UM simply quantifies the flows, it does not engage in analysis of environmental burdens. The identification of waste is a major aspect of MFA as the purpose of conducting such an analysis is to minimize the flow of materials while maximizing human benefit generated by the flow. It allows for the monitoring of wastes typically unaccounted for in traditional UM and economic analysis, and is thus a useful method to evaluate the efficiency of the use of material resources. It is an important tool of industrial ecology and serves as the basis for material flow management. MFA is a component of LCA and provides an in-depth snapshot in time of an aspect of LCA.

4.5 *Multi Criteria Analysis (MCA)*

One of the challenges in environmental management is to make decisions, which include environmental, social and economic aspects. These problems may benefit from multi criteria analysis. Multi-criteria analysis (MCA) helps decision makers develop coherent preferences for a given problem so that decisions can be taken with more confidence. This module explains the multi-criteria analysis (MCA) framework and allows student to apply this knowledge in a tutorial using a free spatial software tool (MCAS-S) developed by the MCAS-S Development Partnership. The Australian Bureau of Agriculture and Resource Economics and Sciences (ABARES) have developed this module.

4.6 *Resource Efficient and Cleaner Production (RECP)*

RECP refers to the continuous application of preventive environmental strategies towards processes, products and services in order to increase the efficiency with which they use materials, water and energy, to improve their productivity and, thus, their competitiveness. Its application leads to a reduction in the amount of pollution and waste generated, and reduces threats and risks for humans and the environment. EU4Environment aims to identify, train and coach national experts in RECP methods, applications and specialized resource efficiency topics. It will raise awareness, and improve the understanding of Circular Economy practices and benefits at the national and regional levels among Small and Medium Sized

Enterprises (SMEs), government entities, and civil society. As such, these practices lead to an improved resource productivity and environmental performance by demonstrating RECP in manufacturing industries.

4.7 *Sustainability Assessment*

A sustainability assessment is a blueprint, a tool that companies can use to evaluate their sustainability efforts. Its primary purpose is to provide clarity, direction and methodical procedures to check the level of social responsibility and how green a business's operations are. Moreover, it has to convert vague sustainability goals into concrete, measurable actions and create the opportunity to gain a competitive advantage. From now on, each responsible business will need a sustainability assessment framework, meaning a comprehensive system to enhance its sustainability performance. A sustainability assessment framework includes evaluations of different aspects of a business's operations:

- Environmental Impact Assessment.
- Economic Impact Assessment.
- Social Impact Assessment.

The below diagram show the different management technique for managing the resources in an effective and efficient way therefore the optimum utilization of resources for current and future need.

- **Better reputation:** Practicing sustainable resource management lets your clients and consumers know that you are taking significant steps to make a positive environmental impact. It allows them to be confident that your organization is putting the planet first, and is willing to invest time and resources into becoming sustainable. Comparing your sustainable organization to other organizations that have not yet made the investment to become more environmentally friendly allows you to have an edge over competitors. People can see your organization has a clear understanding of how it affects the environment and is implementing ways to lessen its impact, which can make both old and new consumers want to follow and support you in your environmental journey.

- **Acquire more business:** It also allows consumers to have trust in your organization to uphold environmental standards, for you and them. With the knowledge that you are considering your organization's impact on the environment, it can open up more opportunities for business for you. It will allow your organization to be more appealing to potential clientele, as it reassures them that they are supporting an organization that is doing its part in keeping the future sustainable. Showing them that you have sustainability at the forefront of your business, it allows those with similar standards to work with you, rather than a competitor who may not hold the same environmentally friendly standards.
- **Cost-effective:** Using renewable resources can also help you to save money in the end. By installing your own forms of renewable energy, like solar panels or wind turbines, on your organization's premises, it can then be used to power from your own energy, directly contributing to reducing your energy output. You are the one in control of how much you want to invest in renewable energy, and depending on the size of that investment depend on the energy return from it. With energy prices increasing, using your own form of renewable resources allows you to cover a significant portion of your energy bills from your own resources that you invested in, saving your organization money. As well as helping you to save money, sustainable resource management can also help your company earn it
- **Less waste:** Sometimes, starting small can help set the ball rolling when it comes to being sustainable. As your organization begins to implement large-scale renewable energy, making smaller changes like designated recycling bins, the cycle to work scheme and trying to make the most out of materials used can help to show that you are just as environmentally conscious on a smaller scale. As mentioned above, being cost-effective, such as using energy-efficient light bulbs and turning off the lights when you leave a room can also make an impact on reducing your energy consumption. It also means that you are considering your organization's impact on the environment outside of just renewable energy. By taking an active role towards recycling, reducing your own carbon footprint and being as environmentally

friendly as you can, it reinforces the sustainability standards your organization has set out to achieve.

4.8 *Challenges in SRM*

Governance and Policy Challenges: Governance and policy challenges are common in both global and India natural resources management. These challenges include weak enforcement mechanisms, conflicting interests among stakeholders, limited financial resources, and insufficient coordination among government agencies. Addressing these challenges requires improved governance structures, multi-stakeholder collaboration, and policy coherence (Dahal *et al.*, 2019). While these challenges are universal, India faces specific governance and policy issues, including those related to trans-boundary water management and climate change adaptation.

Challenges in Natural Resources System Management: Managing natural resources systems faces several challenges. One key challenge is the complex interactions between ecological, social, and economic factors, requiring interdisciplinary approaches (Folke *et al.*, 2005). These challenges include governance and institutional issues, conflicting interests among stakeholders, limited financial resources, and the lack of effective enforcement mechanisms. Additionally, the impacts of climate change, population growth, and technological advancements further complicate resource management efforts. Overcoming these challenges requires innovative approaches, multi-stakeholder collaboration, and adaptive governance structures (Olsson *et al.*, 2004).

5. Conclusion

The resources needed to implement aspects of sustainability reporting can be significant. Therefore, many of the concepts in this chapter are relevant to society and medium and large businesses and can be particularly challenging for smaller organizations. Many of the tools and processes discussed in this chapter are activated toward small, incremental change as a part of continuous improvement. All businesses, small or large, new or mature, and the Government can implement aspects of sustainability reporting into their organization to achieve improved operating results while minimizing negative societal impacts and emphasizing positive societal impacts.

References

[1] Bajracharya, B., Furley, P., Newton, A. and Ghimire, S.K. (2013). Factors influencing community participation in the Annapurna Conservation Area, Nepal. *Environmental Management,* 52(1), 200–214.

[2] Berkes, F. (2004). Rethinking community-based conservation. *Conservation Biology*, 18(3), 621–630.

[3] Campbell, B.M., *et al.* (2009). Synthesis: Developing and Applying Indicators of Sustainable Development in Agricultural Systems for Policy Analysis. In: Sustainable Development in Agriculture: Approaches and Opportunities at the Global Level. Accessed from https://link.springer.com/chapter/10.1007%2F978-1-4020-9294-4_10

[4] Costanza, R., *et al.* (1997). The value of the world's ecosystem services and natural capital. *Nature*, 387(6630), 253–260.

[5] Danielsen, F., Jensen, P.M., Burgess, N.D. and Altamirano, R. (2009). Environmental monitoring: the scale and speed of implementation varies according to the degree of people's involvement. *Journal of Applied Ecology*, 46(3), 548–559.

[6] Folke, C., Hahn, T., Olsson, P. and Norberg, J. (2005). Adaptive governance of social-ecological systems. *Annual Review of Environment and Resources,* 30(1), 441–473.

[7] Ojha, H.R., *et al.* (2010). Decentralization, forests, and livelihoods: Theory and narrative. *Sage Publications India.*

[8] Olsson, P., *et al.* (2004). Shooting the rapids: Navigating transitions to adaptive governance of social-ecological systems. *Ecology and Society*, 9(2), 18.

[9] Reed, M.S. (2008). Stakeholder participation for environmental management: a literature review. Biological Conservation, 141(10), 2417–2431.

[10] Walters, C.J. (1986). Adaptive management of renewable resources. MacMillan Publishing Company.

Political Ideologies and the Issue of Environmentalism: An Analytical Debate and Discussion

Sapan Tamang[1]

ABSTRACT: The issue of sustainability and the discussion on Environmentalism has been a matter of grave concern in the International Political System since last several decades. Every notable international organizations of the world such as BRICKS, SAARC, ASEAN and EU have seriously initiated debate and discussion on the very subject of environment. Francis Fukuyama, the great political scientist of the contemporary world has remarked that the world witnessed the last political ideology in the name of the Liberal Democracy. In his book "End of Ideology and the Last Man" published in the year 1989, he asserted that the end of cold war and the victory of capitalist bloc ultimately stopped the further development of any political Ideology in the world. Hence, it is the End of Ideology and the Liberal Capitalist Democracy is the last Ideology of the world. However, the establishment of Liberal Capitalist Democracy as the only Ideology eventually creates a huge imbalance in the entire eco-system. As a consequence, the huge environmental loss has been noticed in different parts of the world. Daniel Bell, a renowned Political Analyst has countered Francis Fukuyama and argued that it is not the end of Ideology rather the content of Ideology has shifted from Liberalism, Democracy, Feudalism, Capitalism etc. to now Environmentalism in contemporary societies of the world. On the basis of the above theoretical framework, the present study attempts to analyze and explores the relationship between political ideologies and environmentalism, highlighting the various issues and concerns that arise in the intersection of politics and environmental protection. It examines how different political ideologies approach environmental

[1] Assistant Professor, Department of Political Science, Dinhata College, India. E-mail: sapanbomzon@gmail.com

concerns, analyses the challenges faced by environmentalism in the context of differing political ideologies, and proposes potential strategies to bridge the gap between politics and environmental concerns for a sustainable future.

Keywords: *Sustainability, Environmentalism, Capitalist Democracy, Political Ideology, End of Ideology.*

1. Introduction

Everyone should live with his need and not by his greed remarked by Mahatma Gandhi has become a true mantra of life in the present day societies of the world. Everybody started embracing the idea of sustainable living and the importance of closed village economy as advocated by Gandhi. The idea of sustainable living without hampering much to environment has become the motto of every government, non-governmental organization and civil societies of the world. It is well evident that the world has witnessed the irreparable loss of environment in the process of establishing and developing the ideology called liberal capitalist democracy throughout the globe. Environmental issues have become central to global discourse as societies recognize the urgent need for environmental protection and sustainable development. However, the approaches taken by different political ideologies towards environmentalism vary significantly, leading to a multitude of challenges, conflicts, and concerns. This paper aims to analyse and discuss the issues and concerns arising from the connection between political ideologies and environmentalism, shedding light on the importance of promoting environmental protection within the framework of varied political beliefs.

2. Political Ideologies and Environmentalism

Political Ideology refers to a set of beliefs, values and principle that shape and guide an individual or group understands of political systems, governance, and social order. It provides for analysing and interpreting political events and issues. There are various political ideologies viz. Liberalism, Conservatism, Socialism, Communism, Fascism, Anarchism etc. Environmentalism refers to a social and political movement that aims to protect and preserve the natural environment. It involves advocating for sustainability, conservation and the reduction of pollution and ecological degradation. Environmentalists work towards creating awareness about environmental issues and promoting policies and practices that promote a healthy and sustainable relationship between humans and the natural world. It encompasses a wide range of perspective and approaches. Some environmentalists focus on individual actions, encouraging people to make environmentally responsible choices in their daily lives. Others emphasize the importance of collective action, advocating for policy changes at local, national, and international levels. Environmental activists often engage in protests, campaigns, and advocacy to raise awareness and push for action.

Some important Political Ideologies such as Liberalism, Conservatism, Socialism and Issues of Environmentalism are as follows;

Liberalism, with its emphasis on individual freedoms and market-based approaches, has traditionally fostered environmentalism through regulations and economic incentives. However, the tension between economic growth and environmental protection remains a challenge.

Conservative ideology focuses on preserving traditional values and limited government intervention. This ideology often faces conflicts with environmental protection due to a perceived threat to property rights and economic stability. Finding common ground through the promotion of responsible, market-based solutions can help bridge this gap.

Socialism highlights social and economic equality, often advocating for centralized planning and state control. While socialism's propensity for environmental protection seems inherent, concerns lie in the risk of prioritizing immediate needs over long-term sustainability.

3. Environmentalism and Bi-Polar World

Environmental issues have increasingly become polarized along political lines, with debates often framed as an ideological battle. Such polarization poses challenges in finding bipartisan solution, hindering progress towards environmental protection. Balancing economic growth and environmental preservation remains a persistent challenge. The tension between short-term economic benefits and long-term sustainability often impedes effective environmental policymaking. Even within ideologies that prioritize environmental protection, the effectiveness of policies often relies on proper implementation and enforcement, highlighting the significance of administrative capacity and regulatory frameworks.

Political ideologies, driven by electoral cycles, often prioritize short-term goals, potentially diminishing the focus on long-term environmental concerns. Strategies to overcome these short-term biases are crucial for effective environmental policymaking.

4. End of Ideology Debate and Issue of Environmentalism

Political Ideology plays a pivotal role in shaping societies and influencing policy decisions. The environment, as a critical of our time, demands an understanding of how different ideologies approach and address environmental challenges. In his controversial work, "The End of History and the Last Man" Francis Fukuyama argued that the collapse of Communism marked the culmination of ideological struggles, indicating the triumph of liberal democracy over other ideological systems. He further asserted that history should be viewed as an evolutionary process, and that the "End of History" means that liberal democracy is the final form of government for all nations. He opines that since the French revolution, Liberal democracy has repeatedly proven to be the best form of government compare to the other alternatives. However, Daniel Bell, a renowned Political Analyst has countered Francis Fukuyama and argued that it is not the end of Ideology rather the content of Ideology has shifted from Liberalism, Democracy, Feudalism, Capitalism etc. to now Environmentalism in contemporary societies of the world. Moreover, the concept of the 'End of Ideology' has been a subject of intense debate among scholars and intellectuals even today. Further, after the collapse of Soviet Union in early 1990s the entire world has accepted the hegemonic rule of USA. As a consequence, three crucial political ideologies viz. Liberalization, Privatization and Globalization became the new fascinating topic for the world for next several decades. Accordingly, the system of Liberalization, Privatization and Globalization (LPG) under the leadership of USA has become successful in establishing the powerful and dominant Ideology called liberal Capitalist Democracy and divided the world into 'Haves and Have Not'. It enhances the capital flow of the world, foster greater opportunities to the people of the world, increased competition among the nations etc. However, in this process of LPG, huge environmental loss, environmental degradation, Environmental depletion has been noticed in every parts of the world. (Fukuyama, 1993)

The End of Ideology debate has been a longstanding discourse in political science, suggesting that ideological differences are diminishing. However, the emergence and significance of Environmentalism as distinct ideology challenge this notion. Environmentalism highlights the importance of ideological frameworks and political debate in addressing environmental challenges and shaping a sustainable future. As Environmental issues become increasingly urgent, it is crucial to recognize the interdisciplinary nature of Environmentalism and its potential to bridge ideological divides in finding solutions to complex environmental problems. The debate on the End of Ideology should hence consider the distinct and influential role of environmentalism in reshaping political discourse and policy agendas. (ibid)

5. Development and Environmentalism

The System of Liberal Capitalist Democracy fosters the enormous opportunity of growth and development for both the individual as well as for the nations of the entire world. People of the world get connected in terms of economy, culture, education, technology etc. Huge employment opportunities have been generated, large socio-cultural assimilation noticed, huge cross educational studies have been initiated among the nations, and the world noticed an unprecedented technological development in last two decades. However, in this process of development we have witnessed huge environmental loss, environmental degradation followed by huge displacement of deprived and downtrodden people. In this process of development, people have become so greedy that they started encroaching the rivers, mountains and jungles also. Similarly, due to technological advancement nations have started demarcating their boundaries not only in the Land area but also in the Sky or in the Ocean. As a consequence, the mother environment is being hampered with all possible accessibility. Various social movements have been noticed in different parts of the globe having only objective of Environment protection. Several movements in terms of Environment have also been noticed in various parts of India such as Chipko Movement of Uttarakhand, Narvada Bhachao Andolan of Gujarat, Nandi gram Andolan of West Bengal etc.

It is undoubtedly true that the establishment of Liberal Capitalist Democracy is largely responsible for the present degradation of environment all over the world. The eco-system involves all living organisms such as plants, animals and human beings, and the non-living entities like air, water and soil, their various interactions with each other. Being an important element of the holistic eco-system, all are interrelated and highly interdependent with each other. Hence, the action of one element of the system automatically affects other elements of the system and vice-versa. Thus, all these elements play a crucial role for maintaining peace and order in the entire eco-system. However, with the growth of human intelligence, men started dominating and suppressing other elements of the eco-system. As a consequence, disorder and chaos erupted in the entire eco-system. It is only the human beings in the entire eco-system who lead their lives with the greed and not by need. Moreover, in the process of development and making life more comfortable, human beings started exploiting other natural elements of the eco-system. Hence, disorder and crisis became prominent and inevitable in the entire eco-system. (Tamang, 2022)

Accordingly, in the process of development and heading towards modernity, human beings forget to live in a collective system of mutual co-existence and sustainability. They forget to live in cooperative system with collective responsibility. Men forget that right to life is an important, basic and fundamental right of all the elements of the entire eco-system. Hence, this endeavour of leading towards modernity, ultimately made human beings greedier, self-oriented and excluded. The situation became worse with the introduction of liberalization, privatization and globalization. The idea of laissez-faireism further accelerated the situation and emerged as a dominant economic system under the banner of larger capitalist ideology. Capitalism became the only dominant ideology or social system all over the world. It decreases human values, morality and ethics, at the same time it encourages human greed, desires and wishes. Thus in this process of steady growth of capitalist development, unprecedented factories and manufacturing companies have been established in different corners of the world. As a result, huge deforestations and land acquisitions are taking place and everybody is busy making money only. In the name of development, the excessive exploitation of nature, viz. plants and animals, minerals and other natural resources are taking place in an unprecedented manner. Hence, the entire eco-system witnessed the great threat from growing capitalist development. Further, it is indeed imperative to understand that when entire eco-system is affected, then automatically it affects the life of human beings because as discussed above there is an integral and vice-versa relationship between human beings and the whole eco-system. (Tamang, Uncertain Future of NH10: Concern and Issues, 2022)

It is clearly evident that the dominant Ideology of Capitalist Liberal Democracy created an ample space for individual liberty and the development. It reduced the national boundaries and introduced trans-national or multi-national trade and commerce amongst the nations. Hence, capital flows increased, economic inter dependence amongst the nations increased. It fosters wider opportunities to people in terms of technological advancement, cultural assimilation or knowledge dissemination. However, in this fascinating development of Capitalist Liberal democracy, somewhere a gap have been created in the world and that gap is popularly known as Gap of Economic Development versus Environmental Degradation. Excessive exploitation of natural resources in the name of development has become a common practice in every parts of the world. Air pollution and Water pollution are some of the crucial negative impact of the Development. As a result, public health issues have become gigantic problems of the present day world. The countries having advanced public health facilities might have addressed the problem but the developing countries like India public health have become really a big challenge. Thus, it is an alarming situation for the world to think about this growing gap and to address the same at the earliest.

6. Strategy for Bridging the Gap

- Promoting environmental education and awareness across political ideologies is crucial to fostering shared understanding and building consensus for sustainable practices.
- Creating platforms for constructive conversations between political ideologies which can help identifying common ground and develop innovative solutions that transcend ideological differences.
- Incorporating Environmental Concerns in Economic Systems, Developing economic models that incorporate the long-term costs and benefits of environmental protection can contribute to aligning economic interests with sustainability goals.
- Encouraging collaborative Governance: Promoting multi-stakeholder collaborations and involving civil society groups, academia, and private sector actors in decision-
- Making processes can lead to more inclusive and effective environmental policies.

7. Conclusion

Political ideologies play a significant role in shaping environmental policies and their effectiveness. Recognizing and addressing the issues and concerns arising from the intersection of politics and environmentalism is crucial for achieving sustainable development. By fostering dialogue, promoting awareness, and creating inclusive governance structures, we can bridge the gap between political ideologies and environmental concerns, ultimately leading to a more sustainable future.

References

[1] Robert, Brulle J. (2010). "Politics and the Environment" Handbook of Politics, pp. 385– 406, Research Gate, DOI:10.1007/978-0-387-68930-2_21.

[2] Francis , Fukuyama (1993). "End of History and the Last Man" Penguin Books Limited.

[3] Kevin, Harrison and Boyd, Tony (2018). "Environmentalism and Ecologism" Understanding Political Ideas and Movements, pp. 274–293, Research Gate, DOI:10.7765/9781526137951.00018.

[4] Jack, Manno P. (2004). "Political Ideology and Conflicting Environmental Paradigms" Global Environmental Politics, 4(3), pp. 155–159, Research Gate, DOI: 10.1162/1526380041748038.

[5] Massaroni Quinn, (2019). "Cognitive Processing and Climate Change: the Impact of Political Ideology on Processing Climate Change Information", Graduate Theses, pp 1–62, Bryant Digital Repository, Bryant University.

[6] Chandra, Roy Gobinda (2022). "Constitutional Safeguards for Biodiversity Protection: Implementation Aspects, Prospects and Problems pertaining to sub-Himalayan Terai and Dooars of West Bengal" Trends in Biogeography (Eastern Himalaya and North Bengal), pp 30–41, ISBN: 978-93-91139-40-7 Rajesh Publication.

[7] Sapan, Tamang (2022). "The Uncertain Future of NH 10: Concern and Issues" Trends in Biogeography (Eastern Himalaya and North Bengal), pp. 207–216, ISBN: 978-93-91139-40–7, Rajesh Publication.

[8] Sapan, Tamang (2022). "Traditional Ethno-healing, Environment and Modernity: An Outlook in Darjeeling Himalaya" Indian Science Cruiser 36(4) pp. Research Gate DOI:10.24906/isc/2022/v36/i4/216412

[9] http://www.britannica.com

[10] www.wikipedia.ac.in

Author Index

A

Adhikary, Sourav 305
Alam, S.K. Rafikul 328
Allay, Sanjita 71

B

Barman, Bishnu 155
Bhattacharyya, Arindam 227
Biswas, Sankar 155
Biswas, Sima 205

C

Chettri, Neetu 217

D

Das, Biswajit 172
Das, Gopal 37
Das, Partha 305
Das, Pinku 129
Das, Sibabrata 145
Das, Sova Rani 240
Das, Sudarshan 278
Dukpa, Pasang Tshering 217

G

Ghosh, Debarshi 17
Gupta, Manjil 100

H

Hoque, Abdul Momin 17

I

Islam, Nazrul 1, 129

K

Khati, Sweata 90
Kundu, Somnath 266

L

Laha, Manash 54

M

Mahato, Roshan 305
Meitei, Khamnam Michael ... 172
Mondal, Keshab 252

N

Nandi, Jagriti 240

P

Pandey, Anirban 199
Parveen, Rumana 293

R

Rahaman, Mosfudar 117
Ray, Mithun 117
Roy, Gobinda C. 199
Roy, Tamal Basu 155

S

Sarkar, Ranjan 37
Sarkar, Tapan 266
Soren, Sabita 145

T

Tamang, Sapan 339

Y

Yonzone, Sachina 82